WHAT IS A LOLLARD?

OXFORD THEOLOGICAL MONOGRAPHS

OXFORD THEOLOGICAL MONOGRAPHS

What Is a Lollard?

*Dissent and Belief in
Late Medieval England*

J. PATRICK HORNBECK II

OXFORD
UNIVERSITY PRESS

OXFORD

UNIVERSITY PRESS

Great Clarendon Street, Oxford OX2 6DP

Oxford University Press is a department of the University of Oxford.
It furthers the University's objective of excellence in research, scholarship,
and education by publishing worldwide in

Oxford New York

Auckland Cape Town Dar es Salaam Hong Kong Karachi
Kuala Lumpur Madrid Melbourne Mexico City Nairobi
New Delhi Shanghai Taipei Toronto

With offices in

Argentina Austria Brazil Chile Czech Republic France Greece
Guatemala Hungary Italy Japan Poland Portugal Singapore
South Korea Switzerland Thailand Turkey Ukraine Vietnam

Oxford is a registered trade mark of Oxford University Press
in the UK and in certain other countries

Published in the United States
by Oxford University Press Inc., New York

© J. Patrick Hornbeck II 2010

British Library Cataloguing in Publication Data

Data available

Library of Congress Cataloging in Publication Data
Library of Congress Control Number: 2010927171

Typeset by SPI Publisher Services, Pondicherry, India
Printed in Great Britain
on acid-free paper by
MPG Books Group, Bodmin and King's Lynn

ISBN 978–0–19–958904–3

Preface

The question in the title of this book has been asked a great many times, by historians and propagandists, theologians and polemicists, bishops, inquisitors, and scholars of English literature. It is no exaggeration that much of the contested historiography of the late Middle Ages and the early Reformation in England rests on its answer. For the sixteenth-century martyrologist John Foxe just as for the twentieth-century historian A. G. Dickens, the claim that lollards and lollardy existed underground into the 1520s provided fodder for their arguments about the causes and the reception of the Henrician Reformation. For Dickens' near-contemporaries Eamon Duffy and Richard Rex, the claim that lollardy, if it were ever a coherent force to begin with, was spent by the early sixteenth century served the opposite purpose: to prove that lollards have received 'disproportionate historiographical attention' and that medieval heretics exerted no discernible influence on the shape of the Reformation in England.[1]

So this is a book, in large part, about terminology: about the words that contemporaries and later historians have used to characterize, and to categorize, those who dissented from the ecclesiastical norms of the late Middle Ages. In addition to the historiographical extremes represented by Dickens and Duffy, there are other terminological issues as well. Some scholars have suggested that lollardy was less an organized movement of dissent than the ecclesiopolitical construct of a Lancastrian government keen to consolidate its hold on power; others have claimed that whatever the case, the extant sources have permanently concealed from us the details of many putative heretics' thought-worlds.

Indeed, this is also a book about beliefs; it argues that the members of the dissenting communities of fourteenth-, fifteenth-, and sixteenth-century England did not subscribe to a static set of theological ideas but, instead, departed from the consensus of the late medieval church in a host of diverse and evolving ways. As I shall demonstrate, the beliefs of individual dissenters were conditioned by a number of social, textual, and cultural factors, including the ideas they discussed with other members of their local communities, the texts to which they had access, and the influence of mainstream religion and spirituality. Careful attention to these dynamics at the local level, as well

---

[1] Richard Rex, *The Lollards* (London, 2002), 143; see also Eamon Duffy, *The Stripping of the Altars: Traditional religion in England c. 1400–c. 1580*, 2nd edn (New Haven, Conn., 2005).

as to the theological content implicit in Wycliffite texts and ecclesiastical records, can disclose the ways in which dissenting beliefs changed over time and varied from individual to individual and community to community. The divergences in doctrine that I document in the following pages show that late medieval dissenters were by no means homogeneous.

The focus of these pages on dissenters' and heresy suspects' beliefs seeks to fill a lacuna created by some recent trends in lollard studies. Since the revival in the late 1970s of interest in Wycliffites, lollards, and the textual remains they left behind—a revival almost single-handedly pioneered by the rigorous textual editor and Oxford professor Anne Hudson—literary scholars have taken a pre-eminent place in the study of lollardy. Hudson's seminal work *The Premature Reformation*, to which any study of this sort must be hugely in debt, includes an extensive discussion of lollard theology or, in Hudson's phrase, 'ideology'. She argues that:

> the fractured and apparently random assertions found in vernacular treatises, episcopal registers, and first-person testimonies can be shown to be a coherent and reasoned set of beliefs if they are to fit to the template of Wyclif's teaching: the writings of the founder form a conceptual matrix that can elaborate and explain the continuing ideology of the movement.[2]

Hudson's students have carried on her rigorous focus on Wycliffite texts, while at the same time refining some of her methodological assumptions. In the field of English literature, critical approaches to the study of premodern texts continue to vie for influence with the more traditional techniques of textual editing and analysis. Kantik Ghosh's monograph *The Wycliffite Heresy* has uncovered the theoretical debates about biblical interpretation that, in his view, account for the appeal of Wyclif's ideas within the University of Oxford.[3] Katherine Little has argued that the Wycliffite controversy 'should be understood in terms of the history and the sources of the self',[4] And Jill Havens has suggested that Hudson's metaphor of 'the grey area', in which texts neither demonstrably Wycliffite nor demonstrably 'orthodox' can be situated, could admit of further gradations.[5] In historical studies, scholars have likewise begun to explore the social and ideological differences which separated

---

[2] Steven Justice, 'Inquisition, speech, and writing: A case from late-medieval Norwich', *Representations*, 48 (1994), 1–29 at 18.

[3] Kantik Ghosh, *The Wycliffite Heresy: Authority and the interpretation of texts* (Cambridge, 2002).

[4] Katherine Little, *Confession and Resistance: Defining the self in late medieval England* (South Bend, Ind., 2006), 1.

[5] Jill C. Havens, 'Shading the grey area: Determining heresy in Middle English texts' in *Text and Controversy*, 337–52.

many of Wyclif's putative followers from one another. Jeremy Catto, for instance, has persuasively described the competing interests of several groups of Oxford fellows who supported Wyclif, and A. K. McHardy and Maureen Jurkowski have provided us with additional biographical details about early Wycliffites.[6] At the same time as these scholars have concentrated on the personalities and convictions of leading dissenters, Craig D'Alton and Ian Forrest have turned traditional methodology on its head by focusing instead on those who investigated heresy suspects.[7] Finally, in philosophical and theological studies, detailed analyses of Wyclif's works by such scholars as Ian Christopher Levy and Stephen E. Lahey have revealed that the Oxford scholar, far from being ahead of his time, was deeply enmeshed in the contemporary debates of the medieval academy.[8]

As the burgeoning literature in the field suggests, the net result of Hudson's efforts to make Wycliffite texts more widely available has been the creation of a new interdisciplinary subfield, 'Lollard studies':

> where scholars of history and literature have met, and drawn upon one another's methods, in order to edit, study, and interpret a body of texts and records which had previously, especially in English departments, received little attention. The field is now firmly established as an important aspect of the study of medieval England, and within the past ten years or so in particular, Lollard studies have not only entered the mainstream, but come to occupy a central place.[9]

Yet the growth of lollard studies and the claims of its practitioners have not gone without question. As we have already seen, a number of historians have argued that lollardy had little (if any) measurable impact on the late medieval church or the Henrician Reformation. Among the most strident of these critics have been the Cambridge scholars Rex, who published a slim monograph challenging many of the assumptions of lollard studies in 2002, and Duffy, whose introduction to the revised edition of his book, *The Stripping of*

---

[6] Jeremy Catto, 'Fellows and helpers: The religious identity of the followers of Wyclif' in *The Medieval Church: Universities, heresy, and the religious life: Essays in honour of Gordon Leff* (Studies in Church History, Subsidia 11, Woodbridge, 1999), 141–61; A. K. McHardy, 'Bishop Buckingham and the Lollards of Lincoln diocese', *Studies in Church History*, 9 (1972), 131–45; Maureen Jurkowski, 'Heresy and factionalism at Merton College in the early fifteenth century', *Journal of Ecclesiastical History*, 48 (1997), 658–81.

[7] Craig D'Alton, 'The suppression of heresy in early Henrician England' (Ph.D. thesis, University of Melbourne, 1999); Ian Forrest, *The Detection of Heresy in Late Medieval England* (Oxford, 2005).

[8] Ian Levy, *John Wyclif: Scriptural logic, real presence, and the parameters of orthodoxy* (Milwaukee, Wis., 2003); Stephen E. Lahey, *Philosophy and Politics in the Thought of John Wyclif* (Cambridge, 2003).

[9] Fiona Somerset, 'Introduction' in *Influence*, 9–16 at 9.

the Altars, approaches the level of polemic.[10] Other scholars have taken a
more moderate approach, suggesting that although lollardy deserves attention as a factor in the ecclesiastical history of late medieval England, its
coherence as an ideology and its significance for both the medieval and
Reformation periods have been exaggerated.[11]

Through all this, studies of late medieval dissent have by and large moved
away from general and toward local approaches away from traditional historical methods and toward more theoretically grounded analyses of the sources;
and away from questions about lollard belief and toward questions about lollard
texts, communities, and social practices. Each of these trends has produced
much illuminating work, but together they account for a certain lack of attention
in the most recent scholarly literature to the religious convictions of medieval
dissenters.

First, as in the field of Reformation studies, the recent historiography of
lollardy has been characterized by a progressively greater awareness of the
substantial differences in social and economic standing, religious practices,
and beliefs that separated dissenters and dissenting communities from one
another. Whereas early historians often embraced the medieval chronicler
Henry Knighton's claim that lollards 'had only one way of speaking and a
remarkably consistent form of doctrine', scholars have now begun to investigate the social and theological fault lines whose existence refutes any attempt
to treat lollard groups as if they were interchangeable.[12] Among the first
contributors to this trend was J. A. F. Thomson, whose pioneering study
The Later Lollards concluded that 'one cannot talk of a single Lollard creed but
must always remember that beliefs varied, not only from group to group, but
even from individual to individual'.[13] A survey of recent work on communities, texts, and heresy suspects demonstrates that local and microhistorical
approaches have become largely *de rigeur*.[14] Since 2003, David Aers has
analysed the eucharistic theologies of two early Wycliffites, Walter Brut and
William Thorpe; Robert Lutton has published a detailed study of testamentary piety in the heresy-prone Kentish village of Tenterden; Maureen Jurkowski

---

[10] See n. 1 above.

[11] R. N. Swanson, *Church and Society in Late Medieval England* (Oxford, 1989), 329–32.

[12] Henry Knighton, *Knighton's Chronicle*, ed. and trans. G. H. Martin (Oxford, 1995), 302:
'unum modum statim loquelae et formam concordem suae doctrinae mirabiliter habuerunt'.

[13] J. A. F. Thomson, *The Later Lollards: 1414–1520* (Oxford, 1965), 239; see also Richard
Davies, 'Lollardy and locality', *Transactions of the Royal Historical Society*, 6th ser., 1 (1991),
191–212 at 194.

[14] One important exception is Shannon McSheffrey's detailed article 'Heresy, orthodoxy,
and English vernacular religion, 1480–1525', *Past and Present*, 186 (2005), 47–80, which (like
this book) argues that lollardy was far less ideologically circumscribed than Hudson and others
have suggested: see especially 73–5.

has continued her meticulous prosopographical research into dissenters in Oxfordshire and Northamptonshire and book producers in London; and Jill Havens has examined the theological affiliations of a series of late medieval texts linked to a single manuscript, Oxford, University College 97.[15]

The popularity of local studies can in part be explained by the influence of critical approaches on the historiography of late medieval dissent. Whilst the field of lollard studies has not yet been shaped by theoretical questions to the same extent as the study of continental heresies such as 'Catharism' and 'Waldensianism', and of such similarly marginal movements as the beguines, a growing number of scholars have begun to voice criticisms of the ways in which lollard specialists have at times made uncritical use of their sources.[16] In particular, the charge has been made that the adversarial nature of suspect–inquisitor discourse and the ways in which heterodox claims were recorded for posterity work together to obscure dissenters' theological convictions and, to an even greater extent, their spirituality.[17] Scepticism has also been voiced about the category of 'Lollardy' itself: is it the construct of late medieval propagandists and their unwitting allies in the historical guild?[18] Does the use of a single label stereotype the beliefs and practices of a highly disparate cohort of individuals, undercutting the very advances that local studies have begun to make? Or were many heresy suspects sufficiently alike that it would be atomistic not to group them into some overarching category? These questions will receive detailed attention below.

---

[15] David Aers, *Sanctifying Signs: Making Christian tradition in late medieval England* (Notre Dame, Ind., 2004), ch. 4; Robert Lutton, *Lollardy and Orthodox Religion in Pre-Reformation England* (Woodbridge, 2006); Maureen Jurkowski, 'Lollardy in Oxfordshire and Northamptonshire: The two Thomas Compworths' in *Influence*, 73–95, and 'Lollard book producers in London in 1414' in *Text and Controversy*, 201–26; Havens, 'Shading the grey area', 339.

[16] For the influence of critical theory on Cathar studies see, among many other works, John H. Arnold, *Inquisition and Power: Catharism and the confessing subject in medieval Languedoc* (Philadelphia, 2001); Mark Gregory Pegg, *The Corruption of Angels: The Great Inquisition of 1245–1246* (Princeton, NJ, 2001); and James B. Given, *Inquisition and Medieval Society: Power, discipline, and resistance in Languedoc* (Ithaca, NY, 1997). For an interesting survey of historiographical challenges in beguine studies, see Jennifer Deane, '"Beguines" reconsidered: Historiographical problems and new directions', <http://monasticmatrix.org/MatrixTextLibrary/3461Text.html> (accessed 29 January 2009). Arnold's article 'Lollard trials and inquisitorial discourse' in Christopher Given-Wilson (ed.), *Fourteenth Century England II* (Woodbridge, 2002), 81–94, discusses the ways in which students of English and continental heresies can learn from each other's methods.

[17] Among others, see *Coventry*, 15; Paul Strohm, *England's Empty Throne: Usurpation and the language of legitimation, 1399–1422* (New Haven, Conn., 1998), 35, 47; and Peter Biller, '"Deep Is the Heart of Man, and Inscrutable": Signs of heresy in medieval Languedoc' in *Text and Controversy*, 267–80.

[18] Swanson, *Church and Society in Late Medieval England*, 335.

Finally, as theoretical approaches to the sources for lollard history have challenged the viability of belief as an object of study, scholars have begun to devote greater attention to the social practices and textual traditions of dissenting communities.[19] In this connection, recent work has analysed the literary and political contexts of the *Twelve Conclusions*, a Wycliffite manifesto of 1395; challenged the long-held assumption that dissenting communities provided an alternative outlet for women's spirituality; considered Wycliffite depictions of labourers; examined the social and economic standing of lollard families within their local communities; and discussed the persistence of dissenting ideas among the gentry in the late fifteenth and early sixteenth centuries.[20] This list could be continued at some length, but it is important to note that it reflects a broader trend in heresy studies, namely the dichotomy between, on the one hand, treating religious dissent as a phenomenon whose causes are mostly social and economic and, on the other, approaching the subject as primarily an intellectual and theological one.[21] In the case of lollardy, recent developments have provided a series of usually implicit reasons to prioritize social factors. Many early studies of English heresy contained such flawed accounts of lollard ideas, at least according to contemporary standards, because they were too closely bound up with confessional agendas. The theoretical critiques I have alluded to suggest that the authentic beliefs of heresy suspects are highly difficult to retrieve from the extant sources. And because so many previous studies of late medieval dissent focused almost exclusively on lollards' beliefs, there has recently been much more work to be done on social and textual, rather than theological, questions.

The cumulative result of these trends has been a rapid advance in our knowledge of the historical and literary contexts within which lollards moved. Nevertheless, these trends have left a gap in our understanding of dissenters'

---

[19] The importance of religious practice over against doctrine was emphasized by Jeremy Catto, 'Religious change under Henry V' in G. L. Harriss (ed.), *Henry V: The practice of kingship* (Oxford, 1985), 97–115.

[20] Wendy Scase, 'The audience and framers of the *Twelve Conclusions of the Lollards*' in *Text and Controversy*, 283–302; Shannon McSheffrey, *Gender and Heresy: Women and men in Lollard communities, 1420–1530* (Philadelphia, 1995); Helen Barr, 'Wycliffite representations of the third estate' in *Influence*, 197–216; and Andrew Hope, 'The lady and the bailiff: Lollardy among the gentry in Yorkist and early Tudor England' in Margaret Aston and Colin Richmond (eds.), *Lollardy and the Gentry in the Later Middle Ages* (Sutton, 1997), 250–77. To this list can now be added Maureen Jurkowski, 'Lollardy and social status in East Anglia', *Speculum* 82 (2007), 120–52.

[21] The contrast between these two approaches is described well by Brian Stock, *The Implications of Literacy: Written language and models of interpretation in the eleventh and twelfth centuries* (Princeton, NJ, 1983), 93.

beliefs and the theological dynamics that led to their formation. It is note-worthy that Hudson's *Premature Reformation*, written two decades ago last year, remains the most recent attempt to provide a comprehensive survey of lollard doctrine. In the wake of that magisterial study, lollard belief has been addressed largely in microhistorical terms, and investigations into the theol-ogies of individual heresy suspects and texts have frequently turned up results at variance with Hudson's portrait of a largely coherent body of doctrines. As local studies have accumulated, no attempt has yet been made to assemble them into an account of lollard belief that describes and seeks to explain local variations among the data.

That is the task that this book seeks to undertake: to discuss the ways in which the beliefs of dissenters in late medieval England varied and shifted over time, and then to consider the complicated, intricate, and interde-pendent relationships between beliefs, texts, and social circumstances that produced a host of different varieties of dissent. I have chosen as the chrono-logical endpoints for this study two dates which, whilst somewhat arbitrary, nevertheless point to important moments in the religious history of late medieval England. I begin in 1381, the year in which Wyclif went into exile from Oxford on account of his ideas about the eucharist, and I conclude in 1521, the year in which Martin Luther's books were first burned in England at the behest of Henry VIII's government.[22] The choice of such a substantial period of time makes it foolhardy to attempt to study all the issues of religious interest to late medieval Christians; it also makes it impossible to study the many interesting and under-explored resonances between English and conti-nental forms of dissent. In the hope that detailed 'case studies' may help to disclose more general trends, I have accordingly chosen five clusters of doctrines for close analysis.

A Note on The Use of Trial Records

Much of what follows relies upon careful readings of the various texts and trial records which comprise the majority of the extant contemporary evidence for the Wycliffite controversy and its aftermath. These texts fall into four general categories, though the boundaries between them are somewhat more fluid than has generally been acknowledged: Wyclif's own writings; the Latin and vernacular texts of his academic followers and later dissenters; the theological

---

[22] On the circumstances which impelled the English government to burn Luther's books, see D'Alton, 'The suppression of heresy in early Henrician England', 102–3.

and polemical texts produced by anti-Wycliffite churchmen and ecclesiastical assemblies; and the records of the examinations, trials, and punishments of heresy suspects. Each of these corpora of texts presents its own set of interpretative difficulties, but none is for that reason to be rejected. Indeed, even the most problematic sources can sometimes be mutually illuminating if juxtaposed with one another.

In the first chapter of *The Premature Reformation*, Hudson has set out the hermeneutical challenges which confront students of Wyclif's writings, the Latin and vernacular texts of later authors, the detailed refutations of Wycliffite ideas produced by the spokesmen of orthodoxy, and chronicles and synodal *acta*. There is not space to rehearse her arguments here, but the records of the trials of heresy suspects deserve further discussion as historical sources. After all, it is primarily from such documents that we can glean detailed information about the beliefs of the majority of dissenters who could not or did not commit their ideas to writing. These records include material preserved in episcopal registers, where most heresy business seems to have been recorded, as well as in separate court books dedicated to heresy trials.[23] Chance entries in visitation records, consistory and archidiaconal court books, and the records of secular administration also contain information about heresy proceedings, though in the latter case, details about the beliefs that suspects were accused of holding are especially rare.[24] Taking all of these sources into account, the extant records identify at least 659 individual heresy defendants; they include information about the alleged religious convictions of at least 420 of them.

It is no coincidence that these records, the most crucial sources for the voice of otherwise voiceless individuals, are also the sources whose value as historical evidence has most often been called into question.[25] Broadly speaking, three sets of objections have been raised. First, the procedures that governed the trial

---

[23] For further details about episcopal registers and their contents, see David Smith's invaluable *Guide to Bishops' Registers of England and Wales* (London, 1981) and its supplement (London, 2004); for church courts and their proceedings, see the first chapter of Richard M. Wunderli, *London Church Courts and Society on the Eve of the Reformation* (Cambridge, Mass., 1981).

[24] As a result, this study relies only occasionally on material preserved in the records of the courts of King's Bench and Chancery. Though it might seem that indictments and significations of excommunication should provide fertile soil for analyses of dissenting belief, hardly any such records contain sufficient detail for defendants to emerge as individuals.

[25] By, among others, Derek J. Plumb, 'John Foxe and the later Lollards of the Thames Valley' (Ph.D. thesis, University of Cambridge, 1987), 12–13; Charles Kightly, 'The early Lollards: A survey of popular Lollard activity in England, 1382–1428' (Ph.D. thesis, York University, 1975), 576; Paul Strohm, 'Counterfeiters, Lollards, and Lancastrian unease' in Wendy Scase, Rita Copeland, and David Lawton (eds.), *New Medieval Literatures*, vol. i (Oxford, 1997), 31–58; Swanson, *Church and Society in Late Medieval England*, 335; *Coventry*, 14.

and sentencing of heresy defendants tended to oversimplify their views. As early as the 1420s, Archbishop Henry Chichele had commissioned his theologians and canon lawyers to produce questionnaires to be administered to heresy suspects. Episcopal registers suggest that this practice was quickly taken up by bishops like Thomas Polton of Worcester, Thomas Bekynton of Bath and Wells, and William Aiscough of Salisbury.[26] Questionnaires were still in use in the sixteenth century; the registers of Archbishop Warham of Canterbury and Bishop Blythe of Coventry and Lichfield both contain similar, though less extensive, sets of questions, and the constant repetition of many articles in surviving abjurations likewise suggests that inquisitorial preconceptions shaped the manner in which defendants' beliefs were recorded for posterity.[27] At the same time, the omission of subjects like christology and soteriology from the extant questionnaires may have obscured some elements of dissenting theology, since defendants would have been unlikely to profess controversial views unless first asked about them.[28] Indeed, the purpose of a late medieval heresy trial was not to provide a suspect with the opportunity to expound her or his belief system; it was instead to establish her or his guilt with respect to a specific set of charges.[29] Defendants may have had very little opportunity to explain themselves, and thus, whilst they may have subscribed to many of the beliefs they abjured, we cannot be certain of the relative theological emphases that they may have placed on individual ideas.[30]

Second, even if a particular trial included an unusually frank exchange of views between defendant and inquisitor, the extant records are often at a remove of several degrees from the original event. As Peter Biller and Leonard Boyle have shown with regard to the abjurations of 'Cathar' heretics in medieval Languedoc, a registrar or scribe would usually have transformed a defendant's English words into a series of Latin articles and then would often have used those articles to compose a vernacular abjuration for the defendant to sign.[31] In addition, the episcopal registers and heresy court books extant

---

[26] Anne Hudson, 'The examination of Lollards', repr. in *Books*, 124–40 at 126–7.

[27] *Coventry*, 161–5; *Kent*, 2–3.

[28] On the discursive differences between self-generated and inquisitorially prompted statements, see L. B. Brown and J. P. Forgan, 'The structure of religion: A multi-dimensional scaling of informal elements', *Journal for the Scientific Study of Religion*, 19 (1980), 423–31 at 424–5.

[29] For an especially pessimistic account of the violations of the church's own procedures that may have occurred in some medieval heresy trials, see H. A. Kelly, 'Lollard inquisitions: Due and undue process' in A. Ferreiro (ed.), *The Devil, Heresy, and Witchcraft in the Middle Ages* (Leiden, 1998), 279–303 at 299–301.

[30] I owe this distinction to Rowan Williams, *Arius: Heresy and tradition*, 2nd edn (London, 2001), 95.

[31] For Biller, see n. 17 above; Leonard E. Boyle, '*Montaillou* revisited: Mentalité and methodology' in J. Raftis (ed.), *Pathways to Medieval Peasants* (Toronto, 1981), 119–40.

today are not always the original records of the trials they document; a scribe's notes would often have been recopied into a more elegant form, and it is unclear when that process resulted in a summary rather than a verbatim transcript of the original material.[32] The consequences for both the accuracy and the comprehensiveness of the records are self-evident.

Third, there is the possibility that heresy defendants may sometimes have dissembled when asked about their beliefs. The experience of inquisitors in the Languedoc is again relevant here; in the early fourteenth century, the Dominican friar Bernard Gui wrote in his *Practica inquisitionis hereticae pravitatis* that heresy suspects were wont not only to lie but also to agree among one another on a set of stories to be told to the church's representatives.[33] An anonymous text, *Sixteen Points on which the Bishops Accuse Lollards*, suggests that English heresy defendants may have done the same; it provides a set of ready-made responses to questions about the eucharist, the papacy, and other doctrines often asked of suspected heretics.[34] If lollards advised one another how to respond to their inquisitors, then it cannot be taken for granted that their answers reflect their authentic religious beliefs.

Objections like these and others deserve serious attention, for they cast substantial doubt on the use of trial records as evidence for dissenters' beliefs. Nevertheless, the limitations of the sources have often been exaggerated, and since the extant court records are usually the only available sources for the religious convictions of English heresy suspects, it is essential for scholars to consider carefully to what extent they are untrustworthy. Far from being the formulaic products of church authorities committed to achieving convictions at any cost, the records instead reveal a surprising number of details about dissenting belief and practice, details that in many cases medieval churchmen never intended to bequeath to posterity.[35]

To illustrate what I mean, I wish to focus briefly on one of the two extant court books dedicated to heresy proceedings.[36] In 1428, Bishop Alnwick of Norwich tried the first of between 80 and 120 suspects to appear before him over the four-year period to 1431. The proceedings of these trials do not

---

[32] For one such instance, see *Norwich*, 2.

[33] Bernard Gui, *Practica inquisitionis hereticae pravitatis* in *Heresies of the High Middle Ages*, ed. and trans. Walter L. Wakefield and Austin P. Evans (New York, 1991), 375–86 at 377.

[34] *Selections*, no. 2.

[35] R. N. Swanson, 'Literacy, heresy, history, and orthodoxy: Perspectives and permutations for the later Middle Ages' in Peter Biller and Anne Hudson (eds.), *Heresy and Literacy, 1000–1530* (Cambridge, 1996), 279–93. The traditional account of the late medieval inquisition as a bloodthirsty and selfish organization can be found in Henry Charles Lea, *A History of the Inquisition in the Middle Ages*, 3 vols. (London, 1888), i.233.

[36] The other court book exclusively concerned with heresy is the so-called 'Lichfield Court Book', now available in print as *Coventry*.

appear, however, in his register, which contains only a single heresy case from the same period; they are instead preserved in a separate, but now damaged, court book, London, Westminster Diocesan Archives B.2, and in Foxe's transcriptions of those other portions of the court book which are no longer extant. According to Norman Tanner, the manuscript contains not the original minutes of the trials but, rather, copies of the original documents which were likely made by Alnwick's registrar, John Excestr, who attended almost all of the trials and seems to have presided at least once.[37] In the trial of William Masse of Earsham, who first appeared before the bishop on 14 March 1430, there is something of an anomaly: one of the eight articles Masse was accused of believing has been struck through in the same ink in which the rest of the court book was written.[38] This erasure might seem unremarkable, but it raises a host of questions. That the article, which accused Masse of denying the doctrine of transubstantiation, had mistakenly been included in the original record is easy enough to account for: some thirty-four other defendants who appeared before Alnwick had been charged with the same heresy, and Excestr might have inadvertently included it in his list of the charges against Masse. But that he then erased it is harder to explain. If medieval inquisitors and their scribes were as keen to stereotype heresy defendants as some critics have suggested, then Excestr would have no reason to regret, much less to correct, his error. Likewise, there would have been little propaganda value in ensuring that the record of Masse's trial was accurate; the extant court book, like all bishops' registers and other trial records, had not been prepared for public consumption but for the internal use of the bishop and his colleagues. And from a legal point of view, the specific heresies that Masse abjured were irrelevant. If he had later been tried again, then conviction of *any* heresy would have constituted relapse.[39] Thus, the most likely explanation for the erasure is that Excestr, as a conscientious scribe, was genuinely concerned for the accuracy of his record.

It would, of course, be ludicrous to propose that just because John Excestr erased one sentence in the record of the trial of an obscure Norwich heretic, historians should throw caution to the wind and return to their former naïveté about the sources. Nevertheless, Excestr's probity cannot be ignored, and other pieces of evidence can be brought together to rehabilitate the reputations of late medieval inquisitors. One of the other curious features of Excestr's court book is the way in which it seamlessly elides the boundaries between Latin and vernacular discourse. In recording the trial of John Burell,

---

[37] *Norwich*, 4.
[38] London, Westminster Diocesan Archives MS B.2, 250.
[39] Lea, *A History of the Inquisition in the Middle Ages*, iii.202.

for instance, Excestr notes that the defendant 'dicit ... quod quidam sutor, famulus Thome Mone, docuit [Burell] quod nullus homo tenetur ieiunare diebus Quadragesimalibus nec sextis feriis nec vigiliis apostolorum, quia talia ieiunia nunquam erant instituta ex precepto divino sed tantum ex ordinacione presbiterorum, *for every Fryday is fre day*'.[40]

I have quoted this passage in the original languages in order to highlight the fact that Excestr, like the scribes of many medieval common law courts, slides without comment from the formal Latin of his notarial voice into a vernacular idiom which, we must assume, represents something of Burell's actual speech.[41] Steven Justice has advanced the audacious suggestion that Excestr was bored and recorded Burell's and other English phrases because 'he thought they were just interesting'.[42] That may be the case; or perhaps the phrase amused Bishop Alnwick, who ordered that it be written down; or perhaps Excestr himself thought it worthy of recording for later use. We shall never know. But whatever the reason, the evidentiary value of interjections such as this cannot be exaggerated, as they provide fleeting glances into what was actually said in the ecclesiastical courtrooms of the late Middle Ages.[43]

In a paradox common to many medieval and early modern texts, it is precisely where trial records are least interested in recording the minutiae of lollard belief that they tend to disclose the greatest detail.[44] In other dioceses as well, many defendants' own words are preserved not in their abjurations, which ecclesiastical officials usually prepared for them, but instead in the surviving depositions of witnesses: thus, for instance, the Coventry tailor Roger Landesdale's vernacular explication of the eucharist as a memorial of Jesus' death appears not in his abjuration but rather in the testimony of Thomas Abell.[45] The dissenters' passwords, 'May we all drinke of a cuppe' and 'God kepe you and God blesse you', were likewise disclosed in Landesdale's own testimony.[46] In this respect, some sets of records reveal a greater volume of detail than others.

---

[40] London, Westminster Diocesan Archives MS B.2, 234, emphasis mine.

[41] Likewise, there are no visual clues in the manuscript; the English words appear in exactly the same handwriting and style as the Latin.

[42] Justice, 'Inquisition, speech, and writing', 8.

[43] R. N. Swanson, '"... Et examinatus dicit ...": Oral and personal history in the records of English Ecclesiastical Courts' in Michael Goodich (ed.), *Voices from the Bench: The narratives of lesser folk in medieval trials* (New York, 2005), 203–25 at 203–5.

[44] This is a point made to great effect by René Girard in the opening chapter of *The Scapegoat*, trans. Yvonne Freccero (London, 1986), 5–8, and also by Strohm, *England's Empty Throne*, xiii, and Arnold, *Inquisition and Power*, 152.

[45] *Coventry*, 183.

[46] *Coventry*, 117.

At the same time, the appearance of radical and otherwise unexpected articles in a number of documents suggests both that late medieval inquisitors were not so narrow minded as to inquire into only those beliefs covered by their questionnaires and that heresy suspects must often be regarded, in Jurkowski's phrase, as religiously 'self-confident' individuals.[47] Margery Baxter of Martham, tried before Bishop Alnwick in 1428, famously admitted that she had prayed to the Wycliffite preacher William White, who, she said, 'is a great saint in heaven and a most holy teacher ordained and sent by God'.[48] The following year, William Colyn of South Creake was accused of having said that he would rather touch a woman's privy parts than the sacrament of the altar.[49] Idiosyncratic ideas can readily be found in other records as well. Even when defendants abjured only those beliefs normally associated with lollardy, many inquisitors seem to have taken care to ensure that their abjurations were accurate. Most registers and court books preserve an individual abjuration for each defendant. Though they follow a standard form and include many of the same articles, these abjurations seem to have been customized for each case. To choose a random example, of the seven defendants who abjured before Archbishop Warham in the month of August, 1511, six confessed to heresies concerning pilgrimages, five to impugning the veneration of images, three to denying the efficacy of confession, and one to refusing to offer prayers to the saints.[50]

Taken together, all these considerations suggest that whilst the lists of beliefs preserved in defendants' abjurations and witnesses' depositions are incomplete, they are nonetheless not normally fabricated. An even more compelling reason to accept that the extant records reflect at least some measure of their subjects' beliefs lies in the harsher realities of the situation. It is inconceivable, particularly during the tenure of a relatively humanitarian archbishop like Warham, that a defendant would maintain a dissenting opinion to which she or he was not wholly committed, knowing that the possible consequences might include her or his death at the stake.[51] This line of reasoning is admittedly less certain in the case of relapsed heretics, who might have chosen to scandalize their audiences knowing that their fates had already been sealed, but the likelihood that any suspect would approach her or his trial in such a mindset is nevertheless not great.

[47] Jurkowski, 'Lollardy and social status', 150.
[48] *Norwich*, 47: 'est magnus sanctus in celo et sanctissimus doctor ordinatus et missus a Deo'.
[49] *Norwich*, 91.
[50] *Kent*, 79–91.
[51] Norman Tanner, 'Penances imposed on Kentish Lollards by Archbishop Warham, 1511–12' in *Lollardy and Gentry*, 229–49 at 234, 242–3.

In this book, therefore, I will treat the records of heresy trials as limited but nonetheless viable sources for the religious convictions of late medieval dissenters. Their greatest limitation is one of perspective; since bishops and their officials were primarily concerned to identify those doctrines which differentiated dissenters from their so-called 'orthodox' contemporaries, abjurations and depositions tend to focus on the ways in which lollards opposed the beliefs and practices of the institutional church. They suggest that lollard culture was overwhelmingly negative, interested more in rejecting mainstream religion than in constructing a more attractive alternative. It may perhaps have been, but Wyclif's treatises and the writings of his followers reveal, as we shall see, that Wycliffism and lollardy were theologically constructive as well as destructive. By juxtaposing the records of heresy trials with texts from the dissenters themselves, we will be able both to explore the theological assumptions that underpinned the beliefs which dissenters abjured and to identify those places where the apparent unanimity of the trial records may conceal the diversity of beliefs to be found in lollard texts. But before anything else, we must confront the central terminological question: what, after all, is a lollard?

J. Patrick Hornbeck II
Bronx, New York

Acknowledgements

This book began life as a doctoral thesis in the Faculty of Theology of the University of Oxford, where it was supervised by Professor Diarmaid MacCulloch; he has kindly reprised that role in shepherding the manuscript through to publication. My interest in lollardy dates back somewhat further, to my undergraduate years at Georgetown University, when in back-to-back semesters I often heard the word come from the mouths of two ferociously gifted teachers, Scott Pilarz, S.J., and Penn Szittya.

More recently, I am grateful to the many individuals, libraries, and institutions without whom the research and writing of this study could not have taken place. Foremost among them is Mishtooni Bose, whom I thank not only for her keen questions and sharp-eyed editorial work but also for her friendship. Andrew Cole, Alastair Minnis, Paul Strohm, Steven Justice, Shannon Gayk, R. N. Swanson, Jeremy Catto, and an anonymous reader for the Oxford University Press all read chapters or sections of this work; it is the better for their suggestions and criticisms, though any infelicities of phrase or thought which remain are mine alone. I am also grateful for conversations with and advice from Anne Hudson, Fiona Somerset, Helen Barr, Ian Levy, Stephen Lahey, Jill Havens, and Ian Forrest. Audiences at seminars and colloquia in Oxford, Cambridge, London, and New York; at the international medieval conferences in Kalamazoo and Leeds; and at two meetings of the Lollard Society helped me to distil my thinking and clarify my arguments at crucial junctures.

Many librarians and keepers of record offices have been willing to respond to detailed questions and requests for access to primary documents. In addition to the kind-hearted staff of Duke Humfrey's Library, I am thankful to the library of Merton College, Oxford; the library of Gonville and Caius College, Cambridge; Cambridge University Library; the Guildhall Library, London; the Westminster Diocesan Archives; the Centre for Kentish Studies, Maidstone; Canterbury Cathedral Archives; the Wiltshire and Swindon Archives; the Worcester Record Office; the Hereford Archive Service; the Hampshire Record Office; the Lichfield Record Office; and the Devon Record Office. For permission to quote from manuscripts in their possession I have to thank the Master and Fellows of Gonville and Caius College, Cambridge; the Diocese of Lincoln and Lincolnshire Archives; Guildhall Library, City of London Corporation; Wiltshire and Swindon Archives; Hampshire Record Office; and the Westminster Diocesan Archives. Sections of two chapters appeared as articles in the *Journal of Ecclesiastical History* and the *Revue d'histoire ecclésiastique*; I thank their editors and editorial boards for helpful suggestions and Cambridge University Press for permission to republish the material in Chapter 4. For funding, I am grateful to the Jack Kent Cooke Foundation; Christ Church, Oxford; the Faculty of Theology of the University of Oxford; and the Timothy S. Healy Scholarship Trust.

A beloved friend and department chair of mine frequently quips that 'theology is a team sport', and I am thankful for the support, questions, and welcomes of so many colleagues at Fordham University where the bulk of the work of preparing this monograph has taken place. In particular, I am grateful to Terry Tilley, Larry Welborn, Elizabeth Johnson, Maureen Tilley, Maryanne Kowaleski, and Brennan O'Donnell. Joyce O'Leary, Anne-Marie Sweeney, and my research assistant Jennifer Illig all deserve recognition for helping to create and maintain an environment in which research can thrive, and thrive humanely.

The greatest debts, as always, are personal. Lewis Allan helped me maintain sanity and perspective as the thesis out of which this book came reached fruition. My parents, Susann and Patrick Hornbeck, have consistently, generously, and selflessly provided their love and their support from the very first day; this book could not have been written without their sacrifices. Finally, about halfway between defending my doctoral thesis and submitting the manuscript of this study I received a gift I could never have expected or deserved. Anthony Keen's fingerprints are not obvious on every page of this text, but the questions he has asked and the love he has shared have made this a better book and me a better person.

Table of Contents

List of Abbreviations

A&M	John Foxe, *The . . . Ecclesiasticall History Contaynyng the Actes and Monuments* (London, 1570)
Arnold	Thomas Arnold (ed.), *Select English Works of John Wycliffe*, 3 vols. (Oxford, 1869–71)
Books	Anne Hudson, *Lollards and Their Books* (London, 1985)
Companion	Ian Christopher Levy (ed.), *A Companion to John Wyclif: Late medieval theologian* (Leiden, 2006)
Coventry	Shannon McSheffrey and Norman Tanner (eds. and trans.), *Lollards of Coventry, 1486–1522* (Camden Fifth Series 23, 2003)
EETS	Early English Text Society
EWS	Anne Hudson and Pamela Gradon (eds.), *English Wycliffite Sermons*, 5 vols. (Oxford, 1983–97)
FZ	W. W. Shirley (ed.), *Fasciculi zizaniorum* (Rolls Series, 1858)
Influence	Fiona Somerset, Jill C. Havens, and Derrick Pitard (eds.), *Lollards and Their Influence in Late Medieval England* (Woodbridge, 2003)
Kent	Norman Tanner (ed.), *Kent Heresy Proceedings, 1511–12* (Kent Records 26, 1997)
Lollards and Reformers	Margaret Aston, *Lollards and Reformers: Images and literacy in late medieval religion* (London, 1984)
Lollardy and Gentry	Margaret Aston and Colin Richmond (eds.), *Lollardy and the Gentry in the Later Middle Ages* (Sutton, 1997)
Matthew	F. D. Matthew (ed.), *The English Works of Wyclif Hitherto Unprinted*, rev. edn (EETS o.s. 74, 1902)
Norwich	Norman P. Tanner (ed.), *Heresy Trials in the Diocese of Norwich, 1428–1431* (London, 1977)
Ockham to Wyclif	Anne Hudson and Michael Wilks (eds.), *From Ockham to Wyclif* (Studies in Church History, Subsidia 5, Oxford, 1987)
OED	*Oxford English Dictionary*
PR	Anne Hudson, *The Premature Reformation: Wycliffite texts and Lollard history* (Oxford, 1988)

Selections	Anne Hudson (ed.), *Selections from English Wycliffite Writings*, rev. edn (Toronto, 1997)
Tanner, *Decrees*	Norman Tanner (ed.), *Decrees of the Ecumenical Councils*, 2 vols. (Washington, 1990)
Text and Controversy	Helen Barr and Ann M. Hutchinson (eds.), *Text and Controversy from Wyclif to Bale: Essays in honour of Anne Hudson* (Turnhout, 2005)
Thomson, *Later Lollards*	J. A. F. Thomson, *The Later Lollards: 1414–1520* (Oxford, 1965)
Titus	Anne Hudson (ed.), *Tractatus de oblacione iugis sacrificii*, in *The Works of a Lollard Preacher* (EETS o.s. 317, 2001)
Wilkins	David Wilkins (ed.), *Concilia Magnae Brittaniae et Hiberniae*, 4 vols. (1737, repr. Brussels, 1964)
Wilks, *Wyclif*	Michael Wilks, *Wyclif: Political ideas and practice*, ed. Anne Hudson (Oxford, 2000)

Notes to the Reader

QUOTATIONS AND PROPER NAMES

All English quotations in the text and footnotes appear as in their original sources, except where I have removed superfluous medieval punctuation or substituted the word *and* for the ampersand. Quotations from other languages have been translated and the original text given in the notes. As far as possible, I have rendered place names in their modern forms. Unless otherwise noted, transcriptions and translations are my own.

THE WORKS OF JOHN WYCLIF

Wyclif's works are cited only by their title; full bibliographical and editorial details can be found in the Bibliography.

BISHOPS' REGISTERS

Bishops' registers are cited only by the name of the see and the bishop concerned: thus John Trefnant's Hereford register is 'Hereford reg. Trefnant.' The Bibliography provides full bibliographical details and indicates whether a particular register is being cited from the original manuscript(s) or from a printed edition.

1

Introduction: Family Resemblances

When, as a 17-year-old, I applied for undergraduate admission to Georgetown University, in Washington, D.C., I discovered that all first-year students were, and still are, required to take an introductory course in theology. The requirement reflects the curricular breadth that has for many centuries been the hallmark of Jesuit education, ever since the publication in 1599 of the *Ratio studiorum* for the Collegio Romano.[1] But more interesting was the way the course appeared in the catalogue: Theology-001, 'The Problem of God.'

What was the problem with God, I asked? The title of the course was wonderfully ambiguous, and the professors who taught it responded accordingly: some discussed the classic philosophical and theological debates about the existence and the attributes of God; some assigned readings that emphasized the problems modern scholars have identified with traditional constructions of God; some lectured on the state of belief and non-belief in the contemporary world; and so forth. In the face of such curricular diversity, it came to seem to us undergraduates that the 'problem' at stake was less about God than about the multifaceted and multi-method enterprise of theology. Why did so many scholars commit their lives and their careers to the study of something whose very definition remained so elusive?

And therein lies the parallel between the study of theology writ large and the particular set of historical and theological issues with which this book is concerned. In the nearly five hundred years since the start of the Henrician Reformation and the writing of the first pre-histories of that event by English evangelical propagandists, the definition of the phenomenon that scholars so commonly refer to as lollardy remains unclear. First, as I briefly indicated in the Preface, there are the natural frictions between disciplines; whilst for many years lollardy was the province of theologians and ecclesiastical historians, not to mention polemicists on both sides of the Reformation divide, in recent years it has been studied much more frequently in faculties of English literature. Second, there have been challenges to the very existence of lollardy as a

---

[1] On the *Ratio*, see most recently the collection of essays edited by the late Vincent Duminuco, *The Jesuit Ratio Studiorum: 400th anniversary perspectives* (New York, 2000).

discrete phenomenon; in the past two decades in particular, and largely in response to earlier, exaggerated accounts of the role that lollardy played in shaping the English Reformation, it has in some circles been quite common to argue that 'lollardy', in scare-quotes, is primarily the construction of medieval and Reformation propagandists and later historians. There may well have been individuals in late medieval England who resisted the theology and the practice of institutional Roman Christianity, the argument goes, but to call them lollards, particularly Lollards with an upper-case L, is to attribute to them far more coherence and significance than they deserve.

The most serious and complex difficulties, however, revolve around questions of terminology. What, after all, is a lollard? The term's etymology remains a source of dispute among scholars: was it coined in the heat of the academic controversies in the University of Oxford in which John Wyclif and his followers played such a prominent role, or was it a pre-existing term of abuse only retroactively applied to Wycliffites and their supporters?[2] Its affiliations remain equally problematic: it has often been paired with *Wycliffite*, with many scholars accustomed, like Anne Hudson, to speaking in one breath of 'the academic disciples of Wyclif and the later, provincial Lollard[s]'.[3] Recent years have seen the appearance of a number of studies which address the language that might best be used to describe the individuals and groups of religious dissenters whose beliefs are chronicled in these pages. They are too numerous to list here, but the collective work of such scholars as Shannon McSheffrey, Andrew Cole, Kathryn Kerby-Fulton, Margaret Aston, and others has urged us to revise the commonplace equation of the term 'lollard' with the term 'Wycliffite'; and, perhaps even more importantly, to resist thinking of all religious dissenters in late medieval England as automatically connected with Wyclif and the communities that sprung up in his wake.[4]

This chapter aims not to resolve forever these and other terminological questions but, instead, to propose a new model for thinking about the category 'lollardy', a model that draws not only on the traditional disciplines

---

[2] For one recent discussion of the etymology and history of the term, see Wendy Scase, '"Heu! quanta desolatio Angliae praestatur": A Wycliffite libel and the naming of heretics, Oxford 1382' in Fiona Somerset, Jill C. Havens, and Derrick Pitard (eds.), *Lollards and Their Influence in Late Medieval England* (Woodbridge, 2003), 19–36.

[3] *PR*, 2.

[4] In particular, I am thinking of McSheffrey's 'Heresy, orthodoxy'; Cole's *Literature and Heresy in the Age of Chaucer* (Cambridge, 2008); Kerby-Fulton's *Books under Suspicion* (South Bend, Ind., 2006); and Aston's 'Were the Lollards a sect?' in *The Medieval Church: Universities, heresy, and the religious life: Essays in honour of Gordon Leff* (Studies in Church History, Subsidia 11, Woodbridge, 1999), 163–91.

of literary, historical, and theological studies but also on those of psychology and biology. This model, inspired largely by the twentieth-century philosopher Ludwig Wittgenstein's theory of family resemblance, has the potential not to solve the mystery of which inhabitants of late medieval England were and were not lollards but, rather, to help students of lollardy ask more helpful questions of the sources. Its implications for future studies are potentially significant.

TRENDS IN RECENT SCHOLARSHIP

Let us begin with the trial of Thomas Denys, who was burned at the stake at the behest of the Bishop of Winchester. At the time of his trial, Denys was living in New Malden, a hamlet some two miles east of Kingston-upon-Thames, in what is now the south-west part of Greater London. Denys was brought before Dr John Dowman, the bishop's vicar in spirituals, and questioned about his religious beliefs and his involvement in dissenting communities. The record of his trial, preserved in the bishop's register, reveals that Denys' theological views had previously landed him in legal trouble; some years earlier, he admitted, he had been living in Waltham Abbey, Essex, to the north-east of London, where he had been 'detected and taken by thofficers of the bisshop of London than being [his] ordinary, for and upon certain and diuerse pointes and articules of heresye and erroneouse opinions contrary to the determination of holy church.'[5] Denys admitted that he had learned these heresies from one Richard Hortop of Waltham, who later moved to Turnmill Street, near the City of London. Denys had done public penance by bearing a faggot of wood both at Paul's Cross and in his home town, as the register records, 'under maner and forme wonte to be used in such matiers.'[6]

But what did Denys believe? The records of his first trial have been lost, and the records of his second provide less information on this point than we might wish to have. This may well be because Denys was being tried as a relapsed heretic, and hence the authorities simply needed to show that he had reverted to any one of his former beliefs in order to secure a conviction. But there are some tantalizing hints. Denys confessed that he had taught:

that the sacrament of thaltar in fourme of brede was not the veray body of criste, but a commemoration of cristis passion, and cristes body in a figure and not the veray body;

---

[5] Winchester reg. Fox, iii, fol. 69r.
[6] Ibid., Fox, iii, fol. 69r.

that oblation doen by man or woman to thimages in the church was but Idolatrie and nothing worth for they were but stokes and stones made by mannys hande; [and] that preestes might not assoile oon man for offenses doen to a noder man, but that oon man shuld aske a noder forgivenes for the said trespass soe doon and not to be assoiled therof of a prist.[7]

Denys also admitted that he had taught these points in conventicles with other local dissenters and that he had been a purveyor of dissenting texts. As we might expect, Denys was duly handed over to the secular arm and burned in Kingston, where three of his associates were also tried and given penances for their crimes.

Read through the lens of the traditional historiography, Denys and his fellows seem to have been model Wycliffites or lollards. On the one hand, the beliefs for which they were punished can be found in the classic statements of Wycliffite doctrine, namely in texts like the long cycle of English Wycliffite sermons, the *Twelve Conclusions* posted by Wycliffite sympathizers on the doors of Parliament in 1395, and later writings such as the *Apology for Lollard Doctrines*. On the other hand, they also seem to be engaging in classically Wycliffite textual practices. We learn from the trial records that they circulated and read to one another from dissenting texts as well as from the vernacular Scriptures, and we even find that these texts facilitated the conversion of new dissenters. When Denys and his associate Philip Braban wished to induct one of their neighbours into their belief system, they brought him books and encouraged him to read and copy them.[8]

But the difficulty with this portrait of Denys and company as model Wycliffites is that Denys was burned in the year 1512. Even taking into account his claim that he had first learned his dissenting beliefs 'about xxti yeres now last passed', more than a century separates the activities of John Wyclif and his early Oxford followers from those of Denys and his teacher.[9] And neither Denys nor any of the other defendants arrested in Bishop Richard Fox's investigations in Winchester referred to themselves as 'Wycliffites' or 'lollards', or cited Wyclif by name, with (as we shall shortly see) one possible exception; the same can be said of the defendants caught up in the roughly contemporary heresy trials of Archbishop William Warham in Canterbury. Likewise, only one of the forty-nine individuals summoned before Bishop Geoffrey Blythe of Coventry and Lichfield in 1511 and 1512 mentioned Wyclif, and that reference is ambiguous at best.[10]

---

[7] Winchester reg., Fox, iii, fos. 69r–69v.   [8] Ibid., iii, fol. 69v.
[9] Ibid., iii, fol. 69r.
[10] For the reference to Wyclif, in the trial of Thomas Abell, see *Coventry*, 182.

So was Thomas Denys a lollard? Was he a Wycliffite? And what do we even mean when we ask such questions?

Whether or not the Irish Cistercian monk Henry Crumpe was the first to use the term 'lollard', as the anonymous compiler of the collection *Fasciculi zizaniorum* seems to suggest, that label has dominated the historiography of late medieval dissent in England.[11] Its use reflects a set of assumptions about the coherence of dissenting belief and practice that was nearly universal among medieval churchmen and early historians: namely, that heretics believed the same sorts of things and expressed their convictions in highly consistent ways. In the late medieval and early modern periods, not only the opponents but also the publicists of Wyclif and his followers subscribed to Knighton's view that all 'lollards' used a distinctive vocabulary and pro-pounded the same theological views. Thus, for instance, John Foxe concluded his account of the several dozen heresy suspects tried in Norwich diocese in the 1420s and 1430s with the claim that there was 'such society and agreement of doctrine to be amongst them, that in their assertions and articles there was almost no difference'.[12] As Steven Justice has put it, 'for Foxe and Reformation historiography, all the truly faithful were truly one, and all fourteenth- and fifteenth-century dissenters were inspired by Wyclif; the same assumptions made all dissenting writing Wycliffite, and indeed Wyclif's.[13]

The assumption of coherence between Wyclif's views and those of later dissenters remained influential until the late nineteenth and early twentieth centuries, when many scholars began to distinguish between the Oxford thinker and those who came after him. The German historian Gotthard Lechler, for instance, described an 'inner circle' of Wyclif's closest followers and an 'outer circle' of those who may have been inspired by his reforming ideas but nevertheless did not endorse all of them.[14] This division became more pronounced in later work on the subject; Ezra Kempton Maxfield, writing in 1924, was following the terminological fashion of his day when he suggested that not all 'Wyclifian' ideas were carried over into the theologies of 'later Lollardry'.[15] Often, lollardy was seen as the intellectually vacuous

---

[11] *FZ*, 311–12.

[12] *A&M*, 661. Here and throughout this volume, I follow the practice recommended by Thomas Freeman of citing from the original editions of Foxe's *Actes and Monuments* rather than the nineteenth-century editions that distort Foxe's work ('Texts, lies, and microfilm: Reading and misreading Foxe's "Book of Martyrs"', *Sixteenth Century Journal*, 30 (1999), 23–46).

[13] Steven Justice, 'Lollardy' in David Wallace (ed.), *The Cambridge History of Medieval Literature* (Cambridge, 1999), 662–89 at 683.

[14] Gotthard Victor Lechler, *John Wycliffe and His English Precursors*, trans. P. Lorimer (London, 1884), 439.

[15] Ezra Kempton Maxfield, 'Chaucer and religious reform', *PMLA*, 39 (1924), 64–74 at 67, 68.

cousin of Wycliffism; K. B. McFarlane, for instance, was perhaps the most influential exponent of the often-repeated view that Wyclif's ideas had been dumbed down as they moved from theologically aware, Latin, scholastic discourse into a vernacular idiom.[16]

Nevertheless, the suggestion that medieval heretics be separated into theologically aware, Latinate 'Wycliffites' and somewhat less sophisticated, vernacular 'lollards' was never unanimously embraced, and it was dealt, historiographically speaking, a crushing blow in the opening pages of Hudson's *Premature Reformation*. There, Hudson argued that no distinction in meaning between the terms 'Wycliffite' and 'lollard' can be traced in the medieval sources, apart from the fact 'that *Lollard* was the clearer mark of opprobrium: the name was intensely disliked by those to whom it was early applied, though it later became a badge proudly worn'.[17] She concluded that the two words must therefore be used synonymously, since 'no useful distinction can be drawn between the academic disciples of Wyclif and the later, provincial Lollard, limited in his apprehensions to English, as has recently been fashionable' and since 'Wyclif must be regarded as the progenitor of views that, even a century after his death, are argued by the Lollards.'[18]

But is this fair? Hudson was right to point to the theological sophistication of the vernacular views McFarlane and others had dismissed, but in some instances her case seems to have been put too strongly. First, as the work of Jeremy Catto has demonstrated, ideological and political fissures existed even among Wyclif's early followers in Oxford. The reforming fellows of The Queen's College, for instance, distanced themselves from some of Wyclif's ideas whilst nevertheless sponsoring, in part, the English translation of the Bible, whereas the more radical group of Wycliffite fellows at Merton College 'continued to maintain and develop Wyclif's more controversial teaching and to propagate it through the work of itinerant preachers'.[19] Second, Paul Strohm has demonstrated that royal and ecclesiastical authorities had every incentive to exaggerate the coherence of lollardy as a means of bolstering their own claims to power. On his account, the fledgling Lancastrian dynasty used anti-heresy proceedings to demonstrate the virtues of Christian kingship. Strohm concluded that Lancastrian propagandists accordingly magnified the threat posed by heresy to the kingdom: 'so crucial was the Lollard heresy

---

[16] K. B. McFarlane, *John Wycliffe and the Beginnings of English Nonconformity* (London, 1952); and *Lancastrian Kings and Lollard Knights* (Oxford, 1972).

[17] *PR*, 3.

[18] Ibid., 2.

[19] Catto, 'Fellows and helpers', 152–3.

to the establishment of Lancastrian orthodoxy and legitimacy that, had it not existed, they would have had to devise something in its stead'.[20]

Third, even if an absolute binary between academic Wycliffites and vernacular lollards is not viable, it remains clear that earlier and later dissenters operated in different intellectual and social milieux. The style of argumentation that characterizes Wyclif's writings would not have been comprehensible to most laypeople.[21] At the same time, although such projects as the English sermon-cycle, the preachers' encyclopaedias the *Rosarium* and *Floretum*, and other vernacular products of Wycliffite scriptoria conveyed the substance of many of Wyclif's ideas in less erudite terms, few such works were produced or recopied after the opening decades of the fifteenth century. As a result, many later dissenters and groups of dissenters found themselves without authoritative guidance as they formulated or reformulated their views on such crucial issues as the eucharist and the papacy. The consequence, as we shall see in the following pages, was that some communities of dissenters formulated idiosyncratic views on particular doctrines. And finally, a number of studies have shown that few dissenters would have identified themselves primarily in terms of their religious convictions: as Catto has put it, 'Lollard consciousness must have had to compete with the neighbourhood loyalties of parish and town, often reinforced by membership of religious guilds or among more prosperous citizens by inclusion among town officers or commissions of government.'[22] Indeed, Derek Plumb and Richard Davies have shown that, in the early sixteenth century at least, a number of dissenters came from the higher social classes of their towns or villages, and a number of those tried for heresy throughout our period regularly attended mass with their neighbours or were in minor or even major orders.[23]

The uncritical use of a single label to encompass the whole range of late medieval dissenters, their texts, and their beliefs thus entails a host of methodological problems. Insufficiently qualified, the use of a blanket term like 'lollardy' for all inhabitants of the religious margins of late medieval England seems to imply the existence of an organized, centrally governed group of dissenters. But if to retain the conventional use of the categories 'lollard' and 'Wycliffite' is to engage in serious oversimplification, to jettison those terms is

---

[20] Strohm, *England's Empty Throne*, 209–10. Maurice Wiles and other scholars of the Arian movement have demonstrated that Athanasius of Alexandria adopted a similar strategy in 'grouping all opponents of Nicene orthodoxy under the single title of "Arian"' (*Archetypal Heresy: Arianism through the centuries* (Oxford, 1996), 27).

[21] On this point, see Fiona Somerset, *Clerical Discourse and Lay Audience in Late Medieval England* (Cambridge, 1998).

[22] Catto, 'Fellows and helpers', 144.

[23] Derek J. Plumb, 'A gathered church? Lollards and their society' in Margaret Spufford (ed.), *The World of Rural Dissenters* (Cambridge, 1995), 132–63; Davies, 'Lollardy and locality'.

equally unpalatable. In the first place, even if the composition, distribution, and reproduction of Wycliffite texts began to decline in the early fifteenth century, more than three hundred sermons and at least fifty other tracts remain extant. Many of these texts do articulate theological views which cohere not only with one another but also with Wyclif's treatises, and copies of some of them continued to be read as late as the early sixteenth century. Perhaps more significantly, there seem to be few viable alternative terminologies. In his recent study *The Detection of Heresy in Late Medieval England*, as well as in the doctoral thesis out of which that monograph came, Ian Forrest prefers not to speak of 'lollards' or 'Wycliffites', instead calling the subjects of his enquiry 'heretics' or 'heresy suspects'.[24] This is, on one level, a very sensible move: by focusing on a particular spiritual crime with a precise legal definition, Forrest has avoided many of the terminological ambiguities which have bedevilled the study of late medieval dissenters and their associates. But was the group of individuals who in one way or another rejected the authority of the institutional church contiguous with the group of those actually brought to trial? For the purposes of this study, speaking simply of 'heretics' or 'heresy suspects' may be too narrow.

Writing only about 'dissenters', on the other hand, is perhaps too broad. Kathryn Kerby-Fulton's recent volume *Books under Suspicion* sharply, and rightly, challenges the tradition of thinking of religious dissent in late medieval England solely in terms of 'lollardy' or 'Wycliffism'. She argues, instead, that English dissenters may have been influenced by ideas whose roots can be traced back to Joachim of Fiore and Joachite thought; or to the so-called 'Heresy of the Free Spirit'; and so forth.[25] And so, if terms like 'lollard' and 'Wycliffite' oversimplify the complex reality of late medieval religion, then there may be an equal, if not a greater, risk in referring to all the men and women we shall encounter in the following pages merely as 'dissenters'.

There is another wrinkle to all this, as well, for in many places there is nearly as much evidence for the *continuities* between groups of English dissenters as for the discontinuities between them. First, even though the majority of trial records show that dissenters did not think of themselves as Wycliffites or lollards, they did think of themselves as part of a group outside the religious mainstream. They were acutely aware of which of their neighbours were and were not of their number; William Lodge of Coventry testified in 1511, for instance, that he had once entered the brewer Thomas Banbrooke's house and found the tailor Roger Landesdale expounding the

---

[24] Ian James Forrest, 'Ecclesiastical justice and the detection of heresy in England, 1380–1430' (D.Phil. thesis, Oxford University, 2003), 2–7.

[25] Kerby-Fulton, *passim*.

Scriptures to his fellow townsman Richard Bradeley and Bradeley's wife Thomasina. 'Immediately Landesdale became silent', he reported, but 'Bradeley's wife said to Landesdale, "Do not fear, I trust he is a son of grace." '[26] Lodge's counterparts elsewhere were equally sensitive to the importance of maintaining both literal and discursive distance from non-members of their group. According to the register of Archbishop William Warham, at Christmas 1510, a group of Kentish dissenters from the villages of Benenden, Boxley, and Maidstone met at Edward Walker's home in Maidstone, where:

> the wife of the same Walker commyned, herd, assentid and affirmed without contradiccion ayenst the blessed sacrament of the aulter . . . And as they were so commynyng . . . the wif of yat said Walker said, 'Sires, it is not good that ye talke moche here of thies maters for the jaylors will take hede of you yf ye come huder. And also beware for som folks will comyn hider anon.' And thereupon furthwith came yn the jaylors wif and they cessed of their communicacion.[27]

Characteristic lollard descriptors such as 'known man' and 'son of grace' do not appear in Warham's register, but utterances like Mrs Walker's confirm that Kentish dissenters, like their fellows in Coventry, identified themselves as members of a group from whose discussions outsiders must be excluded.[28]

If dissenters shared something of a common literature and an in-group identity, then it may not wholly be coincidental that heterodoxy was concentrated in a relatively small number of localities during the period between Wyclif's death and the outbreak of the Henrician Reformation. As Lutton and others have shown, heretical beliefs were often transmitted through the ties of kinship, and it was thus that dissenting communities in Coventry and Kent could trace their roots to at least the 1480s.[29] The heresy-prone Kentish village of Tenterden had deeper roots still; it was home in the 1420s to William White, the roaming evangelist whose converts included many of the Norwich dissenters tried in 1428–31.[30] Further instances of geographical continuity can be found in the communities of Amersham, Norwich, and Steeple

---

[26] *Coventry*, 201.

[27] *Kent*, 55. 'The jaylors' likely refers to local officers of the law who might notice the presence of individuals from outside the village.

[28] Hudson has argued that these epithets, current as late as the 1520s, served as a sort of shorthand to identify members of the sect to one another (*PR*, 143). See also her article 'A Lollard sect vocabulary?' repr. in *Books*, 181–92; and Matti Peikola, *Congregation of the Elect: Patterns of self-fashioning in English Lollard writings* (Turku, 2000).

[29] This point is best made in Lutton's new book *Lollardy and Orthodox Religion*, 19–26; see also his earlier article 'Godparenthood, kinship, and piety in Tenterden, England, 1449–1537' in I. Davis, M. Muller, and S. Rees Jones (eds.), *Love, Marriage, and Family Ties in the Middle Ages* (Turnhout, 2003), 217–34, for the intriguing suggestion that ties of godparenthood should also be considered in this connection.

[30] Thomson, *Later Lollards*, 173; *Kent*, xxi.

Bumstead, to name but the most prominent.[31] At the same time, contemporary sources disclose a number of connections between dissenters in disparate regions. Joan Warde *alias* Wasshingburn, burned in Coventry in 1512, admitted during her trial that she and her husband, having first learned their heresies in their native Coventry, lived with other dissenters in Northampton, London, and Maidstone, where she had abjured and been branded with the letter *H* on each cheek.[32] Thomas Acton of Coventry admitted to having provided lodgings to an anonymous 'knowen man' during his six-night stay in the city; this wandering dissenter and others like him may have linked Acton and his Coventry fellows with communities elsewhere.[33] And John Jonson, who abjured on 16 January 1512, was perhaps Coventry's best travelled heretic, having lived in Gloucester, Maxstoke Priory, Bristol, Taunton, Brittany, Bordeaux, and London, in at least two of which cities he dwelt with local dissenters.[34] These and other continuities, both chronological and geographical, suggest that whilst lollardy may never have been a centralized phenomenon, some heterodox communities were nevertheless connected both with one another and with their past.

A NEW METHODOLOGY

Whilst these data provide a counterweight to arguments against the coherence of lollardy, they are by no means conclusive.[35] Instead, they point to the need for a terminological *via media*, a way of speaking and writing about lollardy that takes into account both the similarities and divergences among

---

[31] D'Alton, 'The suppression of heresy in early Henrician England', 199; Derek Plumb, 'The social and economic spread of rural Lollardy: A reappraisal' in W. J. Sheils and Diana Wood (eds.), *Voluntary Religion* (Studies in Church History 23, Oxford, 1986), 111–29; R. A. Houlbrooke, 'Persecution of heresy and Protestantism in the diocese of Norwich under Henry VIII', *Norfolk Archaeology*, 35 (1972), 308–26; and Diarmaid MacCulloch, *Tudor Church Militant: Edward VI and the Protestant Reformation* (London, 1999), 112–14. However, it is essential to bear in mind D. M. Palliser's warning that 'geographical determinism' cannot fully describe the reception of reforming ideas ('Popular reactions to the Reformation during the years of uncertainty, 1530–70' in Christopher Haigh (ed.), *The English Reformation Revised* (Cambridge, 1987), 94–113 at 104).

[32] *Coventry*, 239.

[33] Ibid., 150.

[34] Ibid., 111–13.

[35] They also provide a reason not to embrace too hastily the recent practice of some writers in the fields of Cathar and Waldensian studies of pluralizing the subject of enquiry: Catharisms, Waldensianisms, lollardies. The suggestion is not without merit, but it implies perhaps too much difference between lollards and lollard communities.

individuals, texts, and communities. The method of squaring this particular circle that I will be employing here has its roots in the thought of Ludwig Wittgenstein, and in particular in Wittgenstein's theory of 'family resemblance'. Seeking to justify why languages frequently use single categories, such as 'game', to describe such disparate phenomena as board games, card games, ball games, and the Olympic Games, Wittgenstein argued that though there may be nothing common to all these activities, they nevertheless participate in 'a complicated network of similarities overlapping and criss-crossing'. He called this network one of '"family-resemblances,"' for the various resemblances between members of a family . . . overlap and criss-cross in the same way'.[36] In Wittgenstein's terms, then, closely related phenomena might be thought of as members of the same nuclear family, whereas less intimately connected individuals would be second and third cousins.[37]

Since his *Philosophical Investigations* first appeared in 1953, Wittgenstein's theory of family resemblance has successfully been applied in many of the natural and social sciences. In one sense, Wittgenstein had formulated in the language of analytic philosophy insights which had independently been developed by psychologists and taxonomers. His work appeared nearly contemporaneously with the research of the Russian psychologist L. S. Vygotsky, who demonstrated that children form mental schemes of classification not in terms of formal logic but, rather, in terms of resemblance. 'Classes can be composed by means of what Vygotsky calls complex thinking: specifically, in a "chain complex" the definitive attribute keeps changing from one link to the next; there is no consistency in the type of bonds, and the variable meaning is carried over from one item in a class to the next with "no central significance," no "nucleus."'[38] Likewise, the eighteenth-century French botanist Michel Adanson had proposed a similar method of classification for plants. In certain cases, Adanson argued, individuals can be grouped together even if each individual lacks one or more of the characteristic features of the class. Adanson's ideas were brought together with Wittgenstein's by Morton Beckner, an American

---

[36] Ludwig Wittgenstein, *Philosophical Investigations*, trans. G. E. M. Anscombe, 2nd edn. (repr. Oxford, 1997), 32e.

[37] An excellent résumé of Wittgenstein's ideas can be found in Renford Bambrough, 'Universals and family resemblances', *Proceedings of the Aristotelian Society*, 61 (1960–61), 207–22, though Bambrough's claims for the broader significance of Wittgenstein's achievement are hopelessly exaggerated.

[38] Rodney Needham, 'Polythetic classification: Convergence and consequences', *Man*, 10 (1975), 349–69 at 350; see also Needham's book *Belief, Language, and Experience* (Oxford, 1972), 111–14.

philosopher and biologist, who formulated a definition of what he called a 'polytypic' class:

A class is ordinarily defined by reference to a set of properties which are both necessary and sufficient (by stipulation) for membership in the class. It is possible, however, to define a group K in terms of a set G of properties $f_1, f_2, \ldots, f_n$ in a different manner. Suppose we have an aggregation of individuals (we shall not as yet call them a class) such that:

1) Each one possesses a large (but unspecified) number of the properties in G.
2) Each f in G is possessed by large numbers of these individuals and
3) No f in G is possessed by every individual in the aggregate.

By the terms of (3), no f is necessary for membership in this aggregate; and nothing has been said to either warrant or rule out the possibility that some f in G is sufficient for membership in the aggregate.[39]

For Beckner, a polytypic or 'polythetic' class, as later taxonomists would call it, includes a set of individuals related in various ways to one another rather than to a centrally posited ideal type. Thus, in a set of four individuals, one might possess the predicates ABC, another BCD, another ABD, and the last ACD, such that there is no predicate common to every member, though each individual shares some of its predicates with others. Beckner's definition remains current in taxonomy, where today it provides natural scientists with a classificatory tool capable of taking into account the genetic, physiological, and behavioural variations commonly found in nature among individuals who would otherwise be identical.[40]

Wittgenstein's scheme has proven helpful in the humanities as well. One of the more complex and contentious debates of the past half-century in the field of religious studies has revolved around the definition of the term *religion*. What does and what does not 'count' as a religion proved to be an intractable question so long as the assumption remained that *religion* should be defined like other terms. Robert McDermott, and later Ninian Smart, proposed instead that the term 'religion' operates as a family-resemblance phenomenon.[41] Smart noted that defining religion in terms of resemblances

[39] Morton Beckner, *The Biological Way of Thought* (New York, 1959), 22; see also Robert R. Sokal and Peter H. A. Sneath, *Principles of Numerical Taxonomy* (San Francisco, 1963), 12–15.

[40] I am grateful to Katherine Jones for discussion of the finer points of taxonomic theory. Whilst Beckner's definition has commanded general approval, note the critical comments of Keith Campbell, 'Family resemblance predicates', *American Philosophical Quarterly*, 2 (1965), 238–44, who suggests that family-resemblance predicates are too inexact for use in the natural sciences. Campbell does allow, however, that 'for the discussion of human affairs' his critique 'is perhaps of no great moment' (244).

[41] Robert McDermott, 'The religion game: Some family resemblances', *Journal of the American Academy of Religion*, 38 (1970), 390–400; Ninian Smart, *Concept and Empathy* (London, 1986).

rather than a static essence has at least two advantages: it obviates the need for proposed definitions to apply to all religious phenomena, past, present, and future; and it enables disparate phenomena to be studied under the same intellectual umbrella.[42] The philosopher of religion John Hick has likewise employed a family-resemblance definition of religion in his ground-breaking study of religious pluralism, *An Interpretation of Religion.*[43] Likewise, in the context of religious history, Daniel Boyarin has recently used a family-resemblance model to describe the nascent groups of Christians and Jews whose emergence he examines in his book *Border Lines.* For Boyarin, family-resemblance classification provides the basis for a richly textured description of religious life in the first century. He writes:

While, as I have said, there is one (analytic) feature that could be said to be common to all groups that we might want to call (anachronistically) 'Christian,' namely some form of discipleship to Jesus, this feature hardly captures enough richness and depth to produce an interesting category, for in so many other vitally important ways, groups that follow Jesus and groups that ignore him are similar to each other, or put another way, groups that ignore (or reject) Jesus may have some highly salient other religious features (for instance, Logos theology) that binds them to Jesus groups and disconnects them from other non-Jesus Jews.[44]

Boyarin has also borrowed from analytic philosophy the concept of 'membership gradience'; that is, the idea that certain individuals within a particular web of family resemblances can be closer to or farther away from the cluster of individuals which most clearly exemplify the category in question. 'Just as certain entities can be more or less tall or red, I wish to suggest they can be more or less Christian (or Jewish) as well.'[45]

The notion of family resemblance, as originally articulated by Wittgenstein and refined in later reflections on religion and its history, offers an illuminating tool for the analysis of religious dissent in late medieval England. In the first place, it removes the need for scholars to agonize over both the formulation and the application of essentialist definitions. Indeed, studies of lollardy have often been handicapped by attempts to reduce the heresy to a set of theological propositions.[46] If a subject believed five key propositions, then she or he was a lollard; if not, then not.

---

[42] Smart, *Concept and Empathy*, 47.

[43] John Hick, *An Interpretation of Religion: Human responses to the transcendent* (Basingstoke, 1989).

[44] Daniel Boyarin, *Border Lines: The partition of Judaeo-Christianity* (Philadelphia, 2004), 23. I am grateful to Mark D. Jordan for drawing Boyarin's work to my attention.

[45] Ibid., 25.

[46] The most recent such study is Andrew E. Larsen's article 'Are all Lollards Lollards?' in *Influence*, 59–72. Though Larsen promisingly begins by rejecting rigid conceptions of Lollardy, he then proceeds to define the heresy in terms of eleven core doctrines.

Not only does this approach ignore the human and textual components of dissent, but it also entails the side-effect of imposing an unhelpfully polarizing distinction between lollard and non-lollard ideas on a much more complex reality. It requires scholars to debate whether a particular individual, group, or text is or is not lollard, when in fact many individuals should be situated within a more complex matrix of social, textual, and theological interactions.[47] Second, family-resemblance definitions admit of gradation, making it easier for students of lollardy to analyse individuals' beliefs, the level of their commitment to those beliefs, and the level of their involvement in both dissenting and mainstream communities in terms of sliding scales. Finally, Wittgenstein's concept facilitates the identification and analysis of subgroups and individual strands of thought within the broader category of lollard dissent. As we shall see, dissenters within the same community or even the same biological family often shared some beliefs but not others; differences in theological emphasis appear across geographical and chronological divides; and some dissenters combined standard lollard tenets with more idiosyncratic views.

To see how a model based on Wittgenstein's notion of family resemblance might work in practice, let us return to the case of Thomas Denys and attempt to situate him within three distinct, but interrelated, sets of resemblances: those dealing with his theological opinions, those dealing with the texts with which he interacted, and those dealing with the communities of which he was a part.

First, Denys' beliefs. What is particularly striking about the three articles to which he confessed at his second trial is that the first of them reflects what we might call a figurative or commemorative theology of the eucharist. Such views about the sacrament were soon to become familiar enough to the theologians and inquisitors of continental Europe in the theologies of reformers like Ulrich Zwingli, but they are relatively uncommon among the records of medieval English heresy trials. As I will argue at greater length in Chapter 3, Wyclif had quite clearly affirmed the presence of Christ in the consecrated elements of bread and wine, despite the fact he had rejected the doctrine of transubstantiation. Indeed, Wyclif wrote in his *De eucharistia confessio* that Christ's presence in the eucharist is more real than his presence in the other sacraments; the mistake the institutional church has made is to describe the *mode* of Christ's presence in philosophically untenable terms.[48]

---

[47] PR, 429. On the importance of treating texts as 'literary individuals', see Brian Stock, *Listening for the Text: On the uses of the past* (Philadelphia, 1996), 81; the same point should be made about heresy suspects.

[48] FZ, 117; cf. *De blasphemia*, 30.

It was Wyclif's doctrine of Christ's spiritual presence that dominated discussions of the sacrament among his early followers; most of the long Wycliffite cycle of 294 vernacular sermons, for instance, describe the consecrated host simultaneously as bread and God's body. But from around the turn of the fifteenth century, a small but important minority of dissenting writers and heresy suspects began to describe the eucharist in commemorative terms instead. Their views are most clearly and eloquently to be found in the vernacular tract *Wycklyffes Wycket*, a text for which there is no medieval manuscript evidence but which was probably composed in the first quarter of the fifteenth century. There, the author writes that the host is not the body of Christ, 'but the lyckenes' of Christ's body and 'the figure or mynde of Christes bodye in earth'. It is, he concludes, 'but a sygne or mynde of a thyng passed or a thynge to come'.[49]

Views such as these can be found in the records of very few heresy trials before the second half of the fifteenth century. And where they do appear, they seem to have been concentrated in particular geographical areas. No fewer than 236 heresy trials between the time of Wyclif's death and the arrival of Luther's ideas in England involved contested questions about the eucharist. Of those, however, only slightly more than twenty involved commemorative or figurative theologies of the sacrament, and of those, more than two-thirds were trials held in the 1490s, 1500s, and 1510s in the dioceses of Salisbury and Winchester, which are adjacent to one another. So Thomas Denys' beliefs about the eucharist, which might seem idiosyncratic in the broader sweep of late medieval English heresy prosecutions, may make more sense in a narrower historical context. What Denys believed was not far removed from what other defendants *of his generation and in nearby localities* believed. And in terms of family resemblance, therefore, it becomes possible to imagine a cluster of dissenters who, regardless of their relationship to the academic Wycliffites of the late fourteenth century, seem to be quite closely bound up with one another.

Turning to our second type of family resemblance, namely the sorts of texts to which dissenters had access, adds a new dimension to these considerations. Unfortunately, Bishop Fox's register does not preserve in detail a list of the books which Denys allegedly distributed to his neighbours. But there is one tantalizing clue to the contents of Denys' personal library. In the record of his trial, we learn that Denys confessed that he had 'brought unto [a fellow dissenter] diuerse bokes of heresie *and specially a boke of heresy called wiclif*, exhorting him to loke vpon it and folowe and beleve the contentes therof'.[50]

---

[49] *Wycklyffes Wycket* (London, 1546), B5r–B6r.
[50] Winchester reg. Fox, iii, fol. 69v, emphasis mine.

It is also unfortunate that we know with certainty nothing else about what this 'boke . . . called wiclif' might have been, but it stands to reason that it may have been a copy of *Wycklyffes Wycket*. On the one hand, we know that the *Wycket* was circulating among nearby dissenting communities in the early sixteenth century. Among other cases, it was mentioned as a gift from one dissenter to another in a Salisbury diocese case of 1508, and it was also part of the library of Richard Colins, a leading dissenter who was investigated by Bishop John Longland of Lincoln in the early 1520s.[51] On the other hand, if Denys owned and valued a copy of the *Wycket*, then the tract's teachings on the eucharist might explain why Denys and those he converted all propounded figurative theologies of the sacrament.

So theology and textuality create two interlocking circles of family resemblance, but we can also situate Thomas Denys in relation to his fellow dissenters in terms of what Anne Hudson has called 'Lollard society'. Whom did he know; who taught him; and whom did he teach in turn? Here, Bishop Fox's register is less helpful, but there are still some important clues to follow up. Two names particularly stand out: those of Richard Hortop, whom Denys confessed had taught him heresy some twenty years previously, and of Lewis John, whom the register identifies as Denys' co-religionist 'nowe of late of heresy abiured'.[52] About Hortop, unfortunately, we know no more than that he had been living in Waltham Abbey in the early years of the 1490s and sometime thereafter moved to London.

Lewis John, on the other hand, is much more interesting. He was apprehended not in Fox's investigations in Winchester diocese, but rather as part of Bishop Richard Fitzjames' near-contemporary series of prosecutions in London. In 1511, he and a group of some ten defendants, including his wife Joan John, were said to have 'denied the carnall and corporall presence of Christes body and bloud in the Sacrament of the altar' and to have 'read and [used] certeine English bookes . . . as the four Euangelistes, Wickleffes Wicket, a booke of the x commaundementes of almightie God, the Reuelation of S. John, the Epistles of Paul and James, with other like'.[53] It is also likely that the Lewis John of Fox's and Fitzjames' investigations is the same man who, then residing in Reading, was reported in 1508 to have been the teacher of another heresy suspect, Edward Parker.[54]

The group of dissenters in Reading of which John and Parker were members can be traced both backward and forward in time. Entries in the Bishop of Salisbury's register indicate that another prominent member of that community was John Stilman, an enthusiastic disseminator of dissenting views

---

[51] *A&M*, 834.   [52] Winchester reg. Fox, iii, fol. 69v.
[53] *A&M*, 803.   [54] Salisbury reg. Audley, fol. 148v.

who continued to be an active preacher in London until he was apprehended in 1518. At his trial, Stilman acknowledged that his teachers were one Stephen Moone and one Richard Smart, the latter of whom had been burned in Salisbury in 1503. Assuming that Moone and Smart had converts other than Stilman, here we have at least two decades of dissenting activity in and around Reading.[55]

But yet none of this evidence points to a firm connection between Thomas Denys, or his teachers, and the early group of scholars and others who gathered around John Wyclif and his academic disciples in Oxford. This is not, however, to say that there were no such connections, and indeed, where the records permit, it is sometimes possible to trace the genealogies of some dissenting groups, say those in the Kentish Weald, over the span of a century. But, in this case, we would have to make the argument from silence. All that can be said with certainty is that Thomas Denys was a local leader of a dissenting community centred on the town of Kingston and some nearby villages; that this community subscribed to a theology of the eucharist which distinguished it from other dissenting communities elsewhere in the country; that their beliefs about the eucharist may have been derived from their reading of a text like *Wycklyffes Wycket*; and that the community of which Denys was a leader was linked, through various personal connections, to dissenting communities in London, Reading, and Essex.

So to return to the problem of terminology: does any of this make Denys a lollard, or a Wycliffite? What the process of situating him in our three-dimensional matrix of belief, text, and social circumstance has shown is why those 'yes/no' questions are problematic. There are ways in which Denys resembles some individuals whom we are prepared, on independent grounds, to call Wycliffites, but there are ways in which he fails to resemble them. The insight to be gained from Wittgenstein's theory is that we should leave the question there, with relational, or family-resemblance, models of lollardy and Wycliffism, rather than essentialist ones. In the end, the historical record will always remain ambiguous. It cannot be determined if Denys and his fellow dissenters thought of themselves as lollards or Wycliffites, and there is not much to indicate that their inquisitors thought of them as such.

There is, of course, some space here to introduce a further distinction between 'lollard' and 'Wycliffite'. In applying these labels, we may be on safer ground with 'Wycliffite', since it is possible to compare a defendant's or a text's opinions with what Wyclif believed about a particular topic; or to show that a

---

[55] *A&M*, 815; see also Dublin, Trinity College MS 775, fol. 125r. Stilman's case is discussed further by Thomson, *Later Lollards*, 171; and Margaret Aston, 'John Wycliffe's Reformation reputation', repr. in *Lollards and Reformers* (London, 1984), 243–72 at 263.

particular individual professed allegiance to Wyclif; or studied with Wyclif or
with one of Wyclif's early followers. But as Hudson and others have pointed
out, the term 'lollard' functions very differently; it is a subjective term, used by
dissenters against their clerical opponents and by clerical opponents against
dissenters. Its semantic range is so wide as to render it highly problematic as
an essentialist category.

LOLLARDY AND THE DEVELOPMENT OF DOCTRINE

This discussion of terminological and methodological issues has taken us
somewhat afield from the other concerns of this book: namely, to study the
ways in which lollard attitudes toward several key religious issues varied
geographically as well as chronologically during the years separating Wyclif's
exile from Oxford from the arrival of Lutheran ideas in England. Just as with
the case of Thomas Denys, in the pages that follow I will bring the theoretical
models generated by Wittgenstein's notion of family resemblance to bear on
the sources for lollard views on salvation, the eucharist, marriage and sexuality, the priesthood, and the papacy. In doing so, I hope to draw attention to
some of the advantages of this approach for historians as well as theologians.

I have already alluded several times to the much-contested place of lollardy
in the debate on the English Reformation, and indeed, from the sixteenth
century up to the beginning of the twenty-first, much scholarly energy has
been expended in attempts either to demonstrate that lollards played a part in
the genesis and reception of the English Reformation, or else to show that not
only did lollards play no such role, there were hardly any individuals or
communities worthy of the name by the time Henry VIII ascended the throne.
The difficulty with both approaches is that they persist in treating late
medieval dissenters as a kind of historiographical football, less important in
their own right than for the contributions they made, or did not make, to later
events. Yet it was precisely those later events, Henry's Reformation and its
successors, that since the time of Foxe have conditioned our understanding of
late medieval heresy. It has been convenient, although for different reasons,
for the various parties to this debate to work with an essentialist definition of
lollardy. For a historian like Dickens, being able to lump together the many
different strands of reformism which continued to trouble the English church
at the beginning of the sixteenth century was integral to his argument for
what he saw as the acceptance of the Reformation at the popular level. For
revisionists like Duffy and Rex, the expectation that if there were lollards at
the beginning of the sixteenth century, they would have to look like a

recognizably discrete group supports the claim that lollardy contributed little to the events of the 1520s and beyond. Unfortunately, however, to approach the data in either mindset is anachronistic at best. Lollardy was a theologically and socially diverse family of phenomena that contributed in varied ways to the already highly complex religious landscape of late medieval England. Nevertheless, doctrinal variations within and among lollard communities were not entirely random, and in what follows I shall note the social and textual factors that facilitated the development and persistence of individual strands of belief.

At the same time, the results of this study may also, in theological terms, suggest one way of filling a gap in contemporary theories of the development of doctrine. Christian theologians and historians of Christianity have long been aware of variations in belief and practice among individuals and communities; it should go without saying that, historically, many such divergences have been condemned as heresies. Nevertheless, as early as the fifth century, Christian thinkers began to reflect upon the possibility that the doctrines of the institutional church might evolve as believers come gradually to penetrate deeper into the mystery of God. The fifth-century writer Vincent of Lérins, more famous for his maxim that a particular teaching is orthodox if it can be shown to have been held 'always, everywhere, and by everyone' (*semper, ubique, et ab omnibus*), also taught that there can be progress or development (*profectus*) in theology. According to Vincent, so long as a development takes place in the same sense (*in eodem sensu eademque sententia*) as the church's original teaching, then it is legitimate.[56] Partly on account of Vincent's association with the so-called 'Semi-Pelagian' faction whose ideas about salvation were condemned at the Council of Orange in 529, his ideas received little attention in the medieval and early modern church.[57] As a result, and despite interest in the subject from several earlier thinkers, it was not until the mid-nineteenth century that the concept of the development of doctrine came into its own.[58] The modern study of doctrinal development begins with John Henry Newman,

---

[56] Thomas G. Guarino, 'Tradition and doctrinal development: Can Vincent of Lérins still teach the church?', *Theological Studies*, 67 (2006), 34–72 at 35; see also Henri Rondet, *Do Dogmas Change?*, trans. Mark Pontifex (London, 1961), 84–5.

[57] On the relative lack of interest in church history and doctrinal development to be found in the writings of scholastic theologians, see Jan Hendrik Walgrave, *Unfolding Revelation: The nature of doctrinal development* (London, 1972), 114.

[58] This may be an oversimplification. Anselm Atkins characterized the study of the development of doctrine as 'in its infancy' as late as 1964 ('Religious assertions and doctrinal development', *Theological Studies*, 27 [1966], 523–52 at 524). Whilst there is now a substantial literature on doctrinal development, especially in Roman Catholic theology, the most influential works were all written during the Second Vatican Council or in its aftermath.

whose *Essay on the Development of Christian Doctrine* remains a milestone in the history of Christianity's self-understanding.

According to Newman, the original deposit of revelation already contains within itself the seeds of all later growth. 'This process will not be a development', he wrote, 'unless the assemblage of aspects, which constitute its ultimate shape, really belong to the idea from the very start.'[59] Like Vincent before him, Newman recognized that to discern what does and what does not belong to the original idea of Christianity is hardly straightforward. Accordingly, he proposed seven 'tests' or 'notes' to distinguish true developments from false ones. On his account, a development is true 'if it retains one and the same type, the same principles, the same organization; if its beginnings anticipate its subsequent phases, and its later phenomena protect and subserve its earlier; if it has a power of assimilation and revival, and a vigorous action from first to last'.[60]

It has been remarked that Newman designed his tests in such a way as to lend credibility to his decision in 1845 to leave the Church of England and convert to Roman Catholicism.[61] Whatever his motives may have been, his theory of development poses at least two substantial problems. First, Newman's notion of doctrinal development as the gradually fuller explication of primordial revelation hardly coheres with the actual history of Christian theology. Even if it were the case in Newman's time that doctrines developed in such an orderly way, and there is little reason to suggest that they did, the theological vicissitudes of the post-Reformation period contradict Newman's scheme. For instance, Clement XI's 1731 bull *Unigenitus* and, later, the Second Vatican Council both abandoned earlier interpretations of the ancient formula *extra ecclesiam nulla salus* in acknowledging the possibility of grace and salvation outside Christianity.[62]

For this reason, theologians since Newman have been quick to call into question the English cardinal's account of doctrinal development, and they

---

[59] John Henry Newman, *An Essay on the Development of Christian Doctrine* (repr. Notre Dame, Ind., 1989), 38.

[60] Ibid., 171.

[61] Owen Chadwick, *From Bossuet to Newman* (Cambridge, 1957); for a different view, see Hugo A. Maynell, 'Newman on revelation and doctrinal development,' *Journal of Theological Studies*, n.s. 30 (1979), 138–52.

[62] For a thoughtful discussion of what one theologian has called these 'dramatic developments' in doctrine, see John Thiel, *Senses of Tradition: Continuity and development in Catholic faith* (Oxford, 2000), 26. Likewise, Nicholas Lash has described this sort of doctrinal development by turning traditional organic metaphors on their head: 'Though the organic analogy has always referred to the growth of plants, there is also a way in which the process of development has sometimes been by pruning' (*Change in Focus: A study of doctrinal change and continuity* (London, 1981), 145.

have also challenged his claim that doctrinal change should be managed exclusively by the magisterium of popes, bishops, and councils.[63] They have been less attentive, however, to a second implication of Newman's *Essay*, one that bears directly on the study of heresy. For Newman, heresies are 'false developments' that do not follow from the original deposit of revelation. In a memorable passage, he describes the life cycle of heresies thus:

The course of heresies is always short; it is an intermediate state between life and death, or what is like death; or, if it does not result in death, it is resolved into some new, perhaps opposite, course of error, which lays no claim to be connected with it. And in this way indeed, but in this way only, an heretical principle will continue in life many years, first running one way, then another.[64]

Whereas Newman depicts true doctrine as a stream which gradually becomes broader and deeper as it flows outward, heresies are stagnant offshoots connected to one another only by virtue of their shared torpor. Thus, for instance, in his work *The Arians of the Fourth Century*, Newman takes it as axiomatic that Arius and his followers all subscribed to the same set of conclusions.[65] Individual heretics, for Newman, are for theological purposes indistinguishable.

It should be clear that what is absent from Newman's *Essay* is any suggestion that the doctrines of dissenting movements develop like the teachings of the institutional church, and that assumption has prevailed in subsequent studies of the development of doctrine. Writers from the Catholic Modernist Alfred Loisy to the liberal Anglican Maurice Wiles have continued to analyse the history of doctrine in terms of distinguishing true or authentic developments from false or heretical ones.[66] At the turn of the twentieth century, Loisy, for instance, borrowed Newman's terminology in arguing that heresy 'is often born from stagnation, i.e. of an ill-judged conservatism'.[67] One consequence of this tendency has been that whilst theologians have frequently studied the interdependencies of heresy and orthodoxy as a means of illuminating how and why orthodox doctrines have developed as they have, few

---

[63] Among many other critics of Newman, see Jaroslav Pelikan, *Development of Christian Doctrine: Some historical prolegomena* (New Haven, Conn., 1969), 144; R. P. C. Hanson, *The Continuity of Christian Doctrine* (New York, 1981), 68; Terrence W. Tilley, *Inventing Catholic Tradition* (Maryknoll, NY, 2000), 35, 81–82; and Maurice Wiles, *The Making of Christian Doctrine: A study in the principles of early doctrinal development* (Cambridge, 1967), 11.

[64] Newman, *An Essay on the Development of Christian Doctrine*, 204.

[65] Williams, *Arius*, 3–6.

[66] Aidan Nichols, *From Newman to Congar: The idea of doctrinal development from the Victorians to the Second Vatican Council* (Edinburgh, 1990), 71–113; Wiles, *The Making of Christian Doctrine*.

[67] Nichols, *From Newman to Congar*, 85.

have considered what happens to unorthodox ideas once they have been rejected.[68]

Theologians and historians, as well as their colleagues in the sociology of religion, would as a result be well served to consider whether a process parallel to the development of doctrine takes place within groups which have separated themselves from the religious mainstream. If it is worth contemplating 'the development of heresy', then additional questions suggest themselves. What factors provoke change in the beliefs and practices of dissenting movements? How do religious and cultural changes, as well as continuities, outside such communities affect the changes and continuities within? Through what internal structures of authority, if any, are developments mediated? And to what extent are the answers to these questions about the development of heresy similar to the answers that theologians and sociologists have already given about the development of doctrine in so-called 'orthodox' contexts? It is beyond the scope of this book to offer systematic answers to any of these questions, but the historical data I will be presenting suggest a number of preliminary responses and directions for future research, points to which I will return in the Conclusion.

PLAN OF THE ARGUMENT

Each of the five subsequent chapters of this book focuses on a cluster of theological ideas, using the techniques suggested by Wittgenstein's model of family resemblance to examine the ways in which Wyclif's writings, Wycliffite texts, anti-lollard polemics, and the records of heresy trials can together disclose variations in the religious beliefs of late medieval dissenters. The clusters of doctrines I have chosen for close analysis have in common two virtues: first, that of appearing with some frequency in the extant sources and, second, that of not already having been studied exhaustively in other works.[69] In general, each chapter is organized chronologically: first I describe Wyclif's views on the topic at hand; then I turn to the strands of his thought that can be discerned in Wycliffite and lollard texts, as well as in the writings

---

[68] Thus M.-D. Chenu, speaking at a conference in the 1960s, observed that 'a sociology of heresy in evolution is required' ('Orthodoxie et Hérésie: le point de vue du théologien' in J. Le Goff (ed.), *Hérésies et sociétés dans l'Europe pre-industrielle* (Paris, 1968), 16).

[69] As a result, I have excluded a number of otherwise interesting topics, including lollard views on images and on the relationship between civil and ecclesiastical authority: on these topics, see respectively Margaret Aston, *England's Iconoclasts* (Oxford, 1988); and Lahey, *Philosophy and Politics*.

of anti-Wycliffite authors; and finally I consider the data from heresy trials. Where the sources cannot be placed in definite chronological relationships to one another, I have organized the discussion topically.

Chapter 2 traces Wycliffite beliefs about salvation, starting with an analysis of Wyclif's doctrines of grace and predestination. Rather than espousing the view that God has arbitrarily elected those who will be saved and condemned those who will be punished, as medieval polemicists and later scholars alike have argued, Wyclif and many Wycliffite writers instead ascribed to good deeds an essential role in the process of salvation. A majority of lay heresy suspects agreed, and only a few defendants endorsed predestinarian views after the turn of the sixteenth century. This trend suggests that many dissenters were hesitant to abandon the dominant religious world view of the Middle Ages. Ecclesiastically sponsored sermons, poems, plays, and other texts often privileged the need to perform good works over and above the operation of grace, and whilst lollard dissenters were not enthusiastic about such practices as indulgences and bequests for soul-masses, the underlying logic of their soteriologies was strikingly similar.

Whereas many lollards never questioned a works-oriented approach to the doctrine of salvation, the dissenting views on the eucharist that I study in Chapter 3 reveal more substantial divergences from orthodoxy. The mass was at the heart of late medieval religious practice and, as we have seen, it was Wyclif's decision to reject the doctrine of transubstantiation that led in 1381 to his exile from Oxford. Scholars have long known that Wyclif believed that Christ is *spiritually* present in the consecrated elements, and it has been held that, in the hands of later dissenters, his theology of remanence slowly evolved into a figurative interpretation of the sacrament. Instead, Wycliffite tracts and court records reveal that figurative and remanence theologies were *both* current in the early fifteenth century, and the patterns of their dissemination reveal the roles that family and civic ties played in the formation of heterodox beliefs. Figurative theologies of the eucharist were especially prevalent among the communities of Coventry and Lichfield, Salisbury, and Winchester dioceses, and it was in these regions of England that texts articulating such views circulated most widely.

Wycliffites often believed that, in adopting theological positions contrary to those of the established church, they were in fact embracing the plain meaning of the Bible and the teachings of the earliest apostles. The fundamentally conservative impetus of much dissenting thought can perhaps best be seen in the areas of lay marriage and clerical celibacy. In Chapter 4, I examine lollard attitudes to marriage and sexuality. After surveying the development of the medieval church's doctrine of marriage, I argue that Wyclif's views were conservative but ultimately pragmatic. Though chaste marriage was his ideal, Wyclif acknowledged that not all have the capacity to abstain from sexual intercourse. In any case, marriage should not be governed by church courts; it is the mutual consent of the partners and not the approval of the priest that creates a marriage. Later writers tended to articulate somewhat more pessimistic views, conceiving of marriage primarily as a remedy for lust. At the same time, Wyclif's grudging acceptance of some married clergymen was taken in the opposite direction by many of those who came after him, who insisted that all clerics should marry in order not to succumb to the temptations which might arise from a lukewarm commitment to chastity. The views articulated in dissenting texts as well as trial records thus call into doubt the traditional view that lollardy was an innovative movement where issues of gender and sexuality were concerned.

Whether married or otherwise, clergymen played an indispensable role in the practice of late medieval Christianity. In Chapter 5, I study lollard ideas about the sacrament of orders, including the ways in which and the persons to whom it is to be administered; the duties of curates; the financing of the clergy; and the papacy. Both Wyclif and the majority of lay heresy suspects envisioned the retention and purification of the clerical estate. Quite contrary to the stereotype that lollards were radical reformers, Wycliffite theologies of the priesthood tended to be conservative ones: dissenters urged priests to follow more closely the example of the apostles and to repudiate the wealth of the church. Nevertheless, even though many dissenters advocated the total disendowment of the church, Wycliffite writers and heresy defendants were hardly of one mind in proposing alternative structures for its financing and governance. In Chapter 6, I demonstrate that a similar approach characterized Wyclif's and many Wycliffites' attitudes toward the pope: they criticized the abuses of the medieval papacy but did not demand its abolition as an institution. Instead, they argued that the papacy, like the clergy as a whole, should be brought back, forcibly if needs be, to an ideal standard of behaviour.

2

Salvation

In 1521, as the English government was intensifying its campaign against the new theology of Martin Luther, Bishop John Longland uncovered a conventicle of dissenters in his diocese of Lincoln. The men and women who were summoned before him admitted to heresies concerning the Eucharist, images, and pilgrimage.[1] They also confessed to a familiarity with vernacular biblical texts, the translation and copying of which had been forbidden in England for more than a century. According to John Foxe, these dissenters had a particular liking for the Epistle of St James; the brothers Robert and Richard Bartlet as well as Richard's sister Agnes Wellis were accused of having memorized portions of the letter.[2] Their co-religionists Thomas Chase, John Barret, and Richard and Thomas Colins also came under suspicion in connection with the epistle, Chase and Barret for having recited it 'perfectly without book' and the Colins brothers for possessing 'a book of Paul and James in English'.[3]

Though Longland's encounter with the biblically literate heretics of his diocese came several years after Luther's theology had attracted the attention of Europe, it is unlikely that rural dissenters like the Bartlet and Colins brothers were aware of the developments which were in the process of transforming the religious life of the Continent. Luther had published his works in Latin and German; his books had barely infiltrated the English market when they were first officially burned on 12 May 1521; and in any case, Longland seems not to have proceeded against his defendants as Lutherans.[4] The bishop and his commissioners instead treated the dissenters as 'knowen men', one of the terms that later historians linked with the sixteenth-century descendants of John Wyclif and his academic followers.[5]

---

[1] A&M, 946.

[2] Ibid., 947–8. Longland's court book is unfortunately not extant, though it has been a century since W. H. Summers convincingly established the veracity of Foxe's account of the bishop's anti-heresy investigations: see *The Lollards of the Chiltern Hills* (London, 1906), 103–8. For more on the trial of Agnes Wellis, see Ch. 4 below.

[3] Ibid., 947–61.

[4] D'Alton, 'The suppression of heresy in early Henrician England', 102–7.

[5] A&M, 946; on the epithet 'known men', see Hudson, 'A Lollard sect vocabulary' repr. in *Books*, 167–8.

But here lies something of a paradox, for it might seem that Wyclif would hardly have recommended the Epistle of James to his disciples. Both medieval polemics and later studies of his thought have routinely emphasized Wyclif's doctrine of predestination, a theologoumenon which, so the argument goes, undergirded his theologies of the church, the priesthood, and secular authority. These scholars have argued that though he did not explicitly anticipate Luther's remark that James' was 'an epistle of straw', Wyclif nevertheless developed a soteriology at odds with the letter's interest in what later reformers would call the salvific value of good works. How was it, the question has arisen, that Wyclif's predestinarianism gave rise to the communities for whose members James was such a foundational text?

Soteriology remains among the more neglected features of Wycliffite belief, not least because English dissenters' theologies of salvation have often been studied anachronistically, in terms of the categories of the Reformation.[6] With very few exceptions, scholars have either emphasized the ways in which Wyclif's theology foreshadowed the contributions of Luther and his contemporaries or else have ignored Wycliffism and lollardy as a possible influence on the doctrinal development of English Protestantism.[7] In order to overcome this ill-fated alliance of anachronism and myopia, this chapter offers a chronological survey of the spectrum of dissenting views about salvation, taking into account the writings of Wyclif and his immediate followers, the contents of anti-Wycliffite polemics, and the evidence available in such documentary sources as court records and episcopal registers. The hope is that such an examination of dissenting soteriologies will help both to resolve outstanding questions about Wyclif's doctrine of salvation and to demonstrate that the vernacular appropriation of his theology only rarely involved his reputed predestinarianism. Indeed, over the course of the fourteen decades from Wyclif's death through the outbreak of the Reformation in

---

[6] Alister McGrath, 'Forerunners of the Reformation? A critical examination of the evidence for precursors of the Reformation doctrine of justification', *Harvard Theological Review*, 75 (1982), 219–42. The same point was made by Bengt Hägglund in his study of the medieval doctrine of justification, but Hägglund's analysis itself strays into the anachronistic (*The Background of Luther's Doctrine of Justification in Late Medieval Theology* (Philadelphia, 1971), 2).

[7] For two of the many studies which illustrate this point, see Robert Doyle, 'The death of Christ and the doctrine of grace in John Wycliffe', *Churchman*, 99 (1985), 317–35, and O. T. Hargrave, 'The doctrine of predestination in the English Reformation' (Ph.D. thesis, Vanderbilt University, 1966), 3. Other commentators who share Hargrave's tendency to ignore the native theology of the later Middle Ages as a source for English evangelicalism include D. D. Wallace, 'The doctrine of predestination in the early English Reformation', *Church History*, 43 (1974), 201–15, and Peter O. G. White, *Predestination, Policy, and Polemic: Conflict and consensus in the English church from the Reformation to the Civil War* (Cambridge, 1992). The first chapter of D. Andrew Penny's study, *Freewill or Predestination: The battle over saving grace in mid-Tudor England* (Woodbridge, 1990), offers a more balanced view of the issues.

Germany, English dissenting theologies multiplied and developed substantially, and many dissenters, if ever they held doctrines of predestination at all, set aside those beliefs in favour of the ideas about the salvific value of works that made the Epistle of James such an appealing text to the men and women of Lincoln diocese.

DIVINE GRACE AND HUMAN FREEDOM: SALVATION IN HISTORICAL CONTEXT

In order to understand the soteriologies of English dissenters, however, it will first be necessary to make a few points about the development of the doctrine of salvation within the Christian tradition more broadly. It should go without saying that the desire to be saved and to know of one's salvation has long been a preoccupation of Christian believers and their theological spokespersons. As successive generations of thinkers formulated their ideas about salvation, they left behind them a bewildering array of terms in which to describe what they believe God has achieved for them through the life, death, and resurrection of Christ. Eastern Christians, who will not otherwise appear in this study, have tended to follow the author of II Peter in speaking of salvation as deification (*theosis* or *theopoesis*). In the West, on the contrary, Christians have focused their attention on the Pauline metaphors of justification and redemption.[8] The interpretation of these and other terms has been extensively contested, with God's grace and human freedom providing the pair of foci around which arguments have most often revolved. Labels such as Pelagian, semi-Pelagian, predestinarian, fatalist, universalist, Calvinist, and Arminian may appear to delineate particularly influential or controversial positions in the history of the doctrine of salvation, but few such terms are free from ambiguity.

The position to which I shall be referring as *single predestinarianism*, or simply *predestinarianism*, holds that human beings can in no way merit grace and that salvation is accordingly dependent on God's gratuitous election, a divine decision without regard to merit. On the strictest version of this account, the logic by which God makes salvific choices is inscrutable; God's election, moreover, is irresistible, and thus the elect cannot forsake their status, nor can those not elect earn salvation. Two variants on basic predestinarianism are *double predestinarianism*, according to which God takes action

---

[8] Jaroslav Pelikan, *The Christian Tradition: A history of the development of doctrine*, 5 vols. (Chicago, 1971–1989), iii.152; Alister McGrath, *Iustitia Dei: A history of the Christian doctrine of justification*, 3rd edn (Cambridge, 2005), 3.

not only to elect some persons but also to condemn others, and *universalism*, according to which God has irresistibly elected and hence will save all human beings.

Whereas it could be said that predestinarianism emphasizes God's grace at the expense of human freedom, the position to which I shall refer as *Pelagianism* teaches that human persons can earn salvation on account of their freely chosen good deeds. This position has most infamously been associated with the fifth-century British monk Pelagius and was condemned several times starting in the year 418. It remains an open question whether or not Pelagius would have endorsed such an account of his teachings, or whether, as in the case of other putative heresiarchs, the process by which his views were refuted made them appear more extreme than in fact they were. The term 'Pelagianism' nevertheless provides a helpful shorthand for the often reviled—but in fact rarely held—view that human beings can, in effect, compel God to save them on account of their deeds.

Other soteriologies appropriate elements of both predestinarianism and Pelagianism. Insofar as a particular theology of salvation borrows from predestinarianism an emphasis on the sovereignty of God's grace, I shall call it *grace-oriented*; likewise, insofar as a particular theory focuses on human freedom and agency, I shall call it *works-oriented*. One epithet that I shall generally avoid is *semi-Pelagian*, which appears too often in scholarly analyses of late medieval literature and religion as a catch-all phrase for ideas about salvation that are neither predestinarian nor Pelagian. Instead, I shall restrict my use of the term semi-Pelagian to the very limited historical context of the fifth- and sixth-century debates for which it was originally coined. Even in that milieu, as Rebecca Harden Weaver has argued, the appellation is something of a misnomer.[9]

Armed with the categories of predestinarian, grace-oriented, works-oriented, and Pelagian soteriologies, then, we can approach several key episodes in the history of the doctrine of salvation. There is not space here to deal with discussions of salvation in such early Christian sources as the letters of St Paul and the writings of theologians like Athanasius of Alexandria and John Chrysostom, nor with Augustine of Hippo's hugely influential doctrines of grace and divine election.[10] The controversies between Augustine and his supporters, on the one hand, and those who favoured a more works-oriented soteriology, on the other, were at least temporarily resolved in 529 by the provincial Council of Orange. Its canons condemned not only the Pelagian

---

[9] Rebecca Harden Weaver, *Divine Grace and Human Agency: A study of the semi-Pelagian Controversy* (Macon, Ga., 1996), 40.

[10] For a thorough survey of these and other thinkers, see McGrath, *Iustitia Dei*.

view that human beings can merit salvation but also the 'semi-Pelagian' stance that the human will can take the first step toward salvation:

> If anyone says that not only the increase of faith but also its beginning and the very desire for faith, by which we believe in him who justifies the ungodly and come to the regeneration of holy baptism—if anyone says that this belongs to us by nature and not by a gift of grace, that is, by the inspiration of the Holy Spirit amending our will and turning it from unbelief to faith and from godlessness to godliness, it is proof that he is opposed to the teaching of the Apostles.[11]

Orange also endorsed Augustine's doctrine of original sin, concluding that the human will was forever impaired by Adam's first transgression. In reaching these conclusions, the council canonized a substantial part of Augustine's soteriological legacy. By insisting upon the corruption of the will and the gratuitousness of grace and by denying a causal connection between merit and grace, the council placed limits on the language available for future Christian thinkers to frame their arguments. Nevertheless, its function was strictly negative; the council did not endorse any particular theology of salvation.

Apart from the much politicized debate between the ninth-century monk Gottschalk of Orbais and the Bishop Hincmar of Reims, discussions of predestination and salvation were dormant for several centuries after Orange. When they emerged again in the high Middle Ages, they began to be formulated in the substantially different vocabulary of scholastic thought. Anselm of Canterbury, for instance, held that the very concept of *predestination* contains a logical inconsistency, for all things are present to God. From God's point of view, he claimed, nothing can be said to occur before or after anything else, so arguments about the causal and chronological relationships between grace, works, and free will are immaterial.[12] Anselm's approach was taken up by such major thinkers as Alexander of Hales, Bonaventure, and Thomas Aquinas. In his account of salvation, Aquinas also introduced categories that would figure prominently in later medieval debates. He distinguished between the necessity of God's grace being given to all people and the contingency of particular human responses, which are nevertheless foreknown by God. Although human beings must act on grace in order to reach salvation, every such action is still prompted by grace.[13]

Aquinas and his contemporaries thus walked the very fine line between Augustine's doctrine of the sovereignty of grace and the Pelagian and

---

[11] *Select Anti-Pelagian Treatises of St Augustine and the Acts of the Second Council of Orange,* ed. William Bright (Oxford, 1880), 385–6, canon 5.

[12] Pelikan, *Christian Tradition,* iii.272–3.

[13] Lee H. Yearley, 'St Thomas Aquinas on providence and predestination', *Anglican Theological Review,* 49 (1967), 409–23 at 417–18.

semi-Pelagian positions condemned in the sixth century. Their theologies of salvation were grace-oriented but nevertheless left room for human responsibility. As in late antiquity, however, no doctrine of salvation received the endorsement of the institutional church, and when the era of the great *summae* gave way to the logical-critical enquiries of the fourteenth century, there remained what the late Jaroslav Pelikan has called a 'pregnant plurality' of soteriological thought.[14] Thomas Bradwardine, for instance, launched a blistering attack on a group of thinkers he called the 'modern Pelagians' in his work *De causa Dei*. A more moderate group of theologians developed the notion of a salvific *pactum* between God and human beings, according to which people who do what is in them (*facere quod in se est*) are rewarded beyond their desserts. These writers were nevertheless careful to point out that any such *pactum* had been established by God irrespective of the actual merit that might at any time be found in any particular person.[15]

James Halverson has proposed an immensely helpful systematization of late medieval soteriologies in his study *Peter Aureol on Predestination: A challenge to late medieval thought*. According to Halverson, when Aureol lectured on Peter Lombard's *Sentences* in Paris in 1317, he shattered a prevailing consensus about salvation. That consensus, which Halverson calls single-particular election (SPE), held that all people exist in a state of mortal sin and deserve condemnation until God, acting without regard to merit, offers grace to and thereby saves some individuals.[16] Aureol agreed that no person can merit predestination, but he did argue against SPE that God offers grace to *all* human beings. Since the human will is corrupt, individuals do not have the capacity actively to accept grace, but they can decide either actively to resist it or passively not to resist it. Those who make the negative act of not resisting grace, Aureol argued, are the elect, and their number is foreknown but not determined by God. Those who positively resist grace deserve and receive condemnation.[17] Aureol's scheme, which Halverson labels general election (GE), provides the best hermeneutical key for understanding the soteriologies of such thinkers as William of Ockham.[18] GE had attracted no small number of adherents in both Paris and Oxford when, in 1343, Gregory of Rimini rejected it as Pelagian. In place of both SPE and GE, Rimini formulated

---

[14] Pelikan, *Christian Tradition*, iv.10.

[15] On Bradwardine, the classic but often misguided study is Gordon Leff, *Bradwardine and the Pelagians* (Cambridge, 1957); see also Alister McGrath, 'The anti-Pelagian structure of "nominalist" doctrines of justification', *Ephemerides Theologicae Lovanienses*, 57 (1981), 107–19 at 110–14.

[16] James Halverson, *Peter Aureol on Predestination* (Leiden, 1998), 2.

[17] Ibid., 91–106.

[18] On Ockham, see among many others Rega Wood, 'Ockham's repudiation of Pelagianism' in Paul Vincent Spade (ed.), *The Cambridge Companion to Ockham* (Cambridge, 1999), 350–74.

an account of double predestinarianism (or double-particular election, DPE), suggesting that God is equally active in condemning the reprobate as in electing the predestinate.[19]

From the mid-fourteenth century to the outbreak of Luther's reformation, then, both predestinarian and grace-oriented schemes of salvation competed for attention. Far from being the uniformly Pelagian system caricatured by evangelical propagandists, the scholastic theologies of the late Middle Ages often emphasized the gratuitousness of grace instead.[20] As we shall see, the reflections of university theologians did not prevent popular religious practice from focusing on good works, but it is nevertheless essential to bear in mind the pluralism of medieval thought. It was this diversity of opinion that characterized the intellectual world within which John Wyclif reached maturity as a philosopher and theologian in Oxford.

WYCLIF'S SOTERIOLOGY: PREDESTINATION, ECCLESIOLOGY, AND MORALITY

We saw in the previous chapter that whilst ecclesiastical authorities in England had encountered scattered and largely unsuccessful protests against the institutional church in the cases of heresy that came to light in the thirteenth and early fourteenth centuries, it was in Wyclif that they first confronted a politically, philosophically, and theologically astute opponent. From the 1360s, Wyclif had earned a reputation as a leading master of the Oxford schools, setting forth first a realist metaphysics and then progressively more radical theological conclusions. There is not space here for a comprehensive assessment of the philosophical system that Wyclif developed during his years in Oxford, but several elements of his metaphysics bear directly on his theology of salvation.[21] Particularly important is Wyclif's philosophy of being, by which he maintained that everything that exists participates in a single extra-mental reality.[22] God, creatures, substances, accidents, and universal essences all partake in a single kind of being (*ens in communi*). But of these, God alone exists in the proper sense of the term; all other things exist

[19] Halverson, *Peter Aureol on Predestination*, 143–57.

[20] McGrath, 'Anti-Pelagian structure', 107.

[21] For a thorough account of Wyclif's biography and theology, see now Stephen E. Lahey, *John Wyclif* (Oxford, 2009).

[22] Alessandro Conti, 'John Wyclif', *Stanford Encyclopedia of Philosophy*, sect. 3.1, <http://plato.stanford.edu/entries/Wyclif> (accessed 5 March 2006).

only insofar as they share in God's being.[23] All things that exist derive their being, in this sense at least, from an eternal source, and this assumption provided Wyclif with a foundation for his conclusions about necessity and contingency.

Meeting some thirty years after his death, the Council of Constance condemned Wyclif for teaching that 'all things that happen, happen from absolute necessity', and until recently the dominant historiographical tradition has followed suit by describing Wyclif as both a predestinarian and a philosophical determinist.[24] Scholars both medieval and modern have concluded that Wyclif's doctrine of being and the realist theory of universals with which he coupled it together entail a rigid fatalism. 'His metaphysics assumed the eternity of being, and hence the immutability of God's acts.'[25] 'Everything therefore is fixed and determined.'[26] 'His construction of what we may call determinism follows clearly and logically from his doctrine of real universals.'[27] On this account, Wyclif's metaphysics required him to articulate a soteriology according to which God's foreknowledge necessitates double predestinarianism. The saved and the damned 'represented two distinct modes of being...two universals which were eternally distinct from one another.'[28]

Recent studies have challenged several elements of this traditional view of Wyclif's soteriology, but before we consider these new perspectives, it may be helpful to note that language traditionally associated with predestinarianism did undergird a host of the doctrines for which Wyclif later became notorious. In his treatise *De ecclesia* and elsewhere, Wyclif distinguished between two 'churches' whose members together constitute the institutional church on earth: on the one hand, an invisible congregation of those who will be saved, and on the other, an equally invisible gathering of those foreknown, but not actively predestined, by God to damnation.[29] His theology recalls Augustine's account of the two cities, but Wyclif moved beyond Augustine by treating the distinction between the churches as true for all time, not only in the eschaton.[30] Predestinarian language also shaped Wyclif's doctrine of civil and ecclesiastical dominion, where he argued that only the predestined can justly exercise temporal and

---

[23] J. A. Robson, *Wyclif and the Oxford Schools* (Cambridge, 1961), 177.

[24] Tanner, *Decrees*, i.426.

[25] Robson, *Wyclif and the Oxford Schools*, 179.

[26] John Stacey, 'John Wyclif as theologian', *Expository Times*, 101 (1990), 134–41 at 138.

[27] Samuel Harrison Thompson, 'The philosophical basis of Wyclif's theology', *Journal of Religion*, 11 (1931), 86–116 at 113.

[28] Stacey, 'John Wyclif as theologian', 138.

[29] For Wyclif's definition of the true church as the congregation of the predestined, see, among others, *De ecclesia*, 2–3, 7, 37, 58; *De civili dominio*, i.288, 358; and *Opera minora*, 176.

[30] Gordon Leff, 'The place of metaphysics in Wyclif's theology' in *Ockham to Wyclif*, 217–32 at 225; see also his 'John Wyclif's religious doctrines', *Churchman*, 98 (1984), 319–28 at 322.

spiritual authority.[31] Finally, Wyclif's distinction between *predestinati* and *praesciti* called ecclesiastical authority itself into question: his conviction that the true church exists independently of the institutional church resulted, as I will argue in later chapters, in substantially attenuated claims about the papacy, episcopate, and priesthood. After all, if the pope were 'on his way to Hell, Wyclif argued, it was obvious that the pope did not have to be obeyed'.[32]

Nevertheless, Wyclif's use of predestinarian imagery should not be taken to imply that he endorsed either the doctrine of necessity imputed to him at Constance nor the strict form of double predestinarianism articulated, among others, by Gregory of Rimini. Ian Christopher Levy has suggested, for instance, that *De ecclesia* 'uses the categories of predestination and reprobation as broadswords, by which to cut grasping prelates down to size. There is little, if any discussion of the soteriological process itself, but rather its outcome.'[33] In a wide-ranging study of the discussions of grace to be found across the corpus of Wyclif's writings, Levy has convincingly demonstrated that Wyclif believed free will, God's foreknowledge, and predestination to be compatible. Both Levy and Anthony Kenny have pointed out that Wyclif's soteriology turns on the distinction between absolute necessity and hypothetical necessity. Whereas absolutely necessary propositions cannot be untrue, hypothetically necessary propositions are constructed 'in such a way that the truth about the connection is absolutely necessary but the truth of the causal antecedent is contingent'.[34] For instance, it is hypothetically necessary, if God knows that I am writing this sentence while sitting in the Bodleian Library, that it is true that I am sitting in the Bodleian Library. But God's knowledge of my sitting is only contingent; God's knowledge depends upon my will to sit, and were I standing, or perhaps not in the Bodleian at all, then God's knowledge would reflect that state of affairs, yet still not be the cause of that state of affairs.

Wyclif leveraged the concept of hypothetical necessity to explain that God's omniscience and foreknowledge do not entail that all events are pre-determined. 'Hypothetical necessity', he wrote, 'is consistent with supreme contingence.'[35] So long as God's knowledge does not irreversibly determine human conduct, human beings remain free. Kenny has argued that Wyclif

---

[31] Lahey, *Philosophy and Politics, passim*; Michael Wilks, 'Predestination, property, and power: Wyclif's theory of dominion and grace', repr. in Wilks, *Wyclif*, 16–32.

[32] Louis Brewer Hall, *The Perilous Vision of John Wyclif* (Chicago, 1983), 228.

[33] Ian Christopher Levy, 'Grace and freedom in the soteriology of John Wyclif', *Traditio*, 60 (2005), 279–337 at 332.

[34] Anthony Kenny, *Wyclif* (Oxford, 1985), 33; see also Levy, 'Grace and freedom', 285–90, and Kenny, 'Realism and determinism in the early Wyclif' in *Ockham to Wyclif*, 165–78.

[35] *On Universals*, XIV/98–100; see also *De veritate sacrae scripturae*, ii. 222.

even took the more radical step of proposing that human actions can *cause* divine volitions, citing another passage from *De universalibus*:

So the proposition 'God wills Peter to grieve' reports many volitions in God, for instance the volition by which he wills to be what is absolutely necessary, the volition by which he wills the specific nature to be, and this depends on no particular man, and the volition by which it pleases God that Peter grieves, which is one that depends upon Peter's grief. Nor does it seem that he causes that grief, but rather the prior antecedent volition.[36]

Thus, Kenny concluded, Wyclif took the 'highly unusual step of safeguarding human freedom by attributing to it control over the eternal volitions of God himself'.[37] Whilst it is unclear whether in his later writings Wyclif would have continued to frame the relationship between divine and human volitions in these terms, and likewise whether this account violates the traditional doctrines of divine omniscience and omnipotence, it is clear that Wyclif was not a wholesale determinist.

As Levy has shown, his claims about hypothetical necessity provided Wyclif with the discursive space to claim that even though human actions are foreknown, they are nonetheless not caused by God. Two things follow: on the one hand, God is not the cause of human actions, especially sinful ones; and on the other, freely performed actions can be said to play a role in the salvific process. But what sorts of actions are decisive? According to Wyclif, God's will is to save all people, and accordingly God makes prevenient grace available to all. Those who accept God's offer receive merit as well as additional forms of grace, including the grace of predestination, whilst those who either reject prevenient grace, or accept it at one point but reject it later, are for that reason excluded from the congregation of the elect. 'Wyclif paints a picture of God knocking on the door of people's hearts, even as some resist and refuse to let him in ... Thus, on the one hand, no one can be excused, since all people do have the capacity to receive God's grace. On the other hand, one can be sure that Christ does assist those wayfarers who efficaciously will to be saved.'[38] Since, for Wyclif, God is outside time, in one sense God's offers of grace happen simultaneously, though in another sense the offer of prevenient grace is causally prior to all the others. Accordingly, then, Wyclif can argue that the *praesciti*, far from being damned by a capricious decree, are 'those whom God foreknew he would punish on account of the sins they freely committed. While all were lost in sin, the predestined are those who have accepted God's grace, and the damned are those who have rejected it.'[39]

---

[36] *On Universals*, XIV/346–54.   [37] Kenny, *Wyclif*, 38.
[38] Levy, 'Grace and freedom', 313.
[39] Ibid., 330; on this point, see also *Trialogus*, 121–3.

Indeed, the very word *praesciti* suggests that God's role in the punishment of the damned is more passive than active: God foreknows that they will sin and that God will punish them, but God does not necessitate their fall.

Thus, Wyclif's soteriology most closely resembles the scheme of general election attributed by Halverson to Peter Aureol. Richard Rex is right to have observed in this vein that Wyclif's soteriology was not nearly as innovative as earlier scholars had suggested, yet Rex's argument nevertheless neglects to account for the fact that few of Wyclif's contemporaries articulated the ecclesiological and political implications of their soteriologies in so thorough a fashion.[40] In fact, it is this discursive gap between doctrine and practice that has so often bedevilled studies of Wyclif's soteriology. Though Wyclif did not articulate a version of double predestination, the predestinarian metaphors which can be found in other areas of his theology have been used by many, not least his antagonists at the Council of Constance, to impute to Wyclif a soteriological fatalism he never embraced. As we shall see, the thrust of Wyclif's doctrine of salvation was appropriated in many different ways by the dissenting authors who looked to him for inspiration.

THE SOTERIOLOGICAL ETHOS
OF LATE MEDIEVAL ENGLAND

Wyclif suffered a debilitating stroke on 29 December 1384, expiring shortly before midnight on New Year's Eve. His death did not, however, prevent his followers from continuing to spread his ideas among both academic and popular audiences. The means by which dissenting views flowed outward from Oxford have been discussed at length by a generation of scholars, but an investigation of the reception of Wyclif's ideas about salvation remains wanting. In particular, though students of English dissent have occasionally nodded at the waning importance of predestinarianism in the closing years of the fourteenth century, the views of those who looked to Wyclif for inspiration deserve more rigorous study.[41]

The soteriological leanings of early Wycliffites and later lay dissenters cannot, however, be studied in isolation. What Eamon Duffy has called 'traditional religion' was thriving in the late fourteenth century, and salvation preoccupied

---

[40] Rex, *The Lollards*, 38.
[41] *PR*, 320–1; Rex, *The Lollards*, 60.

orthodox Christians as much as it did their dissenting neighbours.[42] Before analysing a representative sample of Wycliffite texts, therefore, let us consider some soteriological ideas dominant in late medieval England. Whereas scholastic theologians emphasized the necessity, and in many cases the sovereignty, of God's grace, mainstream religion stressed the ways in which human actions can affect the attainment of salvation.

It is far easier to trace learned debates about soteriology than to unearth the views of generations of anonymous laypeople. Points of contact between scholastic thought and local practice do, however, exist. Among them are the pastoral and confessional manuals, catechisms, primers, and model sermons often produced in academic contexts for broader dissemination. Whilst these and other materials can indicate how the theology of salvation was presented to churchgoers, they were unevenly distributed and, likely, just as unevenly used. In the absence of external evidence, it is difficult to reach firm conclusions about the manner in which their doctrines were received.

From the standpoint of ecclesiastical leadership, Archbishop John Pecham's constitution *Ignorantia sacerdotum* represented the most substantial effort to regulate pastoral practice in medieval England. Promulgated in 1281, the constitution required priests to teach their parishioners about 'the fourteen articles of faith; the ten commandments of the Decalogue; the two precepts of the gospel . . . ; and the seven works of mercy, the seven mortal sins, with their progeny, the seven principal virtues, and the seven sacraments of grace'.[43] In its wake appeared a number of companion volumes intended to help the clergy in their task. One such commentary adopted an Augustinian view of human frailty but also spoke of cooperation between grace and human agency:

Who knoweth the might of man so wel as he þat yaue hym might? For he yaue vs neuer commaundement, but þat we may perfourme it, if we wol, wiþ his grace. For he is so rightwise þat to inpossibilite he byndeth no man. And yet his grace and merci helpeth vs euer, so þat, and we wol not wilfully exclude his helpe, we shulde shyne as steeres in þe myddes of þis shrewede nacioun.[44]

---

[42] Duffy, *The Stripping of the Altars, passim*; on the importance of salvation in the pastoral context, see Dennis D. Martin, 'Popular and monastic pastoral issues in the later Middle Ages', *Church History*, 56 (1987), 320–32.

[43] *The Lay Folks' Catechism*, ed. Thomas Frederick Simmons and Henry Edward Nolloth (EETS o.s. 118, 1901), 21: 'XIIII Fidei articulos; X Mandata decalogi; duo Praecepta evangelii, videlicet, geminate charitatis; et VII etiam Opera misericordiae; VII Capitalia peccata, cum sua progenie; VII Virtutes principales; ac etiam VII Gratiae sacramenta.'

[44] Oxford, Bodleian Library MS Eng. Th. c.57, fol. 7b, quoted in Phyllis Hodgson, '*Ignorantia Sacerdotum*: A fifteenth-century discourse on the Lambeth Constitutions', *Review of English Studies*, 24 (1948), 1–11.

This anonymous writer's doctrine of grace is reminiscent of the *pactum*-theologies we have already encountered. On his account, it is possible to keep God's commandments with the help of grace, but it is also possible for human beings wilfully to resist God's offer of assistance.[45]

Whereas pastoral manuals were intended to offer parish clergy a rudimentary acquaintance with theology, a second category of materials provided curates with model sermons. The vernacular sermon-cycle that remains extant in the greatest number of manuscripts is that produced by academic Wycliffites in the late 1380s and 1390s, but its most influential 'orthodox' counterpart was the *Festial* of John Mirk, an Augustinian canon of Littleshall, in Shropshire. Mirk's sermons, which remained in circulation throughout the fifteenth century and were first printed by William Caxton in 1483, only rarely engage directly with Wycliffite ideas and do not contest dissenting beliefs about salvation.[46] Nevertheless, salvation is a common theme in Mirk's collection, and it is rare that he concludes a sermon without exhorting his audience to pray to God and the saints for the gift of eternal life. Many of these closing passages associate salvation with good deeds; for example, on Good Friday, Mirk encourages his audience: 'þus schull ȝe forȝeue oþyr for Cristis loue, and klip, and kys, and be frendes; and þen woll Crist clyppe and kys you, and ȝeue you þe joy þat euer schall last. To þe whech joy God bryng you and me. Amen.'[47] The works-oriented scheme implicit in this and similar passages also undergirds the *Festial*'s account of purgatory, from which, Mirk tells his audience, living people can rescue their dead relatives in three ways: 'devot prayng, almes-ȝeuyng, and masse-syngyng'.[48]

Whilst Mirk's emphasis on human action and free choice might seem to make his soteriology a nearly Pelagian one, other passages describe the operation of grace. Mirk consistently depicts grace as something that human beings are free either to accept or to reject, as when, for instance, they choose whether or not to confess their sins and accept God's forgiveness.[49] Even though Mirk does not make the suggestion that human beings can compel or even persuade God to grant them grace, he repeatedly stresses that responding positively to grace is the duty of each individual.

---

[45] Hodgson, '*Ignorantia Sacerdotum*', 4.

[46] Alan J. Fletcher, 'John Mirk and the Lollards', *Medium Aevum*, 56 (1987), 217–24 at 219. But see also Judy Ann Ford, *John Mirk's Festial: Orthodoxy, Lollardy, and the common people in fourteenth-century England* (Cambridge, 2006) for the important suggestion that the *Festial* may have attempted to subvert Lollard views without directly engaging in anti-Wycliffite polemic.

[47] John Mirk, *Mirk's Festial: A collection of homilies*, ed. Theodor Erbe (EETS e.s. 96, 1905), 124/20–3; for this point, see Ford, *John Mirk's Festial*, 13.

[48] Mirk, 269/15–16. On purgatory more generally, see Peter Marshall, *Beliefs and the Dead in Reformation England* (Oxford, 2002), esp. ch. 1.

[49] Mirk, 92/24–9; on the same theme, see also 155/20–3, 268/27–30; Ford, *John Mirk's Festial*, 32.

Whilst pastoral manuals, sermon collections, and other religious texts like the vernacular *Lay Folks' Catechism* of the mid-fourteenth century may have enjoyed fairly wide circulation, no medieval religious text provided a closer point of connection between the institutional church and the laity than the primer. Originating with the ninth-century churchman Benedict of Aniane, primers were collections of prayers encompassing the Divine Office, the Office of the Dead, the litany, the hours of the Blessed Virgin Mary, and other texts.[50] They were used throughout Europe in the high and later Middle Ages, were among the first religious texts to be printed in England, and remain extant in both printed and manuscript form in substantial numbers. On Duffy's account, the primer was at the centre of a works-oriented lay religiosity. Its promises of indulgences and other rewards for prayers and acts of devotion strengthened in its users' minds the connection between pious deeds and heavenly rewards.[51] The colophon to the York primers' version of the 'Fifteen Oes' attributed to St Bridget, for instance, comforts the reader with details of the benefits he can accrue: 'Whoso say this a hole yere, he shall deleuer xv soules out of purgatory of hys nexte kindred, and conuerte other xv synners to gode lyf, and other xv ryghtuouse men of hys kynde shall perseuer in gode lyf.'[52] Ironically, however, the Brigittine 'Oes' are among the most grace-oriented texts to be found in primers. A mid-fifteenth-century English translation of the prayers renders their fifth petition thus:

O Iesu, þe mirrour of euerlasting clerenes, recorde þe of þat mynde which þou haddist whan þou beheldist þe predestinacion of þi chosen children in þe mirroure of þi magiste, to be shewid bi þe vertue of þi passion and þe repreuyng of euyl men, þat wil not kepe þi commaundementis, to be dampnet in þe grete multitude. Mine iesu, I praye þe bi þe depnes of þi merci in which þou haddist compassion of us synners and dispeyring of þi ioy, and principalli of dismas þe þefe þat henge on þi riȝt side, 'Forsothe I sey to þe, today þou shalt be with me in paradise,' Swete iesu, I praye þe haue merci on me in þe houre of my dethe.[53]

The author of these prayers seems to have articulated a fairly standard doctrine of single predestination, speaking not only of the condemnation of the evil on account of their sins but also of God's gratuitous election of some of those who, like the biblical thief Dismas, would otherwise have no hope. What the author

---

[50] H. Littlehales, 'On the origin of the prymer' in Edmund Bishop (ed.), *Liturgica Historica* (Oxford, 1918), 211–37.

[51] Duffy, *The Stripping of the Altars*, 289–94.

[52] *Horae Eboracenses: the Prymer or Hours of the Blessed Virgin Mary according to the Use of the Illustrious Church of York*, ed. Christopher Wordsworth (Surtees Society 132, 1920), 76.

[53] Charity Meier-Ewart, 'A Middle English version of the "Fifteen Oes"', *Modern Philology*, 68 (1971), 355–61 at 359.

would have made of the argument that Dismas made a positive choice for Christ, and hence merited his salvation, is of course impossible to ascertain.

Since prayers, sermons, primers, and other ecclesiastically sponsored and regulated texts provide little *direct* evidence for the reception of ideas about salvation among the laypeople of late medieval England, then we must turn to the indirect evidence available in vernacular literature. Yet there are still hermeneutical challenges here; whilst it is true that extant literary works must have enjoyed sufficient popularity to ensure that they were copied and preserved in the Middle Ages and after, it is difficult and often misleading to generalize about vernacular piety from the theological commitments of individual poems or prose texts. For one thing, almost every theologically attuned literary work had its origins in a cultural elite. Despite the evidence that some of them, like William Langland's ecclesio-psychological epic *Piers Plowman*, were also read in less lofty circles, it is by no means straightforward to gauge the extent to which our scanty data on a particular text's circulation reflects its audience's approval of its theological content. The religious views of many texts remain a matter for interpretation and debate; but this not-withstanding, vernacular literary works can provide us with vivid insights into the religious *mentalités* of late medieval England.

The soteriological commitments of literary texts have generally been studied on a case-by-case basis, of which the substantial scholarly literature on salvation in *Piers Plowman* is the prime example. There is space here to consider only one short vernacular text, however: the romance *The Awntyrs off Arthur*. The bulk of the poem comprises an episode in which the integrity of Arthur's knights is challenged by an outsider, but its opening scene is highly relevant here. Sir Gawain and Guenevere are in the forest when they happen upon a creature terrible in appearance: 'Bare was the body and blak to the bone, / Al biclagged in clay uncomly cladde.'[54] The spectre introduces itself as the ghost of Guenevere's mother and announces that she is in need of prayers to rescue her from what appear to be the pains of purgatory. Guenevere asks whether she can pay for matins or masses to help her mother's spirit, and the ghost asks her to commission a massive number of prayers, thirty trentals in all. Guenevere promises 'a myllion of Masses to make the mynnyng' and then asks her mother for advice as to how best to get to heaven. The ghost's answer is instructive: 'Mekenesse and mercy, thes arn the moost; / And sithen have pité on the poer, that pleses Heven king. / Sithen charité is chef, and then is chaste, / And then almessedede aure al other thing. / Thes arn the graceful giftes of the Holy Goste / That enspires iche sprete withoute speling.'[55] It

[54] *The Awntyrs off Arthur*, in *Sir Gawain: Eleven romances and tales*, ed. Thomas Hahn (Kalamazoo, Mich., 1995), ll. 105–6. I am grateful to Mishtooni Bose for drawing my attention to *Awntyrs*.

[55] Ibid., ll. 250–5.

should go without saying that the spectre's prescription for eternal life is primarily a works-oriented one: charity, chastity, mercy, and almsgiving are the ways in which human beings can hope to find salvation, though the ghost does note in passing that such good deeds are done with the help of grace.

Even a cursory survey of the doctrines of salvation implicit in texts representing the many genres of late Middle English religious writing can thus reveal the substantial gap between the predestinarian and grace-oriented views of scholastic thinkers and the works-oriented theologies of pastoral manuals, model sermons, primers, and literary works. Some notable exceptions notwithstanding, the texts with which the lay men and women of medieval England would have been acquainted articulate neither a doctrine of predestination nor the universalism that Nicholas Watson, perhaps quixotically in some cases, has discerned in a host of Middle English texts.[56] That mainstream medieval religion placed such a strong emphasis on the role of human agency in the dynamic of salvation is something that must condition our reading of dissenting literature.

WYCLIF'S FOLLOWERS: IN THEIR OWN WORDS

A representative sample of Wycliffite texts highlights the range of soteriologies that English dissenters embraced.[57] In keeping with Wyclif's suggestion that theology should be made accessible to both clerics and laypeople, an overwhelming proportion of such texts were written in the vernacular. One Latin tract nevertheless merits attention: the Apocalypse commentary *Opus arduum*, likely written in 1389–90 by an anonymous author imprisoned for his dissenting beliefs. Not studied until the late twentieth century, *Opus arduum* develops a number of Wyclif's favourite themes within the context of a detailed exegesis of the book of Revelation.[58] To judge from its language

---

[56] Nicholas Watson, 'Visions of inclusion: Universal salvation and vernacular theology in pre-Reformation England', *Journal of Medieval and Early Modern Studies*, 27 (1997), 145–87.

[57] The texts below have been chosen on account of the length at which they discuss the doctrine of salvation; space has unfortunately prohibited the inclusion of more than these, but other tracts worthy of similar attention are Sir John Clanvowe's moralistic treatise *The Two Ways* and a collection of Wycliffite sermons discovered by Richard Melia. See V. J. Scattergood, 'The two ways: An unpublished religious treatise by Sir John Clanvowe', *English Philological Studies*, 10 (1967), 33–56, soon to appear in modern English translation in *Wycliffism*, ed. and trans. J. Patrick Hornbeck II, Stephen E. Lahey, and Fiona Somerset (forthcoming), and Melia's article '"Non-controversial Lollardy"? The Lollard attribution of the "Diuers Treatises of John Wiclife in English" (John Rylands Library, English MS 85)', *Bulletin of the John Rylands Library*, 83 (2001), 89–102.

[58] Anne Hudson, 'A neglected Wycliffite text', repr. in *Books*, 43–65; see also her 'Lollardy and eschatology' in Alexander Patschovsky and František Šmahel (eds.), *Eschatologie und Hussitis-*

and the mode and complexity of its arguments, its intended audience was a scholarly one: its interest in such 'technical' doctrines as the Eucharist, clerical temporalities, dominion, and predestination locate it closer to Wyclif's own treatises than the writings of later Wycliffites. But the parallels are not exact: *Opus arduum* espouses a strict predestinarianism, defining the church as the number of the predestined and distinguishing, like Wyclif, between the churches of God and the devil.[59] In focusing on 'concerns of a theoretical and theological cast, rather than . . . the more practical direction of much later Lollard polemic', *Opus arduum* possesses a number of similarities with other Latin texts like the contemporary Wycliffite preachers' handbook, the *Floretum*.[60]

Whereas Wycliffite writings in Latin tended to remain within the idiom of the academic milieu within which Wyclif had spent his career, the dissenters' vernacular works looked outward, aiming both to convert the 'orthodox' and to encourage their co-religionists to persevere in the face of opposition. For the sake of convenience, though as a result somewhat arbitrarily, these English Wycliffite texts can be grouped into three categories: sermons and encyclopaedias; prose tracts which set forth Wycliffite beliefs and attack the doctrines and practices of the institutional church; and poems of a dissenting cast.

Preaching the word: Wycliffite sermons and the Middle English *Rosarium*

Wycliffites placed an unusually heavy emphasis on preaching: it was for Wyclif and his followers the principal duty of the clergy, the means by which laypeople were to come into contact with the all-important biblical text.[61] Accordingly, it is hardly surprising that the most significant literary achievements of dissenting authors were closely connected with the sacred page. Pre-eminently, there is the Wycliffite Bible, which despite being an important monument in the history of English biblical scholarship betrays little about the theological convictions of its translators.[62] Not so with many other

---

mus (Prague, 1996), 99–113. It remains a matter of some disappointment that no edition of the *Opus Arduum* has yet appeared.

[59] Hudson, 'A neglected Wycliffite text', 62–3.

[60] Ibid., 63; see also her 'A Lollard compilation and the dissemination of Wycliffite thought', repr. in *Books*, 13–29 at 20, 23.

[61] On this point, see Ch. 5 below.

[62] The prime and perhaps the only exception to this claim is the highly polemical General Prologue to the Later Version, which I treat further in Ch. 4. It was not, however, widely disseminated in the late fourteenth century: see Mary Dove, *The First English Bible* (Cambridge, 2008).

Wycliffite texts in the vernacular, among them the long cycle of some 294 sermons, a separate collection of sermons for major feasts, and the preachers' encyclopaedia the *Rosarium theologie*.

Containing five sets of texts for the Sunday gospels and epistles, the common and proper of saints, and a number of important liturgical celebrations, the long sermon-cycle provides a comprehensive, if hardly systematic, glimpse into the theological and devotional worlds of Wycliffite dissenters. Its contents range from detailed arguments about the nature of the church, the freedom of the will, and the relationship between ecclesiastical and temporal government to earthy attacks on the wealth and other failings of the monastic and fraternal orders. The question of salvation appears frequently, but perhaps surprisingly, the sermons articulate no single, coherent soteriology. Instead, they reflect three divergent strands of thinking.

In slightly more than half of their references to salvation, the sermons articulate doctrines of predestination, none so carefully nuanced as Wyclif's. They appropriate Wyclif's treatment of the two churches of God and the devil, speaking of the division of humankind into the congregations of the saved and the damned: 'men seyn comunly þat þer ben here two manerys of chirches: holy chirche or chirche of God, þat on no maner may be dampnyd; and þe chirche of þe feend, þat for a tyme is good and lasteþ not, and þis was neuere holy chirche ne part þerof'.[63] One sermon from the common of saints repeats Wyclif's distinction between the predestined, who are *of* the church, and believers on earth, who are simply, and only temporarily, *in* the church; another clarifies that the two churches have existed from the beginning of time: 'þer ben two kynredus þat Crist spekuþ ofte of, þe kynrede of Godis children, and kynrede of feendis children; and at bygynnyng of þis world bygan þese two kynredis.'[64] But yet, some of the sermons move beyond Wyclif in adopting a full-blown determinism.[65] Those whom God has elected to salvation cannot but be saved; the converse applies to those whom God has foreknown as condemned.[66] A Sunday epistle sermon insists that the elect can do nothing

---

[63] *EWS*, i.20/66–9; similar definitions of the church in terms of salvation appear at ii.79/100–6 and iii.233/19–26.

[64] Ibid., ii.84/92–6, ii.74/6–8. See also ii.91/9–11, a sermon from the proper of saints in which the same ideas find expression in nearly identical terms: 'þer ben two kynredus; good kyndrede, and yuel, of whiche ben mansleerus fro þe bygynnyng of þe world to þe laste martir'. But cf. i, E1/72–4, where the preacher maintains that though Adam was the first predestinate man, God marked him out for salvation only after he (and, presumably, the world) had begun to exist.

[65] Ibid., i.43/96–101, i.E4/119–26, ii.107/19–21, ii.108/48–50, iii.150/67–9, and iii.182/29–30.

[66] Ibid., i.2/95–7. See also iii.173/34–6; for the fate of the foreknown, see ii.117/24–7.

to change their status in the eschaton, not least because the grace they have received is wholly unmerited:

Noo man may putte fro hym þat ne he schulde be a choson of God, to fiȝte here wiþ goostly enemyes, and by victorie to gete blisse; and hoolynesse stonduþ in þis, for wiþ hoolynesse schulde men fiȝte. And al þis is a stronde of loue, þat strengore may no loue be. For where is welle of more loue þan chesyng of God byfore þe world, for to brynge men to blisse, and to alle menys nedful þerfore? Or where is more charite þan God hymself to make us hooly, and droppe to us of his owne grace wiþowton owre disseruyng byfore?[67]

Some sermons also discount any necessary connection between salvation and good deeds and, likewise, between damnation and evil actions. 'For þese þat God wot schulle be sauede, al ȝif þei synne for a tyme, neþeles here synful liȝf schal turne to hem to fruyt of heuene. And so þese men þat schal be dampnyde, al ȝif þei don good for a tyme, ȝit þei han an yuel maner þat qwencheþ þe good þat þei don.'[68] This predestinarian sermon thus rejects the view that good works can merit salvation, though another likens the relationship between salvation and good deeds to that between a medical condition and its symptoms: 'siþ a fysisyan lerneþ diligently his signes in vryne, in pows and oþre þingus, wheþur a mannys body be hool, how myche more schulde he knowe syche signes þat tellon helþe of mannys sowle, and how he haþ hym to God'.[69] Despite this last argument, however, the majority of sermons claim that it is impossible in this life to distinguish the predestined from the foreknown. God has hidden his choices from human beings, who consequently have the duty neither to condemn nor fulsomely to praise one another.[70]

A second set of texts shies away from the full implications of predestinarianism, instead discussing salvation in terms of the interplay between God's grace and human freedom. One sermon, for instance, maintains that though God calls many people, only those who respond by living 'in loue of God to þer ende' actually attain salvation.[71] Two others allude to the maxim *facere quod in se est*, the scholastic dictum according to which human beings can reach salvation by doing that which is within their power to do. Thus, one ferial sermon insists that 'for do a man þat in hym is, and God is redy to his dedis', and another exhorts its audience, 'Do we now þat in us is, and God wole haue us excusid.'[72]

---

[67] Ibid., i.E12/15–23. See also i.E7/31–42.
[68] Ibid., ii.55/53–8.
[69] Ibid., i.52/5–8.
[70] Ibid., ii.55/77–81, 84–5. See also ii.69/109–12, ii.73/41–5.
[71] Ibid., i.2/24.
[72] Ibid., iii.176/99–100, iii.229/47–8. This group of sermons shares its soteriological assumptions with the interpolated Wycliffite version of the *Lay Folks' Catechism* (72; see also 41, 58).

A third, smaller group of texts goes further still, articulating a theology of salvation in which meritorious acts alone seem to be able to earn one a place in heaven. The most explicit statement of this position appears in a sermon for the proper of saints that Wyclif's early biographer H. B. Workman disastrously attributed to the Oxford thinker himself: 'for eche man þat schal be dampned, is dampned for his owne gylt, and eche man þat schal be saued, is saued by his owne meryȝt'.[73] Similar, though not as unambiguously Pelagian, sentiments can be found elsewhere: one sermon argues that only those are members of the church who 'beron fruyt, and han loue wiþowton ende'; another suggests that the damned will receive their punishment 'for synnes þat þei han don bifore'; and a third reserves heaven only for those who 'haue . . . som degree of feiþ and hope and charite'.[74]

What can the apparent contradictions of the sermon-cycle's approach to the theology of salvation reveal about the reception of Wyclif's soteriology? On the one hand, the radical inconsistencies between the views expressed in the sermons suggest that the cycle was likely the work of multiple authors. The sermons' editors, Anne Hudson and Pamela Gradon, have expressed agnosticism about their authorship, tentatively suggesting that several individuals of equal learning may have collaborated to produce the cycle. Multiple authors may have been involved in the production of each sermon, some working to unearth and verify biblical and patristic citations, others maintaining consistency of rhetoric. Hudson and Gradon also allow, though to a lesser extent, for the possibility of what they call a vertical division of labour, in which individual writers may have been responsible for individual sermons.[75] This latter model seems more effectively to explain the diversity of theological opinion within the cycle, and something of a concentration of non-predestinarian views in the sermons for the common and proper of saints lends credence to the possibility that the cycle owes its existence to independent authors or teams of authors.[76]

On the other hand, the sermon-cycle's conflicting views about salvation highlight the diversity of Wycliffite theologies of salvation. Hudson and Gradon have tentatively dated the sermons to the period from the mid- to late 1380s to the first few years of the fifteenth century, with earlier *termini*

---

[73] *EWS*, ii.100/82–4; H. B. Workman, *John Wyclif: A study of the English medieval church*, 2 vols. (Oxford, 1926), ii.9.

[74] *EWS*, ii.55/26–8, iii.141/60–3, ii.103/28–32. Curiously, the first of these passages occurs in the same sermon whose author also maintains that salvation and good deeds are unconnected.

[75] Ibid., iv.29–32.

[76] While predestinarian and non-predestinarian views can be found in all but one of the sermons' five sets, seven of the eight instances of works-oriented or Pelagian soteriologies I have cited occur in the common and proper of saints and the ferial set.

ante quem for the Sunday gospels, the proper of saints, and the ferial set.[77] It seems quite possible, then, that even some early Wycliffites did not subscribe to the predestinarian soteriology imputed to Wyclif by his antagonists. Before turning to the reasons why, though, let us first consider another collection of Wycliffite sermons.

Since their appearance in an Early English Text Society volume in 1989, the *Lollard Sermons* edited by Gloria Cigman have not always been thought to deserve that title. Among the early reviewers of Cigman's edition, A. S. G. Edwards and John Frankis both questioned the link between the sermons and Wycliffism. 'Indubitable Wycliffite views are in fact not at all frequent in these sermons, which seem to emanate from the centre of the religious spectrum', wrote Frankis. 'There must clearly be a careful consideration of what these sermons have in common with known Lollard writings.'[78] Whilst the sermons do not adopt clearly heterodox positions on prominently controversial issues such as the sacrament of the altar or the adoration of images, they do replicate many of the nuances of Wyclif's theology of salvation.

The sermons begin with a statement which Wyclif could wholly have embraced as his own. Explicating the passage from Matthew's gospel in which Jesus prepares to enter Jerusalem, the preacher likens Jerusalem to 'þe syth of pees', bi whiche may wel be vndurstonde al holi cherche: þat is, þe general congregacion of alle þat schullen be saued'.[79] In other sermons, the preacher articulates other elements of Wyclif's soteriology: that human persons cannot in their earthly lives know with certainty whether they are destined for heaven or hell[80] and that preaching 'ministriþ to a man greet hope þat he is þe childe of God and a membre of God ordeynid to blis by þe wordis of God'.[81] A thorough analysis of the sermons' soteriology, however, reveals that the preacher's dominant perspective on the theology of salvation is not, as the conventional wisdom about Wycliffism might have it, wholly predestinarian.

Far more often than he discusses predestination, the preacher emphasizes the salvific value of good works. Postillating on the text 'Mani men ben clepid, and fewe ben chose', he argues *not* that those who have been chosen are the

---

[77] *EWS*, iv.10–20.
[78] John Frankis, review of *Lollard Sermons*, *Review of English Studies*, 42 (1991), 437–8; A. S. G. Edwards, review of *Lollard Sermons*, *Speculum*, 67 (1992), 124–6. It must be acknowledged that Cigman has explained that her comments on the sermons' religious outlook were omitted from the edition at the request of an anonymous EETS reviewer (letter, *Review of English Studies* 43 (1992), 250).
[79] Gloria Cigman (ed.), *Lollard Sermons* (EETS o.s. 294, 1989), sermon 1, ll. 86–8.
[80] Ibid., 2/10–11; DM/473–5.
[81] Ibid., 16/218–20.

lucky recipients of predetermined grace but, rather, that the chosen are those who 'wirchen þeraftir to *make* þat þei moun be chose'.[82] Likewise, he maintains that 'no man bee dampned but if he wole himself',[83] that following the commandments of God is the surest way toward heaven,[84] and that the account to be taken at the Last Judgement has everything to do with good deeds.[85] The preacher describes at length the manner in which a person's sins will affect her or his standing in the afterlife: 'aboue men in þat day shal apere þe iuge þat is offendid, shewing hymself ful wraþful to hem þat shullen be dampned. Vnderneþe shal be þe blake hydous pit of helle . . . On þe riȝt side, alle a mannys synnis, redy to accuse him.'[86]

The preacher's most extended discussion of salvation likewise revolves around a works-oriented metaphor. In his sermon for Septuagesima Sunday, he dissects the Matthean parable of the labourers in the vineyard:

þe hure þat þis Lord haþ bihiȝte hem for hire daies iorne (þat is, for þe trewe trauaile of þis liȝf) is a peny, þat is: þe euerlastynge blisse of heuene, whiche mai wel be likened to a peny for þe roundenesse þat bitokeneþ euerlastyngnesse, and for þe blessed siȝt of þe kyngis face þat is in þat peni, and also for þe Scripture þat is þerinne, þat is: þe Booke of Liȝf, in whiche al þo þat schullen see þat siȝte beþ euerlastyngli writen.[87]

The notion that God offers salvation as a reward for honest living (*trewe trauaile,* which in its connections with the distinctive Wycliffite use of *trewe* may well mean good deeds performed apart from the perceived corruptions of institutional piety) follows the broad contours of Wyclif's doctrine of salvation yet casts them in a less grace-oriented light. Using monetary images that would later recur in the *pactum*-theologies of thinkers like Gabriel Biel, who likened good deeds to a copper coin, the preacher stresses that both divine grace and human agency are at work in the dynamic of salvation.[88] The faithful Christian hoping for a bright eschatological future does indeed perform the Lord's work, but it is God who has so constituted the world that good deeds have salvific consequences. As the preacher argues in the same sermon, 'þis gospel techeþ vs to wirche faste and be not idel while we

---

[82] Gloria Cigman (ed.), *Lollard Sermons* (EETS o.s. 294, 1989), sermon 1, 8/189–96, emphasis mine.

[83] Ibid., 2/17–18.

[84] Ibid., 9/83.

[85] Ibid., DM/548–57.

[86] Ibid., DM/640–5.

[87] Ibid., 8/52–8.

[88] See, for instance, Gabriel Biel, 'The circumcision of the Lord' in Heiko A. Oberman, *Forerunners of the Reformation: The shape of late medieval thought illustrated by key documents* (Philadelphia, 1981), 165–74.

been here wandrynge in þis wei, for þe hure of þe hiȝe blisse of heuene þat God haþ behiȝte to alle suche.'[89]

Unless the preacher intentionally disguised a stricter doctrine of predestination in the hope of encouraging his audience to perform good deeds, it seems clear that the *Lollard Sermons* witness to his works-oriented views about salvation. That the church is the congregation of all who will be saved need not mean that those who will be saved have been chosen by God before the beginning of time; instead, the preacher may be alluding to a communitarian concept of the church very much like that which dominates the closing *passus* of Langland's *Piers Plowman*. That people cannot know whether they will spend eternity in heaven or hell can still be true in a world in which good conduct rather than divine fiat is the key criterion for salvation. And that preaching helps people to know that they are ordained to salvation 'by the words of God' may mean that preachers are responsible for guiding their listeners to understand the moral obligations laid upon them by Scripture.[90]

Not all lollard preachers adopted works-oriented soteriologies, however. We have already seen that some of the texts which comprise the Wycliffite sermon-cycle articulate views closely in line with predestinarianism. So also do the theological encyclopaedias produced by Wycliffites, likely in Oxford, as guidebooks for dissenting preachers. The most extensive of these was entitled the *Floretum*, though its more than 500 dense and highly abbreviated Latin entries must hardly have proven conducive to daily use. Indeed, two shorter versions, the *Rosarium sive floretus minor* and the *Rosarium*, were also produced.[91] Fourteen manuscripts of the *Rosarium* have survived, one of which is a faithful Middle English translation of the Latin original.[92] Its entry under *predestination* sets forth what appears to be a doctrine of single predestination. God has chosen those whom God wills to be among the saved; the number of the saved 'is so certayne þat nouþer be added to þam ne be mynisthed of þam'; though God predestines to salvation, God does not actively intend but only passively countenances the damnation of the foreknown; and no number of evil deeds can keep the predestined from heaven. Elsewhere, the text emphasizes that grace can never be merited: 'grace freely

---

[89] Cigman, *Lollard Sermons*, 8/5–7.

[90] This account of Cigman's sermons draws heavily on my article '*Lollard* sermons? Soteriology and late-medieval dissent', *Notes and Queries*, 53 (2006), 26–30.

[91] Hudson traces the textual relations between the three versions in 'A Lollard compilation and the dissemination of Wycliffite thought', repr. in *Books*, 13–29 at 14–18.

[92] A partial edition of the manuscript has been published by Christina von Nolcken as *The Middle English Translation of the Rosarium Theologie* (Heidelberg, 1979); fuller details can be found in her doctoral thesis, 'An edition of selected parts of the Middle English translation of the *Rosarium Theologie*', 2 vols. (Oxford University, 1977).

geffen is god signe or tokne of þe grace of god and noȝt of meritteȝ afore goyne ... grace went afore þe merite, not grace of merite, but merite of grace'.[93] Finally, in its entry on *arbitrium*, the *Rosarium* sets limits to the operation of human freedom vis-à-vis divine grace: not only can the good only be chosen through grace, but a sinful person cannot will to receive grace without divine prompting.[94]

In terms of its ecclesiology, the encyclopaedia follows Wyclif particularly closely; it first distinguishes between material church buildings and the church as a theological reality, conceding that in the latter sense, the word *church* 'is taken ... for noumbour of chosen bi þamself, or for noumbour of reproued be þamself, or medely for noumbour of þam to be saued and reproued togedere'.[95] Later, however, it becomes clear which of these definitions is the more preferable: 'holi chirche is þe congregacion of trew men predestinate and iustified'.[96] It seems clear, then, that the *Rosarium* contains a vernacular account of Wyclif's thought outwardly similar to the original, though without some of the key nuances of Wyclif's theology. There is, for instance, little here that would reflect Wyclif's notion of hypothetical necessity; one conclusion might be that with both the *Floretum* and *Rosarium* having been composed in Oxford, but for mixed audiences of scholars and preachers, their anonymous compilers may have (intentionally or unintentionally) oversimplified Wyclif's views.

Encouraging the faithful: *The Lanterne of Liȝt* and *Speculum de Antichristo*

Wycliffite authors did not, however, confine their propaganda to the genre of sermon-literature. There remain extant dozens of prose tracts betraying evidence of Wycliffite authorship; many of these have been published since the mid-nineteenth-century revival of scholarly interest in lollardy, though a number remain in manuscript. Addressing themselves primarily to such issues as pilgrimage, the monastic and fraternal orders, and the Eucharist, these texts tend to make few overt comments about salvation. At least two, however, do make salvation an explicit concern.

---

[93] Cambridge, Gonville and Caius College MS 354/581, fol. 44r.
[94] Ibid., fols. 12r–12v.
[95] Christina von Nolcken (ed.), *The Middle English Translation of the Rosarium Theologie* (Heidelberg, 1979), 66/24–6.
[96] Ibid., 67/12.

The Lanterne of Liȝt is perhaps the latest surviving systematic exposition of Wycliffite belief, dating from the years 1409–15. Like the Middle English translation of the *Rosarium*, the *Lanterne* sets forth what seems to be a standard account of Wycliffite ecclesiology. The author acknowledges that the church can be defined in a variety of ways, including 'þe chosun noumbre of hem þat schullen be saued'.[97] Nevertheless, he maintains that 'how euere we speken in diuerse names or licknessis of þis holi chirche, þei techen nouȝt ellis but þis oo name, þat is to seie þe congregacioun or gedering togidir of feiþful soulis þat lastingli kepen feiþ and trouþe, in word and in dede to God and to man'.[98] The text distinguishes, as Wyclif did, between God's church of the saved, the material church on earth, and the devil's church of those unfortunates 'þat ben encombrid to serue him after his tising'.[99] Contrasting various types of members of God's and the devil's churches, the author suggests that it is not only possible but indeed incumbent upon every Christian to distinguish between the good and evil elements which together constitute the material church.[100]

The *Lanterne*'s wholesale appropriation of Wyclif's ecclesiology might suggest that its author also shared the reformer's doctrine of salvation. An exhortation in the very last section of the text which has puzzled some critics confirms this view. After prophesying that judgement is about to strike the devil's church, the author encourages his readers to assess the moral quality of their own lives. He then proposes a remedy for those who find themselves wanting: 'Neþeles assay in þis lijf, if ȝe may leeue þe fendis chirche and brynge ȝoure silf boþe bodi and soule in to þe chirch of Iesu Crist while grace and mercy may be grauntid, axe of him þat offrid him silf...to saue vs alle whanne we were loost.'[101] Such language is hardly compatible with predestinarianism: it should go without saying, for instance, that an individual irreversibly condemned to damnation would have little chance of succeeding in his or her efforts to leave the devil's church. The author appears to consider such a change of eschatological condition a real possibility, however, for he also urges his readers to 'mystrist þou not on þe merci of God, for more is his mercy þan þi wrecchidnes'.[102] His comments seem to imply something like the grace-oriented position that human cooperation with the offer of divine

[97] *The Lanterne of Liȝt*, ed. Lilian M. Swinburne (EETS 151, 1917), 23/3–4.
[98] Ibid., 25/1–4.
[99] Ibid., 127/21–2. On this point, see further D. S. Dunnan, 'A note on the three churches in *The Lanterne of Liȝt*', *Notes and Queries*, 38 (March 1991), 20–2.
[100] *Lanterne*, 48/1–13.
[101] Ibid., 136/13–17.
[102] Ibid., 136/31–2. See further on this point Nicholas Watson, 'Vernacular apocalyptic: On *The Lanterne of Liȝt*', *Revista canaria de estudios ingleses*, 47 (2003), 115–26.

grace brings about salvation, yet like Wyclif he does not shy away from coupling this position with rigorously predestinarian imagery.

The second of our prose tracts, the Middle English *Speculum de Antichristo*, presents a less ambiguous situation. Undatable on the basis of either internal or palaeographical evidence and slightly less than five pages in its printed form, the tract frames its claims about salvation in terms of traditional Wycliffite criticisms of the abuse of ecclesiastical authority. Thus, for instance, the author asserts that by restricting public preaching, 'anticrist wolde quenche and owtlaue holy writt and make alle men dampnyd'.[103] The notion that persons can be *made damned* on account of temporal events—in contrast to the less flexible position that those doomed to hell have been condemned to be there from all eternity—is again implied later in the text, where the author asserts that those who fail to keep the commandments will 'goo to helle for bregynge of goddis hestis'.[104]

The author's comments about the saved reveal a similar logic. He insists that 'for siþ eche man haþ a free wille and chesyng of good and euyl, no man schal be sauyd but he þat willefully hereþ and endeles kepiþ goddis hestis', a clear repudiation of determinism.[105] The text also explains in two places that God has ordained preaching as a particularly efficacious means to salvation; it can thus be seen as a Wycliffite appropriation of the classic scholastic trope of the dialectic between God's absolute and ordained powers.[106] Even without access to preaching, though, salvation may still be a real possibility: 'who knoweþ þe mesure of goddis mercy, to whom herynge of goddis word schal þus profite?'[107]

If *Speculum* thus adopts a works-oriented viewpoint, why did its nineteenth-century editor assign it a place among Wyclif's supposedly predestinarian writings? F. D. Matthew explained that though the text asserts the freedom of the will, 'predestination is treated as a recognized truth'.[108] On the contrary, however, the text places its predestinarian assertions squarely in the mouths of Antichrist and his allies. Among their arguments against preaching, the tract

---

[103] *Speculum de Antichristo*, in Matthew, 108–13 at 109/24–5. Line numbers are my own.

[104] *Speculum*, 113/4. The same idea seems to inform the author's claim that 'men shullen by dampnyd ʒif þei failen in bodily werkis of mercy, þat is prechynge, ordeyned to hem' (112/29–31).

[105] Ibid., 111/18–20. The text's earlier formulation that 'god ʒeueþ to eche man a free wille to chese good or euyl and god is redi to ʒeue hem grace ʒif þei wolen resceyuen it' also seems to emphasize the significance of cooperation between divine grace and human agency (110/25–7).

[106] Ibid., 110/21–2, 111/9–11. On the dialectic between the two powers, see among others Heiko A. Oberman, '*Facientibus quod in se est Deus non denegat gratiam:* Robert Holcot, O.P., and the beginnings of Luther's theology', *Harvard Theological Review*, 55 (1962), 317–42 at 327–8.

[107] *Speculum*, 111/15–17.

[108] Matthew, 108.

claims, is that '*þei seyn þat* good men schulden be sauyd þou3 no prechynge be, for þei may not perische, as god seiþ. And summe wicked men schullen neuere come to blisse for no prechynge in erthe.'[109] That the only account of predestination in *Speculum* is attributed to Antichrist rather than to the 'trewe men' who reject his falsehoods should suggest that the author's sympathies lie rather with the works-oriented soteriologies that we have encountered in a number of other Wycliffite texts.[110]

Dissent in verse: *Pierce the Ploughman's Crede*

The period of Wycliffism's emergence from academic obscurity was a time when many authors used vernacular literature to interrogate and nuance traditional understandings of theology. As Andrew Cole has recently suggested, Wycliffism provided medieval authors with 'an emergent fund of ideas, forms, and rhetorics that helped various medieval authors think anew about the past and the present . . . about, fundamentally, what it means to write'.[111] Like many of their contemporaries, Wycliffites also employed poetry to convey their criticisms of the institutional church, borrowing from literary conventions in order to construct indictments of the fraternal orders, the sacramental system, and the interpenetration of secular and ecclesiastical hierarchies. Among the texts which exemplify this variety of versified dissent, *Pierce the Ploughman's Crede* is the most familiar member of what has come to be called the '*Piers Plowman* tradition' of alliterative poetry.[112]

Crede, almost surely written between 1393 and 1401 and first printed by the leading Protestant printer Reyner Wolfe in 1553, takes as its frame story its narrator's search for someone who can teach him the Creed, without which, he ruefully comments, his parish priest will not lightly accept his annual confession.[113] 'Whan y schal schewen myn schrift schent mote y worthen, / The prest wil me punyche and penaunce enioyne; / The Lengthe of a Lenten flech moot y leue / After that Estur ys ycomen and that is hard fare.'[114] Forty days without meat during Eastertide might be 'hard fare', but harsher still, the

---

[109] *Speculum*, 111/6–9, emphasis mine.

[110] Ibid., 111/9.

[111] Cole, *Literature and Heresy*, 186.

[112] Helen Barr, *Signes and Sothe: Language in the Piers Plowman tradition* (Cambridge, 1994). On the '*Piers Plowman* tradition', see further D. A. Lawton, 'Lollardy and the "Piers Plowman" tradition', *Modern Language Review*, 76 (1981), 780–93. On *Crede* in particular, see John Scattergood, '*Pierce the Ploughman's Crede*: Lollardy and texts' in *Lollardy and Gentry*, 77–94.

[113] On the date of *Crede*, see PR, 13.

[114] *Pierce the Ploughman's Crede*, in Helen Barr (ed.), *The Piers Plowman Tradition* (London, 1993), ll. 9–12.

narrator points out, will be Jesus' dissatisfaction with an ill-educated believer. A quote from John's gospel provides the context for the poem's subsequent action: 'Jesu hym-self to the Iewes he seyde, / "He that leeueth nought on me he leseth the blisse."'[115] As he searches for an instructor, the narrator meets members of the four fraternal orders, each of whom he asks to teach him the Creed, a symbol of the salvation that he hopes to achieve. That the narrator feels himself capable either of losing or else of attaining heaven suggests that his thought-world is less a predestinarian than a works-oriented one.

A tacit emphasis on the salvific value of good works pervades the poem. It specifically recurs during each of the narrator's encounters with his four fraternal interlocutors. During his first meeting, with a Franciscan he meets by the roadside, the narrator reveals his despair at being unable to find someone to teach him the Creed, 'Crist for to folwen'.[116] The same language, somewhat amplified by a more explicit focus on Christian living, occurs at the beginning of his subsequent conversation with a corpulent Dominican. He asks: 'Gode syre, for Godes loue canstou me graith tellen / To any worthely wijght that wissen me couthe / Whou y schulde conne my Crede *Crist for to folowe*, / That leuede lelliche him-self and lyuede therafter, / That feynede non falshede but fully Crist suwede?'[117] As at the beginning of the poem, the narrator identifies right belief and right practice as the criteria of Christian discipleship. Similar concerns inform his subsequent encounters with Austin and Carmelite friars.

The first half of *Crede* thus lacks any reference to predestinarianism. The energy with which the narrator approaches his search for a teacher of the Creed suggests that he believes authentic faith in Christ—and the salvation it entails—to be within the grasp of anyone sufficiently motivated to resist the temptations to which the friars have succumbed. In the second half of the poem, the narrator encounters the destitute farmer Peres the ploughman, whose remarks confirm his soteriological instincts. Peres comments that Christ 'the clene hertes curtysliche blissed, / That coueten no katel but Cristes ful blisse, / That leeueth fulliche on God and lellyche thenketh / On his lore and his lawe and lyueth opon trewthe.'[118] These lines hearken back to the characteristics that the narrator praised earlier in the poem. The *Crede*-poet, then, describes Christ not as the arbitrary ruler of a predestinarian universe

---

[115] *Pierce the Ploughman's Crede*, in Helen Barr (ed.), *The Piers Plowman Tradition* (London, 1993), ll. 14–15.

[116] Ibid., l. 101.

[117] Ibid., ll. 232–6, emphasis mine.

[118] Ibid., ll. 639–40.

but as a kindly judge who considers the quality of human works in choosing those upon whom to bestow grace.

Neither Peres' extensive speech about the corruption of the fraternal orders nor his version of the Creed with which the poem ends departs from this works-oriented approach to the doctrine of salvation. Peres' remarks about the friars' worldliness, their gluttony, their relentless pursuit of the poor, and their pride in their academic degrees all reflect the *Crede*-poet's central concern with the behaviour of those who claim to imitate Christ. Indeed, no predestinarian Wycliffite could consistently have written that 'it mot ben a man of also mek an herte, / That myghte with his good lijf that Holy Ghost fongen'.[119] And no predestinarian could have prayed, as Peres does in the poem's final lines, that the friars might 'swiche dedes to werche / That thei maie wynnen the lif that euer schal lesten!'[120] Thus *Crede*, like other Wycliffite texts, implicitly endorses the assumptions of a works-oriented soteriology rather than a doctrine of predestination.

THROUGH THE LENS OF 'ORTHODOX' RELIGION

The dissenters' own words, however, are not the only sources which attest to the doctrines of salvation current within dissenting communities. The far more extensive corpus of texts which constitute the institutional church's response to the emergence of Wycliffism and other forms of religious nonconformity likewise reveals that while some individuals articulated doctrines of predestination, the majority of those who challenged the ecclesiastical *status quo* adopted a works-oriented perspective instead. Anti-Wycliffite polemics, lists of propositions condemned by church councils, and the records of suspected heretics' trials all disclose that over time, ecclesiastical authorities came less and less frequently to associate dissent with predestinarianism.

The earliest opposition to Wyclif's teachings came in the context of the Oxford schools, but it was not until the 1420s that his views found their most able opponent in the person of the Carmelite friar and later Prior Provincial Thomas Netter.[121] His *Doctrinale antiquitatum fidei ecclesiae catholicae* remains the most comprehensive near-contemporary refutation of Wyclif's ideas. As Hudson has shown, Netter's massive work displays his familiarity with many of Wyclif's later writings; though surprisingly it omits reference to *De ecclesia*, it repeatedly cites *Trialogus, Opus evangelicum, De veritate sacrae*

---

[119] Ibid., ll. 830–1. [120] Ibid., ll. 849–50. [121] *PR*, 45–9.

scripturae, and other texts we have encountered.[122] Netter's writings reveal him to have been a perceptive critic of Wyclif's thought, one who concluded that the Oxford scholar's doctrines of necessity and salvation were at the heart of his theology. Netter pointed out, for instance:

> as he says in the third book of *Trialogus*, in chapter eight, *I recall what I said in the first book, that all things which happen, happen by absolute necessity*. From this most evil foundation [he says that] every *praescitus*, by divine necessity, will be damned and is a devil, before anyone will have known whether he is good or evil . . . Now let the faithful pay attention, for here he errs even more, when he says that all the *praesciti* are made devils immediately by God's eternal decree, before they exist in nature.[123]

Though he treated Wyclif's doctrine of necessity as the foundation upon which the heresiarch had constructed his errant theological system, Netter did not hesitate to affirm contemporary orthodoxies about divine foreknowledge. God's foreknowledge is necessary and infallible, and like Wyclif, Netter also distinguished between absolute and hypothetical necessity.[124] Unlike Wyclif, however, Netter argued that the grace of predestination cannot be used as a criterion for membership of the church, whose members hold that status by virtue of their common baptism:

> Therefore, predestination alone, or the result of election, does not make the Church the body of Christ: since on that account the elect and predestinate will err eternally; but the congregation of Christ is consequently comprised by baptismal regeneration. And because Wyclif says that our faith does not speak of this sort of church, but only of a church of the elect, can it be that he did not hear what Christ said?[125]

Though Netter seems to have grasped much of Wyclif's soteriology, his acquaintance with dissenters in his own day was much less profound. It might seem as if the Carmelite was perfectly placed to understand the beliefs and practices

---

[122] Anne Hudson, '*Robustissimus Antichristi Achilles*: Thomas Netter, Wyclif, and the Lollards', Open Lecture, Society for the Study of Medieval Languages and Literature, Oxford, 28 February 2004.

[123] Thomas Netter, *Doctrinale antiquitatum fidei catholicae ecclesiae*, ed. B. Blanciotti, 3 vols. (Venice, 1757–9), i. col. 118: 'ut dicit tertio *Trialogus*, capitulo VIII, *Recolo me dixisse in liber I quod omnia, quae evenient, necessario absolute evenient*. Ex hoc pessimo fundamento eradicate omnem praescitum, necessitatione Divine, fore damnandum, et esse diabolum, priusquam quidquam boni cognoverit, sive male . . . Iam animadvertant Fideles, an iste plus erravit, qui dicit omnes praescitos statim ex aeterna Dei praeordinatione, antequam sint in natura, esse diabolos.'

[124] Ibid., i, col. 124.

[125] Ibid., i, cols. 282–3: 'Praedestinatio ergo sola, vel electione, non facit Christi corpus Ecclesiam: quia electi, et praedestinati, hoc aeternaliter errant; sed congregatio Christi per regenerationem baptismalem, consequentem. Et quia dicit Wicleffus, quod de hac Ecclesia non loquitur fides nostra, sed tantum de Ecclesia electorum; an quod dixit Christus non audivit?'

of some of those who looked to Wyclif for inspiration; he participated in the trials of Sir John Oldcastle in 1414, William Taylor in 1420, and William White in 1428, and he also attended the councils of Pisa and Constance.[126] To judge from the evidence of the *Doctrinale*, however, Netter's familiarity with contemporary heretics was slight. He seems to have been aware that Wyclif's successors had moved beyond his views to different positions, but he did not describe their opinions in detail.[127]

Though we have already seen both that the most extreme predestinarian and deterministic views ascribed to Wyclif at the Council of Constance do not do justice to the many nuances of his thought, and that many early Wycliffites articulated works-oriented soteriologies, the evidence for the prevalence of doctrines of predestination among later dissenters is slimmer still. By way of demonstrating this point, let us consider a series of documents from the early decades of the Wycliffite controversy. The first is a list of twenty-four heresies and errors condemned by the so-called 'Blackfriars Council' meeting in 1382 under the presidency of Archbishop William Courtenay.[128] Among the propositions it anathematized was the claim that 'if the pope be an evil man and foreknown to damnation, and as a result a member of the devil, he has no power over Christ's faithful beyond that which may be granted him by Caesar'.[129] Second is a list of twenty-five articles placed by the monastic chronicler Henry Knighton under the year 1388. Among 'the Lollards' errors', Knighton identified the propositions that 'the saints ought not to be asked to pray for the living, nor ought the litany to be recited, for they say that all things are done by God' and that 'the festivals of the saints, such as Stephen, Lawrence,

---

[126] *PR*, 51.

[127] This short discussion of Wyclif's academic opponents might be thought to neglect the anti-Wycliffite writings of Reginald Pecock, Bishop of St Asaph and Chichester, who was condemned for heresy in 1457. Pecock's agenda, however, was radically different from those of Netter and his predecessors; he aimed to bring dissenters back to the orthodox faith rather than to reply to their arguments, and hence his tracts neither describe nor rebut the soteriologies of Wyclif and his followers. Instead, Pecock set forth an account of the ways in which free will and grace cooperate in the attainment of salvation: though the means 'bi whiche we schulde deserve and wynne and purchace oure seid final perfeccioun and souereyn supernatural good ben our owne werkis freely willid and chosen bi oure free will', God nevertheless offers various graces, 'of which gracis oon kynde of grace is helping grace forto make vs stronge to do þo seid vertuouse dedis' (*The Reule of Crysten Religioun*, ed. William Cabell Greet (EETS, o.s. 171, 1927), 132, 135)). On Wyclif's opponents, see the thorough account of Mishtooni Bose, 'The opponents of John Wyclif' in *Companion*, 407–46.

[128] On the council and its ecclesiopolitical ramifications, see Cole, *Literature and Heresy*, ch. 1.

[129] *FZ*, 278, no. 8: 'Item quod si papa sit praescitus, et malus homo, ac per consequens membrum diaboli, non habet potestatem supra fideles Christi ab aliquo sibi datam, nisi forte a Caesare.' The condemnations of the Blackfriars council also appear in Henry Knighton's chronicle, whose most recent editor has mangled the sense of this article by mistranslating *praescitus* as *prescient* (255).

Margaret, Catherine, and others, ought not to be observed or celebrated, for, they say, we do not know whether they be damned or not'.[130] Although Knighton's interest in these beliefs had less to do with their soteriological underpinnings than with their implications for the practice of intercessory prayer, both articles nevertheless betray official suspicion of soteriologies which underplay the significance of works. They both may also echo certain features of Wyclif's thought: the proposition that all things are done by God may have its roots in the Oxford scholar's doctrines of necessity and being, and the idea that those whom the church recognizes as saints cannot with certainty be said to dwell in heaven may draw inspiration from Wyclif's belief that it is impossible to distinguish the members of God's and the devil's churches.

Additional lists of articles mark important stages in the confrontation of institutional religion and Wycliffite dissent. In 1396, the provincial convocation of Canterbury condemned eighteen propositions, including the familiar claim that 'all things which happen, happen according to absolute necessity' alongside the more idiosyncratic notion that 'those people are presumptuous and stupid who argue that the children of the faithful who die without sacramental baptism will not be saved.'[131] Fifteen years later, an Oxford commission appointed to investigate Wyclif's writings sent a colossal list of 267 errors to the Archbishop of Canterbury.[132] The commission repeated the two propositions condemned in 1396, adding an additional item to emphasize Wyclif's supposed determinism and delving at greater length into his views about the *praesciti*.[133] Among the articles that the commissioners included were the claims that 'a baptized child who is foreknown as damned will necessarily live long enough to sin in the Holy Spirit, by reason of which it will deserve to be condemned forever'; that 'none of the predestinate can sin mortally'; and that 'if Paul is foreknown as damned, he cannot truly repent; that is, he cannot cancel the sin of final impenitence by contrition, or else not commit that sin'.[134] The Council of Constance, meeting in 1415, used Oxford's list as the basis for the Wycliffite propositions it condemned. Only

---

[130] Knighton, *Knighton's Chronicle*, 435–9, nos. 7 and 20, emphasis mine.

[131] Wilkins, iii.229–30, nos. 17 and 4: 'quod omnia, quae eveniunt, absolute necessario eveniunt'; 'quod definitent parvulos fidelium sine baptismo sacramentali decedentes, non fore salvandos, sunt in hoc praesumptusi et stolidi'.

[132] Hudson, 'Notes of an early fifteenth-century research assistant, and the emergence of the 267 articles against Wyclif', *English Historical Review*, 108 (2003), 685–97.

[133] Wilkins, iii.344–5, nos. 124, 139; the new article is no. 250: 'sicut Deus necessitat futurationem partium, sic necessitat ad omnes eventus, qui in illis partibus sunt futuri'.

[134] Ibid., iii.349, nos. 251–3: 'infans praescitus et baptizatus necessario vivet diutius, et peccabit in Spiritum Sanctum, ratione cujus merebitur, ut perpetuo condemnetur'; 'nullus praedestinatus potest peccare mortaliter'; 'Paulus praescitus non potest vere poenitere, hoc est, contritione peccatum finalis impoenitentiae delere, vel ipsum non habere.'

three articles touching on the theology of salvation appear in its decree, however, and they comprise the last three items on the council's list, namely the doctrines that all things happen from absolute necessity; that a foreknown, baptized child will live long enough to sin; and that the foreknown cannot truly repent.[135] Finally, another sort of list can be found in the questionnaire commissioned in 1428 by Bishop Thomas Polton of Worcester. Among its sixty-one propositions, there occurs only a single, veiled reference to the theology of salvation: the question 'whether the evil are part of the church'.[136]

Can these ostensibly sterile lists reveal anything about the doctrines of salvation to which late medieval dissenters might have subscribed? It might be said that they illustrate not the evolution of Wycliffite theology but, rather, only the institutional church's evolving understanding of Wycliffism. This judgement, however, fails to grasp the situation in its entirety. For one thing, the rapidity with which other bishops appropriated Polton's questionnaire for use in their own anti-heresy proceedings suggests that it, at least, may have achieved more than marginal success as a tool for the identification of dissenters in the late 1420s and early 1430s. At the same time, the interests of the Canterbury convocation, the Oxford commission, and the Council of Constance were not merely academic. The members of those bodies were likely to prioritize the beliefs they found being articulated by the individuals for whose repression they were responsible. Seen in this light, the manner in which the participants at Constance selected their lists of articles from the 267 with which the Oxford commission had presented them takes on a different meaning. That Constance chose to mention soteriology only in passing, and toward the conclusion of its decree, suggests that the predestinarianism imputed to Wyclif by early councils and authors may have lost significance for ecclesiastical leaders in the years after his death. The very scanty references to salvation, as well as the substitution of the word *mali* for *praesciti* in Polton's list, both seem to confirm this trend.

Such a line of argumentation is, of course, highly circumstantial. Nevertheless, records from the prosecutions of suspected dissenters confirm that few expressed belief in predestination. In this respect, a distinction may helpfully be made between Wyclif's early academic followers, on the one

---

[135] Tanner, *Decrees*, i.426, nos. 56–8. Interestingly, whilst the council seemed somewhat reticent to involve itself in the intricacies of Wyclif's doctrines of necessity and salvation, it showed no such reserve in the case of John Hus, whose condemnation and sentence of execution it also pronounced. Of the thirty Hussite propositions which incurred the council's wrath, nine explicitly refer to Hus's predestinarianism and its ecclesiological corollaries (Tanner, i.429–31, nos. 1–3, 5, 6, 11, 20–2).

[136] Hudson, 'The examination of Lollards', 134, no. 40: 'item an mali sint pars ecclesie catholice'.

hand, and their lay counterparts and later descendants on the other. Members of the former group, including the anonymous author of the *Opus arduum*, did often profess doctrines of predestination. Thus, for instance, the priest William Sawtre affirmed in 1400 that he would rather adore a predestinate man than an angel of God, and John Purvey was charged with believing that any predestinate man is a true priest.[137] By way of contrast, two early lay prosecutions neglected to uncover predestinarian soteriologies among layfolk; neither the articles administered by Archbishop Courtenay to suspected heretics in Leicester in 1389 nor the abjurations of defendants in Lincoln diocese in 1393 mention predestination or its theological corollaries.[138] It is unclear to which category belongs the letter purportedly sent by an anonymous Wycliffite to his former co-religionist Nicholas Hereford in the wake of the 1393 trial of Walter Brut. The letter, which John Foxe implausibly catalogued under the year 1388, ends with a statement of five beliefs about salvation; they include the claims that 'no perversion of any reprobate is able to turn the congregation of the elect from the faith, because all things that shall come to pass, are eternally in God' and that 'like as the mystical body of Christ is the congregation of all the elect, so Antichrist mystically is the church of the wicked and all the reprobates'.[139]

After a gap of more than a decade, questions about the doctrine of salvation next emerged in the 1415 trial of the London currier John Claydon, who was accused of having commissioned a copy of *The Lanterne of Liȝt*. Among the fifteen propositions excerpted from the *Lanterne* and charged against Claydon was the claim that 'no reprobate is a member of the church, but only such as be elected and predestined to salvation; seeing the church is no other thing but the congregation of faithful souls'.[140] This article rather imperfectly characterizes the soteriology of the *Lanterne*, but combined with other propositions about the papacy, the fraternal orders, and ecclesiastical wealth, its force was nevertheless sufficient to procure Claydon's condemnation to the stake.

---

[137] *FZ*, 387. On the implications of this for Purvey's views about the priesthood, see pp. 166–7 below.

[138] James Crompton, 'Leicestershire Lollards', *Transactions of the Leicestershire Archaeological and Historical Society*, 44 (1968–9), 11–44 at 23; A. K. McHardy, 'Bishop Buckingham', 131–45. See also J. H. Dahmus (ed.), *The Metropolitan Visitations of William Courtenay, Archbishop of Canterbury, 1381–1396* (Urbana, Ill., 1950), 48, 164–6.

[139] *A&M*, 598–9.

[140] Ibid., 757–8. Foxe was particularly anxious to claim this article as an ancestor of Protestant ecclesiology, writing in the margin that 'this is true, speaking of the invisible church'. On Foxe's ecclesiology, see among others Catharine Davies, '"Poor Persecuted Little Flock" or "Commonwealth of Christians": Edwardian Protestant concepts of the church' in Peter Lake and Maria Dowling (eds.), *Protestantism and the National Church* (London, 1987), 78–94.

The year in which Claydon met his unhappy end also saw the failed rebellion of Sir John Oldcastle. In its aftermath, as we have seen, not only did Wycliffite literary production decline markedly, but the prosecution of suspected dissenters also became more sporadic. Nevertheless, several anti-heresy initiatives undertaken by bishops in the fifteenth and sixteenth centuries turned up dissenters whose views on salvation appear in the extant records. From 1428 through 1431, Bishop William Alnwick of Norwich launched an extensive investigation into heresy in his diocese, accusing at least eighty defendants of holding a range of heterodox beliefs about the sacraments, the saints, and the wealth of the church. One of the first dissenters he examined, the parchment-maker John Godesell, confessed that he had believed that 'the catholic church is the congregation of only those who are to be saved'.[141] The following year, his confrere John Burell, servant of the leading local dissenter Thomas Mone, told the bishop that he had heard Mone and others teaching that the church is 'the soul of any good Christian'.[142] The skinner William Colyn was accused of, but denied, having declared publicly that 'from the time of the incarnation of Christ no soul has entered heaven'.[143] Another prominent dissenter, Margery Baxter, was accused by her neighbour Joan Clifland of teaching that 'the holy church exists only in those places where her sect exists'.[144] Finally, in 1430, the tailor William Hardy abjured the otherwise unexplained belief that 'ther is no Churche but oonly hevene'.[145] Of these four defendants, only Godesell articulated a doctrine that might appear to be a version of predestinarianism, and in the wake of his testimony, it is possible that Alnwick and his commissioners would have been on the lookout for suspect claims about salvation and its relationship to the composition or definition of the church. Burell's and Baxter's statements seem to imply a form of separatism, but neither defendant appears to have linked his or her ecclesiological claims with the doctrine of salvation. Hardy's and Colyn's views go against both Wyclif's doctrine of the two churches as well as the institutional church's teachings on heaven and hell; they must in the end be regarded as idiosyncrasies.

Some fifty-five years separate Alnwick's trials from the next major prosecutions of suspected dissenters. Indeed, only a small number of cases from the

---

[141] *Norwich*, 61: 'Item quod Ecclesia catholica est congregacio solum salvandorum.'

[142] Ibid., 73: 'quod Ecclesia catholica est anima cuiuslibet boni Christiani'. Burell later abjured the same belief himself (77).

[143] Ibid., 91: 'quod a tempore Incarnacionis Christi nulla anima intravit celum'.

[144] Ibid., 49: 'quod sancta Ecclesia est tantum in locis habitacionum omnium existencium de secta sua'. For Baxter's case, see further Justice, 'Inquisition, speech, and writing', 21–6.

[145] *Norwich*, 154; for modern English translations of the trials of Godesell and Baxter, see the forthcoming volume *Wycliffism* (n. 57 above).

years 1428–86 are extant; even fewer deal with the question of salvation, though the words of those defendants are instructive. In 1429, Bishop John Stafford of Bath and Wells questioned William Emayn, a Northamptonshire man who previously had been imprisoned on suspicion of heresy. Asked his opinion of Wyclif, Emayn replied that the Oxford thinker 'was a just and catholic man, who if he were alive would prove all his opponents heretics and Lollards'.[146] Thomson has argued that Emayn's testimony demonstrates the extent to which later dissenters invoked Wyclif's memory, though recent research has suggested that that claim may have been overstated. More interesting for our purposes is Emayn's ecclesiology. 'He considered that virtuous living was the qualification for membership of the Church, and that those who were in deadly sin were of the synagogue of Satan, even if they were pope.'[147] Lexical echoes can be found here of Wyclif's thought—the claim that not even the pope is immune from sin and a veiled reference to the idea of the devil's church.[148] For Emayn, as to a more nuanced extent for Wyclif, good deeds and not divine fiat determine one's membership in the church of God.

Bishop Robert Neville of Salisbury encountered in 1437 another dissenter who had appropriated for his own ends the terminology of Wyclif's doctrine of the church. William Wakeham had abjured six heresies in 1434 but relapsed three years later, maintaining, among other things, that a layman gains no more benefit from saying the Lord's Prayer in Latin than from saying 'Bibull babull'. A witness at his second trial accused Wakeham of also believing 'that every man was the church of God, and that the church made with hands was no more than a house built of stone and wood'.[149] From the paucity of the data, it is impossible to determine precisely what Wakeham meant, but the notion that *all* people are somehow the church of God could not be further removed from a predestinarian bifurcation of humankind into *praedestinati* and *praesciti*.

Nevertheless, at least one other defendant articulated a soteriology like the one imputed to Wyclif. The clerk Thomas Bikenore, questioned in 1443 by William Aiscough, Neville's successor in Salisbury, denied the value of baptism and confirmation and argued that God chooses whether or not to give grace to each person before birth.[150] Pressed to explain his stance, Bikenore

---

[146] Thomson, *Later Lollards*, 29. Thomson was following the terminological fashion of his day in capitalizing the word Lollard, but ironically, Emayn's case demonstrates precisely the polyvalence of that term.

[147] Ibid., 29.

[148] On Wycliffite views of the papacy, see Ch. 6 below.

[149] Thomson, *Later Lollards*, 33.

[150] Ibid., 65.

confessed to a strict predestinarianism, abjuring the belief that 'holichirche catholike is a aggregacion of . . . men . . . [who] only shulbe saued'.[151]

The fifteenth century was nearing its end by the time another heresy trial involved assertions about salvation. In 1486, Bishop John Hales of Coventry and Lichfield interviewed ten suspects in his diocese, recording fairly detailed summaries of their beliefs in his register. Though the majority of the defendants' claims concerned images of and prayers to the saints, the value of pilgrimages, and the theology of the Eucharist, two interrogations also dealt with soteriological issues. Richard Hegham confessed to having taught 'that Christians at the hour of death should renounce all their works, both good and bad, and submit themselves to the divine mercy'.[152] His fellow defendant Thomas Butler admitted that he had said that 'whoever dies in the faith of Christ and of the church, no matter how he has lived, will be saued'.[153] Hegham and Butler seem to have been of a uniformly negative opinion as to the salvific value of works, though Butler's formulation came closer to universalism.

Hales' prosecutions bridge the gap between Alnwick's Norwich trials and the investigations that were to mark the early years of Henry VIII's reign. In the interim, only the records of four heresy trials involve the doctrine of salvation. First, Stephen Swallow, tried in London diocese in July 1489, was accused of denying purgatory in addition to believing a series of heterodox propositions about confession, the Eucharist, and the papacy.[154] In February 1491, William Carpenter told his inquisitors in Salisbury diocese that ecclesiastical authorities had no right to canonize saints, since no priest 'can tell or showe weather thes sayntes whom we call seyntes be in hevyn or in helle'.[155] In an isolated Rochester diocese case in 1499, Christopher Morthrop abjured the single article that a person has no soul but only breath.[156] Some years later, Elizabeth Sampson of London confessed, equally cryptically, that she had taught that 'moo soules then is in hevyn all redy shall never come to hevyn'.[157] Whether Sampson intended to articulate the doctrine that God had already chosen who would be saved or whether she was simply a pessimist about the prospect of her contemporaries' salvation remains unclear.

Like Carpenter and Sampson, few of those caught up in the systemic prosecutions of 1511–12 can with certainty be labelled predestinarian. In 1511, Bishop William Smith of Lincoln tried the influential and well-connected dissenter

---

[151] Salisbury reg. Aiscough, ii, fol. 53r.
[152] *Coventry*, 66.
[153] Ibid., 70. Butler's case is noted by Watson, 'Visions of inclusion', 151.
[154] J. B. Sheppard (ed.), *Literae cantuarienses*, 3 vols. (London, 1887–89), iii.312.
[155] Salisbury reg. Langton, ii, fol. 40r.
[156] Rochester reg. Fitzjames, fol. 24r.
[157] London reg. Fitzjames, fol. 7r.

Thomas Man, who ultimately met a heretic's end at Smithfield on 29 March 1518 and who (according to John Foxe) stood at the centre of a network of heresy in and around Lincoln diocese.[158] Of the nine articles that Man abjured in 1511, two are particularly reminiscent of Wyclif's views, namely the notions that the word of God is 'all one' and that 'the popish churche was not the Church of God, but a synagogue: and that holy men of his sect, were the true church of God'.[159] The former proposition hearkens back to Wyclif's view that God's *ens in communi* implies the unity of Scripture; the latter, though not explicitly predestinarian, reiterates the traditional Wycliffite distinction between the churches of God and the devil.[160]

In the same year that Man first came to trial, both William Warham, the Archbishop of Canterbury, and Geoffrey Blyth, the Bishop of Coventry and Lichfield, initiated large-scale investigations into heresy in their respective dioceses. It is particularly fortuitous that detailed records of their investigations survive in Warham's register and a court book, now Lichfield Record Office MS B/C/13, respectively. To judge from the relative uniformity of the abjurations which appear in both volumes, Warham and Blythe likely employed questionnaires to identify suspects' beliefs. Neither Warham's nor Blyth's defendants regularly confessed to errors concerning the nature of the church or the doctrine of salvation, so it seems highly improbable that the bishops' questionnaires included questions of this sort. Accordingly, little can be deduced from the fact that not a single suspect volunteered irregular beliefs about ecclesiology or soteriology, though as we shall see in subsequent chapters, the appearance in these records of idiosyncratic beliefs on other topics is nevertheless illuminating. A rare statement on matters of salvation can be found in the testimony of the Coventry mercer William Lodge, who acknowledged that his fellow dissenters called one another 'sons of grace'.[161] This epithet, like the phrase 'known man', might well be a vestige of Wyclif's soteriology, but neither Lodge's testimony nor the words of other Coventry or Kent defendants reveals its provenance.

Finally, we return at last to the Buckinghamshire defendants in whose company we first encountered the affection of later dissenters for the Epistle of James. Though the loss of Bishop Longland's court book has obscured some of the evidence for their theological convictions, Derek Plumb has

---

[158] In the 1570 and later editions of *A&M*, Foxe printed an extensive table illustrating the interrelationships between dissenters in Lincoln diocese. Man appears more often than any other individual (947–61).

[159] *A&M*, 941.

[160] Maurice Keen, 'Wyclif, the Bible, and transubstantiation' in Anthony Kenny (ed.), *Wyclif in His Times* (Oxford, 1986), 1–14 at 4.

[161] *Coventry*, 201.

uncovered an important correlation between dissenting religious beliefs and bequests for the poor and public works such as highways. 'Lollard wills... point to one particularly defined Lollard belief being carried out; they followed the teaching of one particular epistle, that of St James.'[162] It is perhaps less than wholly accurate to identify the normativity of James' letter as a 'defined Lollard belief', but Plumb's study nevertheless suggests that many dissenters felt an impulse to contribute to the temporal welfare of their local communities.[163] They may have been interested in concealing themselves from investigation, or they may have believed that good works were of soteriological significance, but whatever the reason, their deeds betray little connection with the predestinarianism articulated by some of their spiritual ancestors.

CONCLUSIONS

Like the corpus of vernacular Wycliffite texts, the trials of these and other individuals reveal that dissenters in the fifteenth and sixteenth centuries did not in general subscribe to the deterministic view of salvation imputed to John Wyclif. Yet although few native English heretics were either willing or able to articulate a doctrine of predestination, they continued to use much of the language in which Wyclif had formulated his theology of salvation. Thomas Man's distinction between the true church of God and the popish synagogue, for instance, revisits Wyclif's bifurcation of the world into two similar categories, and likewise William Carpenter's views on intercessory prayer suggest a debt to Wyclif's notion that it is impossible to recognize the members of the true church in the present life. These lexical similarities aside, not many later dissenters demonstrated an understanding of the soteriological principles which may have once undergirded the terminology they inherited from their predecessors.

Is it possible to identify a point at which dissenters definitively exchanged predestinarianism for a works-oriented theology of salvation? The question

---

[162] Plumb, 'The social and economic spread of rural Lollardy', 116.

[163] It is nevertheless important to note R. A. Houlbrooke's cautionary remarks in his study of heresy in Norwich diocese in Henry VIII's reign. Records there highlight local dissenters' opposition to good works, though such feelings ran highest in the 1530s, well after our period ('Persecution of heresy and Protestantism in the diocese of Norwich under Henry VIII', 318). On this point, see also Jurkowski, 'Lollardy and social status', 147, as well as Robert Lutton's account of testamentary piety in the heresy-prone Kentish village of Tenterden, *Lollardy and Orthodox Religion*. Lutton has shown that many dissenters practised what he terms 'parsimonious piety', leaving little of their goods to traditional devotions or public works.

mistakenly assumes that even all early Wycliffites were predestinarians. Some
authors, such as those responsible for parts of the English sermon-cycle, the
conclusion to *The Lanterne of Liȝt*, and the poems of the *Piers Plowman*
tradition, seem soon after Wyclif's death to have opted for soteriologies which
stress the significance of good works over against the grace of God. Dissenting
texts' perspectives on salvation were, however, hardly uniform, and the
cultural milieu within which a particular text was composed seems roughly
to correlate with its perspective on salvation. Scholastic, Latinate texts like
Opus arduum are much more likely than vernacular tracts to espouse predestinarian or grace-oriented views.

Likewise, the information we can glean from institutional sources like anti-
Wycliffite polemics, lists of condemned articles, and trial records confirms
that native English dissenters articulated a plurality of soteriologies. Early
accounts of dissenting belief concerned themselves in large part with Wyclif's
supposed doctrines of necessity and salvation, but as ecclesiastical authorities
found themselves confronting new appropriations of the reformer's teachings,
propositions about the predestinate and the *praesciti* gradually disappeared
from lists of suspect articles. A similar trend can be identified in the surviving
court records. Late-fourteenth-century heretics like John Purvey and the
author of the anonymous letter to Nicholas Hereford may have spoken or
wrote of predestination, but many of the fifteenth- and sixteenth-century
dissenters prosecuted in Norwich, Salisbury, and Coventry and Lichfield
dioceses seem to have lost interest in their predecessors' soteriological language. A few, like William Wakeham and Thomas Bikenore, seem to have
clung to some version of predestinarianism. After the accession of the Tudors,
however, perhaps only Thomas Man did so.

Though it is therefore inappropriate to speak of a chronological decline in
predestinarianism from Wyclif's day to the outbreak of the Henrician Reformation, it is true that far fewer dissenters in the 1510s than in the 1380s would
have been sympathetic to strict doctrines of predestination. Those who were,
like the clerk Bikenore, tended either to have been among the leaders of their
communities or else to have received at least the basic theological education
that was meant to accompany holy orders. Unsurprisingly, this pattern reflects
the situation in the early Wycliffite movement, when, as we have seen, some of
Wyclif's university-trained followers valued the doctrine of predestination
more highly than their lay counterparts did.[164]

---

[164] It also reflects the situation in the Henrician period, when university-educated reformers
such as William Tyndale and John Bale were quick to appropriate Wycliffite terminology for
their own purposes.

The motivations which impel human beings to choose one system of belief rather than another are obscure at the best of times, and to offer hard-and-fast explanations for these developments in Wycliffite belief is to pry into those corners of the psyche for which the evidence is weakest. Nevertheless, three dynamics may begin to explain why later dissenters did not embrace predestinarianism. First, though they often denounced the institutional church and its ministers as the instruments of Antichrist, dissenters usually continued to participate in the activities of their local communities. Individual heresy suspects often served in civil and ecclesiastical office as a way of obscuring their heterodoxy; thus, for instance, Alice Rowley and Joan Smyth of Coventry were both married to former mayors of the city, and William Sweeting of Chelsea served as a holy-water clerk.[165] In these and other roles, dissenters would have been immersed in the thought-world of mainstream religion. As we have seen, the predominant soteriological ethos of the later Middle Ages was a works-oriented one: both ecclesiastically sponsored texts like John Mirk's *Festial* and independent works such as *The Awntyrs off Arthur* privileged the need to perform good works above the operation of grace. Duffy has written that many lay men and women participated in a communal 'determination to use the things of this world to prepare a lodging in the next', and a range of activities from the founding of Oxbridge colleges to small donations to parish churches attests to the strength of that commitment across the socioeconomic spectrum.[166] Though most dissenters were hardly enthusiastic for such institutionally enshrined practices as indulgences and bequests for soul-masses, the underlying logic of their works-oriented soteriologies was strikingly similar. Indeed, it would be mistaken to assume that the majority of dissenters were first predestinarian and then works-oriented. It is far more likely that many of those who opposed the institutional church never departed from their long-held works-oriented views when they embraced other elements of Wycliffite heterodoxy.

Second, predestinarian texts tended to enjoy relatively limited circulation in comparison with their works-oriented counterparts. *Opus arduum*, for instance, would have been accessible to only a small number of Latinate dissenters, and there is no evidence that it was ever translated into English. Something similar can be said of both the Latin and English versions of the *Floretum* and *Rosarium*; they were originally intended to provide guidance to Wycliffite preachers rather than to the rank-and-file members of dissenting

---

[165] *Coventry*, 27; Thomson, *Later Lollards*, 137, 162.
[166] Duffy, *The Stripping of the Altars*, 303.

communities, and their scholastic idiom would have made them impenetrable to those without formal theological training. Indeed, of the Wycliffite texts known to have been widely disseminated, firmly predestinarian views can be found only in a few of the sermons which comprise the English sermon-cycle. Even there, as we have seen, their soteriological commitments are in tension with the works-oriented views to be found elsewhere in the cycle. Other works-oriented texts, like *The Lanterne of Liȝt* and the poems of the *Piers Plowman* tradition, appear to have been distributed more broadly.

Finally, something must be said about the psychological appeal of predestinarianism itself. It is of course difficult to judge whether late medieval men and women would have joined many modern people in expressing dismay at the thought of a loving God who condemns much of creation without regard to merit, but it is possible that many dissenters may have found predestination rather uncomfortable. Not only its stark implications for the afterlife but also its sheer novelty may have made the doctrine less palatable. Like Lancelot Andrewes, who centuries later stressed the value of good works and embraced what one critic has called a 'reverent agnosticism' about predestination, some Wycliffites may have quailed at the notion that they could in no way affect their place in the eschaton.[167] The extent to which this sort of anxiety was at play must have varied widely, but it is reasonable to assume that the confluence of social and psychological influences led at least a few dissenters not to opt for predestinarianism.

It seems clear that lollards were not the theological automata that many studies have implicitly envisioned them to have been. Instead, they were quite capable of formulating and maintaining a host of views alongside and frequently in opposition to traditional Wycliffite doctrines; witness, for instance, Elizabeth Sampson's strange claims about the capacity of heaven, or William Hardy's perplexing denial of the church's existence. As I suggested in the previous chapter, perhaps the most successful model for evaluating the complexities of dissenting belief is Ludwig Wittgenstein's notion of 'family resemblance'. We can now add that the absence of a central core of Wycliffite beliefs about salvation suggests that it may be best to understand the convictions of English dissenters in terms of interlocking networks of theological claims. These networks changed over time and in response both to one another and to the pervasive influence of broader cultural mores. This investigation into

---

[167] Nicholas Lossky, *Lancelot Andrewes the Preacher (1555–1626): The origins of the mystical theology of the Church of England*, trans. Andrew Louth (Oxford, 1991), 145; Paul A. Welsby, *Lancelot Andrewes, 1555–1626* (London, 1958), 44.

the development of lollard soteriology has revealed that doctrinal development was a highly complex process, taking different forms in respect of dissenters' geographical, social, and educational backgrounds. In future chapters, we will see that similar factors shaped the reception of dissenting ideas about the eucharist, marriage, and the priesthood.

3

The Eucharist

One of the more colourful anecdotes from the early years of the Wycliffite controversy involves Laurence of St Martin, a knight who in 1381 was accused of having desecrated the sacrament of the altar. According to the chronicler Thomas Walsingham, Sir Laurence had been to church, heard mass, and received the consecrated bread in his mouth. Rather than consuming it, however, he secretly removed the host and took it home with him, eating it later that day with his oysters.[1] The same story also circulated about another knight, John Montagu.[2]

The horror with which contemporary chroniclers narrated these events reflects the deeply eucharistic piety of the fourteenth century. As Miri Rubin has put it, 'at the centre of the whole religious system of the later Middle Ages lay a ritual which turned bread into flesh—a fragile, small, wheaten disc into God'.[3] To deny that the mass accomplished the transformation it claimed to effect was not merely to reject a metaphysical proposition but also to challenge the authority of the institutional church. It is unsurprising, therefore, that eucharistic heresy was for many bishops and inquisitors the most pernicious of Wycliffite errors.

In 1381, his controversial views on the sacrament of the altar finally forced Wyclif from the University of Oxford. The sacrament also figured prominently in the trials of many of those who came after him. At least 236 heresy defendants who appeared in ecclesiastical courts between the years 1381 and 1521 faced the charge of eucharistic heterodoxy, making the sacrament of the altar numerically the most contested theologoumenon of the period. Only dissenting views on the adoration of images, with approximately 220 appearances, occur with comparable frequency. Heresy defendants articulated a range of views about the eucharistic, yet a comprehensive account of the

---

[1] Thomas Walsingham, *Historia anglicana*, ed. Matthew Parker and Henry Thomas Riley, 2 vols. (London, 1863–4), i, 450–1.

[2] John Capgrave, *Abbreuiacion of Cronicles*, ed. P. J. Lucas (EETS o.s. 285, 1983), 191.

[3] Miri Rubin, *Corpus Christi: The Eucharist in late medieval culture* (Cambridge, 1991), 1.

eucharistic beliefs of Wycliffite texts and heresy suspects has not thus far been attempted.[4]

Among the reasons may be the difficulty of reconciling the vague and frequently misrepresented opinions of lay dissenters with the clarity of the theological propositions they were accused of holding. To return to Sir Laurence and his oysters, the knight's purported disrespect for the host provides few certain data about his beliefs. Sir Laurence's actions do not, for instance, confirm that he rejected the doctrine of transubstantiation, nor do they indicate that he thought of the mass as merely a commemoration of the Last Supper. From our perspective, we can say with certainty little more than that they constitute a transgressive act, the motivation for which can only be conjectured. Even in more conventional sources like abjurations and depositions, questions often remain unanswered. When, for instance, the court book of Bishop William Alnwick of Norwich records that the defendant John Godesell argued in 1429 that the eucharist was 'pure material bread', it seems that Godesell had denied the physical presence of Christ in the consecrated bread and wine.[5] It cannot be resolved, however, whether Godesell believed that Christ was *spiritually* present in the host, whether he perceived the eucharistic liturgy to be a wholly figurative act, or whether he held different views altogether.

To secure their suspect's abjuration was sufficient for Godesell's inquisitors. Whilst in his case his examiners seem to have left his words largely intact and hence preserved their theological ambiguity, other records produced the opposite effect. Paul Strohm has argued that inquisitors frequently attempted to ensnare less educated suspects in the complexities of eucharistic theology: 'the uneven terrain of eucharistic discussion, riddled with theological pitfalls and places of potential doctrinal entrapment, rendered a perfect ground for the analysis and discovery of error'.[6] As a result, suspects unschooled in the intricate vocabulary of scholastic

---

[4] The only two studies which have focused exclusively on the eucharistic views of later dissenters are Anne Hudson, 'The mouse in the pyx: Popular heresy and the Eucharist', *Trivium*, 26 (1991), 40–53; and Aers, *Sanctifying Signs*. Among those who have noted in passing the differences in eucharistic views articulated by English dissenters are Rubin, *Corpus Christi*, 327–9; Anne Hudson, 'A Lollard Mass', repr. in *Books*, 111–23 at 118; Malcolm Lambert, *Medieval Heresy: Popular movements from the Gregorian Reform to the Reformation*, 2nd edn (Oxford, 1992), 259–60; Margaret Aston, 'William White's Lollard followers', repr. in *Lollards and Reformers*, 71–100 at 91–2; and Craig James Fraser, 'The religious instruction of the laity in late medieval England with particular reference to the sacrament of the Eucharist' (D.Phil. thesis, Oxford University, 1995), 294.

[5] *Norwich*, 61.

[6] Strohm, *England's Empty Throne*, 49.

discourse about the eucharist seem in some records to be familiar with Latinate distinctions like those between real, substantial, and sacramental modes of presence. Since only a minority of the defendants whose trial records are extant would have possessed theological knowledge of this calibre, it is reasonable to assume that Strohm was largely correct in suggesting that an inquisitor's drive to secure the submission of suspects, many of whom may have attempted in vain to reconcile their views with the orthodox position, sometimes elicited speculative answers that may have been composed on the spot. The process may also have pigeonholed suspects' views according to the preconceptions of their inquisitors.[7] In sum, the beliefs which dissenters held and taught among themselves were likely hazier and less technical than those they are recorded to have confessed.

Dissenting texts and ecclesiastical records thus present a limited view of their authors' and subjects' beliefs, but they are not completely opaque. As I argued in the Preface, there are good reasons to believe that late medieval inquisitors approached their task conscientiously, even if their presuppositions about heresy, its content, and its means of transmission coloured their treatment of individual defendants. Read in a critical light, the records reveal that heresy suspects were not always of the same mind, nor did they uniformly adopt Wyclif's doctrine of the eucharist. Broadly speaking, dissenters tended to take one of two parallel attitudes to eucharistic theology. Though both rejected transubstantiation, one group of writers and defendants argued that though Christ is also spiritually present in the eucharist, the substances of bread and wine remain in the consecrated elements, whilst the other described the sacrament in figurative terms.[8] Both sets of views about the eucharist have their roots in the tangled web of Wyclif's ideas.

---

[7] At least one lollard text advises its readers to consider the ways in which inquisitors attempted to trip up heresy suspects. Presenting sixteen points with which his fellows are often charged, the anonymous author writes: 'Whoeuer schal see þes sixteen poyntis, be he wele ware þat in eueriche of hem is hidde trewþe and falsehed, and who þat euer grantiþ al, grantiþ myche falsehede, and who þat euer denyeþ al, denyeþ many trewþes. Þerfor witte welle þis þat, wane a coupulatif is madde, þou3 þer be many trewþes, if it afferme a falshed, it schal be denyed al togidur; falseness is so venemus' (*Selections*, 20).

[8] General studies such as those listed at n. 4 above have noticed the commemorative eucharistic theologies of many Wycliffite dissenters, but the full extent and provenance of these ideas have gone unnoticed. Whilst some scholars have overlooked the commemorative views of early defendants, others have over-generalized about the extent to which later dissenters described the eucharist as a memorial; for an example of the latter tendency, see Fraser, 'The religious instruction of the laity', 285.

WYCLIF'S DEPARTURE FROM
EUCHARISTIC ORTHODOXY

Scholarly assessments of Wyclif's eucharistic theology have fluctuated since the revival of Wycliffite studies in the late nineteenth century. Nearly all critics have agreed that Wyclif rejected the doctrine of transubstantiation as it was articulated by Aquinas and his successors, but two questions have been more contested. Why did Wyclif reject this tenet of late medieval Christianity? And what did he teach instead?

Following in the footsteps of the German historian Gotthard Lechler, who had argued that Wyclif's doctrine of the sacrament was a necessary outgrowth of his metaphysics, early twentieth-century students of Wyclif's thought tended to ascribe his eucharistic teachings to his philosophical ultra-realism.[9] For H. B. Workman, for instance, Wyclif's attack on the eucharist was primarily a critique of John Duns Scotus' voluntaristic doctrine of transubstantiation, according to which it is God's unlimited power that annihilates the substances of bread and wine.[10] On this account, Wyclif specifically rejected annihilation, since in his philosophical world, the annihilation of one substance would entail the annihilation of all. Thus a Scotist approach to transubstantiation was 'a doctrine of illusion that seemed the "abomination of desolation" to so thorough-going a realist. For above all else, Wyclif was a metaphysician. He approached the eucharist from the standpoint not of abuses, but of a metaphysical system.'[11]

John Thomas McNeill, an admirer of Workman's biography, agreed that Wyclif 'did not begin with a horror of the idolatries practiced in connection with the eucharist'.[12] Like Workman, McNeill ascribed Wyclif's controversial theology of the sacrament to his philosophical doubts about annihilation; he also emphasized that Wyclif believed in the spiritual presence of Christ in the elements.[13] For McNeill, as for Workman, Wyclif's 'characteristic teaching

---

[9] Lechler, *John Wycliffe*, 343–6.

[10] For a survey of high and late medieval doctrines of the eucharist, and for the important important that the theological consensus had not firmly settled on transubstantiation even by Wyclif's time, see Gary Macy, 'The dogma of transubstantiation in the Middle Ages', *Journal of Ecclesiastical History*, 45 (1994), 11–41.

[11] Workman, *John Wyclif*, ii.30.

[12] John Thomas McNeill, 'Some emphases in Wyclif's teaching', *Journal of Religion*, 7 (1927), 447–66 at 455.

[13] A similar account of Wyclif's opposition to the annihilation of the bread can be found in the equally philosophical treatment of Thompson, 'Philosophical basis', 111. C. W. Dugmore, in a short section in *The Mass and the English Reformers* (London, 1958), emphasizes Wyclif's belief in a real though spiritual presence (52–5).

on the eucharistic is rightly described as consubstantiation. Yet it is consubstantiation in its most spiritual form.'[14] It is worth noting that both Workman
and McNeill anachronistically employed the eucharistic vocabulary of the
sixteenth-century Reformation to evaluate Wyclif's theology of the sacrament.

Closer to the end of the twentieth century, interest in Wyclif's ideas shifted
away from the philosophical. In an article comparing Wyclif's eucharistic
theology with the censured ideas of William of Ockham, Gordon Leff asserted
that Wyclif had developed a doctrine of remanence or coexistence—the idea
that the sacrament consists in the addition of Christ's spiritual presence to the
material bread and wine.[15] That was conventional enough, but Leff placed a
new emphasis on Wyclif's concern that the sacrament of the altar should not
become an occasion for idolatry. It was not merely, as McNeill had put it, that
Wyclif discovered the possibility of sacramental idolatry as he proceeded from
one philosophical idea to another; on Leff's account, Wyclif was critical of
idolatrous practice from the start.[16]

Leff's ideas were formulated far more strongly in an article published in
1985 by the Oxford historian Jeremy Catto. Emphasizing the importance of
the eucharistic cult in late medieval England, Catto exploded the notion that
Wyclif's philosophy had led him inexorably to deny transubstantiation.
Difficulties with the orthodox doctrine had been apparent to Wyclif, Catto
suggested, long before he developed an alternative approach: 'Wyclif's adjec-
tives reveal the quality of his dissent: transubstantiation was improper, material, horrible, gross. He held, then, no coolly philosophical notion of logical
impossibility.'[17] Arguing that Wyclif's writings on the eucharist reveal a
profound interest in the place of the sacrament in Christian life, Catto forcibly

---

[14] Workman, *John Wyclif*, ii.37; McNeill, 'Some emphases in Wyclif's teaching', 457.

[15] Gordon Leff, 'Ockham and Wyclif on the Eucharist', *Reading Medieval Studies*, 2 (1976),
1–13. Macy has suggested that 'coexistence' is a more accurate descriptor than either 'consubstantiation' or 'remanence' for the position I am discussing here ('The dogma of transubstantiation in the Middle Ages', 13). In a pan-European context he is assuredly right, but since the
sources for eucharistic dissent in England consistently treat belief in the remanence of the
original elements as a litmus test for heterodoxy, for convenience I will retain that term.

[16] McNeill, 'Some emphases in Wyclif's teaching', 455–6; Leff, 'Ockham and Wyclif on the
Eucharist', 9. For a similar analysis, though one which describes Wyclif as a logician more than a
metaphysician, see Heather Phillips, 'John Wyclif's *De Eucharistia* in its medieval setting' (Ph.D.
thesis, University of Toronto, 1980), 241–303.

[17] Jeremy Catto, 'John Wyclif and the cult of the Eucharist' in K. Walsh and D. Wood (eds.),
The Bible in the Medieval World: Essays in memory of Beryl Smalley (Studies in Church History,
Subsidia 4, Oxford, 1985), 269–86 at 274. A similar perspective can be found in Dallas G. Denery
II, 'From sacred mystery to divine deception: Robert Holkot, John Wyclif, and the transformation of fourteenth-century Eucharistic discourse', *Journal of Religious History*, 29 (2005), 129–44,
who discusses Wyclif's rejection of transubstantiation in terms of his 'horror' at the possibility
that God would appear in the world in so deceptive a manner as to cloak the divine presence
within foreign substances.

maintained that Wyclif had primarily sought to correct what he considered the corrupt practices of his day:

Idolatry, it seems, was Wyclif's name for the common response of wonder and awe evoked by the sight of the host at the elevation or in procession at Corpus Christi. The doctrine of transubstantiation . . . emphasized the gulf between humanity and the Eucharist. The doctrine of remanence, with which he proposed to replace it, minimized the difference between human and sacramental being.[18]

Catto's article belied the suggestion that Wyclif's objections to transubstantiation were purely philosophical, and later scholars have accordingly engaged with the cultural as well as the intellectual context of Wyclif's ideas.

Wyclif's theology of the eucharist

Useful though they have been, the debates about Wyclif's motivations have sometimes occluded the more fundamental question of what, in fact, he actually taught. Whether on account of his developing metaphysics or his growing horror at contemporary eucharistic practice, or both, it is certain that Wyclif radically changed his public position on the eucharist in the 1370s. His fellow schoolman William Woodford, with whom Wyclif had exchanged notebooks in advance of their disputations and who was later to write an extensive refutation of Wyclif's ideas, claimed that Wyclif's views on the sacrament had developed in several stages.[19] Whilst the development of Wyclif's eucharistic views is interesting, the opinions for which he was finally condemned are more relevant here. Wyclif's mature theology of the sacrament appears in a number of the Latin works he produced in the wake of his 1379 lectures on the eucharist; those lectures, as we have seen, ultimately became his *De eucharistia*. In 1381, Wyclif produced a statement of his beliefs in response to his condemnation in Oxford, and the sacrament continued to figure prominently in the treatises he wrote in exile: *De apostasia*, *De blasphemia*, and *Trialogus* all devote substantial sections to the eucharist. It might seem natural to focus here on the extensive *De eucharistia*, but the revival of scholarly interest in Wyclif's eucharistic theology has already produced an excellent summary of that treatise.[20] In what follows, then, I shall concentrate

---

[18] Catto, 'John Wyclif and the cult of the Eucharist', 281.
[19] Robson, *Wyclif and the Oxford Schools*, 192–3; for additional views on Woodford, see Jeremy Catto, 'William Woodford, O.F.M. (*c.*1330–*c.*1397)' (D.Phil. thesis, University of Oxford, 1969); and *PR*, 46–50.
[20] In Aers, *Sanctifying Signs*, ch. 3.

instead on *De eucharistia confessio*, a shorter tract that nevertheless captures the salient features of Wyclif's thinking.[21]

Wyclif begins by affirming Christ's presence in the consecrated elements; for proof, he asserts that Christ, who cannot lie, has said so.[22] As Levy has pointed out, Wyclif frequently uses as an argument in defence of his eucharistic theology the claim that Christ's words at the Last Supper could not have been other than true.[23] Nevertheless, Wyclif's views on the sacrament went beyond the simple question of Christ's presence or absence, and he dedicated much of the *Confessio* to an analysis of the ways in which Christ is and is not present in the sacrament. Wyclif argues that Christ is not in the bread and wine essentially, substantially, corporeally, or identically (*essentialiter, substantialiter, corporaliter, vel identice*); he is, however, present virtually, spiritually, and sacramentally (*virtualis, spiritualis, et sacramentalis*).[24]

What did Wyclif mean by each of these modifiers? Christ's presence is virtual, he explains, because it extends throughout all of creation; it is spiritual because it is effected through grace; and it is sacramental because Christ's presence is concentrated in the consecrated elements.[25] It cannot be overstated that Wyclif neither here nor elsewhere denies that Christ is present in the elements; indeed, Christ's presence in the eucharist is more real than in the other sacraments. Nevertheless, Christ is not present in the host in the same way that he is present in heaven. Christ's glorified body is in heaven substantially, corporeally, and dimensionally (*substantialiter, corporaliter, et dimensionaliter*), all three of which are modes of presence more real than those Wyclif ascribes to that of Christ in the eucharistic elements.[26]

Wyclif is careful to disclaim the idea that the sacrament is merely a sign or figure of an absent Christ. He argues that whilst the body of Christ comprises what he calls the corporeal substance of the host, Christ's body is present there in a way specific to the *ratio* of the host. The *ratio* of the host, for Wyclif, means

---

[21] A shorter version of the *Confessio*, almost certainly Wyclif's, is known in Trinity College Cambridge MS B.14.50, fols. 56–8, and was printed by S. Harrison Thomson under the name *De Fide Sacramentorum* in *Journal of Theological Studies* 33 (1932), 361–5. Two vernacular confessions, both attributed to Wyclif, appear in Henry Knighton's *Chronicle*, where Knighton records them under the year 1382 (253–61). Hudson has pointed out that the two English statements cannot with certainty be said to be Wyclif's works, though they, like the *De Fide Sacramentorum*, contain the essentials of his eucharistic teaching (*Selections*, 141–3).

[22] *FZ*, 115: 'Probatio est, quia Christus, qui mentiri non potest, sic asserit.' Wyclif makes the same argument in *Trialogus*, 250, 266.

[23] Ian Christopher Levy, '*Christus Qui Mentiri Non Potest*: John Wyclif's rejection of transubstantiation', *Recherches de Théologie et Philosophie Médiévales*, 66 (1999), 316–34 at 328.

[24] *FZ*, 115; cf. *De blasphemia*, 22; *Trialogus*, 248, 278. See also *De eucharistia*, 11–13, 84–6.

[25] *FZ*, 116.

[26] Ibid., 117; cf. *De blasphemia*, 30.

something intermediate between the substantial presence on which his opponents insisted and the position that the sacrament is merely symbolic. For
Wyclif, there are different ways that signs can signify, and the way in which
Christ is present in the eucharist is the most real of them. Through the power of
the words of institution, the eucharist is a sign 'infinite and more outstanding
than the signs of the body of Christ in the old law, or images in the new law'.[27]

In subsequent passages, Wyclif aims to refine his notion of a real, spiritual,
and yet not substantial presence. He turns a barrage of rhetorical fire on his
opponents, whom he calls the glossers of Scripture. Their doctrine would have
the faithful barbarously eating Christ's body corporeally rather than spiritually, and they imagine that an accident can become the body of Christ. In
doing so, Wyclif argues, they display an ignorance of the distinctions and
gradations among signs and hence are worse than infidels.[28] He proceeds to
make a second attempt to position his eucharistic theology between a doctrine of substantial change and the figurative stance that he claims is being
imputed to him by his opponents, writing that the union between the body of
Christ and the bread is neither an identical nor a hypostatic union, but it is
the next strongest sort of union that can exist.[29] Indeed, for Wyclif, the union
between the bread and body finds its most appropriate parallel in the doctrine
of the incarnation; just as two natures are there joined in a single person, so
also through the words of institution are the substances of Christ's body and
the bread present in the consecrated host. Wyclif employs another series of
adverbs to summarize his position: Christ, he writes, is present *bene, miracu-
lose, vere, et realiter, spiritualiter, virtualiter, et sacramentaliter*.[30]

Wyclif dedicates the second half of the *Confessio* to a tripartite assault on his
opponents. He first reiterates his earlier distinction between substantial and
sacramental presence, arguing that whilst the sacrament remains in its essential nature bread and wine, it becomes spiritually the body and blood of
Christ. His opponents, on the contrary, 'imagine that the sacrament is a
strange accident without a substantial subject'.[31] Second, Wyclif maintains
that he and his followers—whom he collectively designates with the phrase
secta nostra—adore in the sacrament not the substantial bread and wine but

---

[27] *FZ*, 119: 'Hoc tamen signum infinitum est praestantius quam signa corporis Christi in
lege veteri, vel imagines in lege nova.' It is on this point that the analysis of T. C. Hammond, in
his article 'The schoolmen of the middle ages', is most perceptive (in A. J. Macdonald (ed.), *The
Evangelical Doctrine of Holy Communion* (Cambridge, 1930), 118–50 at 141).

[28] *FZ*, 119–20; see also *De eucharistia*, 38.

[29] Ibid., 120.

[30] Ibid., 122.

[31] Ibid., 125: 'Sed secta contraria fingit ipsum sacramentum unum esse ignotum accidens
sine substantia subjecta.'

the body and blood of Christ present sacramentally.[32] Others, however, mistakenly adore what they believe is an accident without its proper subject; what is worse, he argues, is that they venerate the elements in the same way as they venerate the cross and other images in the church, which are less worthy of adoration.[33] Finally, Wyclif charges his opponents with creating unnecessary difficulties for eucharistic theology by introducing the language of substance and accidents into a matter already decided by the words of Christ, who, he repeats, cannot lie.[34]

The treatise ends with a series of citations from Ignatius of Antioch, Cyprian, Ambrose, Augustine, Jerome, Berengar's confession on the eucharist, and the canon of the mass.[35] Wyclif repeats that to teach that the eucharist consists of accidents without a subject, even if such a thing is philosophically possible, is to debase and dishonour the body of Christ.[36] In the final paragraphs of the *Confessio*, then, Wyclif's metaphysical challenges to traditional eucharistic theology and his pastoral concerns about the growth of idolatry converge. Whilst he consistently asserts the presence of Christ in the consecrated elements, he defines Christ's presence in his own idiosyncratic vocabulary. For Wyclif, only by thinking in terms of a spiritually or sacramentally present Christ can the eucharist be properly venerated and the philosophically problematic doctrine of substantial annihilation avoided. Nevertheless, the complexity and subtlety of Wyclif's views may have had the unintended consequence that later dissenters, if they were influenced by his eucharistic theology at all, would stress either the remanence of the elements or the figurative character of the sacrament at the expense of the other.

REMANENCE AND FIGURATION: THE
EUCHARIST IN WYCLIFFITE TEXTS

Unlike ideas about salvation, the doctrine of the eucharist makes more than passing appearances in dissenting texts. Indeed, the sacrament figures in the majority of extant Wycliffite writings, which condemn transubstantiation as

---

[32] It is interesting that whereas in the first half of the *Confessio* Wyclif writes in the first-person singular, in this section he shifts to the first-person plural. That he intends to include others in his statement is confirmed by his use of *secta nostra*, a phrase highly liable to misreadings. See Aston, 'Were the Lollards a sect?'

[33] *FZ*, 125.

[34] Ibid., 126.

[35] Ibid., 126–9. Wyclif cites Berengar again at 130 and also in *De blasphemia*, 23.

[36] *FZ*, 129; cf. *Trialogus*, 263.

unequivocally as Wyclif had done. Though they uniformly rejected the eucharistic theology of the institutional church, Wycliffite authors did not articulate a consistent set of teachings on the sacrament. Some texts maintain that the substances of bread and wine remain after the words of consecration and that the host is simultaneously bread and Christ's body. Others eschew the notion of Christ's presence altogether, formulating figurative theologies of the sacrament.

Among the texts that best illustrate the differences of opinion among dissenting writers are those which constitute the long English sermon-cycle, that comprehensive catalogue of Wycliffite ideas we have already encountered. The cycle's editors have opined that the sermons reflect 'with some accuracy' Wyclif's mature doctrine of the eucharist. 'The teaching on this central Wycliffite doctrine in the sermons is remarkably constant.'[37] It is true that the sermons agree on a number of crucial points: they reject in unequivocal terms the doctrine of transubstantiation and argue that the accidents of bread and wine cannot exist without their subjects. Like Wyclif, the sermons cite Christ's words at the Last Supper as an authoritative statement of eucharistic doctrine: 'As Crist seiþ, and seyntis aftir, þat þe hoost, whan it is sacrid, is uerrili Cristis owene body in forme of breed, as cristen men bileuen, and neyþer accident wiþoute sugett, ne nouʒt as heretikis seien.'[38]

But if the elements are not transubstantiated into Christ's body and blood as the institutional church would have its members believe, then what, instead, happens at the consecration? A majority of the sermons adopt the position that the elements consist of both bread and Christ's body and wine and Christ's blood. A sermon for the second Sunday of Lent puts it this way: 'þanne men schulden here Godis word gladly, and dispuyse fablis, and erre not in þis sacrud oost but graunte þat it is two þingis, boþe bred and Godus body, but principally Godus body.'[39] Several texts attempt to clarify how the host can be bread and Christ's body at the same time, deploying Wyclif's distinction between the substantial presence of the bread and the spiritual presence of Christ. As the sermon for the feast of Corpus Christi explains, 'þis oost is bred in his kynde, as ben oþere oostis vnsacrid, and sacramentaliche Goddis body, for Crist seiþ so þat may not lye'. If the sacrament is desecrated, or in the classic scholastic dilemma eaten by a mouse, it 'be foulid in þat þat it is bred or wyn, it may not þus be defoulid in þingis whiche it figuriþ'.[40]

Three sermons gloss a dictum of St Ambrose in support of the distinction between natural and sacramental presence. Ambrose had written that the host was not bread but rather God's body, and orthodox theologians often cited

---

[37] *EWS*, iv.50.   [38] Ibid., i.E47/76–9.   [39] Ibid., i.E17/70–3.
[40] Ibid., iii.206/17–25. See also i.46/68–70, ii.75/149.

the Bishop of Milan in defence of transubstantiation. Wycliffite writers, however, insisted that Ambrose had been misconstrued: what he had meant, one sermon claims, is that the host 'is not aftur *principally* breed, but Godis body in maner as Austyn seiþ'.[41] Indeed, Augustine is a favourite authority in several sermons, one of which maintains that 'as Austyn telliþ heere, þis bred uarieþ from oþer bred . . . . þis bred þat is Crist, etyn gostly of man.'[42]

A significant minority of the sermons instead describe the eucharist in terms of a commemoration of Christ's passion. An epistle sermon for Easter Sunday puts the figurative case most clearly:

For, riȝt as fadris maden þerf breed for to ete þer pasc lomb, so men eton þe sacred oost to ete Crist goostly, þat is to have muynde of hym, how kyndely he suffrede for man. And such a fruytous muynde of Crist is gostly mete to þe soule, and goostly etyng of Cristus body þat þe gospel of Iohn spekuþ of.[43]

The phrase 'þat is to have muynde of hym' seems to move beyond the notion of Christ's localized presence, however spiritual. For this preacher, to receive the host is to call to mind Christ and his passion, not to receive Christ as present in the eucharistic elements. Other sermons compare the eucharist to more commonly acknowledged scriptural symbols. John the Baptist is not Elijah personally, one sermon argues, but he is Elijah figuratively. 'And riȝt so þe sacrid oost is uery bred kyndely ant Goddis body figuraly, riȝt as Crist hymsilf seiþ.'[44] Other comparisons are made with the seven oxen of Pharaoh's dream and the fattened calf of the parable of the Prodigal Son.[45] 'Þis fat calf þat men shulden ete is Cristis body þat men offeren; and so it is þe sacrid oost þat is in figure Cristis body. Crist was deed in his tyme, and ordeyned for to fede men gostly by his body, for it is fat bred herto.'[46]

Of the twenty-one sermons that discuss the eucharist at length, five articulate clearly figurative views. A sixth sermon's position is ambiguous, comparing Christ's passion and death to the passage of the Israelites through the Red Sea and then describing the eucharist as 'oure mete and dryng to fede oure soule in byleue of hem'.[47] Nevertheless, the presence of figurative views across several of the sets of texts that comprise the cycle seems to indicate that dissenting authors held a variety of opinions about the sacrament even as they consistently rejected transubstantiation and the metaphysical claims that surrounded it. The total absence of figurative views in the sermons for the common and proper of saints seems to confirm the previous chapter's

---

[41] *EWS*, i.44/40, my emphasis. See also ii.111/56–8, iii.166/13–15.
[42] Ibid., iii.162/59–62.   [43] Ibid., i.E22/37–42. See also iii.176/70–2.
[44] Ibid., iii.125/39–41.   [45] Ibid., i.30/47–50.   [46] Ibid., iii.158/124–7.
[47] Ibid., i.E13/50.

hypothesis that the sermon-cycle was produced through a vertical rather than a horizontal division of labour; authors and editors whose eucharistic views tended toward the figurative likely worked only on the sermons for the Sunday gospels and epistles as well as the ferial set.[48]

Written about the same time as the sermons, the Wycliffite preaching encyclopaedia the *Rosarium* contains a far more coherent theology of the sacrament. Two entries are particularly relevant. Under *Xtus*, the anonymous author sets forth an account of the eucharist nearly identical to Wyclif's own:

þe body also of Criste is seid brede on tuo maners: þat is to sey spirituale brede, refetyng of þe soule wiþout visibile forme or sacramentale . . . þe 2., it is seide þat white Hoste and rounde halowed of þe preste, after þe consecracion þe body of Criste no noþer þan þat was borne of þe Virgine, bot þe same. Neþerlesse it is oþerwise þer þan it was in þe wombe of þe Virgine or in þe crosse, for in þe crosse it was fleschely and mesurably, bot in þe Oste sacramentaly and multiplyngly. Neþerlesse boþ maners of beyng, þat is to sey fleschely and sacramentaly is þingly ynoʒ.[49]

For the author, the 'body of Christ' can mean both the host as well as the grace given by Christ without the mediation of any sacrament. He chooses to concentrate on the former, arguing that Christ is not present in the eucharistic elements in the same way that he was on earth. Like Wyclif's distinction between material and sacramental presence, the author's distinction between fleshly and sacramental modes of being enables him to speak of Christ's spiritual presence in the eucharist without believing that Christ is materially there.

Whereas the *Rosarium* and the English sermon-cycle mention the eucharist within the context of larger theological projects, two later texts focus specifically on the sacrament of the altar. As its name suggests, the *Tractatus de oblacione iugis sacrificii* is highly concerned with eucharistic theology. Preserved in a single manuscript, London, British Library MS Cotton Titus D.v, the *Tractatus* can fortuitously be dated to a period of eleven months. Its author refers to 'king Herri þe fourþe þat nouʒ late diʒid', placing its composition after Henry's death on 20 March 1413; he also alludes in the present tense to Thomas Arundel, the heresy-hunting Archbishop of Canterbury, whom he describes as 'þe grettist enmy þat Crist haþ in Ynglond'.[50] Arundel's death on 19 February 1414 provides a *terminus ante quem* for the tract; its nearly 4,000 lines were, therefore, written during a time when lollardy was prominent in the public eye. Sir John Oldcastle had been accused of heresy

---

[48] See Ch. 2, pp. 44–5 above.
[49] von Nolcken, 'Edition of selected parts', i.187.
[50] Titus, ll. 174, 405.

during the summer of 1413, and on 23 September he was examined before Arundel for the first time.[51]

The *Tractatus* seems at first glance to focus almost exclusively on the doctrine of the eucharist, though Hudson has observed that 'considerable weight attaches to the question of discernment of authority on that subject'.[52] It would be fair to suggest that the tract is an examination of the source and right use of ecclesiastical authority more generally. Indeed, the eucharist is not mentioned within the first two hundred lines of the printed edition, which are instead given over to a wholesale condemnation of Antichrist and hypocritical churchmen. Like the roughly contemporaneous text *The Lanterne of Liʒt*, the *Tractatus* exhorts its readers to persevere in the face of persecution.[53] Antichrist is described as the agent of the devil, who 'haþ a grete wraþ aʒenst þe peple þat kepiþ Goddis commaundementis and han his lawe . . . for to wiþdraw hem from þis blessed lawe, and so to lett þe fulfilling of þe chosyn number, and so to tari þe dai of dome, in which dai he schal haue final euerlasting confusioun wiþ alle his'.[54]

An explication of the sacrament occupies the majority of the tract. The author rejects the view, which he attributes to Antichrist and the friars, that the sacrament 'is neiþur Cristis bodi, ne brede but accidentis wiþout soget'.[55] He alleges that such a theology of the eucharist can be sustained only by a radically misaligned account of the relationship between divine and human authority. True Christians acknowledge Christ as God and do not follow Antichrist in his tendency to exalt the decrees of the pope over the words of Scripture.

But if the eucharist is not a bundle of accidents without their subject, what is it? The author answers that 'bi þe wordis of seint Poule we most beleue þat þe pure brede bi þe consecracioun is not after þe consecracioun onli brede but olso verri Cristis bodi, and þe wyne is blode'.[56] It is to give greater honour to Christ to call the sacrament his body, though it is also correct to refer to it as bread, since the substance of bread remains after the consecration. In support of his doctrine, the author cites a host of church fathers, but their views are ultimately superfluous; Christ's own words make it plain that the elements are both bread and wine *and* Christ's body and blood, while the insights of even the most learned churchmen pale in comparison.[57]

---

[51] Hudson, *The Works of a Lollard Preacher* (EETS o.s. 317, 2001), xlix–l.

[52] *PR*, 286.

[53] Titus, ll. 4–6, and *Lanterne*, 2.

[54] Titus, ll. 23–5, 26–9. It might seem that the phrase 'þe chosyn number' here might bespeak the author's predestinarianism, but the tract's soteriological affiliations are ambiguous.

[55] Ibid. ll. 402–3.

[56] Ibid. ll. 513–15.

[57] Ibid. ll. 2581–6.

The institutional church's doctrine of the eucharist is symptomatic in the Titus author's mind of a larger problem: the usurpation of divine authority by contemporary ecclesiastics. The tract insists that Christ, not the pope, must be revered as head of the church, and as I will argue at greater length in Chapter 6, its author offers a radical reinterpretation of the key Matthean passage on which the papacy based its claims to power. There is not space here to mention all the areas of doctrine and practice that the Titus author alleges have been corrupted by the sort of presumptuousness that turned Peter's successors into papal monarchs. It will suffice to note that they include the secular lordship of priests and prelates, the begging of able-bodied friars, the letters of fraternity sold to unwitting laypeople, the abuse of the sacrament of penance—and that old standby, clerical lechery. The tract suggests that these and other novelties have given rise to an irreconcilable and inappropriate diversity of opinions about the sacrament. These conflicting theologies include the views that Christ secretly consecrated bread and wine at the Last Supper using a formula unknown to his disciples and their successors; that in saying 'this is my body', Christ was pointing not to the host but to his material body; that the Latin word *transsubstanciatur* should be substituted for *est*; and most notoriously, that after the consecration, what is perceived to be bread consists in accidents without a proper subject or substance.[58] The author rejects all these explanations, returning to his maxim that doctrine and tradition must firmly be grounded in Scripture: 'Whoso wol loke antecristis tradicions in þis mater, he schal se houȝ þis uyolens is do wiþout auctorite of Goddis reson and old determynacion of Cristis chirche.'[59]

Whereas the *Tractatus de oblacione iugis sacrificii* deploys the classically Wycliffite distinction between Scripture and contemporary practice in defence of its doctrine of remanence, a later tract also turns to Scripture, but to justify a figurative theology instead. *Wycklyffes Wycket*, one of the few Wycliffite texts for which no medieval evidence survives, was first printed in 1546 by the reform-minded London printer John Day.[60] With its attribution to Wyclif, the *Wycket* proved a commercial success, and Day produced three more editions between 1546 and 1548. One of these, overseen by the biblical translator and later bishop Miles Coverdale, also included the evangelical testament of William Tracy along with two commentaries on it by William Tyndale and John Frith.[61]

---

[58] Ibid., ll. 1984–2011.   [59] Ibid., ll. 1674–7.

[60] *Wycklyffes Wycket* (London, 1546; STC 25590); for more details on its printing history and provenance, see Hudson, '"No Newe Thyng": The printing of medieval texts in the early Reformation period', repr. in *Books*, 231.

[61] STC 25591; the other editions of 1546 and 1548 are STC 25590.5 and 25591a, respectively.

As Hudson has argued, the *Wycket* stands out among Wycliffite treatments of the eucharist: the terms in which the sacrament is discussed 'are not altogether those found in Lollard treatments of that subject and, though biblical passages are amply quoted, there is not the usual Wycliffite citation of patristic proof texts'. The text nevertheless appeared as evidence in a series of heresy trials from 1511 to 1532; it was composed, therefore, certainly before 1518 'and more probably well before this'.[62] Unique though the chronological place the *Wycket* occupies among dissenting texts may be, the tract nevertheless articulates the sort of figurative theologies of the eucharist that we have already encountered in the long sermon-cycle and that were also voiced by a vocal minority of lay heresy defendants. Its views on the sacrament repay careful attention.

After an introductory prayer, the *Wycket* first asks whether a human being can claim to make God: 'And thou then that art an earthely man, by what reason mayst thou saye that thou makest thy maker. Whether maye the made thynge saye to the maker, why hast thou made me thus? Or maye it turne agayne and make him that made it?'[63] This scepticism about the eucharist is soon replaced by a sophisticated reinterpretation of the scriptural passages on which the institutional church based its theology of the sacrament. When Christ took bread and blessed it, the author argues, 'it semeth more that he blyssed hys disciples and apostles, whom he had ordained witnesses of his passion . . . He sayd not this bread is my body or that the brede shuld be geuen for the lyfe of the world.'[64] If Christ did make his body out of bread, then it could not have been the words of institution which effected the change, 'for they be the words of gyuynge and not of makynge which he said after that he brake the breade'.[65] It might seem, on this logic, that either Christ secretly consecrated the bread and chalice and then presented them to his disciples, or else the traditional words of institution were a lie. Like other dissenting writers, the author is hesitant to impute dishonesty to Christ; his conclusion, therefore, is that Christ did not consecrate his body and blood at the Last Supper and that no priest has done so since.

In the second half of the tract, the author turns his fire on the ritual celebration of the eucharist. One of his more fatuous arguments criticizes priests for using the first person in pronouncing the words of institution: they must either be presuming to refer to themselves as Christ, he writes, 'or els there is a false God, for yf it is thy body as thou sayest, then it is the bodye of a

---

[62] Hudson, 'No Newe Thyng', 247. On the *Wycket*, see shortly J. Patrick Hornbeck II, '*Wycklyffes Wycket* and eucharistic heresy: Two series of cases from sixteenth-century Winchester' in Hornbeck and Mishtooni Bose (eds.), *Wycliffite Controversies* (forthcoming).
[63] *Wycklyffes Wycket*, A8v.   [64] Ibid., A9v–A10v.   [65] Ibid., A12r.

false knaue or of a dronken man, or of a thefe, or of a lecherour or full of other synnes, and then ther is an uncleane bodye for any man to worshyp for god'.[66] He proceeds to ask whether the consecration happens once or twice and whether when the priest and congregation adore the consecrated host, they are simultaneously worshipping nothing more than wine in the as-yet-un-consecrated chalice.[67] Finally, and most crucially for our purposes, the writer rejects the view that Christ is not split into many parts in the many hosts consecrated each day. He notes that his scholastic opponents reconcile the unity of Christ with the multiplicity of the hosts by saying that the hosts are like a mirror split into many parts in each of which can be seen reflected the same object. But the writer argues in response that what is reflected in the pieces of the mirror is not the object itself 'but the lyckenes' of that object, and hence 'the breade is the fygure or mynde of Christes bodye in earth'.[68] The sacrament of the altar, like all the other sacraments, simply commemorates an absent Christ; it is 'but a sygne or mynde of a thyng passed or a thynge to come'.[69] *Wycklyffes Wycket*, therefore, articulates a theology in which the central question is not, as it was for Wyclif, *how* Christ is present in the eucharist. For the author of the *Wycket*, the crucial fact about the sacrament is that it does not effect Christ's presence at all, nor was it ever intended to; it instead calls to mind Christ's earthly ministry and passion and inspires its recipients to perform deeds of charity.[70]

The English sermon-cycle, the *Rosarium*, the *Tractatus de oblacione iugis sacrificii*, and *Wycklyffes Wycket* illustrate significant differences in the trajectories of Wycliffite eucharistic theologies. A host (no pun intended) of other vernacular texts also mention the eucharist but contribute little new to the debate. The Wycliffite *Sixteen Points on which the Bishops Accuse Lollards* argues, as Wyclif did, that the host is God's body only sacramentally and spiritually; among others, the texts that we know as *Seven Heresies*, *An Apology for Lollard Doctrines*, the *Exposition of the Pater Noster*, and *Upland's Rejoinder* maintain that it is both God's body and bread.[71] Articulating the same doctrine of remanence, the *Praier and Complaynte of the Ploweman vnto*

---

[66] Ibid., B1v–B2r.   [67] Ibid., B3v.   [68] Ibid., B5r–v.   [69] Ibid., B6r.
[70] On the *Wycket*, see further Aston, 'John Wycliffe's Reformation reputation', repr. in *Lollards and Reformers*, 243–72 at 257.
[71] *Sixteen Points on which the Bishops Accuse Lollards*, in *Selections*, 19–24 at 20; *Seven Heresies*, in Arnold, iii.441–6 at 443; *An Apology for Lollard Doctrines*, ed. J. H. Todd (Camden Society 20, 1842), 45–6; *The Pater Noster*, in Arnold, 98–110 at 106; and *Upland's Rejoinder*, in P. L. Heyworth (ed.), *Jack Upland, Friar Daw's Reply and Upland's Rejoinder* (London, 1968), l. 380. On the eucharistic theology of the Upland series, see Fiona Somerset, 'Here, there, and everywhere? Wycliffite conceptions of the Eucharist and Chaucer's "other" Lollard joke' in *Influence*, 127–33.

Christe insists that the eucharistic debate has gained undue prominence: the first duty of priests should be to preach and teach, not to consecrate hosts.[72] Several other vernacular texts, among them *Of the Leaven of Pharisees*, *De Papa*, and *De Sacramento Altaris*, all reject the notion that the eucharist is an accident without a subject; *De Sacramento Altaris* explicitly attributes that doctrine to the friars.[73] Finally, the poem *Pierce the Ploughman's Crede* encourages its readers to believe that the sacrament is Christ's body and blood without dwelling too long on the metaphysics of eucharistic transformation:

> And though this flaterynge freres wyln for her pride,
> Disputen of this deyte as dotardes schulden,
> The more the matere is moved the masedere hy worthen.
> Lat the losels alone and leue you the trewthe,
> For Crist seyde it is so, so mot it nede worthe;
> Therfore studye thou nought thereon, ne stere thi wittes,
> It is his blissed body, so bad he vs beleuen.[74]

Whether they adopted a theology of remanence or a figurative one, however, dissenting authors all rejected the doctrine of transubstantiation. We shall examine the institutional church's response to their ideas in the following sections.

WYCLIFFITE DOCTRINES IN ANTI-WYCLIFFITE SOURCES

Although figurative theologies of the eucharist appear in dissenting texts as early as the last decade of the fourteenth century, official accounts of Wycliffite belief focus for the most part on the issue of remanence. Understandably so: despite the fact that some dissenters spoke of the eucharist in figurative terms, Wyclif himself, as we have seen, defended the notion of a spiritual but nevertheless real presence of Christ in the consecrated elements. The chroniclers, scholastic theologians, and canon lawyers who formulated

---

[72] Douglas H. Parker (ed.), *The Praier and Complaynte of the Ploweman vnto Christe* (Toronto, 1997), l. 667.

[73] *On the Leaven of Pharisees*, in Matthew, 1–27 at 19; *De Papa*, in Matthew, 458–82 at 466; *De Sacramento Altaris*, in Matthew, 356–8 at 357.

[74] *Pierce the Ploughman's Crede*, ll. 819–25. *Pierce the Ploughman's Crede* was first printed in 1553 by the evangelical printer Reyner Wolfe (STC 19904), who in the spirit of the 1552 *Book of Common Prayer* omitted the claim made here and elsewhere that the eucharist is indeed Christ's body and blood; see Barr, *Piers Plowman Tradition*, 244–5.

the institutional church's responses to the Oxford reformer and, later, to his successors quite naturally assumed that dissenters had taken their theological cues from Wyclif, the putative heresiarch who reportedly had sent them out to preach dissent across the countryside.

The *Historia anglicana* and the *Chronicon Angliae*, likely the work of the St Albans chronicler Thomas Walsingham, both record under the year 1377 that Wyclif had resurrected the eucharistic heresies of Berengar and Ockham, teaching that bread and wine remain after the consecration of the elements.[75] The date is likely inaccurate; all evidence suggests that Wyclif delivered his controversial lectures on the eucharist no earlier than 1379, before which time he had articulated orthodox or else agnostic views. Walsingham was not alone, however, in describing Wyclif's eucharistic heresies in terms of remanence. In 1381, the chancellor of Oxford and a committee of twelve doctors condemned two propositions as heterodox: that 'in the sacrament of the altar the substances of material bread and wine, which existed before the consecration, really remain after the consecration', and that 'in the venerable sacrament the body and blood of Christ do not exist essentially, substantially, or even corporally, but figuratively; so that Christ is not present there in his own corporeal person'.[76] The second proposition might seem to articulate the figurative view favoured by later tracts like *Wycklyffes Wycket*, but read in the terms of Wyclif's *Confessio*, it seems more likely to have been intended to anathematize Wyclif's distinction between Christ's spiritual and material (that is, 'corporeal') presence.

When in 1382 Archbishop Courtenay summoned twenty-four doctors to meet him at the London house of the Blackfriars, the first five of the ten propositions they condemned as heretical concerned the eucharist. Like the Oxford committee, the council rejected the views that the substances of bread and wine remain after the consecration and that Christ is not corporeally present in the sacrament.[77] It also anathematized three additional propositions: that an accident cannot exist without its subject; that Christ did not institute the mass; and that a priest in mortal sin cannot ordain, baptize, or consecrate.[78] The Blackfriars Council thus became the first body to impute the ancient heresy of Donatism to Wyclif, who, though not named, was clearly

---

[75] *Chronicon Angliae*, ed. E. M. Thompson (London, 1874), 281; Walsingham, *Historia anglicana*, i.324–5.

[76] *FZ*, 110: 'Primo, in sacramento altaris substantiam panis materialis et vini, quae prius fuerunt ante consecrationem, post consecrationem realiter remanere. Secundo, quod execrabilius est auditu, in illo venerabili sacramento non esse corpus Christi et sanguinem, essentialiter nec substantialiter, nec etiam corporaliter, sed figurative seu tropice; sic quod Christus non sit ibi veraciter in sua propria persona corporali.'

[77] Ibid., 277–8, nos. 1, 3.   [78] Ibid., 278, nos. 2, 4, 5.

the target of its condemnations.[79] Bishop Thomas Brinton of Rochester, an avid opponent of Wyclif's ideas who attended the council, condemned in a roughly contemporary sermon the doctrine of remanence and the view that priests in mortal sin cannot celebrate the sacraments.[80]

Six years later, the chronicler Henry Knighton was the first indisputably to reject a figurative theology of the sacrament. In his list of twenty-five of 'the Lollards' errors', Knighton accused the heretics of believing that 'the thing which was bread before its consecration in the sacrament of the altar is not thereafter the body of Christ, being a symbol of that thing, and not the thing itself'.[81] The members of the Canterbury convocation must also have had a figurative theology of the sacrament in mind when in 1396 they drew up a list of eighteen Wycliffite articles, one of which was that 'just as John [the Baptist] was figuratively but not personally Elijah, so also is the bread figuratively but not naturally the body of Christ. There is as much ambiguity in the figurative saying "This is my body" as in the words of Christ, "John is Elijah".'[82]

Ecclesiastical authorities did not draw up another list of Wycliffite errors until the year 1412, when preparations for the Council of Constance were underway, but in the interim, at least two writers assailed Wycliffite views of the sacrament. In 1395, the Dominican friar Roger Dymmok produced an extensive Latin refutation of the twelve conclusions that dissenters had posted in the vernacular on the doors of St Paul's Cathedral and Westminster Abbey. The fourth of those conclusions was the relatively vague assertion that 'þe feynid miracle of þe sacrament of bred inducith alle men but a fewe to ydolatrie, for þei wene þat Godis bodi, þat neuere schal out of heuene, be uertu of þe prestos wordis schulde ben closed essenciali in a litil bred þat þei schewe to þe puple'.[83] Dymmok responded with an enthusiastic defence of eucharistic orthodoxy. Citing Aquinas, Dymmok specifically rejected the view that Christ's body is present only spiritually in the eucharist:

---

[79] Ian Christopher Levy, 'Was John Wyclif's theology of the Eucharist Donatistic?', *Scottish Journal of Theology*, 53 (2000), 137–53.

[80] Mary Aquinas Devlin (ed.), *The Sermons of Thomas Brinton, Bishop of Rochester (1373–1389)*, 2 vols. (Camden Third Series 85–6, 1954), ii.406; see also ii.495. For further background on Brinton, see Siegfried Wenzel, *Latin Sermon Collections from Later Medieval England* (Cambridge, 2005), 45–9.

[81] Knighton, *Chronicle*, 435–9.

[82] Wilkins, iii.229, no. 2: 'Item, quod sicut Johannes fuit figuraliter Helias, et non personaliter; sic panis est figuraliter corpus Christi, et non naturaliter corpus Christi. Et quod absque omni ambiguitate haec est figurative locutio, "Hoc est corpus meum," sicut illa in verbis Christi, "Johannes ipse est Helias." Haeresis est.'

[83] *Selections*, 25.

It is clear, therefore, that what the heretics say is false: that it can be understood that the body of Christ is only *habitudinaliter* in the sacrament. If the body of Christ is in the sacrament only *habitudinaliter* and not *realiter*, then although the body of Christ is a body in its type of substance, of which type it is a real thing and not only a habitudinal one, the body of Christ is therefore a real thing and not a habitudinal one wherever it appears in the sacrament of the altar.[84]

Dymmok concluded by citing a series of miracles in support of Christ's real presence in the eucharist. He also insisted that were the eucharist only bread and wine and not Christ as well, it would have been an unworthy parting gift to have been left by Christ, who on earth had given his body to the Church.[85]

Like Dymmok, the Carthusian friar Nicholas Love also attempted to refute dissenting theologies of the eucharist. Rather than writing in Latin for an audience of courtiers and clerics, however, Love produced a vernacular defence of eucharistic orthodoxy in his *Mirror of the Blessed Life of Jesus Christ*.[86] Love's *Mirror* is the only complete English translation of the early-fourteenth-century Tuscan text *Meditationes Vitae Christi*, but it is not a straightforward rendition of the original Latin. Instead, Love significantly amended his source, inserting a number of passages which criticize the 'lollardes', 'heritykes', and 'disciples of Anticrist' who have arisen in England.[87] He appended a treatise on the sacrament that denigrates his opponents' views still further. Both the text and its appendix reveal how the official church likely perceived dissenting eucharistic theologies in the years immediately before the Council of Constance. That Love's polemical translation echoed the views of the hierarchy seems evident from a prefatory note that came to be attached to most manuscripts of the work:

Memorandum: that around the year 1410, the original copy of this book, that is, *The Mirror of the Life of Christ* in English, was presented in London by its compiler, N, to the most reverend father and lord in Christ, lord Thomas Arundel, archbishop of Canterbury, for inspection and due examination before it was freely published. Who

---

[84] Roger Dymmok, *Liber contra XII errores et haereses Lollardorum*, ed. H. S. Cronin (London, 1922), 98–9: 'Patet igitur falsum esse quod isti heretici dicunt, quod scilicet corpus Christi solum habitudinaliter est in sacramento. Si enim corpus Christi sit in sacramento altaris solum habitudinaliter et non realiter, igitur cum corpus Christi sit corpus in genere substancie, cuius generis quelibet res est res realis, et non respectiua tantum siue habitudinalis, igitur corpus Christi, ubicunque est in sacramento altaris, est res ibi realis et non habitudinalis tantum.'

[85] Ibid., 99–103.

[86] On Dymmok's audience, see Scase, 'Audience and framers'.

[87] Nicholas Love, *The Mirror of the Blessed Life of Jesus Christ: A reading text*, ed. Michael G. Sargent (Exeter, 2004), 90, 225, 236. A useful discussion of the eucharistic views of Love's *Mirror* can be found in Aers, *Sanctifying Signs*, 12–28.

after examining it for several days, returning it to the author, commended and approved it personally, and further decreed and commanded by his metropolitan, indeed his universal, authority that it be published universally for the edification of the faithful and the confutation of heretics or lollards.[88]

As the *Mirror*'s most recent editor has noted, 'this submission was not performed out of fear that his work would not be approved; for Love had altered the text substantially, turning it into a weapon for the archbishop's campaign'.[89]

Love's primary target in the *Mirror* appears to have been belief in the remanence of the substances of bread and wine. His interpolations frequently compare dissenters to Judas, their betrayal of the church's teachings no less repugnant than Judas' original crime. In one such passage, Love wrote that heretics 'falsly byleuen and seyene þat þe holy sacrament of þe autere is in his kynde brede or wyne as it was before þe consecracion, bycause þat it semeþ so to alle hir bodily felyng, as in siht, tast and touching, þe whech bene more reprouable as in þat part þan Judas, for þei seene not Jesus bodily byside þat sacrament as he dide'.[90] Love described his opponents in equally unflattering terms in his appendix, where he again claimed that they 'falsly trowene and obstinately seyne þat it [the host] is brede in his kynde as it was before þe consecration, so þat þe substance of brede is not turnede in to þe substance of goddes body'.[91] Unlike the dissenters, he wrote, the church maintains that the eucharist is God's true body in the form of bread and God's true blood in the form of wine; it is the same body that suffered on the cross; and it exists in the sacrament under accidents which have lost their original subjects.[92] Orthodox believers, therefore, do not commit idolatry when they adore Christ in the consecrated bread.

Whilst refuting the doctrine of remanence seems to have been Love's priority, he also railed in passing at figurative theologies of the sacrament. When he spelled out the beliefs of the institutional church, Love wrote of the sacrament that 'verrey cristes body þat suffrede deþ vpon þe crosse is þere in þat sacrament bodily vnder þe forme and liknes of brede, and his verrey blode

---

[88] Love, *The Mirror of the Blessed Life of JesusChrist*, 7: 'Memorandum quod circa annum domini Millesimum quadringentesimum decimum, originalis copia huius libri, scilicet Speculi vite Christi in Anglicis presentabur Londoniis per compilatorem eiusdem, N, Reuerendissimo in Christo patri & domino, Domino Thome Arundell, Cantuarie Archiepiscopo, ad inspiciendum & debite examinandum antequam fuerat libere communicate. Qui post inspeccionem eiusdem per dies aliquot retradens ipsum librum memorato eiusdem auctori proprie vocis oraculo ipsum in singulis commendauit & approbauit, necnon & auctoritate sua metropolitica, vt pote catholicum, puplice communicandum fore decreuit & mandauit, ad fidelium edificacionem, & hereticorum siue lollardorum confutacionem.'
[89] Ibid., xviii.   [90] Ibid., 151.   [91] Ibid., 225.   [92] Ibid., 151, 226.

vndur likenes of wyne substancially and holely, without any feynyng or deceit, and not onley in figure as þe fals heritike seiþ'.[93] The word *figure* seems to imply the view that the consecrated bread and wine merely symbolize Christ and are not actually the site of his presence, but whether Love had such a target in mind is beyond the pale of the evidence, for no similar statements are to be found elsewhere in the *Mirror*.

The two decades after Love completed his translation of the *Mirror* witnessed a number of significant events for Wycliffites and their clerical antagonists. When in 1412, the commission of Oxford scholars appointed to investigate Wyclif's writings submitted to the Archbishop of Canterbury a list of the 267 errors they had discovered in them, nearly 10 per cent of the errors touched on the subject of the eucharist.[94] Most frequently condemned were the ideas that the elements remain bread and wine in their respective natures (seven articles, one rejecting Wyclif's appeal to Berengar's confession) and that accidents cannot exist without their subjects (five articles).[95] Three of the condemned articles assert that Christ is present in the eucharist figuratively, in the same way that the seven oxen of Pharaoh's dream symbolize seven years of prosperity and that John the Baptist is a figure of the prophet Elijah.[96] As we have seen, these articles take Wyclif's words out of context; to represent his theology as figurative is to occlude the distinctions that he drew between corporeal and spiritual modes of presence. The list of errors does, however, also include several of Wyclif's authentic objections to the doctrine of transubstantiation; among the condemned propositions are his views that annihilation is metaphysically untenable, that two bodies cannot be co-extended, and that God cannot multiply a single body in different places.[97]

The list of errors produced by the Oxford commission were the basis for Wyclif's formal condemnation by the Council of Constance. On 4 May 1415, the council declared Wyclif a 'pseudo-Christian' whose teachings had included, among others, the five eucharistic heresies anathematized at the Blackfriars Council of 1382.[98] On 6 July, after it had deposed the rival popes John XXIII, Gregory XII, and Benedict XIII but before it proceeded to elect a new pontiff, the council condemned fifty-eight additional errors drawn from the list prepared in Oxford. Of these, seven concerned the eucharist.[99]

---

[93] Ibid., 151–2.
[94] Hudson, 'Notes of an early fifteenth-century research assistant', 685–97.
[95] Wilkins, iii.342–9, nos. 70, 121, 169, 239, 248, 261; nos. 67, 68, 160, 161, 170.
[96] Ibid., iii.342–4, nos. 70, 71, 122.
[97] Ibid., iii.346, nos. 159, 165, 167, 173.
[98] Tanner, *Decrees*, i.411, nos. 1–5.
[99] Ibid., i.422, 426, nos. 1–5, 49–50.

Taken together, the lists of articles condemned from 1381 through the Council of Constance and beyond suggest that ecclesiastical authorities perceived Wycliffite eucharistic theologies to be relatively stable. No document from Wyclif's lifetime mentions an unambiguously figurative approach to the eucharist; the proximity of early inquisitors to Wyclif and his doctrine of Christ's spiritual but nevertheless real presence may well explain why their accounts of Wyclif's theology were among the most accurate. From 1388, however, lists of anathemas began with some regularity to include figurative theologies of the sacrament alongside, but never in isolation from, their less radical counterparts. Either inquisitors had on their own initiative begun to consider alternative modes of eucharistic heterodoxy, or else they had begun to encounter heresy suspects whose views on the sacrament did not tally with received ideas about what Wycliffites would say.

LOCAL THEOLOGIES: THE EUCHARIST IN HERESY TRIALS

It is fortunate for our purposes that the eucharist was the theologoumenon most frequently contested in English heresy trials between 1381 and 1521. As I argued at the beginning of this chapter, bishops and inquisitors found the eucharist a useful litmus test for dissenting belief. It is not only that the intricacies of eucharistic theology could trap unsuspecting defendants into making heterodox claims, but that the centrality of the mass in popular religious practice made the sacrament of the altar a likely site for dissent. The inclusion of eucharistic articles in the questionnaires administered to heresy suspects further increased the likelihood that ideas about the sacrament would figure prominently in the testimony of witnesses and the abjurations of suspects.

An inspection of the more than 200 cases in which defendants' eucharistic beliefs were judged to be heretical reveals a number of parallels with the theological differences we have already encountered in Wycliffite texts. For reasons ranging from conviction to confusion and simply incomprehension, heresy defendants articulated a spectrum of views about the sacrament. Nevertheless, whereas Wyclif's eucharistic theology has been studied at length, few scholars have turned their attention to the opinions of later dissenters. Only two studies have focused exclusively on English dissenters' ideas about the eucharist. In her 1991 article 'The mouse and the pyx', Hudson surveyed a number of extant heresy cases; more recently, David Aers has described the eucharistic theologies of Walter Brut and William

Thorpe, calling for further studies of individual Wycliffites and their opinions on particular theological topics.[100]

Since Aers has provided an accurate and sensitive account of Brut's and Thorpe's eucharistic views, it seems unnecessary to do more here than to call to mind their most salient features. As Aers has noted, Brut's theology of the sacrament had its source in liturgical rather than philosophical questions. To receive the sacrament, for Brut, is more important than to consecrate it, for it is the act of reception that most closely recalls the Last Supper and anticipates the eternal feast of heaven.[101] Brut did nevertheless address the metaphysics of the eucharist, concluding that the gospels do not require a materialist view of the sacrament like that enshrined in transubstantiation. He maintained that whilst the physical host is consumed carnally, the true body of Christ is eaten spiritually through faith.[102]

The emphases of Brut's theology of the sacrament stand in contrast to the eucharistic views of his intellectual descendant Thorpe, who almost alone among English dissenters penned an account of his examination, in Thorpe's case a conversation with archbishop Arundel.[103] Hudson has set out the striking evidence in favour of the historicity of Thorpe's text, which circulated in at least three medieval manuscripts and was first printed in 1530 along with the examination of Sir John Oldcastle.[104] Though Thorpe may have caricatured Arundel's discomfort in the face of heterodox opinions, it seems reasonable that his account fairly accurately reflects the questions that he and other dissenters would have been asked at trial. According to Thorpe, Arundel was most interested in the eucharist, images, pilgrimage, ecclesiastical temporalities, and oath-taking. Thorpe himself raised two further issues: 'those of the nature of the Church, and hence the claims of the contemporary hierarchy to authority, and the prime obligation of the priest to preach even without licence'.[105] Thorpe, like Wyclif, understood the church to be the

---

[100] Hudson, 'The mouse in the pyx'; Aers, *Sanctifying Signs*, ch. 4.

[101] Aers, *Sanctifying Signs*, 73–4. The original record of Brut's trial is Hereford reg. Trefnant, 278–365.

[102] Hereford reg. Trefnant, 279; Aers, *Sanctifying Signs*, 77; see also *PR*, 284 n. 33. On the gaps in the records of Brut's trial, and that of his fellow Herefordshire dissenter William Swinderby, see Anne Hudson, 'The problems of scribes: The trial records of William Swinderby and Walter Brut', *Nottingham Medieval Studies*, 49 (2005), 80–104.

[103] The only other dissenter known to have produced an autobiographical account of his trial is Richard Wyche, who appears later in this chapter.

[104] *The Testimony of William Thorpe*, in Anne Hudson (ed.), *Two Wycliffite Texts* (EETS o.s. 301, 1993), xlvii–lii: 'On almost every issue where Thorpe can be checked . . . he can be shown to be reasonably reliable.' On Thorpe, see further John Fines, 'William Thorpe: An early Lollard', *History Today*, 18 (1968), 495–503.

[105] Anne Hudson, 'William Thorpe and the question of authority' in G. R. Evans (ed.), *Christian Authority: Essays in honour of Henry Chadwick* (Oxford, 1988), 127–37 at 131.

congregation of the predestined; accordingly, he argued, he would submit to the correction only of those whom he knew to be members of God's true church. His responses to the archbishop's questions about the eucharist were thus subsidiary to a broader concern about the proper exercise of ecclesiastical authority.[106] He argued that the gospels do not require Christians to believe anything about the eucharist more complex than what Christ himself taught:

I bileue þat þe niȝt bifore þat Crist Iesu wolde suffire wilfulli passioun for mankynde on þe morwe, after hee took breed in his holi and worschipful hondis and, 'liftynge vp his iȝen he dide þankynges to God his fadir, and blessid breed and brake it, and he ȝaf to hise dissciplis, seiinge to hem 'Takiþ þis and etiþ of þis alle; þis is my bodi.' And þat þis is and owiþ to be alle mennes bileue, as Mathew, Mark, Luk and Poul witnessen. Oþir bileue, ser, siþ I bileue þat þis suffisiþ in þis mater, haue I noon, neiþir wole haue ne teche.[107]

Pressed by Arundel as to whether the eucharist remains bread in its substance, Thorpe argued that the language of substance was unbiblical. When the archbishop forced him to give a clearer answer, he proceeded to cite Paul, Augustine, the canon of the mass, and the obscure church father Fulgentius in support of his claims that the consecrated host should be called bread and that the eucharist contains more than a single substance.[108] For the host to contain only the substance of Christ's body, Thorpe insisted, would be for it to be an accident without a subject, a belief that Thorpe dismisses as unnecessary: 'I dar neiþer denye it ne graunt it, for it is scole-mater aboute whiche I neuer bisied me for to knowe.'[109] Throughout his testimony, Thorpe's reverence for the eucharist remained unequivocal, but it is clear that he articulated a theology according to which if the consecrated host is indeed the body of Christ, it also retains the substance of bread.[110]

How closely did Brut's and Thorpe's views resemble those of other suspects? On 31 October 1389, just months before Brut stood trial in Hereford diocese, Archbishop William Courtenay visited the town of Leicester and heard accusations against nine of its citizens, among them a priest and a married couple. Heading the schedule of beliefs they were accused of holding was a proposition about the eucharist: that in the sacrament of the

---

[106] Aers, *Sanctifying Signs*, 88. In this way, Thorpe's testimony resembles the *Tractatus de oblacione iugis sacrificii*, whose author, as we have seen, cites the eucharist in his polemic against the perceived illegitimacy of ecclesiastical authority.

[107] *Testimony of William Thorpe*, 53/958–66.

[108] Ibid., 54/999–1014.

[109] Ibid., 55/1030–1.

[110] Aers, *Sanctifying Signs*, 84. On Thorpe, see further David Aers and Lynn Staley, *The Powers of the Holy: Religion, politics, and gender in late medieval English culture* (University Park, Pa., 1996), 52.

altar the body of Christ exists after the words of consecration alongside the material bread.[111] Excommunicating his defendants *in absentia* on the testimony of five priests and three burghers, Courtenay also interdicted the performance of divine services in any church of the town as well as any neighbouring monastery the heretics might enter.[112] Four of the defendants, the priest Richard Waystache, William Smyth, Roger Dexter, and Dexter's wife Alice, submitted to the archbishop in Dorchester on 17 November, where he assigned them penances and lifted the interdict.[113] The other five suspects remained at large, and the next episcopal visitation of the town, that of Philip Repingdon in 1413, found that dissenting feelings remained strong.[114]

In the same year that Courtenay visited Leicester, Bishop John Waltham of Salisbury brought to trial perhaps the only English heresy suspect accused of having celebrated a form of the mass altered in accordance with Wycliffite doctrines. In addition to other articles about tithes, confession, clerical marriage, images, and the papacy, William Ramsbury was charged with having accepted ordination from one Thomas Fishbourn and with having subsequently presided over unlicensed and heterodox liturgies. In particular, Ramsbury was said to have omitted the prayers of consecration, though he retained the elevation of the host and chalice. Hudson has quite rightly noted that, whilst Ramsbury's liturgical innovations were controversial, 'the use of the established liturgy, albeit abbreviated, for this mass goes some way to explain how Lollards could often survive for a long time unsuspected by their orthodox fellows'.[115] Ramsbury abjured his opinions on 3 July 1389, and Waltham required him to renounce his heresies in Salisbury cathedral and, on three successive days, to prostrate himself beside the altar from the time of the elevation until the communion.

The beliefs and practices of few other early lollards are recorded in equal detail. The peripatetic preacher William Swinderby was recorded by the chronicler Henry Knighton as having taught that priests who live against God's commandments are not priests at all and commit idolatry when they attempt to consecrate the eucharist.[116] For three of Wyclif's closest associates, Nicholas Hereford, Philip Repingdon, and John Aston, we have only short vernacular confessions in which they affirm transubstantiation but do not

---

[111] Wilkins, iii.208; see also Walsingham, *Historia anglicana*, ii.53–4.
[112] Dahmus, *Visitations*, 48.
[113] Crompton, 'Leicestershire Lollards', 24.
[114] Ibid., 26.
[115] Hudson, 'Lollard Mass', 118.
[116] Knighton, *Chronicle*, 315–23.

repudiate any specific doctrines.[117] Among Wyclif's other disciples, John Purvey seems best to have understood his master's theology of the sacrament. In 1400, he abjured a complexly worded article on the eucharist that cannot but have its roots in Wyclif's thought: 'that in the sacrament of the altar after its consecration there cannot be an accident without its subject, but there truly remains there the same substance and nature of the bread, visible and corruptible, and similarly the same substance of the wine, that were put on the altar before the consecration to be consecrated by the ministry of the priest'.[118] Purvey also maintained that the mass, as his contemporaries celebrated it, was a human and not an evangelical tradition, and he argued that priests would do better to neglect the mass than to neglect preaching.[119]

Three notable cases were heard nearly contemporaneously with Purvey's. Sometime before 27 July 1400, a man named John Seynon came to the attention of authorities in Lincoln diocese. His case was soon transferred to the provincial convocation of Canterbury, where his abjuration and penance were recorded in the register of Archbishop Arundel. He confessed that he had taught that the eucharist was instituted in Christ's memory and that, accordingly, it is only a figure of Christ's body and blood.[120] The convocation that heard Seynon's case also heard that of William Sawtre, the priest who later became the first English dissenter to be burned for his beliefs. Sawtre at first 'attempted to equivocate ... on all three questions put to him on the eucharist; after some time for reflection he still claimed he did not know, later that he would stand by the determination of the church "ubi talis determinatio non esset divinae voluntati contraria [where such determination is not contrary to the divine will]," and only finally was brought to admit that after the consecration, in his view, bread, and the same bread, remained'.[121]

---

[117] Knighton, *Chronicle*, 277–81. Nevertheless, that Hereford, Repingdon, and Aston all abjured *in English* is itself testament to the importance of the vernacular in early English dissent. See Margaret Aston, 'Wyclif and the vernacular' in Anne Hudson and Michael Hudson (eds.), *From Ockham to Wyclif* (Studies in Church History, Subsidia 5, Oxford, 1987), 281–330.

[118] Wilkins, iii.260: 'Quod in sacramento altaris post sui consecrationem non est nec esse potest accidens aliquod sine subjecto; sed ibi remanet veraciter eadem substantia, et natura panis, visibilis et corruptibilis, et idem vinum similiter, quae ante consecrationem in altari ponuntur, sacerdotis ministerio consecranda.' He also abjured a second eucharistic article, that Innocent III and the bishops of the Fourth Lateran Council were 'haeretici et blasphemi, ac seductores populi christiani' for teaching that in the eucharist accidents can exist without their subject.

[119] Knighton, *Chronicle*, 291–3.

[120] Lambeth reg. Arundel, fol. 411v. Maureen Jurkowski shrewdly points out to me that Seynon was most likely not 'a real name, but a sobriquet applied because he said "no" a lot (i.e., denied transubstantiation, the worship of the crucifix, etc.)', personal communication, 14 July 2008.

[121] *PR*, 284, quoting *FZ*, 411.

A third trial from the early years of the fifteenth century was that of Richard Wyche, who recanted before Bishop Walter Skirlaw of Durham in 1401 or 1402. Though his formal recantation includes fourteen condemned articles, none of them concern the eucharist.[122] The sacrament apparently did, however, occupy a substantial part of his examination before Skirlaw and his inquisitors, as a letter Wyche wrote shortly after the trial to an unknown 'reverende domine et frater' suggests. Asked repeatedly whether he believed that material bread remains after the words of consecration, Wyche said he maintained that Christ had called the host his body and that that no further belief is required of a Christian.[123] Scripture does not use the term 'material bread', and hence to introduce such a term is unnecessary. Wyche did give his inquisitors more ground for suspicion when he described the host as the body of Christ in the form of bread; according to the archdeacon who apparently was in charge of his examination, the correct formula was rather that the host is the body of Christ under the *species* of bread.[124] Though he did not state it explicitly, he seems to have taken the position, not unlike Wyclif's, that the material bread and the spiritual presence of Christ together comprise the sacrament.

Such a belief in the remanence of the elements was deadly for John Badby, the first victim, in 1410, of the statute *De heretico comburendo*.[125] Indeed, remanence was the form of eucharistic heterodoxy most frequently abjured in pre-Reformation England, with defendants from London, Ely, Norwich, Lincoln, Canterbury, and Coventry and Lichfield dioceses all confessing to having held the belief that the substances of bread and wine remain after the consecration.[126] Among the most infamous of these suspects was Sir John Oldcastle, whose examination before Arundel and a host of ecclesiastical worthies was preserved in *Fasciculi zizaniorum* and published, with interpolations from other sources, in 1530.[127] Fortunately so: the formal record of Oldcastle's abjuration, which also appears in *Fasciculi zizaniorum*, does not

[122] *FZ*, 501–5.

[123] Matthew, 'The trial of Richard Wyche', *English Historical Review*, 5 (1890), 530–44 at 532, 539; von Nolcken, 'Richard Wyche, a certain knight, and the beginning of the end' in *Lollardy and the Gentry*, 133.

[124] Matthew, 'The trial of Richard Wyche', 532.

[125] *A&M*, 621.

[126] It was also the form of eucharistic heterodoxy imputed to John Claydon, the London currier burned in 1415 for possessing the dissenting text *The Lanterne of Liȝt*. Despite the fact that the *Lanterne* itself does not comment on the metaphysics of the eucharist, it was judged before Claydon's trial to contain the view, as Foxe recounted it, 'that after consecration of bread and wine . . . the same bread and wine that was before, doth truly remain on the altar' (quoted in *Lanterne*, x).

[127] On the printed work, see Hudson, 'No Newe Thyng', 244–5.

include any specific articles on the eucharist or other theological topics.[128] In the *Fasciculi,* as in the early modern print, Oldcastle was repeatedly asked whether material bread and wine remain on the altar after the words of consecration. According to the printed version, Oldcastle responded three times that 'the moste blessed sacrament of the altare is very Christes body in forme of bread', but when pressed, he ultimately admitted that 'yt is Christes body and breade'. Asked specifically about the material presence of bread and wine, he averred that 'the gospell spekith not of the terme materiall'.[129] In the *Fasciculi,* Oldcastle's response is more complex but nevertheless can still be called a doctrine of remanence: 'just as Christ had in him divinity and humanity when he lived on earth...so also in the sacrament of the altar there is true body and true bread; that is to say, bread which we see, and the body of Christ hidden under it, which we do not see'.[130]

In many other cases, however, it must remain unclear whether suspects believed that the material bread and wine coexist alongside the spiritual presence of Christ. Belief in a spiritual or sacramental presence is entirely compatible with the continued existence of the original substance of the elements, but so also is the figurative view of the eucharist we have found, for instance, in *Wycklyffes Wycket.* Many of the formulae employed in the extant depositions and abjurations can be construed either way; thus, John Wardon of Loddon's confession that he had believed that after the words of consecration there remains 'panis purus et materialis' cannot provide definitive answers about his eucharistic theology.[131] Similar phrases appear in the abjurations of several of his fellows also cited for heresy in bishop Alnwick's investigations in Norwich diocese in 1428–31. Neither Wardon nor his contemporaries spoke Latin, and hence the documentary remains of their trials remain open to scribal corruption. They nevertheless all appear to have believed that the original elements remain after the consecration. Margery Baxter was said to have described the bread as 'tantum panis materialis'; John Skylly's vernacular abjuration uses the words 'pure material bred'; and John Godesell called it 'purus panis materialis', as did John Spyr.[132]

As Margaret Aston has noted, these and other phrases likely have their origin in the teachings of the itinerant evangelist William White, who first

---

[128]   *FZ,* 414–16.
[129]   *The examinacion of Master William Thorpe...* [with] *The examinacion of...syr Jhon Oldcastell* (Antwerp, 1530), n.p.
[130]   *FZ,* 443–4: 'sicut Christus hic in terra degens habuit in se divinitatem et humanitatem... sic in sacramento altaris est verum corpus et verus panis; panis videlicet quem videmus, et corpus Christi sub eodem velatum, quod non videmus'.
[131]   *Norwich,* 33.
[132]   Ibid., 41–64, 202–4.

abjured heresy in Canterbury diocese, then moved to Norwich, was tried again on 13 September 1428, and was executed soon thereafter.[133] At his trial in 1428, he was confronted with the evidence of his previous abjuration, in which he had confessed to teaching that 'in the sacrament of the eucharistic there remains material bread after its consecration on the altar; nor does it cease to be material bread, but it is simultaneously the flesh of Christ and substantial bread'.[134] That stance seems remarkably similar to Wyclif's, but White's subsequent examination in Norwich suggests that his position may have changed. There, he again argued that Christ's words *Hoc est corpus meum* do not imply the annihilation of the material bread. He asserted that it is sufficient for a good Christian to believe that the sacrament is the body of Christ 'in memoria' and bread in its nature.[135] The precise meaning of the phrase *in memoria* remains unclear; it may imply a figurative theology of the sacrament and hence that White had ceased believing that the sacrament is in any substantial way the body of Christ, or it may simply have been that White's original inquisitors in Canterbury diocese had not fully understood his position. In either case, none of the Norwich suspects who may have been White's disciples approached the sophistication of his eucharistic beliefs. Though some produced idiosyncratic views on the sacrament, none explicitly described it as figurative. In 1429, the skinner William Colyn said that he would rather touch a woman's genitals than the host, and in 1431 Nicholas Canon of Eye reasoned that if the sacrament is indeed Christ's flesh, then priests who consume the host on Fridays are committing a sin.[136]

Many later defendants also argued that the original substances of bread and wine persist after the consecration. On 27 May 1457, the brothers William and Richard Sparke of Somersham appeared before Bishop John Chedworth of Lincoln and confessed their belief that the host remains true bread.[137] In 1461, James Wyllis of Lincoln diocese insisted that the substance of the bread remained, as did two other suspects, William Stevyne and John Baron, tried by Bishop Chedworth in 1467.[138] The London suspect Thomas Wassyngborn

---

[133] Margaret Aston, 'William White's Lollard followers', 91–2, traces what Aston calls the adulteration of sophisticated eucharistic views in the Norwich trials. The date of White's trial appears in *FZ*, 417.

[134] *FZ*, 418: 'in sacramento eucharistiae manet substantia panis, post ejus completam consecrationem in altari, nec desinit esse panis materialis, sed est simul caro Christi, et panis in substantia'.

[135] Ibid., 424.

[136] *Norwich*, 89–92; *A&M*, 789.

[137] Lincoln reg. Chedworth, fols. 12v–14.

[138] Ibid., fols. 57v–58v, 62v.

articulated a similar view of the sacrament in 1482.[139] Belief in remanence remained popular among defendants into the sixteenth century, when Archbishop William Warham of Canterbury and his inquisitors included it in the formulaic abjurations that over forty defendants signed in the years 1511 and 1512. We shall see that at least one of Warham's suspects also spoke of the eucharist in figurative terms, but it is worth noting that the majority of defendants for whose trials the depositions of witnesses are preserved in the archbishop's register simply maintained that the sacrament is 'not Crists very body, flesshe and bloode, but oonly materiall bred, affermyng that God made man but man cowde not make Gode'.[140]

This rejoinder is typical of what Hudson has called the eucharistic 'pragmatism' of many lollards.[141] The quip that priests cannot make their maker appears in approximately a dozen trials from 1429 to 1514.[142] At least one other suspect raised the classic problem of whether a mouse which finds its way into a pyx eats God's body; another enquired into the fate of Christ's body after it has finished making its way through the digestive system of the communicant; another observed that the orthodox doctrine of the eucharist implies that over 20,000 gods are made in England every year; and several others joked that it would be possible to buy several dozen gods for half a penny.[143] A more idiosyncratic claim appears in the trial of the Pembrokeshire knight Sir Roger Burley, who around 1487 asserted that he himself could consecrate the host.[144] Burley's is the first Welsh case we have encountered, a fact that may owe less to the religious quiescence of the principality than to the scarcity of its records.[145] It is important to note that he was accused only of appropriating to himself the powers of the priesthood and not of having

---

[139] William Hale (ed.), *A Series of Precedents and Proceedings in Criminal Causes from 1475 to 1640, extracted from the Act-Books of Ecclesiastical Courts in the Diocese of London* (London, 1847), nos. 34–35.

[140] *Kent*, 65; see also the cases of William Olberd and Robert Reignold, 66–7; Christopher Grebill, 27–8; and John Browne, 43–9.

[141] Hudson, 'The mouse in the pyx', 43.

[142] The defendants were John Kynget (*Norwich*, 79–84, in 1429), William Wakeham (Salisbury reg. Nevill, fols. 52–52v, 57v, in 1437), William Apleward and Robert Spycer (Lincoln reg. Chedworth, fol. 61–61v, in 1467), Margery Goyte (*Coventry*, 87–94, in 1488), Richard Petesyne *alias* Sawyer (Winchester reg. Courtenay, fols. 26r–27r, in 1490), Thomas Boughton (Salisbury reg. Blythe, fols. 74–5, in 1499), Robert Silkby (*Coventry*, 102–4, 108–9, 146–50, 205–6, 283–5, in a series of hearings from 1511–22), and Margery Swayne *alias* Bernard (Salisbury reg. Audley, fols. 155v–156, in 1514).

[143] See Hudson, 'The mouse in the pyx', 43–8, for a full inventory of such beliefs.

[144] R. A. Roberts and R. F. Isaacson (eds.), *The Episcopal Registers of the Diocese of St David's, 1397 to 1518*, 3 vols. (Cymmrodorion Record Series 6, 1917–20), ii.479.

[145] No bishops' registers or other heresy material are extant for Llandaff and St Asaph's dioceses, and only a few such volumes survive from St David's.

denied the doctrine of transubstantiation. Any such denial, had it been made, would surely have been recorded, and hence it seems safe to think of Burley as an isolated malcontent.

To return closer to the mainstream, another discernible strain of dissenting eucharistic belief can be found alongside the theology of remanence. We have already encountered the figurative doctrines of *Wycklyffes Wycket* and the early heresy suspect John Seynon, but it is important to note that a number of defendants were accused of subscribing to figurative or commemorative positions on the sacrament in the late fifteenth and early sixteenth centuries. John Qwyrk, tried in Lincoln diocese in 1463, was the first dissenter in that period to describe the sacrament as a memorial.[146] No other fifteenth-century defendants in Lincoln diocese articulated such a theology of the eucharist, and hence it is especially unlikely that Qwyrk's inquisitors fabricated the beliefs he abjured on 30 March. His views gained greater currency in subsequent decades, especially in Salisbury and Winchester dioceses. In 1491, John Tanner of Steventon, in Salisbury diocese, described the eucharist as a sign of Christ's passion.[147] John Godson, tried in 1499, said that the sacrament was 'not the body of cryste, but preestys offer vp the said sacrament oonly in the comemoracon of the passion of cryste'.[148] A number of Godson's near-contemporaries may have held similar views. In 1507, John Benet junior testified that he had believed that the eucharist is 'not verey goddes body ... but the wordis that the prist speketh in tyme of consecracon be verey good and holy', a statement which may indicate the persistence of figurative or commemorative views in Salisbury diocese.[149]

Similar opinions cropped up in sixteenth-century Winchester diocese. Joan Haddam *alias* Brede of St Olave's parish in Southwark testified in January 1508 that the eucharist signifies God's presence but is 'not very god'. She added, 'and I wold dye in the same quarrel'.[150] Haddam abjured and received her penance, but other Winchester defendants articulated the same view. In the next heresy case to appear in Bishop Richard Fox's register, Thomas Denys, who some two decades earlier had been tried for heresy in the diocese of London, was accused of teaching 'that the sacrament of thaltar in fourme of brede was not the veray body of criste but a comemoration of cristis passion and cristes body in a figure and not the veray body'.[151] Denys was allowed to abjure, though subsequent entries in Fox's register make it clear that he was

---

[146] Lincoln reg. Chedworth, fols. 59v–60.
[147] Salisbury reg. Langton, 81–2.
[148] Ibid., Blythe, fols. 77–77v.
[149] Ibid., Audley, fols. 147v–148r.
[150] Winchester reg. Fox, iii, fols. 87–87v.
[151] Ibid., Fox, iii, fols. 69–70.

among the most prominent dissenters in the local community. He appears in the records of the trials of Philip Braban, Margery Jopson, and John Jenyn *alias* Broderer, to the last of whom, as we saw in Chapter 1, he was accused of delivering 'a boke called Wiclif'.[152] If this book is indeed *Wycklyffes Wycket*, as is likely, then the text was quite possibly the source of Denys' figurative view of the eucharist. It may also have informed the beliefs of Braban, Thomas and Anne Wattys, Laurence and Elisabeth Swaffer, William and Alice Wickham *alias* Bruar, and Robert Winter, all of whom abjured the belief that the host is a figure of Christ's body.[153]

Some suspects detected in the purge of Coventry and Lichfield diocese in 1511–12 also articulated figurative theologies. One of them, John Blumston *alias* Phisicion, was said by his neighbour and disciple Thomas Banbrooke to have believed that the eucharist was 'not the very body of our Lord but a figure'.[154] In addition to Banbrooke, Blumston's nephew, John Bull, testified that his uncle had taught him the same thing.[155] This might appear to be merely the case of a belief being transmitted along family lines, but a third suspect, Agnes Corby, also confessed that the eucharist was a memorial of Christ's passion.[156] In none of these cases was the *Wycket* implicated, nor was it mentioned among the books confiscated from any defendant in Coventry and Lichfield diocese in the early sixteenth century.

Isolated figurative views of the sacrament were still being discovered through the outbreak of Luther's reformation. Alone among the suspects examined by Archbishop Warham in Canterbury diocese, Edward Walker of Maidstone, executed in 1511, was said by his fellow dissenter Robert Reignold to have argued that the eucharist is 'a thing made in mynde and for the remembraunce of Criste for the people'.[157] Christ's body, Walker believed, remains always in heaven. In nearby London diocese, Bishop Fitzjames' heresy court book is no longer extant, but John Foxe reported that both William Sweeting (tried 1511) and Christopher Shoemaker (tried 1518) believed the eucharist to be a memorial or a figure 'bearing the remembrance of Christ'.[158]

---

[152] Winchester reg. Fox, iii, fol. 70v.
[153] Ibid., Fox, iii.70v–76v. *Wycklyffes Wycket* reappeared at the very end of our period, when the Lincoln diocese suspect Richard Colins of Ginge, whose servant Philip Braban had become sometime between 1512 and 1521, admitted to having read it (*A&M*, 958). Both Colins and Braban were detected to Bishop Longland by John Edmunds, whose eucharistic views were also of the commemorative variety. See *A&M*, 960; McSheffrey, 'Heresy, orthodoxy'; and my article '*Wycklyffes Wycket*'.
[154] *Coventry*, 195–6.   [155] Ibid., 215–16.   [156] Ibid., 234–7.
[157] *Kent*, 53.   [158] *A&M*, 929, 944–5.

CONCLUSIONS

The extant records of English heresy trials thus confirm what we have already discovered about Wycliffite texts: that dissenters approached the eucharist from a variety of sometimes conflicting vantage points. Though almost every suspect we have encountered denied the doctrine of transubstantiation as it was understood by the institutional church, dissenters did not express nearly so unanimous a view as to what happened instead at the words of consecration. Some spoke of Christ's spiritual presence alongside the material substance of the bread; others described the sacrament in figurative terms. It seems clear that Wyclif endorsed the former point of view; his doctrine of Christ's spiritual presence in the consecrated bread and wine is more than figurative. But it is not beyond the pale of credibility to think that some dissenters may have misunderstood Wyclif's nuanced use of the terms sacramental and virtual presence. Other advocates of figurative theologies may not have been aware of Wyclif's ideas at all, instead drawing their inspiration from apocryphal texts like *Wycklyffes Wycket.*

Students of Wycliffism and lollardy have long been aware of the shades of eucharistic opinion to be found in dissenting texts and trial records. It has become commonplace to acknowledge that figurative interpretations of the sacrament appeared in the late fifteenth and early sixteenth centuries, but the evidence seems to suggest that such views were current even in the 1380s. Several sermons of the long vernacular cycle describe the eucharist in the same terms as biblical parables and encourage their hearers to receive the host in memory of Christ. The trial in 1400 of John Seynon in Lincoln diocese revealed that figurative views had penetrated into the lay as well as the clerical consciousness by the turn of the fifteenth century.

To describe the evolution of dissenting eucharistic theology in terms of a unidirectional shift from the doctrine of remanence to that of figuration is, therefore, to oversimplify. Whilst it cannot be doubted that a greater number of dissenters in the years after 1450 spoke of the eucharist in figurative or commemorative terms, what may also have changed were inquisitors' attitudes toward heresy suspects and their beliefs. With the important exception of the anathemas of the Council of Constance, few sets of condemned doctrines included the figurative views articulated by Seynon and a host of later defendants; both Roger Dymmok and Nicholas Love trained their polemical fire on the notion of remanence; and the inquisitorial questionnaire of Bishop Thomas Polton likewise focused on the issue of the persistence of the bread and wine. With bishops and their associates concentrating elsewhere, figurative theologies were more likely to have escaped detection in the late fourteenth and early fifteenth centuries.

Whether suspects became more likely to hold figurative views or whether inquisitors became more likely to notice them, or both, it remains significant that figurative doctrines of the eucharist were concentrated in a few geographical areas. Heresy hunters in Salisbury, Winchester, and Coventry and Lichfield dioceses seem to have encountered more proponents of figurative views than their counterparts in Norwich and Lincoln dioceses. Such a disparity may again have something to do with the theological acumen of the inquisitors concerned, but it is far more likely that particular sets of theological views were perpetuated within individual communities. That the Winchester dissenter Thomas Denys shared a copy of *Wycklyffes Wycket* with several of his neighbours can begin to account for their views, as can the family relationship between the Coventry suspects John Blumston and his nephew John Bull. The limitations of the evidence make such connections difficult to trace in many cases, but it is through further prosopographical research that historians and theologians will better be able to explain the transmission of dissenting views within and across networks of family, trade, and local community.

It must be acknowledged that our study of dissenting eucharistic theology has said little or nothing about eucharistic piety. Like much else about lollard religious culture, the reasons that individual men and women found condemned ideas about the eucharist appealing are in many ways lost to us. The (admittedly slim) evidence for the celebration of the mass in dissenting circles does to some extent confirm the hypothesis that Lollards retained respect for the celebration of the eucharistic liturgy even as they described its effects in terms not at all like those employed by their orthodox counterparts.[159] Careful studies of Wycliffite writings will likely be able to tease out some sense of the spirituality favoured by the suspects whose depositions and abjurations are, understandably in the circumstances, often all too wooden.[160]

Until then, however, lollard texts and trial records can disclose that the eucharistic beliefs of the men and women who broke from the ecclesiastical consensus of late medieval England were as diverse as the suspects themselves. It has admittedly been somewhat artificial to describe the more than 200 defendants who confessed to eucharistic heterodoxy in terms either of remanence or figuration, but even that facile binary has helped to reveal the many

---

[159] Hudson, 'A Lollard Mass', 116–19.

[160] Fiona Somerset has been engaged in groundbreaking studies of lollard spirituality: see her preliminary findings in 'Wycliffite spirituality' in *Text and Controversy*, 375–86. I am grateful to have had the opportunity to discuss this research with her.

shades of dissenting opinion. Lollards did and did not believe that the eucharistic elements contained the spiritual presence of Christ; they did and did not believe that the eucharistic liturgy was primarily a commemoration of the Last Supper; and they did and did not condemn the mass as an entirely human invention. What they believed had much to do with when and where they lived, what they read, and especially whom they knew. Dissenters, in short, were human beings bound by the circumstances of time, place, and society. It cannot be surprising that they failed to reach consensus on the central ritual of late medieval religion.

4

Lay Marriage and Clerical Celibacy

We have already encountered John Longland, the Bishop of Lincoln whose anti-heresy initiatives in the early 1520s turned up more than a hundred defendants, including a clutch of suspects familiar with the Epistle of St James.[1] One of them was an Amersham woman named Agnes Wellis, who had come to Longland's attention through the testimony of her brother, Richard Bartlet.[2] Agnes and Richard were members of an extended family of dissenters: their father; their siblings, Robert and Isabel Bartlet; and Isabel's unnamed husband were all implicated in heresy by Longland's inquisitors. Forced under oath to name their sympathizers, Agnes and her relatives were also asked a series of questions about their beliefs and religious practices. Had they conversed with anyone suspected of heresy? Had they attended the 'readings' of a heretic? Had they appeared on charges of heresy before Longland's predecessor, William Smith?[3]

The list of enquiries put to Agnes Wellis was among the most extensive of the questionnaires preserved in Longland's court book, perhaps because the bishop and his assistants thought that a woman would be less able than a man to keep the secrets of her sect. Agnes was asked about her relationships with four prominent local dissenters, about her attendance at secret gatherings, and about her views on the sacrament of the altar and the adoration of images. Alongside these familiar staples, however, appears another query: 'whether she knew that those of the sect only married each other?'[4] Her reply does not survive, and her husband John Wellis was never summoned before a heresy tribunal, but the question is striking nonetheless. Not only does it suggest a concern on the part of her inquisitors that heterodox views could circulate through the ties of kinship and marriage, but it also prompts us to investigate a largely unexplored dimension of dissenting belief. What did late medieval English heresy suspects think about marriage and sexuality, both for laypeople and for clerics? And did their views change over time?

Scholarship on Wycliffite and lollard attitudes toward marriage and sexuality is scarce indeed. There are only two articles dedicated to the

---

[1] See Ch. 2 above. [2] *A&M*, 947. [3] Ibid., 946. [4] Ibid., 948.

topic, of which the first, published in 1973, was unable to make reference to a number of Wycliffite and anti-Wycliffite texts which have since come to light.[5] Brief sections on marriage do appear in a number of more recent studies, but most discussions have tended to concentrate on the issue of clerical celibacy, likely because dissenting views on the marriage of priests and nuns have been thought to anticipate those of sixteenth-century refor-mers.[6] Alcuin Blamires rightly suggested in 1989 that 'further research is needed to determine whether the movement developed a consistent doctrine on sexuality', but the problem is not merely one of scholarly awareness.[7] Medieval and early modern sources only rarely make sexuality a primary concern. As I hope to demonstrate in this chapter, the situation is not therefore hopeless, but it is true that discussions of sexuality and lay and clerical marriage were for dissenters and their antagonists often incidental to broader theological arguments.

A more substantial body of work, however, has been produced in the related sphere of lollardy and gender. In 1978 and 1980, respectively, Claire Cross and Margaret Aston published groundbreaking articles on the role of women in dissenting communities. They both argued, with some success at the time, that English dissenters, 'like Cathars and Waldensians, derived a large measure of support from members of the female sex. In the fourteenth and fifteenth centuries, as earlier, unorthodoxy offered women outlets for religious activity that were not to be found in the established church.'[8] Cross focused on the ways in which women disseminated their views by circulating Wycliffite texts, hosting gatherings of dissenters, and learning portions of the Bible for later recitation in public. Aston, on the other hand, concentrated on the claims advanced among some dissenters that women were capable of exercising the powers of priesthood.[9]

Attractive though it may be to think of lollards as equal-opportunity dissenters, the suggestion that heresy provided an alternative context for female religiosity in late medieval England has largely been discredited. In 1995, Shannon McSheffrey forcefully argued that 'gender was a crucially

[5] Henry Hargreaves, 'Sir John Oldcastle and Wycliffite views on clerical marriage', *Medium Aevum*, 42 (1973), 141–6; and Dyan Elliott, 'Lollardy and the integrity of marriage and the family' in Sherry Roush and Cristelle L. Baskins (eds.), *The Medieval Marriage Scene: Prudence, passion, policy* (Tempe, Ariz., 2005), 37–53.

[6] Thus *PR*, 292, 357–8; McSheffrey, *Gender and Heresy*, 149, 81–6.

[7] Alcuin Blamires, 'The Wife of Bath and Lollardy', *Medium Aevum*, 58 (1989), 224–42 at 232.

[8] Claire Cross, ' "Great reasoners in Scripture": The activities of women Lollards 1380–1530', in Derek Baker (ed.), *Medieval Women* (Studies in Church History, Subsidia 1, 1978), 358–80, and Margaret Aston, 'Lollard women priests?', repr. in *Lollards and Reformers*, 49–70 at 49.

[9] Aston, 'Lollard women priests?', 59–60.

important variable in participation in a heterodox movement—but not necessarily in the direction often assumed . . . Heterodoxy did not mean gender equality: challenges to orthodoxy did not lead inexorably to questioning of patriarchal social categories.'[10] Although several women, especially widows of substantial wealth and social status, did play important roles in individual dissenting communities, McSheffrey observed, most such groups tended to be dominated by men. At the same time, Wycliffite texts reinforced prevailing medieval notions about the proper structure of relationships between men and women, husbands and wives, and parents and children. 'Since Lollardy recognized no other roles for women than as wives and mothers, it removed the possibility that at least some orthodox women had of living outside the structures of the patriarchal family.'[11]

Whilst McSheffrey's conclusions have generally been accepted by scholars of late medieval dissent, they have also raised further questions.[12] Fiona Somerset has suggested that the nature of the extant sources has worked to occlude women's participation in dissenting communities: misogynist prosecutors may have assumed that women existed only at the margins of heretical groups; male dissenters may have underestimated the contributions of their wives, sisters, and daughters; and no Wycliffite text can conclusively be said to have been written by a woman.[13] Indeed, even the eye-catching claim of the early heresy defendant Walter Brut that women may be ordained to the priesthood was a statement neither of fact nor of aspiration. As Somerset has shown, Brut intended simply to acknowledge that women *can* be priests without endorsing the idea that they *should* be ordained.[14] At the same time, Margaret Aston has revised her earlier, optimistic claims about women's

---

[10] McSheffrey, *Gender and Heresy*, 2.

[11] Ibid., 81.

[12] Dyan Elliott's thoughtful article on the role of marriage and the family in lollard communities echoes McSheffrey's thesis (see n. 5 above). On Elliott's account, Wycliffite writers portrayed 'these intimate institutions as beleaguered and urgently in need of vigorous defence' from church courts, friars, and other ecclesiastics partly in order 'to undercut the orthodox coalition between women and the clergy' ('Lollardy and the integrity of marriage and the family', 38, 53).

[13] Fiona Somerset, '*Eciam Mulier*: Women in Lollardy and the problem of sources' in Linda Olson and Kathryn Kerby-Fulton (eds.), *Voices in Dialogue: Reading women in the Middle Ages* (Notre Dame, Ind., 2005), 245–60 at 247.

[14] Ibid., 248–56. Similar points are made by Alastair Minnis, "Respondet Walterus Bryth . . . ': Walter Brut in debate on women priests' in *Text and Controversy*, 229–49; and Aers, *Sanctifying Signs*, 81–2. Kathryn Kerby-Fulton, responding to Somerset's article, has suggested that Brut's ideas ought to be considered in the context not merely of English dissent but also of pan-European movements like the *Devotio Moderna* and the heresy of the Free Spirit ('*Eciam Lollardi*: Some further thoughts on Fiona Somerset's "*Eciam Mulier*: Women in Lollardy and the Problem of Sources"' in Linda Olson and Kathryn Kerby-Fulton (eds.), *Voices in Dialogue: Reading women in the Middle Ages* (Notre Dame, Ind., 2005), 261–8); see also her more recent *Books under Suspicion*.

participation in lollardy.[15] Both Somerset and Aston rely on arguments from the silence of the records, and though it is sensible to assume that some women influenced the shape of English dissent, it is often impossible to determine to what extent they did so.

At least one limitation of McSheffrey's work deserves additional attention. She has acknowledged that her analysis relies more on the records of heresy trials and other sorts of legal evidence than on the theological and polemical texts produced by Wycliffites and their clerical antagonists.[16] Texts of this second kind portray dissenters from the perspective of 'clerical males of considerable education' writing in an academic environment, but when read alongside the trial records, they can disclose essential clues to the theologies of sexuality and marriage with which late medieval dissenters were conversant. This notwithstanding, McSheffrey has provided an important description of the gender roles and power relationships that operated among English dissenters. Her thesis that 'Lollardy was made by, and in a sense for, men' offers a necessary corrective to earlier ideas about the connections between heresy and gender, and her study demonstrates that marriage and family life were important to the members of dissenting communities.[17] In particular, she has confirmed bishop Longland's suspicions that dissenters often married one another and that their weddings provided occasions for lollard gatherings. 'Fully half the women who were involved in Lollardy were married to other Lollards, suggesting that this was a critical element in recruitment of women to the movement.'[18]

In light of the considerable body of research into the roles that marriage and family played in the transmission of dissenting belief, it is odd that Wycliffite ideas about marriage and sexuality have rarely been examined. Questions about marriage—the circumstances in which and the partners between whom it is valid, the involvement of church courts in its regulation, and the boundaries of marital sexual activity—appear in the records of no fewer than seventy-four heresy trials between the years 1381 and 1521; they likewise figure in a number of vernacular texts written by dissenters and their opponents, some of which have hitherto escaped attention. In addition, marriage was not contested only among dissenting Christians, and any study of their attitudes must accordingly take into account the broader cultural context. Using all of these sources, then, this chapter will chronicle

---

[15] Margaret Aston, 'Lollard women' in Diana Wood (ed.), *Women and Religion in Medieval England* (Oxford, 2003), 166–85.
[16] McSheffrey, *Gender and Heresy*, 15.
[17] Ibid., 149.
[18] Ibid., 95–6.

the development of Wycliffite and lollard views about sexuality, starting in the time of John Wyclif and focusing on the closely related but nevertheless separate constellations of questions about lay and clerical marriage. Wyclif's Latin writings suggest that he professed caution about clerical marriage and also articulated a culturally traditional theology of lay marriage. Whereas his hesitation at the prospect of a married clergy gave way to enthusiasm among later dissenters, Wyclif's ideas about lay marriage resonated with heterodox and orthodox writers alike. What we shall find in vernacular Wycliffite tracts and trial records, therefore, shall call even further into doubt the view that lollardy was an innovative movement on issues of sexuality and gender.

MEDIEVAL MARRIAGE: THEOLOGY, LAW, AND PRACTICE

The theory and practice of marriage in the Middle Ages involved a series of interrelated yet distinct elements: the theological and philosophical under-pinnings provided by Christian and other ideas about sexuality, the economic and political consequences of marriage-making, the procedural requirements of the institutional church, and, perhaps most important, the extent to which clerics and laypeople were cognizant of these rules. Before it is possible to consider dissenting ideas about marriage, it will be important first to describe the theology of marriage that claimed the support of the medieval church.

There is not space here to reprise the development of beliefs and practices about marriage in the Christian West, but several points are particularly relevant. From the fourth and fifth centuries, Christian reflections about marriage assumed the shape of a debate about its status relative to celibacy, a debate which achieved something of a resolution, if not quite a synthesis, in the monumental writings of Augustine of Hippo, himself no stranger to sexual experience. In *De bono coniugali*, Augustine argued that marriage is 'the first natural union of human society'.[19] He identified three goods of marriage: *fides* (the fidelity of the partners to one another), *proles* (their offspring), and *sacramentum* (the inseparability of the union).[20] Nevertheless, Augustine warned that sexual intercourse between husbands and wives is almost invariably evil in practice; he therefore counselled married couples

---

[19] Augustine of Hippo, *De bono coniugali, c. 401. The Good of Marriage*, trans. C. T. Wilcox (Washington, DC, 1955), 1.1.

[20] Christopher N. L. Brooke, *The Medieval Idea of Marriage* (Oxford, 1994), 61.

to put aside sexual acts as quickly as possible.[21] He also argued that Christian marriages are indissoluble by virtue of the *sacramentum* created between the partners, even though spouses can be allowed to separate in the case of infidelity on the part of either husband or wife.[22] Augustine's teachings survived largely unchallenged into the medieval period: 'the plain fact is that whatever the political changes and chances of the Middle Ages, the Christian churches continued to teach the precepts hammered out in the patristic age with very little modification, and the legacy of Augustine remained dominant'.[23]

What did the medieval church require of marriages? From the middle of the twelfth century, canon law identified the exchange of consent in words of the present tense (*verba de presenti*), or else the exchange of consent in words of the future tense (*verba de futuro*) followed by intercourse, as the form of the sacrament of marriage.[24] Theologians, including Thomas Aquinas and Jean Gerson, concurred, describing the verbal exchange of consent as the efficient cause of marriage.[25] In England, the church formally adopted these principles at the provincial council of Westminster in 1175.[26] That council provided that marriage could be contracted either by words *de presenti* or by a pledge to marry in the future (*verba de futuro*) followed by sexual intercourse. Conditional marriages could also be contracted. A would-be spouse might make a vow *de futuro* with conditions attached: 'I will take you as my wife if your father agrees.' Once its conditions were met, a conditional vow was as binding as a present one. The consent of the partners, symbolized by the exchange of their vows, thus became the *sine qua non* of medieval marriage.[27] Since the exchange of vows could not easily be verified in the absence of unbiased witnesses, it became important from the church's point of view that marriages be solemnized in public. Announcements of an impending marriage, known

---

[21] Augustine, *De bono coniugali*, 3.3.

[22] Peter Coleman, *Christian Attitudes to Marriage: From ancient times to the third millennium* (London, 2004), 145–6.

[23] Ibid., 148.

[24] Conor McCarthy, *Marriage in Medieval England* (Woodbridge, 2004).

[25] Thomas Aquinas, *Summa theologica*, Suppl.III.45. 1–2; Jean Gerson, 'Considérations sur saint Joseph' in P. Glorieux (ed.), *Oeuvres complètes* (Paris, 1960–73), vol. 7, part 1, 81.

[26] Michael M. Sheehan, 'Marriage and family in English conciliar and synodal legislation' in *Marriage, Family, and Law in Medieval Europe: Collected studies* (Cardiff, 1996), 77–86 at 86.

[27] McCarthy has argued that the consent model was sometimes overlooked or intentionally superseded by the medieval church when issues of social order were at stake (*Marriage in Medieval England*, 41–4). Underage marriages between children incapable of consent were often arranged between socially prominent families, and church courts had the ability to force repeated fornicators to marry against their will.

as banns, would be read in both partners' parish churches on three consec-
utive Sundays, and the partners would marry each other on a Sunday
morning at the church door. With a priest officiating, they would exchange
vows *de presenti* in front of witnesses and then proceed into the church for
a nuptial mass.[28]

Despite the best efforts of ecclesiastical regulators, however, couples frequently contracted their marriages privately. In doing so, they had theology
on their side; since it is the two partners who marry one another, any cleric
present acts merely as a witness. Private or clandestine marriages were sacramentally valid but were seen as less than ideal; the canonist Gratian cited a
letter of the second-century pope Evaristus to the effect that clandestine
marriages were 'infected' though nevertheless valid.[29] Since it circumvented
the public processes of betrothal and the reading of banns, clandestine
marriage posed a significant challenge to the church's authority and also
increased the likelihood that a marriage would be contested at a later date.
In his study of a fourteenth-century register from Ely diocese, for instance,
Michael Sheehan pointed out that more than four-fifths of matrimonial cases
involved clandestine unions.[30]

Not only did the church mandate that marriages were to take place
publicly, but canon law also regulated who could marry whom. The reforms
of the eleventh century had provided that no person could marry a relative
within seven degrees of consanguinity, though Lateran IV lowered the requirement to four degrees.[31] Other impediments prohibited forced marriages,
marriages involving a partner who was already married, and marriages
involving men younger than fourteen years and women younger than twelve.
Infertility and adultery could also impede a marriage, as could 'disparity of
cult'—that is, a marriage between two partners of different religions.[32] But for
our purposes, most important was the requirement that no person who had
taken major orders or religious vows could marry.

Even this short survey has revealed the bewildering array of regulations that
the medieval church hedged around the theory and practice of marriage. Did

---

[28] Peter Fleming, *Family and Household in Medieval England* (Basingstoke, 2001), 43.

[29] Eric Josef Carlson, *Marriage and the English Reformation* (Oxford, 1994), 19.

[30] Michael Sheehan, 'The formation and stability of marriage in fourteenth-century England: Evidence of an Ely register' in *Marriage, Family, and Law*, 38–76 at 62.

[31] Tanner, *Decrees*, i.257. Against the traditional view that consanguinity rules provided
many disaffected medieval couples with the opportunity to escape the marriage bond and that
the rules remained impracticable even after having been relaxed at Lateran IV, R. H. Helmholz
has shown that few divorces actually took place on such grounds (*Marriage Litigation in
Medieval England* (Cambridge, 1974), 77–9).

[32] Fleming, *Family and Household in Medieval England*, 13–16. The category of cultic
disparity also included cases in which one partner was guilty of heresy.

laypeople understand the rules? In his classic survey of medieval marriage litigation in England, Richard Helmholz argued that confusion was frequent, especially as regards the status of vows made with words *de futuro*. The word *volo*, as in the phrase *volo habere te in uxorem* ('I wish to have you as my wife'), was particularly problematic, and Helmholz has suggested that it was not uncommon for a layman to enter into a legally binding marriage when he had merely intended a betrothal:

> Whereas the canon law regarded the contract by *verba de presenti* as a complete marriage, many laymen continued to regard it simply as a contract to marry. There was a clear difference between the formal law and the popular attitude on this score. Many people had simply not accepted the Church's definition of what constituted a complete and indissoluble marriage . . . Though the evidence is neither as thick nor as free from ambiguity as one would like, it appears that the English courts normally construed the phrase 'volo habere te in uxorem' as a contract of present consent.[33]

A substantially different view appears in a more recent study of English marriage disputes by Frederik Pedersen. Rather than depicting the average layperson as uninformed about the legal aspects of marriage, Pedersen cited a number of cases in which appellants and witnesses demonstrated extraordinary familiarity with the requirements of canon law. In one case, the domestic servant Maud Schipyn testified that she had intentionally left a room where two people were about to exchange vows *de presenti*, knowing that had she heard them speak, she could have been called to testify at an ecclesiastical trial.[34] It is undoubtedly the case that some laypeople knew more about marriage law than others, but as we shall see in this chapter, the sophisticated arguments of some dissenting texts and heresy defendants tend to corroborate Pedersen's argument.

Having considered the theology and practice of marriage in the Christian West and its regulation in late medieval England, it only remains for us only to describe more concretely the state of affairs around the time of John Wyclif's rise to notoriety. Women usually married between the ages of seventeen and twenty-four; men between twenty-one and twenty-six. Most marriages were formed between partners of roughly equal age, and one out of ten people never married. Whilst the men and women of the Middle Ages would not have recognized modern notions of marriage for romantic love, neither did any but the exceptionally well-off enter into unions solely for strategic social or financial reasons.[35] Church courts continued to hear a large

---

[33] Helmholz, *Marriage Litigation in Medieval England*, 31, 38.
[34] Frederik Pedersen, *Marriage Disputes in Medieval England* (London, 2000), 65; see also 69, 77.
[35] Fleming, *Family and Household in Medieval England*, 20–3, 31, 53; McCarthy, *Marriage in Medieval England*, 92–3.

number of matrimonial cases in the fourteenth and early fifteenth centuries. The volume of business dropped off in the last decades of the 1400s, however, likely on account of a parallel decline in the number of clandestine marriages.[36] The church's procedures, it seems, had made greater inroads into lay consciousness.

WYCLIF'S THEOLOGY OF MARRIAGE

The preceding chapters have uncovered in Wyclif a thinker at once conservative and radical. Even as he challenged accepted notions of merit and transubstantiation, he did so within the framework of scholastic logic and the tradition of the early church. Wyclif's writings on marriage and sexuality follow a similar pattern, combining reverence for the ideal of chastity with scepticism about the authority of the church and its courts. Unlike the doctrines of salvation and the eucharistic, however, marriage and sexuality appear only infrequently in Wyclif's works. Even when he did write about lay and clerical marriages, he did so highly unsystematically, and the reader sometimes has the impression that Wyclif may have felt himself to be on less than certain ground. What I shall call his theologies of marriage and sexuality, therefore, are less reasoned syllogisms than occasional observations.

Wyclif's ideas about marriage appear most prominently in his late works, written during his exile in Lutterworth. *Trialogus* and *De veritate sacrae scripturae* both contain sections on marriage and sexuality, and passing references can also be found in *De ecclesia, De officio regis,* and the *Responsiones ad Radulphi Strode.* It was in his unfinished polemical tract *Opus evangelicum,* however, that Wyclif set forth his views on marriage most clearly. He quoted at length from Augustine's tract *De sermone Domini in monte,* arguing that whilst divorce was permitted in the time of the Old Testament, Christ's law demands that his followers observe a higher set of sexual standards.[37] Just how high a set of standards Wyclif made clear in his commentary:

It seems that this saint intends that all these temporal things which in this life we do be postponed in love for Christ and the goods of heaven . . . And so Augustine seems to say that the good of matrimony, figuring the blessedness of heavenly marriage, is better than the procreation of children in this life. And this good was in Joseph and

---

[36] Helmholz, *Marriage Litigation in Medieval England,* 167.
[37] *Opus evangelicum,* 165–9.

the Blessed Virgin and can exist among married people who do not render to each other the marital debt.[38]

Like other medieval theologians and canonists, Wyclif held up the marriage of Mary and Joseph as a model. Although he acknowledged that an earthly marriage involving sexual consummation can prefigure a heavenly union, he nevertheless urged that temporal sexuality be put aside.[39] He later repeated the same argument: marriage in which the partners help each other toward blessedness (*beatitudinem*) is preferable to marriage for the sake of procreation or the release of libido.[40]

Whilst chaste marriage was his ideal, Wyclif, like St Paul, acknowledged that not all have the charism of lifelong celibacy. In *Trialogus*, his character Phronesis defines marriage as 'legitimate conjugal copulation, by which the law of God permits the procreation of children without guilt'.[41] Phronesis proceeds to set forth a relatively positive account of marriage: God ordained it for Adam and Eve; Christ approved of it by saying 'what God has joined, let man not separate'; Christ intended for married people to have intercourse; and Augustine was right to identify *fides, proles,* and*sacramentum* as the three goods of marriage.[42] In response to an objection from his interlocutor Pseustis, Phronesis then qualifies his remarks. Marriage does not exist when any two people have intercourse. It requires a distinction between the sexes and hence a male and a female partner; it must entail the partners' consent; and it cannot exist where there is no possibility of procreation. Phronesis insists: 'As for the aged who on account of a desire for temporal goods, out of hope for mutual help, or on account of satisfying their libido have intercourse with each other without a desire for children, their union is not true matrimony.'[43] In some cases, however, it is impossible for a disinterested observer to learn

---

[38] *Opus evangelicum*, 169/11–21: 'Videtur istum sanctum intendere quod omnia hec temporalia que in vita presenti nobis proficiunt debemus postponere in amore propter Christum et bona celestia . . . Et sic videtur Augustinus dicere quod bonum matrimonii figurans beatitudinem celestis coniugii sit melius quam prolis procreacio hic in via. Et illud bonus fuit in Joseph et beata virgine et potest esse in coniugatis sine debiti solucione.'

[39] The case of the marriage of Mary and Joseph proved to be a model as well as a stumbling point for theologians as well as canonists. See Irvin M. Resnick, 'Marriage in medieval culture: Consent theory and the case of Joseph and Mary', *Church History*, 69 (2000), 350–71.

[40] *Opus evangelicum*, 171/8–13.

[41] *Trialogus cum supplemento trialogi*, 315: 'matrimonium est conjugum legitima copulatio, qua secundum Dei legem licet eis sine crimine filios procreare'.

[42] Ibid., 315; see also 205, where Phronesis argues that genital sexual acts can be meritorious if they occur in the correct circumstances.

[43] Ibid., 317: 'Unde antiqui ex cupiditate temporalium, ex spe mutuorum juvaminum aut ex causa excusandae libidinis, licet desperent de prole, copulantur ad invicem, non vere matrimonialiter copulantur.'

why a couple are proposing to marry. Phronesis argues that in such situations it must remain uncertain whether a particular union is approved by God.

It is at this point that Wyclif's theology of marriage began to stray outside the ecclesiastical consensus. Whereas mainstream theology and canon law placed emphasis on the *words* of consent, Wyclif argued that it is the approval of God and the *mental* consent of the partners that actually makes a marriage. An exchange between Phronesis and Alithia, his other dialogue partner, makes his distinction clear:

Alithia: But say, I ask, with what words and signs marriage should be celebrated; for it is often said, that it should be celebrated with *verbis de praesenti*, and not with *verbis de praeteritio vel futuro*, nor indeed an affirmation about the future.
Phronesis: In this matter I do not take much delight from the lips, especially since this custom was established by human beings and without much foundation. The truth seems to me, that the consent of the partners and the approval of God, leaving aside any sensible sign, will suffice . . . In words of whatever extrinsic appropriateness there is the possibility of deception.[44]

What matters for Phronesis, and (as his other writings indicate) for Wyclif as well, are not the words of the mouth but rather the words of the heart. The precise form of the vows which the partners exchange is less important than their internal consent.[45] For that reason, Phronesis concludes that the practice of rendering judgements about the existence of a marriage on the basis of the precise language of the partners' vows is not only unhelpful but in fact against the gospel: 'Judges who reach verdicts on the basis of the bare words judge against the verdict of God's law; and cursed be that law, by which a judge forces the persons he is judging to work against the law of God on account of his made-up censures!'[46] He also objects to two additional elements of medieval marriage practice: the idea that intercourse can create a marriage and the tradition that partners should pledge their troth both at home and then again in church, 'commonly in words which are worthless and falsely observed'.[47] If Phronesis' views represent Wyclif's, then Wyclif was here

---

[44] Ibid., 322–3: '*Alithia*: Sed dic, quaeso, cum quibus verbis vel signis debet matrimonium celebrari; dicitur enim communiter, quod cum verbis de praesenti, et non cum verbis de praeterito vel futuro, imo expressa affirmatione de futuro . . . *Phronesis*: Non delector multum labi in ista materia, specialiter cum sit humanitus et saepe infundabiliter instituta. Veritas quidem mihi videtur, quod assistente consensus conjugum et Domino approbante, subducto quocunque signo sensibili foret satis . . . In verbis enim qualitercunque aptatis extrinsecus potest esse deceptio.'
[45] Ibid., 324.
[46] Ibid., 323: 'Judices ergo qui ex nudis verbis judicant pro matrimonio, judicant contra judicium legis Dei; sed maledicta sit lex hujusmodi, qua judex coartabit per censuras fictas jugum personarum, ut faciant contrarie legi Dei!'
[47] Ibid., 324: 'per verba nugatoria et falsa communiter celebrato'.

employing the same logic that governed his theologies of confession and excommunication. His fundamental principle remained constant: that the church can only effect something if God has already effected it.[48]

Wyclif recommended that ambiguous marriage disputes should be left to the consciences of the partners involved. The church, he wrote, has taken the opposite route, tightening the laws of marriage and restricting the rules of consanguinity so that marriages which previously would have been allowed are now illicit.[49] In particular, Wyclif inveighed against what he took to be the church's superfluous regulations on 'divorce', a term which in *Opus evangelicum* encompasses a range of possible terminations of marriage. Wyclif argued that the bill of divorce (*libellus repudii*) had been invented not by God but by Moses; furthermore, Christ had forbidden its use 'on account of its imperfection'.[50] Nevertheless, prelates have revived the practice of divorce and have drastically skewed the criteria on the basis of which separations are to be granted.[51] Wyclif criticized the institutional church for applying inappropriate penalties in particular cases. Referring to the distinction between a divorce *a vinculo* (which freed the partners from the marriage bond and left them able to remarry) and a divorce *a mensa et thoro* (which simply enacted a separation, leaving the marriage intact and the partners unable to marry again), Wyclif pointed out that whereas cases of adultery normally result in a divorce *a vinculo*, the far more serious crime of heresy, or 'spiritual fornication', is not even punished by a divorce *a mensa et thoro*.[52] In contrast to what he viewed as inconsistent and un-evangelical jurisprudence, Wyclif insisted that questions of marriage and divorce should be resolved by an appeal to conscience: 'human laws seem to be shut away and to be made subject to the arbitrariness of the judges on account of demons coming in against the law of Christ'.[53] Whether such an appeal to conscience could provide a practical solution to actual marital disputes remains uncertain.

It is unsurprising that when ecclesiastical censors began to scour Wyclif's writings for erroneous propositions, they rejected only a few of his ideas about marriage and sexuality. Three articles about marriage condemned first

---

[48] This point was originally made to great effect by Gordon Leff, *Heresy in the Later Middle Ages: The relation of heterodoxy to dissent, c. 1250–c. 1450*, 2 vols. (Manchester, 1967), ii, 531.

[49] *Opus evangelicum*, 172/21–33.

[50] Ibid., 175/11–16.

[51] Ibid., 175.

[52] Ibid., 175/33–7; on the different types of divorce, see McCarthy, *Marriage in Medieval England*, 41. Wyclif's treatment of divorce in *Trialogus* is slightly different. Phronesis echoes Wyclif's preference for the commands of Scripture rather than the laws of human judges and, in a discussion of Matthew 5, repeats that whoever divorces his wife, except on account of fornication, makes her an adulterer (319–22).

[53] *Opus evangelicum*, 177/15–19.

at a provincial convocation in 1396 and again by an Oxford committee in 1411 all revolved around his objections to the institutional church's regulations around marriage. One was the proposition that 'divorce on account of consanguinity or affinity is a purely human ordinance'; the second was the view that 'the words "I will take you as my wife" are more suitable for the contract of matrimony than the words "I take you as my wife", and in the case of a person contracting with one woman in *verba de futuro* and then with another in *verba de presenti*, the first vow must not be frustrated by the second'; and the third was that 'those who, without hope of children, marry in old age for temporal goods, for mutual succour, or to provide an outlet for their lust are not truly married'.[54] Each of these propositions either appears in or follows logically from Wyclif's arguments in *Trialogus*.[55]

Perhaps surprisingly for early historians accustomed to seeing Wyclif as the so-called 'morning star' of the Reformation, none of the condemned propositions concerned the marriage of priests and nuns. Wyclif was not an ardent advocate of clerical marriage, but nor did he follow other medieval thinkers in holding that the sacrament of orders is an impediment to that of marriage. The crucial question, for him, was not whether priests *can* marry but whether, in fact, they *should*.

According to Wyclif, enforced celibacy is often the source of sexual vice, and although he did not exempt secular priests from criticism, he singled out members of the fraternal orders for special abuse: 'Now it is a legal custom that the lady of the house can have a friar hear her confession in the absence of her husband; yet widows and especially nuns are seduced by their confessors in this way.'[56] Friars give off a false aura of holiness and lure women into their confidence through prayers, fables, and long orations; in this way, Wyclif argued, the sects resemble the devil who seduced Eve in her husband's absence.[57] He made what would have been perceived to be a more serious charge in *Trialogus*, where Phronesis suggests that celibacy among male religious can lead to sodomy:

---

[54] Wilkins, iii.229–30, nos. 7–9, iii.339–49, nos. 129–31: 'Causae divortii ratione affinitatis vel consanguinitatis sunt infundabiliter humanitus ordinatae'; 'Haec verba "accipiam te in uxorem" eligibiliora sunt in contractu matrimonali, quam ista "ego te accipio in uxorem"; et quod contrahendo cum una per haec verba de futuro, et post cum alia per haec verba de praesenti, non debent frustrari verba prima per verba secundaria de praesenti'; 'Antiqui, qui ex cupitate temporalium, ex spe mutuorum juvaminum, aut ex causa excusandae libidinis, licet desperent de prole, copulantur adinvicem, non vere matrimonaliter copulantur.'

[55] *Trialogus*, 319, 323, 317.

[56] *Opus evangelicum*, 40/27–30: 'Jam enim consuetudo pro lege admittitur quod domina in mariti absencia fratrem habeat confessorem; vidue autem et specialiter sanctimoniales per confessores huiusmodi sunt seducte.'

[57] Ibid., 41/26–8.

It seems to me, therefore, that . . . the devil knows to teach youths this most grievous sin apart from the company of women, and especially when a number of virile young men are separated from women, living delightfully and at leisure from work. Whence Ezekiel 16, 'This was the sin of your sister Sodom: pride, fullness of bread, and an abundance of wine and leisure.' For this reason it is to be feared among the private orders, lest they fall into this sin.[58]

The institutional church, Wyclif argued, has mistakenly focused on clerical marriage when greater sins deserve attention. In his political tract *De officio regis*, Wyclif used a New Testament metaphor to compare clerical celibacy with the wealth of the church: 'And like the Pharisees we focus on the gnat [of clerical marriage] and yet swallow the camel, fearing marriage among priests like venom, but approving simoniacal transactions . . . for the health and defence of the church.'[59] He pursued a similar line of argument in *De ecclesia*: 'It is less foreign to Christ's priesthood for priests to receive from secular lords the use of their wives . . . than to receive civil dominion. Both are horrible, but the second more horrible, *since carnal procreation can exist along with priesthood*.'[60] In *De veritate sacrae scripturae*, Wyclif made an argument from history, appealing to the practice of the primitive church, when married bishops lived continently with their wives.[61]

Whilst it seems that Wyclif neither endorsed nor rejected the possibility of clerical marriage, it remains an open question whether he would have been a proponent of married priests had he lived in a time of greater (perceived) ecclesiastical virtue. What is clear is that Wyclif's views on clerical marriage were more complex than some commentators have heretofore remarked.[62]

---

[58] *Trialogus*, 206: 'Videtur tamen mihi . . . cum diabolus scit docere juvenes extra mulierum consortium hoc pecatum turpissimum, et specialiter assistente copia juvenum masculorum separatorum a feminis, voluptuose viventium et a laboribus otiantium. Unde Ezech. xvi. "haec fuit iniquitas Sodomae, sororis tuae, superbia, saturitas panis, habundantia vini et ostium." Ideo cavendum est privatis ordinibus, ne incidant in hanc culpam.' It may strike a modern reader as odd that Wyclif feared both the seduction of wives and daughters as well as sodomy among the clergy, but it is more likely that Wyclif, unaware of later ideas about sexual orientation, simply saw both opposite-sex and same-sex activity as equally possible consequences of enforced celibacy.

[59] *De officio regis*, 29/27–31: 'et sic phariseice colamus culicem et deglutimus camelum, horrentes in sacerdotibus corporale coniugium ut venenum, sed negociacionem eciam simoniacam . . . sanitavam ac defensivam ecclesie approbamus'.

[60] *De ecclesia*, 365/7–13: 'Unde minus remotum est a sacerdocio Christi recipere a dominis temporalibus alternatum usum uxorum suarum secundum copulam carnalem . . . quam quod recipient a seculari domino dominacionem civilem; utrumque enim istorum foret horribile, sed secundum horribilius, cum carnalis procreacio stat cum sacerdocio' (emphasis mine).

[61] *De veritate sacrae scripturae*, ii.262/2–6.

[62] In the early twentieth century, Henry C. Lea observed that Wyclif tentatively endorsed clerical celibacy; his analysis did not, however, take into account the full corpus of Wyclif's writings (Lea, *A History of the Inquisition in the Middle Ages*, i.474–5).

It seems less than accurate to argue, as McSheffrey has, that Wyclif's position was that 'clerks should be allowed to take wives . . . because they fornicate if they are not allowed to marry'.[63] Like his ideas about lay sexuality, Wyclif's position on clerical celibacy was fundamentally a conservative one. Neither was fully adopted by those who followed in his footsteps.

LAY CHASTITY, CLERICAL MARRIAGE: SEXUALITY IN WYCLIFFITE TEXTS

Just as Wyclif's Latin works contain no systematic discussion of marriage, so also the majority of Wycliffite authors addressed the subject only in passing. With the exception of the vernacular tract *Of Weddid Men and Wifis and of Here Children Also*, ideas about marriage and sexuality are peripheral to the concerns of many English dissenting works. Where they do occur, comments about the marriages of clerics and laypeople are commonly to be found embedded in the course of larger arguments about ecclesiastical authority, the status of canon law, and the sins of the clergy and prelacy. Read with care, however, such oblique references have the potential to disclose dissenters' attitudes toward marriage and sexuality. In general, Wycliffite texts adopt a more pessimistic view of lay sexuality than Wyclif's. On the question of clerical marriage, however, they depart from Wyclif in the opposite direction, strongly advocating the marriage of priests, minor clerics, and nuns.

In the last two chapters, one of our primary sources for the beliefs of English dissenters has been the cycle of *English Wycliffite Sermons* edited by Anne Hudson and Pamela Gradon. The sermons, however, reveal relatively little about their authors' views here. The text for the *Missa pro sponsalibus*, where ideas about marriage and sexuality might seem most likely to be found, is a highly compressed exegesis of the Matthean passage in which Jesus responds to the Pharisees' question about divorce: 'Wher it be leeueful to a man to leeue his wif for ony cause?'[64] The preacher does little more than to emphasize that God instituted marriage for the end of procreation; to cite Augustine's claim that the benefits of marriage are 'feiþ, children and chastite'; and to argue that the marital bond will survive death and endure even in

---

[63] McSheffrey, *Gender and Heresy*, 82; see also *PR*, 357–8; Hargreaves, 'Sir John Oldcastle and Wycliffite views on clerical marriage', 144–5.

[64] *EWS*, iii.239/3–4.

heaven. He proceeds from these premises to a typically Wycliffite diatribe against the glossing of Scripture.[65]

Other components of the sermon-cycle have little to add. Four sermons utilize the trope of describing the relationships between God, Christ, and the church in terms of a marital union. Thus, for instance, one Sunday gospel sermon employs the metaphor of a wedding feast to discuss the church's role in salvation:

The kyngdam of heuene is þe chirche þat takiþ name of þe hed, as þe gospel spekiþ comunly; and so þis rewme is lych a kynge, þat is þe Fadyr in Trinnyte. And þis kyng made a mariage to Crist, þat ys his Sone, and to þis cherche, þat is his spowse, and to damyselys þerof. For as Salamon seyth fowre degrees ben in þis chirche: summe ben qwenes, and summe ben lemmanys, and somme damyselys, but oone is spowse þat conteneþ alle þese þre and þat is al hooly chyrche . . . Þes seruauntis of þis spowse bidden men to þe feeste, whanne þei meue men to come to blisse by þer iust lif.[66]

Another sermon comments on the wedding at Cana, which, following medieval tradition, the preacher takes to be the wedding of John the evangelist. He suggests that Christ's presence at the wedding and the miracle of turning water into wine 'bytookneþ loue þat God hadde to his chirche, how he wolde bycome man and be newe weddit to it'.[67] Whereas Christ has been faithful to his spouse, the church has not been equally loyal; Christ is now wedded 'wiþ newe wenchis', though he continues to seek the salvation of his spouse.[68]

Only once does the sermon-cycle mention the marriage of priests. In a short sermon for the vigil of John the Baptist, the preacher argues that:

Here men may dowte and trete of þe staat and lif of preestis, how þei ben dowyde and wifles aʒen Godis auctorite; for Crist forfendid dowyng boþe in hym and hise apostles and approuyde weddyng in apostles and money oþre. And þis is þe cast of þe feend to kyndely fuyre in herdis; for or þei moten boþe brenne, or þe kepere mut leue his craft, and traueyle to kepe þis fyer. And preestis schal not do boþe wel.[69]

Hudson has commented that 'it seems unclear whether this [passage] is intended to encourage clerical marriage or to discourage it,' and indeed, the text seems to lean in both directions.[70] The first sentence in the excerpt I have quoted suggests that Christ had prohibited his disciples from gaining worldly lordship but encouraged them and others to marry but, on the contrary, the church validates worldly lordship and prohibits marriage. The following sentences, however, somewhat complicate the picture. The preacher appears

---

[65] Ibid., iii.239/7.   [66] Ibid., i.20/24–35; see also i.13, i.E27.
[67] Ibid., i.33/39–40.   [68] Ibid., i.33/42–51.   [69] Ibid., ii.104/38–44.
[70] Ibid., iv.114.

to be suggesting that the devil encourages lust among clerics so that they will either pursue destructive affairs ('þei moten boþe brenne') or else lose sight of their pastoral responsibilities and divide their time between family and church ('leue his craft and traueyle to kepe þis fyer'). Though the sermon remains ambiguous, it may be that the preacher is subtly reproducing Wyclif's argument that even though it is not against God's law for priests to marry, it is nonetheless unseemly.

Like the *English Wycliffite Sermons*, the prose text *An Apology for Lollard Doctrines* touches briefly on sexuality. The *Apology* was attributed to Wyclif by its nineteenth-century editor but is unlikely to have been composed by the Oxford thinker. It does, however, bear the marks of having been composed in a learned environment and shares many of Wyclif's views. For instance, though the tract does not express an opinion on clerical marriage per se, its author maintains that priests should be held to a higher standard of behaviour than laypeople; thus, 'þe prest in doing fornicacoun doþ sacrile, and brekiþ his wow; for bi þe vertu of his degre, he made þe vow of chastite'.[71] Like Wyclif, the *Apology* also expresses scepticism about the church's regulations concerning marriage. Its author suggests that the church has mistakenly prohibited both clerical marriage as well as marriages between those whose relationships fall within the third and fourth degrees of consanguinity.[72] The ensuing discussion is strikingly reminiscent of Wyclif's ideas about the relationship between ecclesiastical and divine authority: the church can only solemnize a marriage if God has already ratified it, 'and if it be ratified of God, þan þe kirk mai not depart it, for no man may depart þe þing þat God haþ joinid'.[73] Thus, when the church makes marriages on the basis of its own authority, and not on God's, it effectively forces people to commit sin. Marriages can be made that are not true marriages, and people whom God wishes to be joined can be kept from marrying.[74]

Though the *Apology for Lollard Doctrines* confirms that at least some of Wyclif's arguments about marriage remained current after his death, the text provides few other details about its author's views. Far more helpful are the anonymous *Lollard Sermons* edited by Gloria Cigman. Like Wyclif himself, the preacher of Cigman's collection argues that the marriage of Mary and Joseph should be taken as a model. In the first place, the union of Mary and

---

[71] *An Apology for Lollard Doctrines*, 38.
[72] Ibid., 70–1.
[73] Ibid., 70.
[74] *The Lanterne of Liȝt* and *The Great Sentence of Curse Expounded*, two other vernacular Wycliffite tracts, both argue that many of the church's marriage regulations were implemented in order to boost ecclesiastical profits (*Lanterne*, 124–6; Arnold, iii.284).

Joseph demonstrates that a marriage need not be consummated to be perfect: in his sermon for Christmas Day, the preacher argues that the story of the nativity gives 'autorite aȝenst hem þat seiyn þat fleschli couplynge of man and womman makeþ matrymonie, for a blessider matrimonie or wedlok was þer neuere þan was þis, vnder whiche was born þat blesside chyld þat was boþe God and man'.[75] Whether the preacher intended to subvert the practice of judging a marriage valid if it involved words *de futuro* followed by consummation is unclear. Not only is it right that a marriage need not be consummated, he argues, but the spiritual marriage of two chaste people is the best of all possible unions: 'þus it is preued þat hooli wylles of man and womman, faste knytted wiþ þe sacrament of matrimonie in þat entente to dwelle togedere in maydenhood to her lyues ende, is perfite matrimonie and pleseþ God as wel, oþer bettere, as þat þat is ioyned in fleschly couplinge'.[76]

The preacher allows that married people who engage in sexual activity within marriage are committing no sin, but they are not perfect in chastity. In his sermon for Septuagesima Sunday, he offers advice to people in the various states of life: single men should not seek wives, widows should not seek second husbands, and married men should abstain from sex on feast days and during their wives' menstrual periods.[77] If people are to marry, however, the preacher would prefer to see couples living together abstinently. In his sermon for Sexagesima Sunday, he describes three ascending degrees of sexual virtue. Borrowing his language from the Matthean parable of the sower, he argues that chastity exists thirtyfold among married people who faithfully render to each other the marital debt. Sixtyfold chastity obtains among widows, who avoid 'al manere flescli couplynge þat hee mai þe more freliere ȝeue tente to Goddis seruice'.[78] But hundredfold chastity exists only among lifelong celibates, by whose virginity 'þe mynde is couplid alweie to God as to þe spouse . . . [To] maidens, and to martiris, and to prechouris, longiþ a special worschipe in heuene'.[79] The *Lollard Sermons* thus leave the reader with the impression that virginity is a supreme good that cannot be equalled in marriage; and that although sexual acts are not always sinful, they are nevertheless to be avoided.

A similarly conservative, but somewhat more pragmatic, view of marriage is embedded in the vernacular text *Of Weddid Men and Wifis and of Here Children Also*, edited by Thomas Arnold in his three-volume collection of English works attributed to Wyclif. Whilst it is almost certain that the tract is not Wyclif's own, and whilst Anne Hudson has called the text only 'questionably' Wycliffite, the fact that *Of Weddid Men and Wifis* is the

---

[75] *Lollard Sermons*, 5/123–7.   [76] Ibid., 5/56–60.   [77] Ibid., 8/82.
[78] Ibid., 9/383–5.   [79] Ibid., 9/390–1, 397–8.

only tract with potential Wycliffite affiliations dedicated primarily to marriage, child-rearing, and sexuality means that it deserves particularly close
attention.[80] As in the case of many such works, the scant palaeographical
and bibliographical evidence makes it difficult to locate the text within the
matrix of dissenting and orthodox belief. At the same time, since its focus
is almost exclusively on married life, it is difficult to compare its theological content with unquestionably Wycliffite works. Nevertheless, in at least
two of the manuscripts in which it is preserved—Cambridge, Corpus
Christi College 296 and Westminster School 3—the tract keeps company
with other heterodox writings.[81] It employs several elements of the Wycliffites' distinctive polemical idiom; the friars, for instance, it calls the 'newe
religions' and the 'newe ordris'. Finally, the tract borrows Wyclif's language
around the themes of salvation and clerical marriage. A careful study of its
contents reveals that it also shares many features with Cigman's sermons
and could very well have been produced within a similar theological
milieu.

The tract begins, conventionally enough, by comparing marriage between
persons to the spiritual relationship between Christ and the church. The
author writes that God established matrimony in Paradise, that Christ
could not have been born outside of wedlock, and that Christ sanctified the
institution of marriage by attending the wedding at Cana. For this reason, the
author argues, we know that marriage is a sacrament created for the purpose
of preserving the human race until the Last Judgement. Twice, the author
suggests that when men and women procreate, they 'fulfille þe chosen noumbre of seyntis in blisse', a comment that seems to allude to the predestinarian
language of Wyclif and some early Wycliffites.[82] In another passage, he adds
that since marriage was ordained by God, it must be superior to the 'newe
religions' of the friars.[83] The remainder of the tract articulates a pessimistic
theological anthropology: men and women are so frail, and fornication is so
great a temptation, that God established marriage not only for laypeople but
also for clerics: 'God ordeynede prestis in þe olde lawe to have wyves, and
nevere forbede it in þe new lawe, neiþer bi Crist ne bi his apostlis, but raþere

---

[80] *PR*, 425.

[81] On London, Westminster School, MS 3, see Amanda Moss, 'A merchant's tales: A London
fifteenth-century household miscellany', *Yearbook of English Studies*, 33 (2003), 156–69. Jill C.
Havens has proposed one methodological approach for handling texts, like *Of Weddid Men and
Wifis*, that fall within the 'grey area' between dissent and orthodoxy: see her 'Shading the grey
area', 350.

[82] *Of Weddid Men and Wifis and of Here Children Also*, in Arnold, iii.188–201 at 191. On
predestinarianism, see Ch. 2 above.

[83] *Weddid Men*, 189.

aprovede it.'[84] Likewise, Christ never forbade marriage for his disciples, 'but now, bi ypocrisie of fendis and fals men, manye bynden hem to presthod and chastite, and forsaken wifis bi Goddis law, and schenden maydenes and wifis, and fallen foulest of alle'.[85] The author does not, however, wholeheartedly commend matrimony. Virginity, he writes, is far superior to marriage: Christ himself maintained lifelong chastity, as did his mother and John the evangelist. Were human beings less prone to temptation, more might follow in their footsteps, but virginity is a virtue that only a few may hope to attain. 'And þerefore Poul ȝaf no comaundement of virgynite, but ȝaf counseil to hem þat weren able þerto.'[86]

The author proceeds to spell out the rights and duties of married men and women. Marriage must be made with the consent of both parties and should be contracted between two partners of roughly equal age. A young man should not marry an old widow, for instance, since she will be unable to bear him children. Sexual relations within marriage should take place for three reasons only: 'þe firste for to geten children, to fulfille þe noumbre of men and wymmen þat schullen be savyd; þe secunde to kepe his wif fro lecherie of oþere men; þe þridde is to kepe himself fro lecherie of oþere wymmen'.[87] Two people might agree to live together in marital chastity, but a partner should not deny his or her spouse in other circumstances. *Of Weddid Men and Wifis* quotes at length from the Epistles of Peter and Paul to justify a traditional view of the relationship between husband and wife.[88] Wives, its author writes, should dress modestly, learn in silence, and not presume to teach publicly.[89] Husbands should take care not to consume too much drink or delicate meat and should exercise restraint in demanding the marital debt; wives, on the other hand, should seek to soften their husbands. Both spouses should take it upon themselves to teach their children God's commandments, a duty that should not be left only to a child's godparents.[90] What parents should *not* teach their children the author spells out at length: stories of battles, songs, needless crafts, and 'fals cronyclis' are all proscribed.[91]

Of Weddid Men and Wifis is thus in many ways a paradigm of dissenting ideas about marriage and sexuality. Whilst the tract acknowledges that marriage is licit for both clerics and laypeople, not least because it helps them to avoid falling into fornication and adultery, it sets its discursive sights much higher. Virginity is an ideal that few can hope to achieve, but even those who

---

[84] Ibid., 190.   [85] Ibid., 190.   [86] Ibid., 190.   [87] Ibid., 192.

[88] The subjugation of women to men is also urged by the author of the sermon *Of Mynystris in þe Chirche*, *EWS*, ii.l. 504, and by the Wycliffite writer William Thorpe in his testimony before Archbishop Thomas Arundel (*The Testimony of William Thorpe*, 49/836).

[89] *Weddid Men*, 193.   [90] Ibid., 196.   [91] Ibid., 196–7.

do not attempt to lead a celibate life should regulate themselves to the greatest extent possible; married people, for instance, should have intercourse only to procreate and to keep one another from lust. The text also articulates traditional notions about the relationships of husbands and wives and parents and children. In this way, the tract further substantiates McSheffrey's thesis that many dissenters retained the patriarchal structure of the medieval family whilst disputing other aspects of the contemporary theological consensus.

Whereas the texts considered so far have expressed almost ascetic ideas about lay sexuality, Wycliffites' views on clerical marriage were frequently more radical. Both the *Apology for Lollard Doctrines* and *Of Weddid Men and Wifis* make the point that Christ did not prohibit his disciples either from getting married or from enjoying intimacy with their wives, and we have already seen that a passage from the English sermon-cycle can be construed similarly. Other Wycliffite authors likewise argue for the legitimacy, if not in fact the necessity, of clerical marriage.

The third and eleventh of the *Twelve Conclusions* posted on the doors of Westminster Hall in 1395 call for an end to celibacy among clerics and religious women.[92] The relevant passages deserve to be quoted at length:

Þe thirdde conclusiun sorwful to here is þat þe lawe of continence annexyd to presthod, þat in preiudys of wimmen was first ordeynid, inducith sodomie in al holy chirche...Resun and experience prouit þis conclusiun. For delicious metis and drinkis of men of holi chirche welen han needful purgaciun or werse. Experience for þe priue asay of syche men is, þat þei like non wymmen; and when þu prouist sich a man mark him wel for he is on of þo. Þe correlary of þis conclusiun is þat þe priuat religions, begynneris of þis synne, were most worthi to ben anullid...

Þe xi conclusiun is schamful for to speke, þat a uow of continence mad in oure chirche of wommen, þe qwiche ben fekil and vnperfyth in kynde, is cause of bringging of most horrible synne possible to mankynde. For þou sleyng of children of þei ben cristenid, aborcife and stroying of kynde be medicine ben ful sinful.[93]

The suggestion that the combination of exclusively male company and fine food and drink leads to homosexual activity had already been made by Wyclif in his *Trialogus*, and the anonymous author or authors of the *Conclusions* extend his warning about sodomy among friars to the clergy as a whole, though the corollary to the third conclusion still lays blame for sodomy primarily at the doors of the fraternal orders. Nevertheless, the writers of the *Conclusions* appealed not to Wyclif, who had died a decade earlier, but

---

[92] For a useful discussion of the conclusions, see Blamires, 'The Wife of Bath and Lollardy', 231–2.

[93] 'Twelve conclusions of the Lollards' in *Selections*, 25, 28.

rather to the categories of reason and experience. Like the tract *Of Weddid Men*, the *Conclusions* depict marriage as an antidote to the potentially disastrous consequences of repressed sexuality, but yet they do not suggest that virginity is preferable to marriage.

At least three other vernacular texts attribute the prevalence of sexual sin among the clergy and religious orders to their vows of celibacy. *Of Prelates*, for instance, argues that Scripture does not prohibit clerical marriage and that the tradition of clerical celibacy was instituted by the devil: 'Prelates . . . forsaken as venym matrimonye, þat is leffel bi holy writt, til newe vowis of contynense of worldli clerkis weren brouȝt in bi disceit of þe fend.' Because priests cannot marry, they now 'defoulen wyues, maidenes, widewis and nunnes in eche manere of lecherie, and children ben morþerid, and synne aȝenst kynde is not clene fleed'.[94] In general, the tract's arguments follow those of the *Twelve Conclusions*, even as to the details of the sins—sodomy and infanticide—that male clerics and nuns are most likely to commit. The text *Of the Leaven of Pharisees* makes similar charges, adding that lecherous priests also kill women who withstand their sexual advances.[95] The *General Prologue* to the Wycliffite Bible specifically warns against lechery, simony, and sodomy among the scholars of Oxford, though it does not explicitly associate these vices with the discipline of clerical chastity.[96] Only one English text, *De Papa*, appears to sanction celibacy: 'We graunten þat prestos ben of mannus kynde, as ben lordis and weddid men, but ȝit þey shulden not haue þis lordchip ne kyndely gendrure of children, but ȝif þey wolden leeue þis staat and bicome weddid men, for we bileuen þat maydynhot and goostly gendrure is betere þan þis.'[97] Even here, traditional Wycliffite concerns emerge: whilst the author maintains that priests should not have wives or children, he is also concerned that clerics should not enjoy temporal lordship.

Thus, English dissenting authors embraced a range of opinions about marriage and sexuality. On the one hand, whether they considered marriage a good in and of itself or merely a means to avoid fornication, Wycliffite writers endorsed an end to mandatory vows of celibacy. Those who wrote about lay sexuality, on the other hand, tended to take a more cautious line. Not only did the preacher of Cigman's sermons and the author of *Of Weddid Men* call for sexual restraint even between spouses, but they also upheld virginity as superior to marriage. In doing so, dissenters moved away from

---

[94] *Of Prelates*, in Matthew, 100.
[95] *Of the Leaven of Pharisees*, in Matthew, 6.
[96] *The Holy Bible . . . Made from the Latin Vulgate by* John Wyclif and His Followers, ed. Josiah Forshall and Frederic Madden, 4 vols. (Oxford, 1850), i, 51. I am grateful to Mishtooni Bose for this reference.
[97] *De Papa*, in Matthew, 474.

Wyclif, whose arguments had instead reflected his scepticism about the church's regulation of marriage. Apart from the suggestion in the *Apology for Lollard Doctrines* that the church has sinfully prohibited some marriages, such as those between partners related in the third and fourth degrees, Wycliffite texts are generally unconcerned with Wyclif's distinction between marriages endorsed by God and those approved by the church. Likewise, no vernacular writer expressed Wyclif's cynicism about the words of the marriage contract. The reason may have to do with the sexual politics of dissenting communities; McSheffrey has shown that many such groups were led by men, and if she is right, then it is unsurprising that writers already in a dominant position would have sought no change in the sexual *status quo*.

THE ORTHODOX CONTEXT: CONTESTED VIEWS OF MARRIAGE IN LATE MEDIEVAL ENGLAND

It may be helpful at this point, before turning to the records of the heresy trials where ideas about marriage and sexuality were contested, to remember that Wycliffites were not the only medieval English writers to discuss the theory and practice of marriage. There remain extant a number of late-fourteenth- and fifteenth-century texts whose authors articulate theologies of marriage which, however controversial, were perceived to remain within the bounds of orthodoxy. Whilst those texts which explicitly respond to dissenting ideas uniformly reject the position that religious men and women should not be bound by vows of chastity, other writings express a range of opinions on the relative merits of marriage and virginity. Just as dissenting authors did not always find consensus among themselves, so also did those who stood within the mainstream of late medieval religion hold widely disparate views. A survey of several tracts to be found outside the culture of Wycliffite dissent will help to contextualize the ideas that we have already encountered.

An overt refutation of Wycliffite views on clerical marriage can be found in Roger Dymmok's *Liber contra XII errores et hereses Lollardorum*. Dymmok's discussion of marriage focuses on the third and eleventh of the *Twelve Conclusions*, the text of which I have set out above. His reply is part an argument from church history and part an apology for the intrinsic holiness of the fraternal vocation. Responding to the charge that priestly celibacy provides an occasion for sodomy, particularly among members of religious orders, Dymmok first argues that vows of chastity have their origin in Christ's earthly ministry. He acknowledges that priestly celibacy was prohibited in the time of the Old Testament and that the first person to take a vow of chastity was Jesus' mother, Mary, who, 'before she was married, took a conditional vow of virginity, such that, if it pleased God, she would remain in chastity after the marriage made between her and Joseph by divine inspiration, her husband consenting'.[98] The coming of Christ definitively cancelled the prescriptions of the old law, so vows of celibacy need no longer be conditional. Dymmok writes that Christ and his disciples all observed chastity: those who had wives did not have intercourse with them, and those who did not have wives never married.

But why should Christ's priests be chaste, if their predecessors in the Old Testament took wives? Dymmok offers three reasons. First, he argues that the Christian priesthood is more sacred than its Levitical counterpart: Christian priests administer holier sacraments, especially insofar as they consecrate and distribute the body of Christ. Second, he notes that since the Levitical priesthood was hereditary, it required sex to perpetuate itself; the Christian priesthood has no such limitation. And finally, Dymmok points out that since priests must abstain from sex before consecrating the sacrament, it is fitting for priests to be perpetually chaste. On a practical note, he adds not only that priests with wives would be less likely to devote themselves wholly to their ministry but also that married priests would require additional benefices to support their families.[99]

Prescinding from these quasi-historical arguments, Dymmok also responds to what he takes to be the Wycliffites' pessimistic account of human beings' capacity for continence. He argues that Christ and the apostles would not have required priests and other clerics to remain chaste if it were not, in fact, possible for them to do so. In what strikes the modern reader as an odd turn of argument, Dymmok suggests that if married people can remain faithful to their spouses, then clerics can do the same for Christ.[100] With that analogy in hand, he argues that the law of priestly celibacy does not hinder women from finding spouses, since a priest is no less available to a single woman than a man already married.[101]

Dymmok dedicates a more substantial portion of his text to the Wycliffite accusation that male clerics, in the absence of female company, will turn to sodomy. His argument attempts, with varying degrees of success, to distinguish between the discipline of clerical chastity and individual clerics who break

---

[98] Dymmok, *Liber contra XII errores et haereses Lollardorum*, 72/23–7: 'Et ideo Uirgo gloriosa uotum condicionaliter emisit uirginitatis, antequam esset desponsata, scilicet, si Deo placeret, set post matrimonium inter ipsam et Ioseph celebratum ex divino inspiracione, marito consenciente.'

[99] Ibid., 75–7.   [100] Ibid., 81/25–32.   [101] Ibid., 74/5–13.

their vows. Dymmok first points out that male clerics do not avoid the company of women at their own behest; the ordinance of the church and, more important, the command of the Holy Spirit require them to do so. He emphasizes that many male clergy find it difficult to abstain from women and that some even require medicine to help them do so.[102] Whilst he thus builds up a picture of the clerical world as one in which priests' sublimated desires are exclusively heterosexual, Dymmok does admit that some clerics commit sodomy. He argues, however, that neither the church nor the fraternal orders are at fault; after all, the orders' rules prohibit sodomy just as they prohibit heresy and blasphemy. If an individual friar commits a sinful act, his order cannot be held responsible for a crime that its rules proscribe: 'if a religious commits sodomy or any other criminal act, he does not stain his order, but his order remains, as before, untouched'.[103] The same logic, Dymmok claims, applies to the church as a whole. Besides, he notes in conclusion, sodomy can be traced back long before the founding of the religious orders.

Dymmok's response to the eleventh Wycliffite conclusion, which links chastity among female religious with infanticide and abortion, proceeds along similar lines. The Dominican again argues that dissenters have taken too pessimistic a view of human capacities: women, he writes, are indeed capable of remaining chaste, not least with the help of God's grace.[104] In supposing that women are so frail as to be unable to honour their vows, Dymmok chides, lollards must be judging all women by themselves.[105] He admits that abortion and infanticide are indeed great crimes, especially if the children involved were not baptized. Nevertheless, employing the same logic that governs his treatment of sodomy, Dymmok argues that those crimes are not *caused* by the vow of chastity; instead, all that can be said is that the vow provides an *occasion* for sin. Not everyone is called to chastity, Dymmok concludes, and the fact that some people fail to keep their vows implies neither that virginity is impossible nor that it should be abolished.

Dymmok's text betrays the sense that its author was caught somewhat off guard by dissenting views on clerical sexuality. There is not to be found here the stately rhythm of his arguments against Wycliffite ideas about the eucharistic, for instance; instead, there are admissions of vice among religious

---

[102] Ibid., 83/32–7.

[103] Ibid., 85/21–3: 'si religiosus sodomiam committat siue quodcunque aliud criminale, suam religionem non maculat set seipsum, sua religione, ut prius, illibata manente'.

[104] Ibid., 280/11–15. Nevertheless, Dymmok was no proponent of the equality of the sexes; as Fiona Somerset has pointed out, his text contains no 'genuine evaluation of women's capacity for learning'. It is 'always foreclosed . . . by remarks on either their seductability or their seductiveness' ('*Eciam Mulier*', 246).

[105] Dymmok, *Liber contra XII errores et haereses Lollardorum*, 282/24–7.

and attempts to shift the blame from structures to individuals. At the same time, it is important to note that neither Dymmok nor the later anti-Wycliffite writer Thomas Netter wrote at length about the marriage of laypeople, instead dedicating their energies to the task of refuting the view that marriage is licit for clergy and religious. It is to texts closer to the day-to-day lives of medieval Englishmen that we must turn to find mainstream treatments of lay marriage.

One such is *Dives and Pauper,* a tract of the early fifteenth century which discusses a series of theological topics by means of a dialogue between a poor man, Pauper, and a rich one, Dives. Though the text appeared as evidence against at least one heresy suspect, Hudson has justifiably written that 'the well-instructed reader cannot suppose the author of *Dives and Pauper* to have been a Wycliffite, of however conservative a cast'.[106] The text's views on marriage can, therefore, serve as a yardstick against which dissenting opinions may be measured.[107]

It is in Pauper's exegesis of the sixth commandment that the text's stance on marriage emerges most clearly. Like the author of *Of Weddid Men and Wifis,* Pauper's view of sexuality and his theological anthropology are pessimistic. Marriage, the character says, was ordained by God, but only for two reasons: 'to bryngyn forth childryn to Godis seruyse. Also into remedie to flen fornycacion and lecherye.'[108] Sexual activity is licit only when it tends to one of these ends; thus, a married person can have intercourse to procreate, or to keep him- or herself from falling into adultery, or to help keep his or her spouse from doing the same. Pauper shares with the authors of the *Twelve Conclusions* an especially strong disregard for women's abilities: husbands must pay close attention to their wives because they are 'mor frele' and hence more likely to fall into sin.[109] Women should, in addition, be subject to their husbands:

Diues. Why made nout God woman be hyrself of þe erde as he dede Adam?

Pauper. For to moryn her loue togedere and also to ȝeuyn woman materie of lownesse. For for moryng of loue, for in þat woman is part of mannys body man must louyn her

---

[106] *PR,* 419.

[107] *Dives and Pauper* does not, however, present an uncomplicated case. As Ruth Mazo Karras has argued, whilst the text perpetuates the 'double standard' of medieval sexual mores by treating sexual sins committed by men differently than those committed by women, it reverses the normal order of things—*Dives and Pauper* treats sexual failings in men as more sinful than those in women: 'Two models, two standards: Moral teaching and sexual mores' in Barbara A. Hanawalt and David Wallace (eds.), *Bodies and Disciplines: Intersections of literature and history in fifteenth-century England* (Minneapolis, Minn., 1996), 123–38.

[108] *Dives and Pauper,* ed. Priscilla Heath Barnum, 2 vols., 3 parts (EETS o.s. 275, 280, 323, 1976–2004), i, Pt 2, Bk 6, Ch. 2, 60/1–2.

[109] Ibid., i, Pt 2, Bk 6, Ch. 6, 71/7.

as hys owyn flesch and blood, and she must also louyn man as hyr begynnyng and as hyr flesch and hyr blood. Also she owyth takyn gret materie of lownesse and þynkyn þat man is hir perfeccioun and hyr begynnyng and han man in reuerence as hyr perfeccioun, as hyr principal, as hyr begynnyng and hyr first in ordre of kynde.[110]

Whilst Pauper may justly be accused of misogyny, he acknowledges that men too can be guilty of sexual sin, though they are frequently able to escape punishment.[111] The text concludes its commentary on the sixth commandment with a fascinating series of hypothetical disputed marriages. Though there is not space here to detail all the dilemmas that Pauper constructs, the character's familiarity with the intricate casuistry of medieval marriage law substantiates Frederik Pedersen's thesis that some non-lawyers were aware of the complex rules governing marriage.[112]

Dives and Pauper's account of lay sexuality is, in some ways, of a piece with the Wycliffite texts we have discussed. Nevertheless, Pauper allows the institutional church a substantial role in the regulation of marriage. First, he specifies that husbands who discover that their wives have committed adultery must obtain the church's endorsement to dissolve the union.[113] Second, he urges Dives to turn to the observances of traditional religion when tempted by lust: sinful thoughts may be overcome by sparing consumption of fine meat and drink, by fighting against the urge to look at or think about women, and by meditating on Christ's passion.[114]

Whereas there is little about *Dives and Pauper* that suggests that its author intended either to refute or else to endorse Wycliffite ideas about marriage, the same cannot be said of John Mirk's *Festial*, whose Augustinian author was a vocal opponent of early lollardy. Mirk's biographer, Susan Powell, has speculated that though the sermons may not have been disseminated widely, 'it may be that the circulation of the *Festial* in the central midlands, which is well attested by extant manuscripts, was officially encouraged in opposition to the Lollard sermon cycle'.[115] Compared with a text like *Of Weddid Men and Wifis* or even *Dives and Pauper*, Mirk's 'Sermo de nupcijs' contains a relatively positive theology of marriage.

---

[110] *Dives and Pauper*, i, Pt 2, Bk 6, Ch. 4, 67/40–9.

[111] Ibid., i, Pt 2, Bk 6, Ch. 4, i, Pt 2, Bk 6, Ch. 5, 68/44–8.

[112] Ibid., i, Pt 2, Bk 6, Chs. 19–20, 111–18. For additional discussion on this point, see Christine Peters, 'Gender, sacrament, and ritual: The making and meaning of marriage in late medieval and early modern England', *Past and Present*, 169 (2000), 63–96 at 72.

[113] *Dives and Pauper*, i, Pt 2, Bk 6, Ch. 7, 75/12–17.

[114] Ibid., i, Pt 2, Bk 6, Chs. 14–15, 95–9/1–104, 1–4.

[115] Susan Powell, 'Mirk, John', *Oxford Dictionary of National Biography*, <http://www.oxforddnb.com/view/article/18818> (accessed 6 December 2005).

The sermon prominently describes marriage as a sacrament and discusses its benefits under three headings: 'furste for gode begynnyng, sython for gode leuing, and aftur for gode ending'.[116] Mirk proceeds to compare the marriage ritual with the creation of men and women in the book of Genesis. Just as God formed Eve from Adam's rib, so also should couples resemble each other in age, health, and social status. When during the marriage rite the priest gives the woman to the man, he represents God giving Eve to Adam. Under the rubric of 'holy . . . lyuing', Mirk recounts the story of the wedding at Cana, noting that Christ's presence there sanctified marriage for all time.[117] Finally, as for marriage's 'gode ending', Mirk notes that 'þei þat keputh it wel in hure lyuing, þei schul come and ben takon in at þe gret weddyng þat schul ben aftur þe day of dome'.[118] In comparison with Wycliffite writings on the subject, Mirk does not teach that marriage is primarily a remedy for concupiscence; he instead stresses its sacramental aspect and treats it as an independent good. Mirk, however, does urge his audience to conduct their marriages within the bounds of church law: he reminds his hearers of the consanguinity rules and makes it clear that partners should not enter into marriage without the intention of having children.[119] Since Mirk replies elsewhere to dissenting arguments about images and clerical authority, it would not be unsurprising if its author constructed his theology of marriage in such a way as to counter the pessimism about human nature and scepticism about ecclesiastical regulation to be found in such texts as *Of Weddid Men and Wifis*.

A more sympathetic response to dissenting concerns can be found in one of the so-called 'N-Town' cycle plays, composed in the second quarter of the fifteenth century for performance in an unnamed East Anglian community or communities.[120] Emma Lipton has pointed out that the N-Town cycle uniquely dedicates an entire play to the marriage of Mary and Joseph, an event unrecorded in the Bible and rarely discussed among scholastic theologians.[121] Though the play was never implicated in Wycliffism, the manner in which it treats its subject places it on a common footing with many dissenting texts. The play depicts Mary, a virgin of fourteen years, being brought to the temple to be wed. She protests, however, that she wishes never to marry:

---

[116] Mirk, *Festial*, 289/10–11.   [117] Ibid., 292/31–4.   [118] Ibid., 293/14–16.

[119] Ibid., 290/16–20, 31–3. An equally mainstream treatment of marriage is to be found in Mirk's *Instructions for Parish Priests*, ed. Edward Peacock (EETS o.s. 31, rev. edn., 1902), 6–7.

[120] *The N-Town Play: Cotton MS Vespasian D.8*, ed. Stephen Spector, 2 vols. (EETS s.s. 11–12, 1991), i.xxxviii–xli. For the suggestion that the play was itinerant, see i.xiii.

[121] Emma Lipton, 'Performing reform: Lay piety and the marriage of Mary and Joseph in the N-Town cycle', *Studies in the Age of Chaucer*, 23 (2001), 407–35 at 408; see more recently her monograph *Affections of the Mind: The politics of sacramental marriage in late medieval English literature* (South Bend, Ind., 2007).

'Aʒens þe lawe wyl I nevyr be, / But mannys felachep xal nevyr folwe me. / I wyl levyn evyr in chastyté / Be þe grace of Goddys wille.'[122] A character who bears the anachronistic title *Episcopus* insists that Mary find a spouse, and he bids every eligible man of the house of David to come to the temple bearing a wooden rod. Joseph, an elderly man, at first refuses to join in, pleading age and impotence. He lurks behind the crowd of suitors, but in the end, his rod is the one that bursts into flowers. Like Mary, he resists marriage, but the couple are wedded nonetheless; they exchange rings and take mutual vows to live together in chastity.[123]

At first glance, the N-Town play might seem to be no more than a spirited defence and pious dramatization of Mary's perpetual virginity. Lipton, however, has suggested that the religious politics of early-fifteenth-century East Anglia provide an important context for the drama: the 'theatrical promotion of lay piety,' she has argued, 'would have appealed not only to moderate constituencies, such as the wealthy merchant patrons of the numerous parish churches in East Anglia, but even . . . to Lollard extremists'.[124] Whilst the play is almost certainly not of Wycliffite composition, not least because many dissenters opposed what they perceived to be the vulgarity of treating scriptural and religious subjects in dramatic form, it does share a number of features with Wycliffite theologies of marriage. By depicting the chaste marriage of Joseph and Mary not as an aberration but as a model, the play reflects the distrust of sexual activity that can be found, for instance, in Cigman's *Lollard Sermons* and *Of Weddid Men and Wifis*. The play takes the stance, as Lipton has put it, that marriage is 'a sacramental and spiritual practice that does not depend on consummation', implicitly ridiculing the sexual criteria of medieval marital jurisprudence and emphasizing that marriage consists in a spiritual bond between the partners.[125] At the same time, however, the play reinforces traditional medieval notions about marriage. It is a clergyman, *Episcopus*, who requires Mary and Joseph to be married, arguably against their will; it is also he who conducts the marriage ceremony, which, as we have already noted, would have been unremarkable to a medieval audience. Unlike the highly traditional seven-sacrament fonts that began to appear throughout East Anglia at roughly the same time, the play straddles orthodox and dissenting positions and can be seen neither as a work of anti-lollard propaganda nor an apologia for Wycliffite concerns.[126]

---

[122] *N-Town Play*, i.97/36–9.   [123] *N-Town Play*, i.106/331, 111/485.
[124] Lipton, 'Performing reform', 409.   [125] Ibid., 433.
[126] From the second quarter of the fifteenth century, seven-sacrament fonts were acquired by many East Anglian parish churches. As Ann Eljenholm Nichols has suggested, their iconography served as a visual riposte to dissenting ideas about the eucharistic and the other sacraments. On their panels depicting marriage, all but one of the fonts include at least one clerical figure, and all

The corpus of texts produced in the late fourteenth and fifteenth centuries by writers who stood within the religious mainstream reveals a surprising diversity of opinions about marriage. Whilst no such author joined extreme Wycliffite writers in advocating clerical marriage, their views of marriage differed substantially. Whereas the clerical polemicists Dymmok and Netter both ignored the question of lay sexuality, Mirk appears to have regarded marriage as an independent good, whilst the author of *Dives and Pauper* seems to have considered it primarily a means of avoiding sexual sin. Finally, the N-Town cycle takes a wholly different view of marriage and sexuality altogether. Combining conventional and dissenting ideas about marriage, the playwright praises the chaste union of Mary and Joseph. Taken together, these texts highlight the inadequacy of the single label *orthodox* for late medieval English texts that cannot be traced back to Wycliffite dissenters. It was not only the theologically deviant who failed to find common ground where marriage was concerned.

MARRIAGE IN HERESY TRIALS

Like dissenters who wrote about these topics, the more than seventy heresy suspects whose depositions and abjurations contain ideas about marriage and sexuality sometimes differed in their approaches. Most common among the defendants was the view that marriages need not be solemnized in church, but they also articulated ideas about the equality of men and women, about the relative worth of marriage and virginity, and about the consequences of clerical celibacy. Nevertheless, as we found with the doctrines of salvation and the eucharistic, records from heresy trials must be read with great care. The stereotyping effects of inquisitorial presuppositions were very much in force where ideas about marriage were concerned, and confusion about the boundaries of orthodoxy complicated the situation further.

After Wyclif's death in 1384, the first heresy trial to involve controversial statements about sexuality was the process in 1389 against William Ramsbury of Salisbury diocese. Whilst, as we saw in the previous chapter, his trial is justly famous for the light it casts on the liturgical practices of early dissenters, more important for our present purposes is Ramsbury's position on questions

---

but six feature lay witnesses as well. By thus reinforcing the church's prohibition of private or clandestine marriages, the fonts implicitly reject the claim that marriage should be solemnized outside of church (*Seeable Signs: The iconography of the seven sacraments, 1350–1544* (Woodbridge, 1994), 274–85).

of sexuality. He confessed to having taught that sex with a nun is no sin; that priests and laymen may rightly have intercourse with any woman in order to propagate the species; that it is better for priests and religious men to take wives and be apostates rather than to live in chastity; and that if a man finds that his wife cannot bear him children, he should put her away and seek another.[127] This last position may have garnered support from some canonists, but Ramsbury's ideas were hardly well received by Bishop Waltham's inquisitors.[128] He abjured these and eleven other articles, received a penance, and apparently performed it well.

As has recently been emphasized, Ramsbury may have been indebted more to continental 'Free Spirit' ideas than to English Wycliffite ones.[129] Indeed, other suspects' views were less permissive. Sir Lewis Clifford, one of the so-called 'Lollard knights' and a retainer first of Edward the Black Prince and then of his son Richard II, was reported by the chronicler Thomas Walsingham to have confessed that marriage, having been ordained directly by God, is superior to virginity and priesthood.[130] Clifford argued that all men and women who are not married should get married, or at least desire to get married; otherwise, he said, they were guilty of having wasted the opportunity to bring forth children. Finally, Clifford suggested that a man and a woman can marry simply by exchanging consent: 'that is sufficient, without major obedience having been made to the church'.[131]

It is possible that Clifford's views were distorted by Lancastrian propagandists keen to associate their Plantagenet predecessors with heresy as well as revolt and nepotism, but at least one of the beliefs that Clifford abjured was common among English dissenters. The view that church weddings are unnecessary and that couples can marry without solemnizing their union in front of a priest occurs frequently in the records. Curiously, this belief, which at least four dozen defendants abjured, was not precisely heterodox, since the institutional church taught that clandestine marriages were valid, even if not ideal.[132]

---

[127] Hudson, 'Lollard Mass', 121, nos. 13, 14, 9, 10.

[128] James A. Brundage, 'Impotence, frigidity, and marital nullity in the decretists and early decretalists', repr. in *Sex, Law, and Marriage in the Middle Ages* (Aldershot, 1993), ch. 10.

[129] Hudson, 'Lollard Mass', 114, and Kerby-Fulton, *Books under Suspicion*, 269–71.

[130] K. B. McFarland, *Lancastrian Kings and Lollard Knights* (Oxford, 1972), 164–6.

[131] Walsingham, *Historia anglicana*, ii.252–3: 'si vir et foemina convenerint in una voluntate nubendi, ipsa voluntas sufficiens est conjugium sine majori obedientia Ecclesiae facienta'. See also *Annales Ricardi Secundi et Henrici Quarti, Regum Angliae*, in *Chronica Monasterii S. Albani*, ed. H. T. Riley (London, 1866), 153–420 at 347–8.

[132] See p. 110 above. Lipton has suggested that dissenters were unaware the church grudgingly considered clandestine marriages valid, but it seems far more likely that overzealous inquisitors recorded as heretical a position that, technically speaking, was not ('Performing reform', 424).

Nevertheless, clandestine marriage remained a litmus test of orthodoxy in the fifteenth and early sixteenth centuries. Twenty-four of the defendants who appeared before Bishop William Alnwick of Norwich during the period 1428–31 admitted to having believed that the consent of the partners alone makes a marriage, as did ten suspects from Salisbury, Ely, Lincoln, and Hereford dioceses and a dozen defendants brought to trial during Archbishop William Warham's purge of Canterbury diocese in 1511–12.[133]

The groups of heresy suspects from Norwich and Canterbury arouse the suspicion that inquisitors may erroneously have attributed identical views to large numbers of suspects. Indeed, all but five of the Norwich suspects whose trials included material about marriage confessed to the belief that solemnization in church is not necessary. Their depositions and abjurations follow a pattern which seems to have been established during the trial of Margery Baxter, the first suspect to admit to heterodox ideas about marriage. Among the witnesses who testified in her case was Joan Clifland, one of Baxter's fellow parishioners in Norwich. Clifland reported that Baxter had said 'that only the consent of mutual love between a man and a woman suffices for the sacrament of matrimony, without any other words or solemnization in church'.[134] The very same text, with only cosmetic changes, appears in the deposition of John Skylly of Flixton, the next suspect to appear in court.[135] It also recurs, again with only minor textual amendments, in the trials of Sybil Godsell of Ditchingham, John Reve and Matilda Fleccher of Beccles, Robert Cavell of

---

[133] In Norwich, the defendants were Margery Baxter of Martham, John Skylly of Flixton, Sybil Godsell of Ditchingham, John Pryre of Martham, John Kynget of Nayland, Richard Fleccher of Beccles, Robert Cavell the parish chaplain of Bungay, John Reve of Beccles, Richard Knobbyng of Beccles, Richard Grace of Beccles, Baldwin Cowper of Beccles, Matilda Fleccher of Beccles, John Eldon of Beccles, Hawisia Mone of Loddon, John Skylan of Bergh, William Hardy of Mundham, William Bate of Seething, Edmund Archer of Loddon, John Pert of Loddon, Thomas Mone of Loddon, John Fynche of Colchester, John Wroxham of Loddon, Robert Gryggys of Martham, Isabel Chapleyn of Martham, and William Masse of Earsham; see *Norwich, passim*. Other defendants were Thomas Bikenore (Salisbury reg. Aiscough, fols. 52v–54v, 1443); William and Richard Sparke (Lincoln reg. Chedworth, fols. 12v–14, 1457); Robert Sparke, John Crud, and John Baile (Ely reg. Grey, fol. 130b, 1457); John Cornewe, John Breche, and Richard Atcombe (Hereford reg. Stanbury, 118–9, 1469); John Croft (Hereford reg. Mayew, 66–7, 1505); and Henry Shercot (Salisbury reg. Audley, fols. 160r–v, 1517). In Canterbury diocese, the suspects Robert Harryson of Canterbury, William Carder of Tenterden, Agnes Grebill of Tenterden, Christopher Grebill of Tenterden, William Riche of Benenden, John Grebill senior of Benenden, Thomas Mannyng of Benenden, Joan Colyn of Tenterden, Robert Hilles of Tenterden, John Browne of Ashford, Edward Walker of Maidstone, and Thomas Church of Great Chart all abjured articles concerning marriage; see *Kent, passim*.

[134] *Norwich*, 46: 'Item quod eadem Margeria dixit isti iurate tunc ibidem quod solus consensus mutui amoris inter virum et mulierem sufficit pro sacramento matrimonii, absque expressione aliorum verborum et absque solennizacione in ecclesiis.'

[135] Ibid., 52.

Bungay, Thomas Mone and John Wroxham of Loddon, John Fynche of Colchester, Robert Gryggs and Isabel Chapleyn of Martham, and William Masse of Earsham. A literal English translation of the same words appears in the records associated with John Pert of Loddon and Richard Fleccher, Richard Knobbyng, Richard Grace, and Baldwin Cowper, all of Beccles. The phrases of Clifland's testimony against Baxter also appear along with other views about marriage in the abjurations and depositions of Hawisia Mone and Edmund Archer of Loddon, John Skylan of Bergh, William Hardy of Mundham, and William Bate of Seething.[136]

Nevertheless, just because Bishop Alnwick's inquisitors employed a stock phrase to describe the defendants' ideas about marriage does not mean that no defendant emerges from the records as an individual. Whilst we know nothing of fourteen defendants beyond what Margery Baxter reportedly told Joan Clifland, in other cases the Norwich records preserve additional details about their subjects. William Hardy, for instance, confessed to having taught that the solemnization of marriage in church was invented by avaricious priests in order to extort money from their flocks.[137] Hawisia Mone said that the consent of the partners suffices to create a marriage 'withoute symbred asking', an obscure phrase which may imply the view that potential partners should not be subjected to the ritual of a public inquisition into their family relationships.[138] And William Colyn of South Creake, whom we have already encountered on account of his infamous claim that he would rather touch a woman's privy parts than the host, maintained that women should be held in common and marriage itself abolished.[139] Whilst it is likely, therefore, that the Norwich records do obscure some of the variations in belief that existed in fifteenth-century East Anglia, it is to the inquisitors' credit that something of the defendants' idiosyncrasies can still be found. In Canterbury diocese, however, the opposite situation obtained: nearly the same form of words was abjured by all twelve defendants who confessed to heterodox ideas about marriage, which makes it all but certain that Archbishop Warham's officials painted their heresy suspects with a single brush.[140]

---

[136] *Norwich, passim.*
[137] Ibid., 153: 'suche solennizacion is but vayneglorie induced be covetise of prestes to gete mony of the puple'.
[138] Ibid., 141.
[139] Ibid., 91.
[140] Almost all of Warham's defendants confessed that 'matrimonii solemnisatio non est necessaria ad anime salutem nec a iure divino instituta' (*Kent*, 2). Six defendants dropped the phrase *nec a iure divino instituta* from their abjurations, and Thomas Church of Great Chart argued that unction as well as matrimony was not necessary, but the sense of all twelve articles is identical.

Apart from the mass persecutions of Alnwick and Warham, defendants' beliefs about marriage ran the gamut from the highly technical to the lecherous. The most complex set of views on lay marriage was abjured sometime between 1400 and 1403 by the leading Wycliffite John Purvey.[141] Of the seven opinions of which he was accused by the Carmelite prior Richard Lavyngham, three are strikingly reminiscent of Wyclif's views: that canon law enables men to circumvent God's rules about marriage; that if a woman knows of an impediment of consanguinity but cannot prove it to the satisfaction of a church court, she should leave her husband anyway; and that it is better to release the parties to a disputed marriage to their own consciences than to run the risk of compelling them to live together adulterously.[142]

Few defendants approached Purvey's legal and theological sophistication. As the complexities of early Wycliffite belief gave way, later defendants who spoke of marriage did so in practical terms. In 1412, the layman William Mundy abjured in Salisbury diocese the view that any married person is equal in status to a priest. Though a number of defendants throughout the fifteenth and sixteenth centuries spoke of what later reformers would call the universal priesthood of all believers, Mundy was the only one to discuss the relative status of marriage and ordination.[143] About half a century later, the Lincoln suspect John Qwyrk confessed that the church cannot separate couples whose marriages had been solemnized, a view that was echoed in Scotland in 1495, when eight suspects from Kyle abjured the claim 'that after Matrimony by [*sic*] contracted, and consummate, the kyrk may make no Divorcement.'[144]

With the sole exception of Ramsbury's inflammatory comments late in the fourteenth century, clerical marriage does not appear in the trial records until 1424. In that year, the Franciscan friar John Russell, an unlikely candidate for membership of a Wycliffite community, appeared in the Canterbury provincial convocation to answer the charge that he had preached that religious men can have sex with women without sinning.[145] It is likely that Russell was no more than a discontented celibate, but his views were echoed four years later by a more obvious lollard, the preacher William White. In 1428, White confessed to Bishop Alnwick of Norwich that after abjuring heresy in Canterbury diocese, he had moved to Norwich, given up his habit and tonsure, and

---

[141] For additional biographical details on Purvey, see Maureen Jurkowski, 'New light on John Purvey', *English Historical Review*, 110 (1995), 1180–90.

[142] *FZ*, 391–2.

[143] Salisbury reg. Hallum, no. 1142; on the concept of universal priesthood, see Ch. 5 below.

[144] Lincoln reg. Chedworth, fols. 59v–60; John Knox, *The Historie of the Reformation of the Church of Scotland* (London, 1644), 2–3, no. 24.

[145] Lambeth reg. Chichele, iii, 91.

married a woman named Joan. He taught that popes had mandated clerical celibacy against the freedom of Christ and argued that once priests in England were prohibited wives, they became both greedy and lecherous.[146] As a relapsed heretic, White was burned in short order. Around the time of his trial, seven other Norwich defendants confessed to believing that marriage is permissible and indeed desirable for priests and nuns. One of them, the servant John Burell, reported that his master Thomas Mone had recommended that priests should take wives, 'just as many priests do in remote regions'.[147] Though a question about clerical celibacy made its way into the questionnaire commissioned in 1428 by Bishop Thomas Polton of Worcester, clerical marriage did not resurface in a heresy trial until 1488, when John Nowers of Lincoln diocese argued that the marriage of men in holy orders is lawful; it recurred again in 1490, when Richard Petesyne of Winchester diocese maintained that prelates should have wives.[148]

It remains to ask if these records reveal any patterns. It is striking that the majority of suspects who expressed opinions about marriage and sexuality articulated roughly similar views. There were not, in other words, the substantial differences of opinion that we have encountered in the cases of salvation and the eucharistic. At their trials, few dissenters expressed the sexual traditionalism that can be found in Wyclif's Latin writings and some of the texts produced by his early followers. It must be acknowledged, however, both that inquisitors were more likely to focus on questions whose answers could be judged clearly orthodox or heterodox and that heresy trials are not the optimum venue for discussions of sexuality and sexual ethics. The high numbers of suspects from Norwich and Canterbury dioceses who confessed to dissenting views about marriage may suggest that inquisitors in those dioceses were more aware than their counterparts elsewhere that marriage could be a site for heterodox discourse.

Two chronological trends also deserve attention. On the one hand, the view that marriage should not be solemnized in church recurs frequently through the fifteenth and early sixteenth centuries, even though the incidence of clandestine marriage seems to have decreased over the same period. On the other hand, it is interesting that with the notable exception of William Ramsbury's trial in 1389, controversial claims about clerical marriage do not enter the records until the 1420s. Whether or not that may have been

---

[146] *FZ*, 420–5.
[147] *Norwich*, 73: 'sicut plures presbiteri faciunt in diversis partibus remotis'.
[148] Hudson, 'The examination of Lollards', 134, no. 39; A. Hamilton Thompson, *The English Clergy and Their Organization in the Later Middle Ages* (Oxford, 1947), 222–6; Winchester reg. Courtenay, fols. 26r–27r.

due to the lingering effects of Wyclif's caution on the topic remains an open question, though it seems unlikely that many lay dissenters would have been more familiar with Wyclif's works than with the many vernacular tracts which urged an end to clerical celibacy.

CONCLUSIONS

Marriage and sexuality have proven to be additional areas where Wyclif and his successors did not always agree. Whereas Wyclif had expressed scepticism about clerical marriage, declaring it to be possible but nevertheless inappropriate, many later dissenters embraced it enthusiastically. The suggestion that priests and nuns should be allowed to marry appears often in Wycliffite texts and trial records, and it was a sufficiently controversial idea for at least two orthodox polemicists, Roger Dymmok and Thomas Netter, to devote considerable energy to its refutation. Wyclif's views on lay marriage met a different fate: only a few features of what I have been calling his theology of sexuality can be found in his followers' tracts on the subject. Indeed, many Wycliffites moved beyond the Oxford thinker in articulating so pessimistic a view of human nature as to render marriage merely a preventative for lust. Likewise, few dissenting authors explicitly concurred with Wyclif's scepticism about the institutional church's ability to regulate marriage, though as we have seen, the belief most commonly abjured by heresy suspects was that marriage need not be solemnized in church.

Our study of dissenting theologies of marriage and sexuality therefore calls even further into doubt the view that Wycliffites and their successors subverted the sexual *status quo* of the later Middle Ages. With the exception of their objections to the practice of church weddings, Wycliffites who wrote about lay marriage often recapitulated traditional themes, and they rarely praised the abilities of women. Against the background of such ideas, even the ostensibly 'liberal' suggestion that clerical celibacy should be abolished can be read in terms that buttress patriarchy and sexual traditionalism. Wycliffite texts repeatedly warn that celibacy has given rise to sins ranging from sodomy to infanticide, and it is no stretch to imagine that their authors regarded the marriage of priests and nuns more as an opportunity to regulate clerical libidinousness than as an exercise in Christian liberty. As McSheffrey has noted, the abolition of celibacy would have struck especially hard at the opportunities available to medieval women, for a slim minority of whom the convent provided 'the possibility . . . of living outside the structures of the patriarchal family'.[149]

But, then, why has lollardy been thought of for several decades as a movement—or, more accurately, a set of more or less interconnected communities—that appealed especially to women? That the first scholarly studies of lollardy and gender were written as feminist theory was flowering cannot be discounted, nor can the fact that some of the texts upon which McSheffrey and I have relied have only become available in the last two decades and have, in a few cases, been studied here for the first time. The notion of lollards as sexual pioneers remains strange indeed, not least because late medieval English heretics were rarely themselves accused of libertinism. James A. Brundage, Vern Bullough, and other historians have documented the ways in which accusations of heresy and sexual immorality tended to go hand in hand among the opponents of sects like the Cathars and Waldensians of southern France. Against this background, it is particularly surprising that few accusations of sexual vice in late medieval English religious controversy were made against Wycliffites by their clerical opponents.[150] The reason may be that English dissenters were not themselves especially scandalous. Only two suspects' views about marriage bordered on indecency, and these two, William Ramsbury and William Colyn, both seem to have existed at the margins of Wycliffite or lollard dissent, if indeed they can be described in these terms at all. At the same time, Roger Dymmok's defensiveness and uncharacteristically specious arguments about clerical marriage suggest that the church may not have stood to gain from comparisons between the behaviour of ecclesiastics and heresy suspects.

The substance of dissenting ideas aside, the history of Wycliffite and lollard attitudes toward marriage and sexuality reveals a pattern of doctrinal change. Whereas with the doctrine of salvation, dissenters appropriated predestinarian terminology whilst for the most part embracing the works-oriented soteriology widespread in the Middle Ages, and whereas with the eucharistic, they tended to embrace either the theology of remanence or that of figuration, with marriage, dissenters seem to have adopted Wyclif's theology of lay sexuality whilst at the same time rejecting his cautions about a married clergy. As in previous chapters, however, it is impossible to speak of a linear transition from one set of ideas to the other. Despite the tendency of the extant sources to pigeonhole ideas about marriage even more noticeably than those

---

[149] McSheffrey, *Gender and Heresy*, 81.
[150] James A. Brundage, *Law, Sex, and Christian Society* (Chicago, 1987), 493, 357; Vern Bullough, 'Postscript: Heresy, witchcraft, and sexuality' in Vern L. Bullough and James Brundage (eds.), *Sexual Practices and the Medieval Church* (Buffalo, NY, 1982), 206–10.

about salvation or the eucharistic, Wycliffite texts and trial records both witness to the multivalent views about marriage and sexuality to be found within dissenting circles. Each side of the dialogue between dissenters and their antagonists reinforced the other: when the former priest William White abandoned his tonsure, got married, and preached about clerical marriage in Norwich, it was unsurprising that inquisitors there asked later defendants about the same topic. But however stereotyped the records might be, careful reading reveals that dissenters' ideas about marriage and sexuality were hardly unitary. We do not know if the Buckinghamshire suspect Agnes Wellis, in whose company we began, told Bishop Longland that she and her fellow dissenters only married one another. But even if they did, it is by no means settled what they thought their marriages entailed.

5

Priesthood and its Discontents

On 5 April 1441, a heresy defendant confessed to Bishop John Stafford of Bath and Wells that he had blasphemed against four of the church's sacraments. John Jurdan's arguments about baptism, confession, and the eucharist were conventional enough; like many of the dissenters whom we have encountered, he claimed that a child born to baptized parents does not herself need baptism, that oral confession to a priest is unnecessary, and that the substances of bread and wine remain on the altar after the words of consecration. But in his abjuration Jurdan made an additional statement: 'that the sacrament of ordre ordeyned for ministres to be in the church is vayne, voyde, superflewe and not necessarie'.[1] Criticisms of the clergy were not unusual in late medieval England, but Jurdan had not merely pointed out that some clergymen were failing to conform to the standards of behaviour expected of them. Instead, it seems, he aimed to undermine the sacred character that distinguished the clergy as one of society's three estates.

It is difficult to overestimate the role that clergymen played in the theory and practice of late medieval Christianity. Even when confraternities, gilds, and 'third orders' provided lay people with the opportunity to participate more actively in spiritual matters, or when popular piety encouraged the institutional church to enshrine devotions like the feast of Corpus Christi, the clergy remained indispensable.[2] Only a priest or bishop could preside at the celebration of mass. It was almost always a priest who baptized newborns and, likewise, it was a priest to whom the dying made their last confessions. Priests witnessed betrothals and marriages, buried the dead, and if their parishioners were sufficiently fortunate to have an educated cleric among them, provided spiritual instruction. For nearly all medieval Englishmen, it was a local priest who connected parish life to the universal church, with its distant Roman head, the pope. With such a wide range of responsibilities and opportunities for error, it should not be surprising that many clergymen were perceived to

---

[1] Bath and Wells reg. Stafford, ii.266–7.
[2] See, for instance, Rubin, *Corpus Christi*.

fall short. Indeed, criticism of the church's ministers suffuses the writings of many mainstream as well as of dissenting authors.

To study lay attitudes toward the clergy is in many ways to step into a historiographical minefield. The first obstacle to be avoided is a terminological one. Until the mid-1980s the dominant interpretation of the origins of the Reformation in England took as one of its foundational categories the concept of anticlericalism. G. G. Coulton, for instance, argued in 1930 that the Reformation would never have happened if medieval clergymen had not been corrupt.[3] In the last three decades, however, revisionist historians have objected that to use the label 'anticlericalism' to describe religious feeling in late medieval and early modern England is to commit a methodological blunder. Christopher Haigh, in particular, has argued that anticlericalism provides no more than a flawed 'explanatory tool' which teleologically connects disparate phenomena like Wycliffism, statutes against benefit of clergy, and the acts of the Reformation Parliament. At the same time, the label elides a host of distinctions: supposedly 'anticlerical' thinkers included erastian political theorists as well as disaffected parishioners and dissenters who embraced the doctrine of the priesthood of all believers.[4]

A broader approach to the study of the late medieval clergy can be found in the work of R. N. Swanson, who in 1990 published an important study of complaints against parish priests.[5] Swanson argued that most medieval critics of the clergy focused on the perceived misbehaviour of individual priests rather than challenging the prerogatives of the clerical estate as a whole. When, for instance, the parishioners of Saltash in Devon complained in 1404 that their vicar was a drunkard, a simoniac, and a failure in the pulpit, they asked the patrons of the living to give them a more qualified priest. 'If

---

[3] G. G. Coulton, *Ten Medieval Studies* (Cambridge, 1930), 137–8; for the most influential restatement of this position, see A. G. Dickens, *The English Reformation*, 2nd edn (London, 1989). In 1987, Dickens admitted the force of many revisionist arguments, granting that 'anticlericalism has become an unduly capacious word', but he continued to insist that the category provides a useful framework for historical discourse: 'The shape of anticlericalism and the English Reformation', repr. in *Late Monasticism and the Reformation* (London, 1994), 151–75 at 151.

[4] Christopher Haigh, 'Anticlericalism and the English Reformation', repr. in *The English Reformation Revised* (Cambridge, 1987), 56–74 at 56–7.

[5] R. N. Swanson, 'Problems of the priesthood in pre-Reformation England', *English Historical Review*, 105 (1990), 846–69. For his more recent contributions to this debate, see among others 'Before the Protestant clergy: The construction and deconstruction of medieval priesthood' in C. Scott Dixon and Luise Schorn-Schütte (eds.), *The Protestant Clergy of Early Modern Europe* (Basingstoke, 2003), 39–59, 200–9; and 'Pastoralia in practice: Clergy and ministry in pre-Reformation England' in T. Clemens and W. Janse (eds.), *The Pastor Bonus: Papers read at the British-Dutch colloquium at Utrecht, 18–21 September 2002* (Leiden, 2004), 104–28.

they were being anticlerical, which is questionable, they were certainly not being antisacerdotal.[6] Indeed, the Saltash parishioners' complaint reflects a keen interest on the part of a group of laypeople to ensure continuity in the traditional ministries of word and sacraments, not a desire to do away with the clergy altogether. It is helpful, then, to distinguish between two sets of ideas that have often been conflated under the rubric of 'anticlericalism'. The position to which I shall be referring as *antisacerdotalism* envisions the abolition of a separate priestly class with the exclusive right to celebrate the sacraments. Antisacerdotal thinkers, of whom John Jurdan may have been one, are to be differentiated from *hyperclericalists*, who subscribed to traditional theologies of the priesthood but desired the restoration of ideal standards of behaviour among clergymen.[7]

Terms such as these will help us to avoid many of the ambiguities entailed in the earlier language, but other challenges still remain. For one, as I have emphasized above, not all manifestations of religious dissent in late medieval England can be traced back to the reforms proposed by Wyclif and his followers. Indeed, from the time of the earliest ecumenical councils, the desire to regulate the behaviour of the clergy has been a perennial concern of senior churchmen. In 325, the Council of Nicaea approved a canon to prohibit clergymen from moving at will between cities; another canon provided for the punishment of clerics who practiced usury.[8] Future councils would legislate against pluralism, drunkenness, incontinence, and excessively sumptuous dress—all topics that continued to attract attention in late medieval England.[9] At the same time, many of those who in our period objected to the behaviour of the clergy went without suspicion of theological heterodoxy. King Edward III, for instance, was not accused of heresy in 1363, when he threatened to disendow the clergy for disrespecting the rights of lay patrons.[10]

Though efforts to reform the clergy have recurred throughout the history of Christianity, they were especially prominent in the later Middle Ages. To be sure, criticisms of the clergy appear so frequently in medieval sources that it would be unwieldy to discuss every dimension of the topic here. There is not

---

[6] Swanson, 'Problems of the priesthood in pre-Reformation England', 868.

[7] Malcolm Beryl Yarnell, 'Royal priesthood in the English Reformation' (D.Phil. thesis, Oxford University, 2000), makes a similar distinction, but he calls the two positions 'extreme anticlericalism' and 'anticlericalism', respectively. The ambiguities of the older terminology thus persist unhelpfully in Yarnell's work.

[8] Tanner, *Decrees*, i.13, 14.

[9] Among many others, see Tanner, *Decrees*, i.92 (Chalcedon), 197 (Lateran II), and 242–3 (Lateran IV).

[10] Michael Wilks, 'Royal patronage and anti-papalism: From Ockham to Wyclif', repr. in Wilks, *Wyclif*, 117–46 at 129.

space to address them at length, but three areas of study do deserve brief mention: the relationship between church and state, the theory of dominion, and the monastic and fraternal orders. First, a number of studies have sought to situate John Wyclif and later English dissenters within a tradition of thinking about the competing jurisdictional claims of the *imperium* and *sacerdotium*. Both L. J. Daly and Michael Wilks have attempted, with varying degrees of success, to document the influence of Giles of Rome, Marsilius of Padua, and the medieval canonists on Wyclif's ideas about the relative powers of king and pope.[11] Whilst it remains unclear whether the lines of intellectual inheritance can be so easily drawn, it is helpful to acknowledge that the relationship between church and state has less to do with the sacrament of orders than with broader questions of ecclesiology and political philosophy. In any case, with the exception of the view that secular lords should take an active part in confiscating the goods of the church, discussions of the relationship between church and state do not regularly appear in the dissenting texts produced after Wyclif's death.

A second area of Wyclif's thought-world in which later dissenters seem to have shown comparatively little interest is his theory of dominion. As Stephen E. Lahey has argued, many of Wyclif's arguments about the authority of the king 'were framed neither in the theocratic kingship language of the Anglo-Saxon and Anglo-Norman tradition, nor were they couched in the more contemporary Aristotelian terms favoured by other champions of secular authority... His arguments were framed in terms of Grace-founded *dominium*.'[12] For Wyclif, *dominium* refers to the ownership or lordship that a person has the power rightly to exercise in either the civil or ecclesiastical realm. Only those presently in a state of grace can wield *dominium*, and thus, sinful lords and bishops cannot properly exercise lordship over their subjects. The place of *dominium* in Wyclif's thought remains a matter of some dispute, but the doctrine ultimately had little effect on the more pragmatic arguments about the clergy that I shall be discussing here.[13]

Finally, objections to the monastic and fraternal orders occur frequently in dissenting texts and heresy trials. The form of these criticisms, which in some cases were raised by secular clergy against their monastic and fraternal

---

[11] L. J. Daly, *The Political Theory of John Wyclif* (Chicago, 1962); Michael Wilks, 'The *Apostolicus* and the Bishop of Rome', *Journal of Theological Studies*, n.s. 13 (1962), 290–317, and n.s. 14 (1963), 311–54.

[12] Lahey, *Philosophy and Politics in the Thought of John Wyclif*, 1. The first chapter of Lahey's study contains an excellent survey of the historiography of Wyclif's doctrine of dominion.

[13] See, for instance, Leff, *Heresy in the Later Middle Ages*, ii.520–1. Leff's views are followed by Lambert, *Medieval Heresy*, 237.

brethren, varies according to the type of religious order under discussion: monks appear as greedy 'possessioners' who grow fat on rents but carry out no public ministry, whereas friars are depicted as false beggars who seek alms without being genuinely needy. Dissenting authors routinely challenged the vocations of both, arguing that Christ had never intended that there be distinct orders of religious independent of parochial and diocesan structures.[14] Whilst it is impossible for a cursory summary to do justice to the substantial corpus of antimonastic and antifraternal literature, it is fortunate that these texts have been examined at length elsewhere. Penn R. Szittya's classic study *The Antifraternal Tradition in Medieval Literature* includes a chapter on Wyclif and discusses a host of vernacular dissenting works, and Wendy Scase has suggested that antifraternal and antimonastic texts were part of a 'new anticlericalism' that derived its intellectual energy from the ideas about poverty and dominion associated with Richard FitzRalph, the mid-fourteenth-century Archbishop of Armagh.[15] Indeed, antimonastic and antifraternal discourses functioned in many ways as microcosms of the arguments that English dissenters were making against the clergy as a whole.

Having thus identified several areas on which we will be unable to dwell, it remains to define the subject of this chapter in more positive terms. Here, I shall be examining the views of English dissenters on three distinct but interrelated topics: the sacrament of orders, including the ways in which and the persons to whom it is to be administered; the duties of curates; and the financing of the clergy. I shall thus be paying particularly close attention to the members of the clergy with whom dissenters would have most extensively interacted. Perhaps surprisingly for those accustomed to thinking of lollards as 'anticlerical', I shall conclude that Wyclif and the majority of English dissenting writers were hyperclericalists who envisioned the retention and purification, rather than the outright abolition, of the clerical estate.

---

[14] For examples, see *Fifty Heresies and Errors of Friars* and *De Blasphemia, Contra Fratres*, in Arnold, iii.366–401 and iii.402–29, respectively. Monks come in for criticism in a smaller number of Wycliffite texts: see, for instance, *Petition to King and Parliament*, in Arnold, iii.507–23 at 511.

[15] Penn R. Szittya, *The Antifraternal Tradition in Medieval Literature* (Princeton, NJ, 1986); Wendy Scase, *Piers Plowman and the New Anticlericalism* (Cambridge, 1989). On FitzRalph, see especially Katherine Walsh, *Richard FitzRalph in Oxford, Avignon, and Armagh: A fourteenth-century scholar and primate* (Oxford, 1981). Scase's 'new anticlericalism' is a way of thinking about late medieval literature which has not met with unanimous approval; see, for instance, Szittya's comments in a review in *Speculum*, 67 (1992), 1040–2.

THE DEVELOPMENT OF THE
SACRAMENT OF ORDERS

Of the sacraments routinely administered in the medieval church, that of orders has been one of the more rarely studied. Whereas the continuing centrality of the eucharist in the worship of many Christian denominations has kept alive interest in the history and theology of the sacrament of the altar, and whereas marriage likewise remains a topic of no small controversy, the sacrament of orders has generated neither theological nor ecclesiopolitical interest on a similar scale.[16] There is not space here to reconstruct the origin and development of orders within the Christian church, but several points are particularly relevant to the concerns of Wyclif, his academic followers, and later English heresy suspects.

First, from the time of the Emperor Constantine, the Christian clergy gradually evolved into a distinct estate of society, first separate from and then superior to the laity. In 314, the emperor transferred the social privileges of pagan priests to Christian bishops and presbyters, an act which the Benedictine historian Jean Leclercq has described as the beginning of a cultural and educational gap between clergy and laity. With the fall of the Roman Empire, the distance between the two estates widened further; in particular, political and social structures previously dominated by lay rulers came to be managed by bishops instead.[17] At the same time, the ecumenical councils of the fourth and later centuries enhanced the jurisdictional role of bishops within the church.[18] The distinction between the episcopal and presbyteral orders was not, however, as sharp as one might imagine; Jerome and John Chrysostom both argued that bishops and presbyters were of equal dignity, apart from the power to ordain new clergymen. Below the bishops and presbyters, a number of minor orders were also developing. Nevertheless, as clerical prerogatives continued to multiply, theological discourse in the patristic period and the early Middle Ages devoted little attention to questions about ministers and the ministry.

---

[16] Among Roman Catholic scholars, however, the reforms of the Second Vatican Council inspired the re-examination of an official theology of orders that had gone largely unchallenged since the Council of Trent: see, for instance, David N. Power, *Ministers of Christ and His Church* (London, 1969); James A. Mohler, *The Origin and Evolution of the Priesthood* (Staten Island, NY, 1970); and Aidan Nichols, *Holy Order: The apostolic ministry from the New Testament to the Second Vatican Council* (Dublin, 1990), among others.

[17] Jean Leclercq, 'The priesthood in the patristic and medieval church' in Nicholas Lash and Joseph Rhmyer (eds.), *The Christian Priesthood* (London, 1970), 53–73 at 57–9.

[18] Nichols, *Holy Order*, 47.

Against this background, 'the attempt to write a more lucid theology of order... begins with the *On the Sacraments* of Hugh of St Victor'.[19] Peter Lombard enlarged Hugh's account of the sacrament in the fourth book of his *Sentences*, where he listed seven orders and argued that the highest order, that of priesthood, is shared between priests and bishops. On Lombard's account, the seven orders are to be distinguished from one another primarily in terms of their relationship to the eucharist, and since priests and bishops can both consecrate the sacrament, they differ from one another only in *potestas jurisdictionis*, not in *potestas ordinis*.[20] Lombard's ideas were taken up by many of the giants of scholastic theology, but his was not the only view of the sacrament of orders. Some theologians, like Durandus of St Pourçain, argued that the only orders are those of bishops and priests; others, like Duns Scotus, envisioned a separate order for bishops and hence a total of eight; and others still, like William of Auxerre, included the episcopate and archiepiscopate in a scheme of nine orders modelled on the *Celestial Hierarchy* of pseudo-Dionysius.[21]

Among the new ideas that scholastic theologians introduced into their discussions of the sacrament of orders, two are especially crucial for our purposes. First, in keeping with the newly rediscovered categories of Aristotle, theologians asked what kind of character orders bestow on their recipients. William of Auxerre described the character of orders as a special disposition to receive grace, whereas the continuator of the third part of Aquinas' *Summa theologiae* argued that ordination imprints an indelible character that remains forever and cannot be removed.[22] The widespread reception of the latter view in the medieval church shored up the distinction between clergy and laypeople. Second, since a clergyman's sacramental power came to be seen as a consequence of his ordination and not of his responsibility to care for a particular community, the medieval church began to condone the practice, technically forbidden in 451 by the Council of Chalcedon, of ordaining a man without first assigning him to a particular cure of souls.[23] Edward Schillebeeckx has described the theological effect of such ordinations thus: 'The consequence of all this is that the old relationship between *ministerium* and *ecclesia*, between ministry and the church, now shifts to a relationship between *potestas* and *eucharistia*... In comparison with the ancient church,

---

[19] Nichols, *Holy Order*, 73.
[20] Ibid., 74.
[21] Power, *Ministers of Christ and His Church*, 115.
[22] Aquinas, *Summa Theologica*, Suppl. III, q. 35, art. 2.
[23] Tanner, *Decrees*, i.90. See also R. N. Swanson, 'Titles to orders in medieval English episcopal registers' in Henry Mayr-Harting and R. I. Moore (eds.), *Studies in Medieval History Presented to R. H. C. Davis* (London, 1985), 233–45.

circumstances here have taken a markedly different direction: a priest is ordained in order to be able to celebrate the eucharist.'[24]

But what effects did these evolving theologies of orders have on the parishes and parishioners of late medieval England? Though estimates of the total numbers of clergy remain contested, it is certain that priests with the cure of souls played a number of public and private roles in the lives of their spiritual subjects. In 1994, Peter Marshall structured an excellent study of the priesthood on the eve of the Reformation around eight functions of the late medieval priest: as confessor, celebrant, teacher, anointed, celibate, pastor, neighbour, and enemy.[25] Several of these functions we have already touched upon; the act of presiding at the eucharist, and to a lesser extent his responsibility for administering the other sacraments, ensured that the priest enjoyed an elevated position in the local community. But what Gabriel Le Bras has called 'the exaltation of the clergy' also entailed a set of moral expectations; many laypeople demanded that their priests be exemplary in virtue and were sometimes prepared to object if a particular curate failed to meet their standards.[26] Parishioners complained when their clergymen refused the sacraments without good cause, demanded excessive fees for the solemnization of marriage, or excommunicated parishioners for failing to pay tithes. Visitation records also include mention of clerics' sexual irregularities, 'but it may be that they were considered less serious from the parishioners' viewpoint than complaints about the clergy's failings in the provision of services and ministrations'.[27]

Despite the reticence of many sources, it is possible to construct an outline of the expectations that both religious superiors and laypeople would have had of their priests. In N. J. G. Pounds' words, 'the would-be priest had to be freeborn and legitimate, sound in body, free of physical blemish, and sufficiently well educated for the performance of his office'.[28] Beyond these basic qualifications, clergymen were expected to live simply, shy away from physical aggression, and approach their priestly tasks with humility. In his collection of vernacular sermons, the *Festial*, John Mirk anachronistically praises St Mark for possessing the ideal qualities of a late medieval priest:

And when he [Mark] was full ylurned of Cristys fayþe, þen Seynt Petyr made hym goo and prech þe pepull Godys word. And for he was soo holy a man, þe pepull allgate wold make hym a prest, he, for gret mekenes of hymselfe, made to kyt of his þombe; neuerþeles when God wold haue hyt, Seynt Petyr wyth gret instaunce made hym to

---

[24] Edward Schillebeeckx, *The Church with a Human Face* (London, 1985), 193–4.
[25] Peter Marshall, *The Catholic Priesthood and the English Reformation* (Oxford, 1994).
[26] Gabriel Le Bras, *Institutions ecclésiastiques de la chrétienté médiévale*, 2 vols. (Paris, 1959), i.150.
[27] Swanson, 'Problems', 847–48.
[28] N. J. G. Pounds, *A History of the English Parish* (Cambridge, 2000), 157.

take þe ordyr of prest. Then was he besy day and ny3t forto prech Godys word to þe pepull; and all þat he sayde wyth worde, he confermed wyth good ensampull and wyth doing of myracles.[29]

In another sermon Mirk emphasizes that priests should not swear, lie, or gossip. His views on the duties of clergymen were echoed at the end of our period by John Colet, the reforming dean of St Paul's.[30]

One of the roles attributed by Marshall to the late medieval priest is particularly relevant to this study: that of the priest as enemy. Indeed, priests were the enforcers of moral discipline and ecclesiastical law at the local level.[31] In theory and sometimes in practice, curates could deny the sacraments to parishioners they considered to be in a state of sin, but far more commonly, tensions between clergymen and laypeople in late medieval England concerned the payment of tithes. 'The medieval ideal was of a single church serving the spiritual needs of a discrete area and supported by the tithes and oblations of its parishioners. It was, however, rarely achieved.'[32] Tithe disputes frequently came before ecclesiastical courts, but until the late Middle Ages few contested the legitimacy of the practice itself; most disagreements concerned whether a particular type of good was tithable or how tithes were to be calculated. *Dives and Pauper*, for instance, takes it as given that laypeople are obligated to pay tithes: 'Swiche fadris arn worþi duble worchepe... for þey ben worþi to ben reuerencyd of her sogetis and to han her lyuynge. Therfor þey owyn to han typis and offeryngis of her chyldryn.'[33] Though the text places an obligation on the clergy not to misspend tithe income, it also cites canon law to the effect that laypeople may withhold tithes from a corrupt priest.[34]

THE PRIESTHOOD IN WYCLIF'S THEOLOGY

Practical calculations about tithes and other church taxes may seem remote from Wyclif's concerns, for scholarly studies of his views on the clergy have often concentrated on his supposedly virulent arguments against the pope

---

[29] Mirk, *Festial*, 135/32–136/6.
[30] Peter Iver Kaufman, 'John Colet's *Opus de sacramentis* and clerical anticlericalism: The limitations of "ordinary wayes"', *Journal of British Studies*, 22 (1982), 1–22 at 8–9.
[31] A. Hamilton Thomson has stressed that the ratio of judicial to pastoral responsibilities increased as a cleric ascended the ranks of the ecclesiastical hierarchy (*The English Clergy and Their Organization in the Later Middle Ages* (Oxford, 1947), 6).
[32] Pounds, *A History of the English Parish*, 42.
[33] *Dives and Pauper*, i, Pt 1, Bk 4, Ch. 13, 330/14–16.
[34] Ibid., i, Pt 1, Bk 4, Ch. 8, 321/38–41.

and other senior churchmen. The Jesuit scholar E. A. Ryan's analysis of Wyclif's *De ecclesia*, for instance, devotes four pages to the doctrine of predestination, five to the power of the pope, and two to the question of disendowment, but spends only a paragraph on the duties of the clergy.[35] Nevertheless, the nearly exclusive focus of some scholars, medieval as well as contemporary, on the Oxford scholar's sensational claims about the papacy and ecclesiastical temporalities has obscured his views on other issues related to the clergy.

The sacrament of orders has occasionally been described as the site of a tension in Wyclif's theology. His early twentieth-century biographer, H. B. Workman, argued that Wyclif articulated a doctrine of the universal priesthood of the predestinate, a position which Workman took to undermine Wyclif's views of the clerical estate and its sacramental powers: 'When faced with the difficulty of the place and value of the sacraments in his system Wyclif goes off at a tangent and never comes to grips with the problem.'[36] On the contrary, however, it is unclear whether Wyclif ever seriously entertained the notion of the priesthood of all believers, and as we have already observed elsewhere, Workman's footnotes reveal that he relied too uncritically on the English works he mistakenly took to be Wyclif's own.[37]

We shall shortly return to Wyclif's putative claims about the priestly powers of the predestined, but it is first necessary to describe formally the Oxford scholar's theology of orders. A chapter in the fourth book of *Trialogus* sets out Wyclif's mature position. Asked by Alitheia to describe what orders are, Phronesis responds that the word *ordo* can be taken in three senses. First, it can describe the position of a creature in God's ordering of the world, 'just as in the angels there are many orders, so are there also in the multitude of creatures under the moon'.[38] Second, orders can refer to the new religious orders which, Phronesis insists, were established by Antichrist against Christ's command. Finally, in the strictest sense, orders refer to the power given by God in order that a clergyman might minister in the church.[39] This last kind of orders is commonly celebrated in church 'with a solemn fast and masses and other rites', but Phronesis seems uncertain as to whether these

---

[35] E. A. Ryan, 'Three early treatises on the church', *Theological Studies*, 5 (1944), 113–40 at 126–36. A similar imbalance can be found in Workman, *Wyclif*, who like Ryan focuses on the papacy and disendowment to the exclusion of other considerations.

[36] Workman, *Wyclif*, ii.13; a similar view can be found in Lechler, *John Wycliffe*, 305.

[37] See, in this context, the citations from Arnold's *Select English Works* at Workman, *Wyclif*, ii.13, nn. 2, 7.

[38] *Trialogus*, 295: 'sicut in angelis sunt multi ordines, sic in qualibet creata multitudine sublunari'.

[39] *Trialogus*, 295.

are necessary.[40] Phronesis then reports on the differences of opinion among scholastic theologians about the indelible character conferred by ordination. He notes that whilst some think it is a quality and a type of grace, others think it is an invisible sign. Failing to resolve these conflicting views, he ultimately concludes that whatever it is, the character remains perpetually imprinted on the soul. For Phronesis, as for Wyclif in *De officio regis*, perhaps the most important function of the character conferred by ordination is that it distinguishes the clergy from the laity: 'By the character of *baptism*, the faithful person is distinguished from the heathen; and by the character of *orders* the cleric is separated from the lay person, and by the ordination of Christ is designated to hold an office superior to the laity.'[41]

Wyclif was here articulating a fairly standard late medieval account of the sacrament of orders, but whilst he accepted the conventional distinction of clergy and laity, and even the supremacy of the clerical estate, he envisioned the clergy in substantially different terms from those of his mainstream contemporaries. In his writings on priesthood as well as the other sacraments, Wyclif consistently emphasized that sacramental grace is given not by the minister but by God.[42] As Phronesis implies, therefore, the ordination rite does not automatically make a man a member of God's true clergy. In *De ecclesia*, Wyclif argues that the sacrament imbues an ordinand with the character of the clergy only insofar as he is worthy. 'God, giving power to the minister, gives grace unless he is hindered by the unworthiness of the ordinand.'[43] Not every ordained priest is a real priest, and vice-versa; hence episcopal consecration, whilst customary, is not absolutely necessary.[44] At this point in the argument, Wyclif offers no criteria for distinguishing genuine clergymen from pretenders, though later he especially condemns as counterfeit those clerics who accept endowments and offices from secular authorities. Despite these caveats, though, it is evident that Wyclif envisioned the retention of a separate clerical estate whose members are distinguished from the laity on account of their uprightness of life and the grace they have received

---

[40] *Trialogus*, 296: 'cum solemni jejunio cum missis et aliis ritibus'. See also Wyclif's *De potestate pape*, 33. In *De ecclesia*, Wyclif further undermines the necessity of ordination rites by arguing that it cannot be known at what point in the liturgy rite God imprints the priestly character (*De ecclesia*, 515).

[41] *Trialogus*, 296: '*Baptismi* enim charactere fidelis ab infideli distinguitur . . . et charactere *ordinis* clericus separatur a laico, ac si ex ordinatione Christi ad officium singulare supra laicum in ecclesia sit signatus' (original emphasis).

[42] Yarnell, 'Royal priesthood in the English Reformation', 43; see, for instance, *De ecclesia*, 511–12, *De potestate pape*, 117.

[43] *De ecclesia*, 511: 'Deus enim dans potestatem ad ministrandum dat eciam graciam ad officium exequendum nisi indisposicio ordinate prepediat.'

[44] *De officio regis*, 147; see also *Dialogus sive speculum ecclesie militantis*, 34.

from God. In an ideal world, according to Wyclif, the clerical estate would be contiguous with those who have actually been ordained.

But what about the passages in Wyclif's works that seem to argue for the universal priesthood of the predestined? In *De potestate pape*, Wyclif argues that 'every Christian and *especially a good presbyter* is a priest, and thus *spiritually* a good doorkeeper, candlebearer, lector, exorcist, subdeacon, deacon, and priest'.[45] Whilst many later heresy suspects seem unreservedly to have subscribed to similar views, Malcolm Yarnell has persuasively suggested that Wyclif may have mooted such a controversial position only in order to use it as a jumping-off point for his arguments against the behaviour of the contemporary clergy.[46] Indeed, in his *Responsiones ad argumenta Radulfi Strode*, Wyclif suggests that unordained Christians must sometimes act as priests when bishops ordain the unworthy. Nevertheless, whilst that there may be cases in which the unordained should exercise the priestly powers they possess, Wyclif held that it would be better if the sacrament of orders were conferred, as God intended it to be, exclusively upon the worthy.[47]

Before moving on to Wyclif's views on the endowment of the church, it remains for us to consider very briefly several other elements of his theology of orders. Though Wyclif seems to endorse the seven traditional orders of the Latin church in the quotation from *De potestate pape* above, elsewhere he argues that the five minor orders are superfluous and that the church should follow the example of the apostles in ordaining only priests and deacons.[48] The apostolic church, he notes, did not distinguish between bishops and priests, and whilst Wyclif did not object to a separate episcopate, he conceived of episcopacy as an office rather than an order *per se*.[49] In doing so, Wyclif endorsed a distinction that we have already encountered: every priest enjoys the same *potestas ordinis*, but some have greater or lesser *potestates jurisdictionis*.[50] Wyclif's views on the number of orders were among the ideas most frequently condemned by his clerical antagonists. In 1396, the provincial convocation of Canterbury criticized him for maintaining that 'in the time of Paul two orders of clergy sufficed for the church, namely priests and deacons'. Similar views appear in the list of articles sent by an Oxford commission to the Archbishop of Canterbury in 1412.[51]

---

[45] *De potestate pape*, 315: 'omnis christianus et specialiter bonus presbiter est sacerdos, sic est spiritualiter hostiarius, ceroferarius, lector, exorcista, subdyaconus, dyaconus et sacerdos' (emphasis mine); see also *De eucharistia*, 98–9.

[46] Yarnell, 'Royal priesthood in the English Reformation', 40.

[47] In *Opera minora*, 174–6.

[48] See, for instance, *De ecclesia*, 515.

[49] *De potestate pape*, 74.

[50] Ibid., 95–6.

[51] Wilkins, iii.229, no. 6: 'quod tempore Pauli sufficiebant ecclesiae duo ordines clericorum, sacerdos et diaconus'; iii.344–5, nos. 109–10, 127, 132; see also Knighton, *Knighton's Chronicle*, 435, no. 10.

Whereas Wyclif's theology of orders displays many of the subtleties we have come to expect from the Oxford scholar, his views on ecclesiastical finance were more straightforward. Taking his place in a tradition of criticism stretching back at least to the early thirteenth-century minstrel Walther von der Vogelweide, Wyclif pinpoints the so-called Donation of Constantine as the source of all the church's corruption.[52] Wyclif's attitude toward Constantine's gift became more critical over time. Nevertheless, whilst Wyclif condemned the Donation, he did not argue that clerics should be totally without material possessions. In *De ecclesia*, for instance, he allows that some financial privileges can benefit the church: 'To put it briefly, the administration of temporal goods is not a privilege for the clergy, except insofar as it stimulates [them] to follow Christ in his behaviour and to seek out the privilege of his love.'[53] In order to provide the clergy with sufficient though not excessive resources, Wyclif encourages the practice of temporary (rather than perpetual) alms and urges secular lords to moderate the quantity of alms they give to clergymen.[54] Wyclif is chiefly remembered, however, for his more radical suggestion that temporal lords should disendow the church altogether and distribute ecclesiastical property among secular lords. He argues at length that it is within the king's power to take temporal goods away from the clergy when clerics abuse their privileges or demonstrate contempt for royal power.[55] William the Conqueror, for instance, took perpetual alms away from some bishops and abbots, and Wyclif cites additional precedents from the history of the Templars and the reign of Edward III.[56] Whilst the programme of disendowment that Wyclif proposed would primarily have affected the sorts of perpetual gifts that only the wealthiest could afford, he also urged laypeople, too, to play their role in divesting an erring clergy of its material goods. 'It is evident, if a cleric does not do his duty as he should, or is a notorious fornicator, that a layman is not bound to give him tithes.'[57]

---

[52] Smalley, *English Friars and Antiquity* (Oxford, 1960), 195. Closer to Wyclif's time, the English poet William Langland also associated the Donation with clerical corruption. In *Passus* XV of the B-text of *Piers Plowman*, the character Conscience notes that 'whan Costantyn of curteisie Holy Kirke dowed / With londes and ledes, lordships and rentes, / An aungel men herden an heigh at Rome crye: "*Dos ecclesie* this day hath ydronke venym, / And tho that han Petres power arn apoisoned alle!"' (XV, 556–60).

[53] *De ecclesia*, 190–1: 'Et breviter ministracio temporalium non est clero in privilegium, nisi de quanto promovet ad sequendum Christum in moribus et impetrandum privilegium amoris sui.'

[54] Ibid., 274; *Dialogus*, 59; *Trialogus*, 305; cf. Workman, *Wyclif*, ii.14.

[55] *De ecclesia*, 329; *De officio regis*, 164; cf. Lechler, *John Wycliffe*, 307.

[56] *De ecclesia*, 331–2.

[57] *De veritate sacrae scripturae*, iii.3: 'et patet, quod, si clericus non facit servicium, ut deberet, vel sit notorius fornicator, tunc laicus non tenetur, ei dare decimam'.

Wyclif's suggestions that secular lords should disendow the clergy and that laypeople should withhold their tithes from sinful priests are of two substantially different orders. With the former he intended to take away from *all* clerics the endowments that contribute to their laxity, whereas with the latter he envisioned only the punishment of wicked churchmen.[58] On Wyclif's account, all clerics should be content to live by the tithes and alms they receive as free gifts.[59] If these funds prove insufficient, there are a variety of ways in which a cleric divested of his endowments could supplement his income: by manual work, by writing in a scriptorium, by teaching grammar, or by taking a modest yearly salary from his parishioners.[60]

It should not be surprising that Wyclif's claims about the Donation of Constantine and the disendowment of the clergy were among the earliest to be anathematized. The sixth article mentioned in the 1377 letter in which Pope Gregory XI condemned nineteen of Wyclif's conclusions was that 'temporal lords may legitimately and meritoriously take away goods from a delinquent church'.[61] In the list of articles prepared in 1396 by the Canterbury convocation, three relevant articles were condemned: two observing that the Aaronic and Levitical priests never had endowments and a third arguing that secular lords have not only the right but indeed the obligation to take temporal goods away from negligent churchmen.[62] Seven propositions about disendowment appear in the list of 267 articles prepared by the Oxford commission of 1412, including one article suggesting that laypeople as well as lords should be prepared to withdraw their alms from the clergy.[63] Finally, the Council of Constance condemned no fewer than ten Wycliffite articles on ecclesiastical finance. The council rejected on two separate occasions the propositions that secular lords can disendow the clergy and that laypeople can withhold their tithes from the unworthy. It likewise anathematized the propositions that it is against Scripture for churchmen to have possessions, that the pope and clergy are heretics for owning property, that it is against Christ's command to enrich the clergy, that the greatest heresy is to approve of

---

[58] As far as this latter point is concerned, Wyclif argues that both an annual stipend and respect are due those clerics who are worthily called priests of Christ (*De ecclesia*, 131).

[59] *Dialogus*, 2.

[60] Ibid., 51.

[61] Wilkins, iii.123, no. 6: 'domini temporales possunt legitime ac meritorie auferre bona fortunae ab ecclesia delinquente'.

[62] Wilkins, iii.230, nos. 11–13.

[63] Wilkins, iii.341–7, nos. 49, 75, 95, 135, 148, 206–7. Proposition no. 95 suggests that 'people should withdraw tithes, oblations, and other private alms from the unworthy disciples of Antichrist, as they are required to do by the law of God' ('subtrahat populus decimas, et oblationes, et alias privatas eleemosynas ab indignis antichristi discipulis, cum hoc facere debeant de lege Dei').

the endowment of the church, and that Silvester and Constantine jointly erred in endowing the clergy. In a move which perhaps reflects the conflation of heresy and sedition in early fifteenth-century England, the council also condemned a view that Wyclif never actually taught: that 'the people can correct sinful lords at their discretion'.[64]

HYPERCLERICALISM OR ANTISACERDOTALISM? ORDERS IN WYCLIFFITE TEXTS

We shall shortly see how Wyclif's programme of disendowment was taken up by a host of dissenting writers, but we must first consider the ways in which the Oxford scholar's more abstract ideas about the priesthood were received among those who followed him. The theologies of orders articulated in vernacular Wycliffite texts have received somewhat uneven treatment. If only as a result of the sheer volume of the relevant source material, sensational claims about the papacy and church endowments have often been privileged over more explicitly theological ideas about the clerical estate.[65] It cannot be denied that the texts lend themselves to such interpretations: since most dissenters were writing polemical rather than academic treatises, their concerns about the wealth and other failings of the clergy came readily to the fore.

The theologies of orders that can be discerned beneath the surfaces of many Wycliffite texts are largely traditional. The tract *The Order of Priesthood*, for instance, begins with the assertion that the priesthood was established by God in both the Old and New Testaments. Throughout, its author treats the clergy as a distinct estate, even if at the present time a corrupt one: 'And many prestis kepen it ful euele, telle we summe errours of prestis to amende hem wiþ goddis grace.'[66] Likewise, the author of *Of Poor Preaching Priests* exalts the simple priesthood founded by Christ above the new orders of monks and friars. Among the claims he sets out at the beginning of the tract is that Christ's true priesthood must always exist: 'þe ordre of presthod wiþ clennest reulis of cristis gospel be holden and meyntened boþe perfiter and esier and sikerer þan ony newe ordre or secte'.[67] With few exceptions, dissenting texts envision the persistence of some distinction between the clergy and laity. Many, like *The Lanterne of Liȝt*, explicitly call priesthood 'þe secounde astate

---

[64] Tanner, *Decrees*, 412–13, nos. 10, 16–18, 32–3, 36; 422–6, nos. 41–3.
[65] Thus, for instance, the sacrament of orders receives only a scanty eight lines in *PR*, 292–3.
[66] *Of Clerks Possessioners*, in Matthew, 164–79 at 166.
[67] *Of Poor Preaching Priests*, in Matthew, 275–80 at 276.

in hooli chirche' and spell out the duties to be performed by conscientious clerics.[68] Indeed, a high proportion of the criticisms that appear in dissenting texts depend for their force on the continued existence of a distinct clergy. Arguments against churchmen holding secular office, for instance, would make little sense if dissenters did not at least implicitly endorse a traditional account of the three estates.

Nevertheless, Wycliffite writers were frequently concerned to establish who are, and who are not, true priests. The vernacular tract *De Papa* follows Wyclif in arguing that no external ceremony or invocation can guarantee that a particular man has received the grace of orders: 'crounne and cloþ maken no prest, ne þe emperours bischop wiþ his wordis, but power þat crist ȝyueþ; and þus bi lif ben prestis knowun'.[69] The second of the *Twelve Conclusions* posted on the doors of Westminster Hall in 1395 articulates a similar view:

Oure usuel presthod, þe qwich began in Rome, feynid of a power heyere þan aungelis, is nout þe presthod þe qwich Cryst ordeynede to his apostlis. Þis conclusion is prouid for þe presthod of Rome is mad with signis, rytis and bisschopis blissingis, and þat is of litil uertu, nowhere ensampled in holi scripture, for þe bisschopis ordinalis in þe newe testament ben litil of record.[70]

Anne Hudson has argued on the basis of texts like these that 'given Lollard views on the clergy, ordination was evidently irrelevant'.[71] Nevertheless, it is far from certain that a majority of late medieval dissenters would have subscribed to such a view. It is true that many texts fail to mention ordination, but in view of their near-unanimous endorsement of a distinct clergy, it seems more reasonable to construe their silence as approval, if not of the medieval ordination rite itself, then at least of a scripturally warranted laying-on of hands. Dissenting authors did not, however, sanction the whole range of orders offered by the medieval church: those texts which comment on the number of orders typically recommend the elimination of all but the biblically 'grounded' orders of priests and deacons.[72]

One doctrine that cannot readily be found in vernacular Wycliffite writings is that of the priesthood of all believers. It does make an appearance in the tract *Sixteen Points on which the Bishops Accuse Lollards*, where the seventh of those points is 'þat þer schulde be bot oo degre aloone of prestehod in þe chirche of God, and euery good man is a prest and haþ

---

[68] *Lanterne*, 34; see also the sermon *Omnis plantacio*, in Hudson, *The Works of a Lollard Preacher*, 2/22.
[69] *De Papa*, in Matthew, 458–82 at 467.
[70] *Selections*, no. 3, 25/13–18.
[71] *PR*, 292.
[72] *On the Seven Deadly Sins*, in Arnold, iii.119–67 at 130.

power to preche þe worde of God'.[73] Here it might seem that the author of the tract is arguing for the view of universal priesthood which Wyclif mooted but ultimately rejected. Nevertheless, the text's gloss on the article makes it clear that whereas laypeople can exercise some priestly powers, their 'spiritual' priesthood must be distinguished from the official priesthood of the ordained:

we graunten þat þe state of prestis schulden be oon in very vnite, and þe order is al oon ... but þe degrees in hem ben diuerse, boþe heier and lower. And as God haþ grauntted hem þe keies of power and knouyng of his lawe, so al prestes of office han euene power of ordere of prestehode ... And þou3 lewde men ben good lyueris and wise men, 3it ben þei not prestes of office, ne þei be not bounden to preche of office, al be it þat þei be prestes spirituali.[74]

According to the author, spiritual priesthood entails relatively limited duties, namely teaching and instructing one's family 'to be of good maners'.[75] Nowhere in the *Sixteen Points* nor in other dissenting tracts are laypeople credited with more traditional priestly responsibilities: public preaching and the celebration of the eucharist are restricted, albeit often implicitly, to ordained ministers. It is for this reason that the claim recently made by one scholar that in lollard writings 'the second estate does not simply become superfluous, it disappears altogether' must be viewed with some caution.[76] Dissenting authors recommended neither that the priesthood should be abolished nor that an ordained ministry should be replaced by what Yarnell has called a 'fractious individualism', according to which all laypeople can exercise priestly powers.[77] Instead, they urged that clergymen should be stripped of many of their privileges and possessions in order that they might be more attentive to their duties.[78]

A reliable guide to lollard views on the rights and responsibilities of the clergy is the text known as the *Thirty-Seven Conclusions*. Extant in three vernacular manuscripts and a shorter, Latin summary, the list of conclusions and their corollaries was likely produced around the last decade of the fourteenth century. The text was first printed in 1851, when it was ascribed without much evidence to the pen of Wyclif's so-called *secretarius*, John

---

[73] *Selections*, no. 2, 19/16–18.
[74] Ibid., no. 2, 22/119–27.
[75] Ibid., no. 2, 22/129.
[76] Helen Barr, 'Wycliffite representations of the third estate', 205.
[77] Yarnell, 'Royal priesthood in the English Reformation', 44.
[78] John H. van Engen, 'Anticlericalism among the Lollards' in Peter A. Dykema and Heiko A. Oberman (eds.), *Anticlericalism in Late Medieval and Early Modern Europe* (Leiden, 1993), 53–63 at 58.

Purvey.[79] Whilst its use of scholastic and biblical authorities makes it probable that its author was an academic, it is impossible in the absence of new evidence to identify him more precisely. The third of the conclusions spells out the fundamental responsibilities of the priestly office: 'to sheewe to the puple ensaumple of holi lyuynge, and to preche truli the gospil bi werke and word'.[80] The collocation of good living and good preaching occurs frequently in Wycliffite texts, not least in the English sermon-cycle, where the sermon for the eighth Sunday after Trinity stresses that clerics must guide those in their cure by deeds as well as words. 'And so hit suffisyþ not to prestys to sey "God be wiþ ȝow," but þei mote sey wel in herte and wel in mouth, and lyue wel, for ellys a man schal not be sauyd.'[81]

For many dissenters, preaching is the first and the most important duty of the clergy. Thus, for instance, the tract *Of Prelates* stresses that 'prelatis ben more bounden to preche trewely þe gospel þan þes sugetis ben holden to paie here dymes . . . Also prelatis ben more bounden to þis prechynge, for þat is comaundement of crist before his deþ and eke aftir, þan to seie matynes, masse, euen song, or placebo, for þat is mannus ordynaunce.'[82] Another Wycliffite text charges that false curates 'dispisen þe principal office comaundid of god' and instead give priority to human traditions.[83] It would be tiresome to note each of the passages in which dissenting writers prioritize preaching above the other responsibilities of the clergy, but an important corollary of this view can be found in lollard invectives against the regime of preaching licences famously augmented in archbishop Thomas Arundel's constitutions of 1407–9.[84] Several English sermons blame the avarice of the fraternal orders for the restrictions on preaching: 'we se þe synne þat þe fend haþ newe brouȝt in, to lette trewe prestis to teche, and kepe þe puple to þes freris—not to profit of þis puple, but to spuyle hem more pryuely'.[85] William Thorpe was among the dissenters who defied Arundel's ban on preaching,

---

[79] *PR*, 214; Josiah Forshall (ed.), *Remonstrance against Romish Corruptions in the Church* (London, 1851), xiii; see also H. F. B. Compston, 'The thirty-seven conclusions of the Lollards', *English Historical Review*, 26 (1911), 738–49.

[80] Forshall, *Remonstrance*, 4.

[81] *EWS*, i.8/63–5; see also Heyworth, *Jack Upland*, ll. 11–14.

[82] *Of Prelates*, in Matthew, 52–107 at 57; see also *The Order of Priesthood*, in Matthew, 164–79 at 172; and *De Officio Pastorali*, in Matthew, 405–57 at 441.

[83] *The Office of Curates*, in Matthew, 141–63 at 150.

[84] Other passages which commend preaching more than the administration of the sacraments occur in *EWS*, ii.83/22, ii.112/20–2, and iii.123/7; *Lanterne*, 34–5; *On the Seven Deadly Sins*, 144; and *An Apology for Lollard Doctrines*, 30–1, among many others. On Arundel's constitutions, the classic, controversial, and in many ways now superseded study is Nicholas Watson, 'Censorship and cultural change in late-medieval England: Vernacular theology, the Oxford translation debate, and Arundel's *Constitutions* of 1409', *Speculum*, 70 (1995), 822–64.

[85] *EWS*, iii.214/6–8; see also ii, 58/11.

writing in his account of his examination that he had told the archbishop that 'we doon not þe office of presthood if we leeuen oure prechinge'.[86] Nevertheless, not every dissenter urged the clergy to accentuate preaching at the expense of the sacraments. The knight in the *Dialogue between a Knight and a Clerk* unusually places the administration of the sacraments before preaching in his enumeration of curates' responsibilities.[87]

Not all of the *Thirty-Seven Conclusions* concern spiritual duties; in fact, articles which seek to limit the clergy's temporal privileges are far more numerous. The first two of the *Conclusions*, along with the sixth of the more famous *Twelve Conclusions* of 1395, demand that clergymen neither exercise worldly lordship nor take offices in secular courts.[88] Unease at the prospect of clerics serving temporal lords as well as Christ occurs frequently in dissenting texts. In his infamous Paul's Cross sermon of 21 November 1406, William Taylor argued that involvement in the affairs of the world impairs the ability of clergymen to carry out their spiritual duties: 'if þei ouȝt haue of kunnyng, encumbringe hemsilf in worldly ocupaciouns and ȝyuyng entent to lustis, þei forȝeten þat litil kunnyng so ferforþ þat þei han no sauour, and also kunnen not comyne of heuenly and goostly þingis'.[89] The vernacular tract *On the Leaven of Pharisees* blames a corrupt system of patronage for driving priests to work ever longer hours in lords' courts as they seek to procure suitable benefices. The net result, the author argues, is that priests are so occupied in temporal affairs that 'vnneþis [only with difficulty] may þei at reste seie metenes or masse with deuocioun'.[90] Several sermons of the long English cycle likewise condemn the involvement of the clergy in secular life.[91]

For many dissenters, the involvement of churchmen in secular affairs was a symptom of what they perceived to be the more substantial problem of the church's wealth. At least three of the *Thirty-Seven Conclusions* touch on the financial standing of the church: the fourth alleges that greedy prelates and

---

[86] *The Testimony of William Thorpe*, 47/788–9.

[87] *Selections*, 134/92; on this text see further Anne Hudson, 'A Lollard quaternion', repr. in *Books*, 192–200.

[88] Forshall, *Remonstrance*, 1–4; *Selections*, no. 3, 26/62–73. Roger Dymmok responded to the sixth of the *Twelve Conclusions* by arguing that both the Old and New Testaments authorize clergymen to act as civil judges and to occupy other temporal offices (*Liber contra XII errores et haereses Lollardorum*, 149). On Dymmok's account, clergymen can exercise the cure of souls in a variety of ways, including by helping the king to rid the realm of adultery and other sins (*Liber contra XII errores et haereses Lollardorum*, 151). Hudson has rightly called Dymmok's response 'one of his briefest and, it seems fair to say, not one of his most persuasive' ('Hermafrodita or Ambidexter: Wycliffite views on clerks in secular office' in *Lollardy and Gentry*, 41–51 at 42–3).

[89] *The Sermon of William Taylor*, in Hudson, *Two Wycliffite Texts*, 4/58–61.

[90] *Of the Leaven of Pharisees*, in Matthew, 1–27 at 22.

[91] See, for instance, *EWS*, ii.64/67, ii, 71/67–70, ii.89/77–80, ii.114/22, iii.154/77.

curates waste the goods of the church, the seventh encourages Christian people to give only the 'necessaries of þis lif' to faithful clergymen, and the thirtieth states that 'symple prestis . . . þat han no beneficis bi doom of þe chirche now . . . owen to be apaied wiþ symple liflode and cloþinge in preiynge deuoutli for hemsilf and þe puple'.[92] Similarly, many vernacular texts distinguish between the tithes whose payment was made mandatory by the institutional church and the alms that Christian people might freely choose to give to their curates. Like Wyclif, the authors of these texts suggest that payments to clergymen should never be obligatory. In his examination before Archbishop Arundel, Thorpe explained that although tithes may have been required in the Old Testament, neither Christ nor his apostles took tithes or commanded that they be paid. Instead, 'Crist tauȝte þe peple to do almes, þat is werkis of mercy, to pore nedi men of þe surpluys of her temperal goodis.'[93]

The argument that tithes are unscriptural but that alms should be given to good curates was echoed in other dissenting writings. For instance, the tract *Why Poor Priests Have No Benefice* joins Thorpe in arguing that priests can follow Christ more closely by taking voluntary alms than by demanding tithes and offerings.[94] Several texts seem hesitant to do away with the traditional language of tithing and instead urge that tithes and offerings be given in moderation.[95] The *Sixteen Points* echo Thorpe's ideas about almsgiving when they propose that tithes should be paid to clerics who 'do þer office as God haþ comanded hem'.[96] An English sermon likewise suggests that if tithes are paid to needy clerics, then they are being given in accordance with Christ's mandate: 'for persouns [i.e., parsons] shulden be pore men, and feble to do boþe þer offys and trauele for þer sustenaunse, þerfore þei may take þis almes'.[97] The Wycliffite preaching handbook the *Rosarium* takes a somewhat more conservative stance, quoting Augustine and Chrysostom to the effect that tithes must be paid on pain of sin but also citing Chrysostom's criticism of clergymen who over-exuberantly pursue delinquent payments: 'prestes þat blameþ þe puple for dymes, and seyng gretter synnes are stille, þei teche for to clense a gnatte and swelowe a camel'.[98]

If tithes should be paid to clergymen who successfully fulfil their duties, then they should likewise be withdrawn from those who fail to do so.

---

[92] Forshall, *Remonstrance*, 7, 12, 97.
[93] *Testimony of William Thorpe*, 67–8/1426–8; see also *The Grete Sentence of Curs Expounded*, in Arnold, iii.267–337 at 309; *EWS*, iii.147/58.
[94] *Why Poor Priests Have No Benefice*, in Matthew, 244–53 at 252.
[95] *EWS*, i.50/101–2; *Þe Seven Works of Mercy Bodyly*, in Arnold, iii.168–82 at 171.
[96] *Selections*, no. 2, 21/81–7; see also *De Officio Pastorali*, in Matthew, 405–57 at 431–2.
[97] *EWS*, iii.147/60–2.
[98] von Nolcken, *Middle English Translation*, 63/12–14.

Nevertheless, the view that negligent clerics have no absolute right to their parishioners' financial support was not exclusively a Wycliffite one. I have already cited Swanson's study of the thoroughly orthodox laypeople of Saltash and other parishes who attempted to use the power of the purse to force ecclesiastical patrons to provide them with more capable curates. They joined dissenting authors in demanding that tithes be withheld from ineffective clergymen. The vernacular tract *De Officio Pastorali* sets forth one of the more sophisticated arguments for the withdrawal of tithes:

cristenmen of þis ground þenken þat pariȝschens shulden drawe fro persouns offer-
ingis and dymes and oþere godis whanne þey faylen opynly in þer offiss, for siche
assent is to blame þat nurshiþ persouns in siche synne. but what meede were it to
pariȝshens to ȝyue her almes to siche a prelat to werre aȝenus crist and his chirche and
mayntene þe fendis part aȝenus crist? . . . Also þe popis lawe biddiþ men to not here þe
massis of prestis þat ben comyn lechours. Þanne ȝif prestis ben in more synne þat is
more knowun to þe puple, þey shulden not take þes prestis seruyss; how shulden þey
herfore ȝyue hem almes?[99]

In this passage, several elements of Wycliffite thinking about tithes and alms come together. First, the author sets his concerns about clerical finance against the background of the eschatological conflict between Christ and the devil: to give money to evil prelates and curates is to contribute to the war against Christ. Second, in an attempt to hoist the clergy by its own petard, the author cites the canonical requirement that laypeople should shun the services of fornicating priests as an argument against giving tithes to the unworthy. Finally, the net effect of the passage is to place judgements about the fitness of the clergy in the hands of their parishioners, a move that subverts the traditional hierarchy of the three estates but yet still is not tantamount to advocating the abolition of the clergy.[100] Similar arguments for withholding tithes can be found in a host of other Wycliffite texts.[101] At least one dissenting writer perceived that his call for the withdrawal of financial support from the clergy might be interpreted as permission for tenants to refuse to pay rents to sinful secular lords as well. We have already seen that the Council of Constance attempted to link Wyclif's views on tithes with charges of sedition, and the author of the tract *Of Servants and Lords* may have been attempting to refute the connection between the payment of tithes and rents when he wrote that 'þis is a feyned word of anticristis clerkis . . . [S]ugetis han þe auctorite of goddis lawe and mannus lawe also, but not to

    [99] *De Officio Pastorali*, 418.   [100] *PR*, 343.
    [101] See, for instance, *On the Twenty-Five Articles*, in Arnold, iii.454–96 at 468; *EWS*, i.10/58–68, i.50/97–105.

wiþdrawe seruyce and rentis fro wickid lordis; but ben chargid of god bi petir and poul to be þus suget to wickid lordis.'[102]

Whilst some dissenters were content to advocate the removal of temporalities from corrupt clergymen, others took the more radical view that all clerical endowment is sinful.[103] Hudson has rightly pointed out that the disendowment of the church was by no means an innovative proposal in the late fourteenth century: 'the notion can find theoretical antecedents in Marsilius, John of Jandun, Ockham, and John of Rupescissa, and practical models in actions by English kings against the bishops and by Richard II's suppression of the alien priories'.[104] A number of Wycliffite texts argue that the endowment of both secular and regular clergymen has led to a host of abuses in the church. The short tract printed by Thomas Arnold under the title *Church Temporalities* gives three reasons why secular lords should take away the material goods of the clergy. First, God has given kings and lords the power to mete out punishment for sin, even among churchmen. Second, disendowment would enable the clergy to lead more holy lives: 'For nowe prelatis and grete religious possessioners ben so occupied aboute worldly lordischipis and plea and bysinesse in herte, þat þei may not be in devocion of preiynge.'[105] Lastly, the goods of the church could more wisely be used to augment the kingdom's defences without having to raise rents or taxes.

Each of these concerns recurs in other discussions of disendowment, as does the suggestion that temporal lords should be the ones to take away the possessions of the clergy. Without delving too deeply into their views on the theoretical dimensions of the balance of power between king and church, it is interesting to note that some dissenters perceived the increasing wealth of the church to threaten royal sovereignty. The author of the *Dialogue between a Knight and a Clerk*, for instance, places an eloquent argument against the financial and legal independence of the clergy in the mouth of the Knight:

For ȝe [the clergy] haue þe þridd parte of þis land in ȝour handes, and ȝit ȝe beþe about to purchase and amortaise euer more and more . . . ; and þan, als ȝe sayne, þe kinge had no more to done þerwiþ, and þan had he lost all his souerainte and

---

[102] *Of Servants and Lords*, in Matthew, 226–43 at 229–30. The connection between heresy and sedition was commonly made by chroniclers and orthodox writers; see further Margaret Aston, 'Lollardy and sedition', 1–44; and Barr, 'Wycliffite representations of the third estate', 197.

[103] Immensely helpful though Hudson's discussion of disendowment remains, it is unfortunate that she seems sometimes to conflate these two sets of arguments (as, for instance, at *PR*, 338). On disendowment more broadly, see Margaret Aston, '"Caim's Castles": Poverty, politics, and disendowment' in R. B. Dobson (ed.), *The Church, Politics, and Patronage in the Fifteenth Century* (Gloucester, 1984), 94–131.

[104] *PR*, 337.

[105] *Church Temporalities*, in Arnold, iii.213–18 at 215.

gouernaile of his land . . . þan were he no kinge, but as kinge in a somer game, or elles as a kinge paintid on a wall.[106]

Other texts focus on the effect of material goods on the spiritual lives of individual clergymen; hence the preacher of one English sermon attributes the multiplication of religious orders to the church's excessive wealth and urges that 'I can see no more mede þan to destruye þis prestis pruyde. Take awey þes brondys ȝif þow wole qwench þe fuyr.'[107] Finally, several tracts make specific recommendations as to how the wealth of the church might be better used. The best known of these texts is the 'Lollard Disendowment Bill', supposedly presented to Parliament in either 1407 or 1410. The document calculates in detail the income the king might gain if he confiscated the temporalities of bishops, abbots, priors, and other churchmen; it estimates that the annual total would be £143,734 10s. 4d.[108] Less ambitious proposals can be found in the tract *Of Poor Preaching Priests*, which suggests that religious endowments should be spent on the 'defence of þe rewme, and releuynge of þe pore comouns', and in Nicholas Hereford's controversial Ascension Day sermon, preached in Oxford in 1382, where Hereford suggested that seizing the possessions of the monastic and fraternal orders would enable the king not to have to tax the poor.[109]

Dissenting authors regularly followed Wyclif in blaming the endowment of the church on the Donation of Constantine, a document they seem to have regarded as authentic. As we have already seen, criticisms of the Donation can be traced back at least two centuries before Wyclif, and lollard writers lost no time in appropriating for their own purposes a ready-made tradition of critique. The first of the *Twelve Conclusions* argued that the English church became corrupt when it 'began to dote in temperalte aftir hir stepmodir þe grete chirche of Rome'.[110] Many discussions of the Donation lay responsibility for its consequences at the feet of Pope Silvester: the tract printed by Matthew under the title *The Clergy May Not Hold Property*, for instance, unfavourably compares the pope with the Old Testament prophet Elisha, who refused the

---

[106] *Selections*, no. 26, 132–3/47–56. The Wycliffite tracts *Of Clerks Possessioners* and *Of Dominion* as well as the twelfth of the *Thirty-Seven Conclusions* all cite clerical immunity from prosecution in the king's courts as another example of the imbalance of power between king and church.

[107] *EWS*, ii, 114/52–4; see also iii.140/57; *An Apology for Lollard Doctrines*, 40; *Lanterne*, 95–6.

[108] *Selections*, no. 27, 137/76.

[109] *Of Poor Preaching Priests*, 279; Simon Forde, 'Nicholas Hereford's Ascension Day sermon, 1382', *Mediaeval Studies*, 51 (1989), 205–41 at 240/31–2.

[110] *Selections*, no. 3, 24/7–8. A similar argument was made by the author of the so-called 'Lollard Chronicle' of the late fourteenth or early fifteenth centuries (Dan Embree (ed.), *The Chronicles of Rome* (Woodbridge, 1999), 117/14–26).

gifts of the Assyrian general Naaman. 'Siluestre in þe same case toke þat þe emperoure proferid hym, boþe þe grete worldly aray and þe wondir grete lordeschipis.'[111] Matthew's tract is a version of a longer sermon on the text 'Omnis plantacio quam non plantavit pater meus celestis eradicabitur', whose preacher criticizes Silvester but concludes a lengthy discussion of the Donation with this eirenic disclaimer:

And in þis writynge I blaspheme no more Siluestir, alþouȝ I reherce and blame his synne, þan I do Petir and his felowis whanne I seie þat þei synfulli forsook Crist, or Poul whanne I seie þat he wickidli pursuede Cristis chirche . . . For Petir wepte sore for his synne as þe gospel seiþ. And seynt Poul, mekeli knoulechinge his synne, seiþ þat he was not worþi to be callid apostle of Crist, and þat because þat he pursuede Cristis chirche. And on þe same wise Siluestir dide, or ellis shulde haue do, for his synne.[112]

Whilst the pope was at fault for originally accepting the Donation from an emperor who was either ignorant or else beguiled by the devil, temporal lords will now be to blame if they do not act to disendow the church. As we have seen throughout this section, the tone of this criticism is hyperclerical and reformist; what the preacher seeks is not so much the abolition of the clergy but instead its reform.

It remains for us only to ask how English dissenters intended to fund the clergy once it had been disendowed. Unfortunately, the answer must be a fragmentary one; most dissenting texts, including the Disendowment Bill itself, do not propose an alternative model for financing the clerical estate. Hudson has proposed that 'by most Wycliffites the ideal seems to have been agreed: the clergy should be satisfied to live on the day-to-day hospitality of those to whom they ministered, and if necessary to earn their bread by practical labour'.[113] This, for instance, is the approach to be found in *Omnis plantacio*, where the preacher rejects the practice of permanent alms and recalls that St Paul continued to work with his hands throughout his ministry.[114] An English sermon likewise cites Paul's example: 'boþe prelatis and prestis shulden holde hem paied wiþ Poulis reule, to take fode of þe puple for goostli trauele þat þei don, and ȝit take not þis of þe folc but bi tytle of almes and loue'.[115] Whilst other dissenting texts offer no clearer models for funding disendowed clerics, they are nevertheless remarkably unanimous in advocating the retention of a reformed clergy.

---

[111] *The Clergy May Not Hold Property*, in Matthew, 359–404 at 378.
[112] *Omnis plantacio*, ll. 1826–36.
[113] *PR*, 341.
[114] *Omnis plantacio*, ll. 2147, 2763–8.
[115] *EWS*, i.E53/19–22; see also ii, 58/89, ii.64/71, ii, 65/42, ii.83/83–94.

A PRIESTHOOD OF ALL BELIEVERS?

It is not until we turn to the records of heresy trials that we can find evidence for the view that orders are altogether superfluous. Whereas both Wyclif and the authors of many dissenting texts took the hyperclerical stance that the second estate need only be purified of corruption, a number of English heresy defendants instead adopted an antisacerdotal position, arguing either that all Christians are already priests or that the sacrament of orders conveys no special character, or both. As we consider these views, it must be borne in mind that the records of heresy trials tend to privilege concrete claims about the endowment of the clergy and the sacramental powers of the priest against more theoretical ideas like the priesthood of all believers.[116] Quite often, however, beliefs about the sacrament of orders are implicit in the ways in which heresy suspects enumerated the failings of the clergy.

The claim that 'any just man, whatever his learning, is a priest' first entered the extant records of English heresy proceedings in the 1389 trial of eight Leicester townspeople by the visiting Archbishop of Canterbury, William Courtenay. The archbishop's visitation records reveal that the defendants, who included the chaplain Richard Waystathe, had articulated an egalitarian theology of orders. In addition to their views on priesthood, they also abjured the propositions that any layman can teach or preach the gospel, that a curate or other priest cannot administer the sacraments whilst under suspicion of wrongdoing, and that tithes should not be given to clergymen in mortal sin.[117] Even though the last of these articles is reminiscent of the petition of the Saltash parishioners against their negligent curate, it is clear that these Leicester defendants did not merely desire the reform of the clergy but instead embraced a version of universal priesthood and, hence, a form of antisacerdotalism. Four defendants in Nottingham in 1395 likewise pledged never again to despise 'states of holy chyrche in no degree'.[118] Similar views were attributed in the early fifteenth century to the Wycliffite scholar John Purvey. Summarizing Purvey's opinions in his *Ecclesiae regimen*, the Carmelite friar Richard Lavynham alleged that Purvey had taught that every good Christian who is predestined is also a true priest, ordained by God in order to offer up

---

[116] See the more extensive discussion of this point in Ch. 1 above. There were, however, a few exceptions: the sophisticated dissenters William Taylor and William Emayn, for instance, both articulated a version of Wyclif's doctrine of dominion. See *FZ*, 413, no. 5; and Bath and Wells reg. Stafford, i.76–8.

[117] Dahmus, *Visitations*, 164.

[118] *Calendar of Close Rolls: Richard II*, 6 vols. (London, 1914–27), 1392–6, 487; the suspects were William Dyvet, Nicholas Taillour, Nicholas Poucher, and William Steynour.

the body of Christ. On Lavynham's account, Purvey had also argued that God has the power to ordain priests outside the context of the ordination rite, that is 'without human operation and the signs of the sins of men'.[119]

As we saw in Chapter 4, the Salisbury defendant William Mundy abjured in 1412 the view that 'any married person who well observes his state is as high in dignity as the highest priest'.[120] His abjuration included no claims about the sacramental powers of married laypeople, and it is impossible to determine exactly whether Mundy believed in the priesthood of all believers, or at least of all married believers. Whilst no other suspects explicitly compared the merits of priesthood and matrimony, at least six defendants in Norwich diocese did articulate the view that all good Christians, including women, have the potential to exercise priestly powers. Margery Baxter, the first woman to appear before Bishop Alnwick and his inquisitors, linked universal priesthood and the criteria of salvation: 'any good man is a priest, and . . . no man will finally come to heaven unless he is a priest'.[121] A more detailed statement can be found in the 1428 trial of John Skylly, who abjured the article that 'every trewe man and woman being in charite is a prest, and that no prest hath more poar in mynystryng of the sacraments than a lewed man hath'.[122] The second part of this article may reveal a tension between suspects' views and inquisitors' expectations. Skylly had also denied that priests (including, presumably, 'lay' priests) have the power to consecrate the eucharist, and as a result, the extension of priestly powers to the laity may have carried less theological weight for him than for the inquisitors before whom he appeared. In addition to Skylly, four other suspects abjured heterodox views about both the priesthood and the eucharist.[123] For these dissenters, the idea of universal priesthood did not mean ascribing to all Christians the exalted character of the late medieval clergy; instead, it entailed the deconstruction of what defendants took to be clerics' exaggerated claims about their own powers.

These Norwich defendants may have been influenced by the ideas of William White, the wandering evangelist who, after having abjured a series of heretical views before Archbishop Chichele, had subsequently preached and made a number of converts in Norwich. At his second trial, White was accused of teaching 'that any faithful person in Jesus Christ is a priest elected for the church of God'.[124] He denied the charge, but he did confess that he had preached against traditional understandings of the eucharist and the

[119] *FZ*, 387: 'sine operatione humana, et signis hominum peccatorum'.
[120] Salisbury reg. Hallum, no. 1142. See p. 137 above.
[121] *Norwich*, 42: 'quod quilibet bonus homo est sacerdos, et quod nullus homo finaliter veniet in celum nisi sacerdos'.
[122] Ibid., 57.   [123] *Norwich*, 59, 66, 142, 144.
[124] *FZ*, 423: 'quod quilibet fidelis in Christo Jesu est sacerdos electae ecclesiae Dei'.

sacrament of penance. It must remain uncertain whether White had in fact taught a version of the doctrine of the universal priesthood of the faithful, but the egalitarian thrust of his preaching could quite readily have given rise to the ideas articulated by later dissenters in Norwich diocese.

After Alnwick's persecutions of 1428–31, the notion of universal priesthood makes only three appearances in the records, appearing each time in quite different terms. First, at the beginning of this chapter I discussed the 1441 trial of John Jurdan, with his claim that the sacrament of orders is 'voyde, super-flewe, and not necessarie'; second, in 1494, the so-called 'Lollards of Kyle' abjured the view that every faithful man and woman is a priest; and finally, in 1518, the peripatetic preacher Thomas Man confessed that he had taught that 'all holie men of his secte were onely Priestes'.[125] In the interim, however, heresy defendants continued to articulate a range of criticisms of the clergy. Three suspects tried before Bishop Thomas Langton of Salisbury admitted in 1491 to having called priests scribes, Pharisees, and the enemies of Christ.[126] Two other defendants caught up in Langton's prosecutions claimed that priests deceive the common people, though in what way the records do not reveal.[127] When in 1511 the English episcopate resumed large-scale anti-heresy initiatives, defendants in Canterbury, Coventry and Lichfield, and Winchester dioceses all confessed to errors about the clergy. In Canterbury, thirteen suspects denied that priests have more power than laypeople to administer the sacraments.[128] In Coventry, inquisitors did not rely as heavily on stereotyped questionnaires as did their southern counterparts, and the records of their trials accordingly reveal more idiosyncratic views. Richard Gilmyn of Coventry argued that 'a priest is a priest while he is in the mass, and after the celebration of the mass until the beginning of another mass he is only a layman and has no power except as a mere layman', and Thomas Villers was said to have taught that 'a priest cannot make even the smallest fingernail, much less the Lord's body'.[129] A group of dissenters from villages around Farnham, tried in March 1512 before Bishop Fox of Winchester, articulated

---

[125] See p. 143 above; John Knox, *The Historie of the Reformation of the Church of Scotland* (London, 1644), 2–3; A&M, 941–3.

[126] Salisbury reg. Langton, 71–73.

[127] Ibid., 75–6, 79–80.

[128] The article 'quod nulla potestas fuit aut est sacerdotibus a Deo collata magis quam laicis in sacramentis ecclesie ministrandis' occurs in the trials of Robert Harryson, William Carder, Agnes Grebill, Christopher Grebill, William Riche, John Grebill senior, Agnes Ive, Thomas Mannyng, Robert Hilles, John Browne, Edward Walker, and Stephen Castleyn (Kent, *passim*).

[129] *Coventry*, 73, 201; see also the 1502 suspect Thomas Widerley's similar view that the priest is only a priest when he is celebrating mass: Maidstone, Centre for Kentish Studies, PRC 3/1, fols. 144v–145r.

roughly similar views, arguing, in the words of the defendant Elizabeth Swaffer, that a priest receives no new sacramental powers when he is ordained.[130]

Quite apart from their views on the relative powers of priests and lay-people, several suspects in the late fourteenth and early fifteenth centuries assailed the link between priestly power and episcopal ordination. We have already seen that Wyclif had taught that God can create priests independently of the institutional church's rites, and at least four defendants articulated similar views. William Ramsbury, tried in 1389, confessed to believing that the pope has no power to consecrate bishops, nor bishops the power to ordain priests.[131] In the same year, William Swinderby was accused of having preached that curates receive their powers of binding and loosing directly from Christ and not through the mediation of the pope or a bishop.[132] Challenged by his inquisitors, he explained in a written response that one man can bestow grace on another only if it is God's will.[133] Similarly, the Norwich defendants John Burell and John Kynget admitted that they had believed that 'God makes all priests.'[134] These claims appear in the context of their beliefs about the eucharist but nevertheless have important conse-quences for their views of the priesthood. If God makes priests, rather than the bishops of the institutional church, then must someone be sacramentally ordained in order to exercise priestly power?

Whereas heresy suspects articulated a range of views about the sacrament of orders, they spoke with far greater unanimity about the duties of the clergy. Like the authors of many dissenting texts, heresy suspects demonstrated a marked preference for preaching as opposed to the administration of the sacraments. Ramsbury was accused of teaching that 'it is more meritorious for priests to walk through the countryside with a Bible under their arm, preaching to the people, than to say matins and celebrate masses and the other divine offices'.[135] Likewise, William Emayn, tried in Bath and Wells diocese in 1428, insisted that it is the duty of every priest to preach.[136] Some suspects argued that the right to preach should not be limited only to the clergy but should be restored to all Christians. In the early sixteenth century, the Winchester defendants Thomas Wattys and Laurence Swaffer both as-serted that priests have no greater power than other Christians to preach.[137] Not all suspects prized preaching, however: the Coventry defendant Richard

---

[130] Winchester reg. Fox, iii, fols. 75r–v.   [131] Hudson, 'Lollard Mass', 120, no. 2.
[132] Hereford reg. Trefnant, 236.   [133] Ibid., 247.   [134] *Norwich*, 77, 81.
[135] Hudson, 'Lollard Mass', 121 no. 11: 'quod maius meritorium esset sacerdotibus transire per patriam cum biblia sub brachio et predicare populo quam dicere matutinas vel celebrare missas vel alia diuina officia exercere'.
[136] Bath and Wells reg. Stafford, 76–8.   [137] Winchester reg. Fox, iii.73v–75r.

Gilmyn asserted that 'no priest speaks better in the pulpit than' his book containing an English translation of the gospels and epistles.[138]

Heresy defendants also articulated roughly consistent views on the financing of the clergy. They echoed for the most part the opinion of dissenting authors that endowments and temporalities should be taken away from ecclesiastical institutions. That the disendowment of the clergy should be the responsibility of secular lords was a frequent suggestion. Swinderby wrote that temporal magnates should seek to withdraw 'pore mennes godes, the whiche they wrongfuly holden', from friars and priests who are living in corruption.[139] A range of suspects—from Walter Brut and the chaplain Robert Chapell of Rochester diocese, to the Norwich defendant Hawisia Mone—likewise urged the first estate to correct the abuses of the second.[140] The Lincoln dissenter William Apleward, took the unprecedented step of blaming the king and other secular leaders for having funded rather than disendowed the church: 'the king and all thoo that maynteyne the Churche shall go to the devyll. And inespeciall the king because of his grete supportacon of the church.'[141]

In addition to the wholesale disendowment of the church, some dissenters proposed the withdrawal of tithes from particularly sinful clerics. In 1393, Brut was accused of teaching that 'no one is bound to give tithes or oblations, and if anyone wishes to give any at all, he should be able to give his tithes and oblations to whom he wishes, even to the exclusion of his own curates'.[142] Replying to his inquisitors, Brut wrote that the obligation to give alms ceased with the coming of Christ.[143] Likewise, both Ramsbury and the Norwich defendant Richard Fleccher denied that anyone should be bound to make offerings or pay mortuaries to churches, 'for such payng of mortuaries and other thinges to the Churche makyn prestes proude'.[144] Later, in 1469, the Hereford defendants John Breche, John Cornewe, and Richard Atcombe all abjured the article 'that personal tithes are not due by divine instruction'.[145] Whilst some dissenters urged that tithes should never be paid, others argued that they should be given only in moderation. Swinderby admitted that Christ

---

[138] *Coventry*, 73.

[139] Hereford reg. Trefnant, 240; see also the related view of John Purvey at *FZ*, 394, no. 3.

[140] Hereford reg. Trefnant, 280; Lambeth reg. Chichele, iv.155–8; *Norwich*, 138.

[141] Lincoln reg. Chedworth, fols. 61–61v.

[142] Hereford reg. Trefnant, 279: 'nullus tenetur dare decimas nec oblaciones, et si quis omnino voluerit dare, poterit dare suas decimas et oblaciones cui voluerit, curatos suos inde excludendo'.

[143] Ibid., 306.

[144] Hudson, 'Lollard Mass', 121, nos. 4–5; *Norwich*, 86.

[145] Hereford reg. Stanbury, 118–9.

commanded his followers to give help to the needy but also argued that such a command could not be relevant to a worldly, well-endowed clergy. 'I can not se be Godes lawe what tytel thai hafe to asken hem, ne how the puple owen to gyf hem tewthes.'[146]

It is highly difficult to ascertain whether dissenters ever attempted to put into action their plans to withdraw financial support from the clergy. Tithe matters accounted for more than one in ten cases in late medieval ecclesiastical courts, but in only a few English trials does it appear that heresy suspects maliciously withheld payment. In June 1428, John Upton of the parish of Edington in Salisbury diocese was accused of having made a pact with others in his parish to withdraw offerings for marriages, purifications, and mortuaries; whether Upton had carried through with his alleged promise or whether the vicar had caught wind of his plans is unclear.[147] The following year, Thomas Ploman of Sizewell in Norwich diocese admitted that he had not paid tithes for seventeen years and had spoken ill of the sacraments.[148] But whether the two matters were connected in his mind cannot be deduced from the proceedings. Just as the records reveal little of Ploman's intent, so also do the extant sources rarely indicate what alternative schemes, if any, dissenters might have had in mind for the financial support of the clergy. One exception is the Norwich defendant John Skylan's suggestion that priests should sustain themselves by the labour of their own hands but, again, whether Skylan's proposal would have found favour among other dissenters must remain uncertain.[149]

CONCLUSIONS

These uncertainties aside, lollard attitudes toward the clergy seem, in general, to have fallen somewhere between the two extremes which have often been mooted in previous studies; with notable exceptions, dissenters in late medieval England neither demanded the abolition of the clergy as a separate estate of society nor articulated a proto-Lutheran doctrine of the priesthood of all believers. As we have scoured Wycliffite texts and trial records for evidence of dissenters' authentic views, one hermeneutical tool has been especially valuable. It has been helpful to follow Haigh, Swanson, Yarnell, and other scholars of recent vintage in distinguishing between the antisacerdotal position that the clergy should be dismantled altogether and the hyperclerical stance that a

---

[146] Hereford reg. Trefnant, 264.   [147] Salisbury reg. Nevill, ii, fol. 32r.
[148] *Norwich*, 103.   [149] *Norwich*, 144.

reformed clergy should remain an integral part of the church. In the next chapter, I shall employ a similar distinction between those who favoured the outright abolition of the papacy and those who called for its reform. In both cases, it bears repeating that to castigate clerics, not to mention popes, for their sins was not to argue that their offices be eliminated.

Despite favouring a theology of orders and an ecclesiology centred on the person of Christ, rather than any of Christ's ministers, Wyclif and the majority of those who followed him did not endorse either a version of the doctrine of the priesthood of all believers nor the principle of congregationalism in church governance, at least not as those concepts were later articulated by the reformers of the sixteenth century. Whilst a not inconsiderable number of heresy suspects did consider 'every good Christian' to be a priest, it seems clear that they were in the minority. It is difficult to say more, not least because of the generic limitations of many of the extant sources. Trial records, as I noted in the Preface, are far more likely to note what doctrines and practices heresy defendants rejected than to indicate what recommendations for reform they might have made. Where it seems that there were such proposals, these tend to be described in the sparsest of terms; hence it is only rarely we learn of such individuals as John Upton of Salisbury diocese, who was accused in 1428 of making a pact with his fellow parishioners to withdraw offerings from their curate. In addition, the suggestions for reform made by the authors of Wycliffite texts tend to differ substantially from one another. Thus, while some authors advocated the removal of temporalities from all clergymen, others recommended the disendowment of only the corrupt. Among the many possible paths of ecclesiastical reform, one which occurs very rarely in discussions of either the clergy or the papacy is that of conciliarism. Only the early Wycliffite John Purvey seems to have gestured in this direction with the recommendation, reported by his interlocutor Richard Lavynham, that 'all priests might well rule the church by common assent'.[150]

Unlike in previous chapters, where we have observed the existence of several branches of dissenting belief, with regard to the clergy Wycliffites and later dissenters seem to have been more of one mind. Almost every dissenting text we have considered emphasized preaching in preference to the administration of the sacraments and the other traditional duties of the late medieval clergy; many sought to restrict the extent to which clergymen might engage in temporal affairs, particularly work in the courts of kings and lords; and a substantial majority criticized mandatory tithes and perpetual endowments as sources of ecclesiastical corruption. With regard to this

---

[150] *FZ*, 388: 'omnes sacerdotes bene possunt regere ecclesiam per communem assensum'.

last claim, there seems to have been a difference of opinion as to whether the endowment of the church is *ipso facto* sinful; some texts advocate for the withdrawal of tithes and endowments from only sinful clergymen, whereas others considered any form of ecclesiastical wealth to be against the gospel. There also seems to have been no clear consensus among Wyclif and Wycliffite authors as to how a disendowed clergy should support itself, though a range of suggestions appear sprinkled throughout the texts we have been considering: that clergymen who were perceived to have failed at their pastoral duties, especially at the task of preaching, might be forced to leave the priesthood; or that clergymen should support themselves by means of manual labour, scribal work, or fees for teaching the young.

It is worth noting, as we have seen in other contexts as well, that the records of heresy trials provide especially few details where questions like these last are concerned. As a result, apart from the interesting hints that a number of defendants believed in something like universal priesthood, the vast majority of heresy trials present an almost wholly negative view of the clergy. It may have been this fact that led earlier historians to assume that lollards, in criticizing the abuses of individual clerics or even vast groups of clergymen, desired that the clerical estate be eliminated altogether. Instead, the absence from the records of positive affirmations about the clergy should highlight the relationship between a particular text's or document's genre and its content, a relationship we will consider at greater length in the next chapter. Where Wycliffites wrote for one another about the rights and duties of the clergy, they tended to affirm the place of a reformed second estate in the church, but where dissenters' words were recorded for posterity by their clerical antagonists, the records shift the focus of attention elsewhere. Nevertheless, some dissenters quite clearly did reject the theological foundations of an ordained clergy, as when John Jurdan declared in 1441 that 'the sacrament of ordre ... is vayne, voyde, superflewe and not necessarie'.[151] He may, however, have been expressing a view that not only the bishop and ecclesiastical officials before whom he appeared, but also many of his fellow dissenters, would have judged controversial.

---

[151] Bath and Wells reg. Stafford, ii, 266–7.

6

The Papacy

J. A. F. Thomson, writing in the final chapter of his groundbreaking study *The Later Lollards*, argued that the heresy suspects whose trials he had examined were 'strongly antipapal, not infrequently describing the pope as Antichrist, and in consequence may have helped to prepare the ground for the popular acceptance of Henry VIII's break with Rome'.[1] The second part of this conclusion remains a bone of no small contention; as I observed in the Preface, the four decades since the publication of Thomson's work have witnessed the emergence of formidable challenges to the traditional historiography, hearkening back to the days of John Foxe, that the remnants of the movement of religious dissent inspired by John Wyclif helped to cause, or at least ease the reception of, the Henrician Reformation.[2] This chapter's interest, however, lies in exploring the first half of Thomson's remark.

It is well known that Wyclif, his early academic followers in Oxford, and later heresy suspects condemned the pope as Antichrist; indeed, they applied similar epithets to all the ranks of the ecclesiastical hierarchy. In 1396, for instance, the tenth Wycliffite article censured by the clergy meeting in the provincial convocation of Canterbury was that 'these twelve are agents of Antichrist, and the disciples of Antichrist: the popes, the cardinals, the patriarchs, the archbishops, the bishops, the archdeacons, the officials, and deans, monks, and canons . . . , pseudo-friars just recently introduced, and pardoners'.[3] But the force of such criticisms, and their implications for Wyclif's programme of ecclesiastical reform, was less transparent than Thomson and some later historians have recognized. As we discovered in the previous chapter with regard to their views on the clergy, what Wyclif and many of those who came after him sought was not the abolition but, rather, the reform of the papacy. They argued not that the papacy should be dismantled but, instead, that it

---

[1] J. A. F. Thomson, *The Later Lollards: 1414–1520* (Oxford, 1965), 249.

[2] See pp. v–viii above.

[3] Wilkins, iii.230, no. 10: 'Item, quod isti duodecim sunt procuratores antichristi, et discipuli antichristi, papae, cardinales, patriarchae, archipraesules, episcopi, archidiaconi, officiales, et decani, monachi, et canonici . . . , pseudofratres introducti jam ultimo et quaestores.'

should be stripped of its extravagant claims to authority and thus made to resemble more closely the ministry of the apostle Peter. It would not be appropriate to call this view *hyperpapal,* by way of analogy with the term *hyperclerical* as I defined it in Chapter 5; that language would seem too much to imply sympathy on the part of lollards for the claims of the late medieval papacy. But nor was it unambiguously *antipapal,* at least as Thomson and most other scholars would construe that term.

It will be helpful to begin by briefly situating Wycliffite ideas about the powers and responsibilities of the pope within their historical context. Though the high Middle Ages has been described as a period of papal monarchy, such absolutism was impossible to achieve in practice.[4] From the mid-eleventh century, nevertheless, the succession of popes associated with the reform programme of Gregory VII made progressively grander claims to universal jurisdiction. Despite the increasing scope of the papal office, however, it would have been a rare inhabitant of late medieval England who would personally have been affected by these developments. For all but the politically connected or the exceptionally affluent, who might have taken advantage of the pope's claims to universal jurisdiction by bringing their lawsuits to the papal curia, the pope would have existed at the periphery of laypeople's devotional world. His name would have been mentioned in sermons, in the bidding prayers at mass, and in some public proclamations, but he would have been largely a symbolic figure.[5]

But if for most late medieval people the pope was a symbol of the universal church, it did not follow that he was a figurehead. To take but one example, John Mirk's *Festial* reflects an exalted view of papal authority. For Mirk, as for other mainstream theologians and preachers, the pope has the power to procure the remission of sins and, hence, the release of the dead from purgatory:

And ȝet yn more confort of all Godys pepull yche fyfte ȝere, þe pope of Rome grauntyþe a full remyssion of all synnys to yche man and weman þat comyth to Rome þat ȝer. But for all men may not come þedyr and haue þys pardon, þerfor þe Pope of Heuen, Ihesu Cryst, of his specyall grace grauntyþe all men and woymen full pardon of hor synnys yn hor deth-day.[6]

---

[4] Colin Morris, *The Papal Monarchy: The Western Church from 1050 to 1250* (Oxford, 1991).
[5] It is telling, for instance, that the index to Duffy's masterful account of 'traditional religion' in England, *Stripping of the Altars*, only refers to the pope in the context of the expurgation of his name from English prayer books.
[6] Mirk, *Festial,* 74.

Lest it appear that he is claiming that Christ has granted salvation to everyone, Mirk proceeds to specify that those who would claim this 'specyall grace' must be contrite, confess their sins, and resolve to sin no more. A peculiar reversal of language betokens Mirk's belief in a close association between the pope and Christ. To call Christ the 'Pope of Heuen' is to imply that the papacy is a title so high that it can rightfully be used of God; it also suggests that the pope's place in the church is analogous to the undisputed supremacy of God over all the other dwellers in heaven. All this notwithstanding, Mirk was composing the sermons of the *Festial* at a time when papal authority was in particular need of support. The schism between the Roman and Avignonese papacies, which from 1378 until 1415 divided cardinals, monarchs, and kingdoms between the two rival claimants to Peter's throne, produced as one of its effects a higher profile for conciliarism, the principle that a general council is the highest form of church government and could end the schism by deposing both would-be popes and electing a new one in their place.[7]

Accordingly, many of John Wyclif's statements about the papacy were made against the backdrop of restlessness about ecclesiastical governance. The schism, in which the English crown opted publicly for Urban but may simultaneously have sounded out the possibility of compromise, figured prominently in the development of Wyclif's thinking about the rights and responsibilities of the pope; and the split between Rome and Avignon ultimately came to stand, for him, as a sign of divine judgement on an institution which had become corrupt.[8] Nevertheless, Wyclif did not categorically reject the papacy, except perhaps in one or two ill-tempered polemical writings near the end of his life. Rather, he articulated an account of the papacy's role in the church which stressed the theological, constitutional, and moral limitations on papal power.

---

[7] It is important to note, however, that conciliarism was not a medieval innovation and that its proponents were hardly of one mind as to the precise legal and theological relationships between councils, popes, and bishops: see Francis Oakley, *The Conciliarist Tradition: Constitutionalism in the Catholic Church, 1300–1870* (Oxford, 2003), esp. 66–72; for the earlier view that conciliarism represented a definite series of positions on political and ecclesiological questions, see Ray C. Petry, 'Unitive reform principles of the late medieval concilarists', *Church History*, 31 (1962), 164–81.

[8] On the willingness of Richard II's government to seek compromise, see J. J. N. Palmer, 'England and the great Western schism, 1388–1399', *English Historical Review*, 83 (1968), 516–22; on other English views of the schism, see among others Margaret Harvey, *Solutions to the Schism: A study of some English attitudes, 1378–1409* (St-Ottilien, 1983). The importance of the schism in shaping Wyclif's view of the papacy is stressed by Ryan, 'Three early treatises on the church', 113–40.

WYCLIF'S VIEW OF THE PAPACY

Regardless of whether we ascribe to Wyclif the predestinarianism that earlier commentators regularly discerned in his thought, the scholarly consensus has long held that among the first principles of his ecclesiology is a distinction between the church as a theological reality and the church as a visible institution.[9] As a theological reality, the church has no head apart from Christ, from whom all authority and sacramental power directly flows.[10] It would be blasphemous to describe the pope, or for that matter any human being, as head of the church, and in *De civili dominio*, Wyclif accordingly interprets Matthew 16:18 to mean that the 'rock' on which Christ promised to build the church is not Peter but, rather, Christ himself: 'After Peter . . . acknowledged the divinity and humanity of Christ, he who was Truth granted to him [the knowledge] that "upon this rock", which according to the apostle was Christ.'[11] In a later work, Wyclif rejected the view that Peter's very name implies his headship of the church: 'And some people, from the father of lies, pretend these things: that Peter was the head of the church and that the name Cephas should be interpreted as "head", and so they say that unless the pope rules the church, it should be *acephalam*, which is to say headless.'[12] Thus, while Wyclif acknowledged Peter's primacy within the church, his exegesis of Matthew 16 draws a firm distinction between primacy and headship. As we shall see, at least two later Wycliffite authors appropriated this interpretation for their own.

But if only Christ can be the head of the church, then what of the pope? Returning to his distinction between the true church and the visible church, Wyclif allows that the pope *can* be head of a *particular* visible church. In Wyclif's ecclesiology, this latter term denotes a circumscribed assembly, a historically instantiated body comprised jointly of the predestinate and those foreknown to damnation. Yet in setting forth this claim, Wyclif is not merely making an empirical observation, that whoever is pope can by virtue of his

---

[9] See Ch. 2 above.

[10] This point has recently been made to great effect by Takashi Shogimen, 'Wyclif's ecclesiology and political thought' in *Companion*, 199–240 at 217, and also by Ian Christopher Levy, 'John Wyclif and the primitive papacy', *Viator*, 38 (2007), 159–89 at 179.

[11] *De civili dominio*, i.281: 'Postquam enim Petrus exclusis heresibus confessus est Christi deitatem et humanitatem, concessit sibi Veritas quod super hanc petram, que secundum apostolum erat Christus.'

[12] *Responsiones ad argumenta cuiusdam emuli veritatis*, in *Opera minora*, 269: 'Et sic fingunt quidam ex patre mendacii, quod Petrus fuit caput ecclesie et quod Cephas interpretatur caput et sic dicunt ecclesiam nisi papa ipsam regeret acephalam, hic est sine capite.'

office exercise leadership in the Roman church. Rather, he is stressing that the proper exercise of the pope's authority, even in the visible church, is subject to conditions. First, the pope must be predestined to salvation, for on Wyclif's account of ecclesiastical and temporal dominion, no person who is not among the elect can rightly claim the obedience of others; second, the pope must govern the church according to the law of Christ, as revealed in Scripture; and third, the moral quality of the pope's own life must be worthy of his office.[13] As Ian Christopher Levy has pointed out, the net effect of these conditions is to emphasize that only those popes who successfully imitate Peter can rightly claim a place of primacy among Christ's people.[14]

Wyclif had articulated the theological foundations of his attitude toward the papacy as early as 1378, when he wrote his treatise *De ecclesia*. Nevertheless, his criticisms of the papacy became more vitriolic in later years. From the late nineteenth century, scholars have traditionally pointed to a three-stage development in his views, though Levy's recent discussion of the references to the papacy in Wyclif's early *Postilla super totam bibliam* renders problematic any rigid scheme of periodization.[15] First, before the schism, Wyclif acknowledged the authority of a morally upright pope over a particular church whose centre was at Rome but, even in this period, Wyclif made much of the long-standing tradition of using the model of the primitive church (*forma primitivae ecclesiae*) as a standard for his own time. Levy has shown that Wyclif's appropriation of the *ecclesia primitiva* tradition provided a link between his views of the papacy and of churchly endowments:

It is not surprising to find Wyclif also gazing nostalgically upon that primitive state of the church. His words mirroring Jerome's, he too spoke of a church that grew rapidly on the strength of the martyrs' suffering. It was the Donation of Constantine, says Wyclif, which marked the church's subsequent fall into the sins of the flesh and worldly wisdom . . . On other occasions, Wyclif will even contend that there were no popes prior to the Donation, at least not in the current sense of the term. For there was certainly no figure (neither Christ, nor Peter, nor Clement) who claimed for himself all temporal and spiritual power over his fellow bishops.[16]

After the outbreak of the schism, Wyclif took a second, somewhat more complex position on the papacy, a stance exemplified in his 1379 treatise

---

[13] *De Christo et suo adversario antichristo*, in *Polemical Works*, ii.672.

[14] Levy, 'John Wyclif and the primitive papacy', 159–61.

[15] For three accounts of this traditional view, ranging over a century of Wyclif scholarship, see Lechler, *Wycliffe*, 312; Workman, *Wyclif*, ii.73–80; and *EWS*, iv.93. Cf. Levy, 'John Wyclif and the primitive papacy', 165–6.

[16] Levy, 'John Wyclif and the primitive papacy', 163.

De potestate pape.[17] Here, Wyclif begins with an extended disquisition on the nature of power and then proceeds to consider the relationship between Peter and Christ's other apostles. His analysis echoes the twenty arguments in support of Peter's primacy set forth by Richard FitzRalph in his *De questionibus Armenorum*: that Christ addressed Peter as if he were the whole church, that only to Peter were given the keys of heaven, that Christ invited only Peter to join him walking on the water, and so forth.[18] In this stage of the evolution of his views, Wyclif also retains FitzRalph's assertion that Christ's commission in Matthew 16 is an argument for Peter's primacy among the apostles.[19] Indeed, Peter held the primacy, but 'he did not receive that primacy only for himself but for his vicars, succeeding him in the church militant. Since Christ cannot desert his church...it is right that he [Peter] should continue to be captain in the church militant.'[20] We shall shortly see that this image of the pope as 'captain', rather than head, of the church recurs in some of the writings of Wyclif's successors.

The thrust of Wyclif's arguments in *De potestate pape* is that Christ intended that there be a pope in the visible church, but that person must be worthy of the name. As in his earlier writings, in this treatise he again places limitations on Peter's successors: they must imitate the apostle in conduct and morals; they must be among those who have received the grace of predestination; and, crucially, they cannot be chosen by merely human means. Wyclif thus rejects the election of popes by the college of cardinals, arguing instead that selecting popes by lot is more faithful to Scripture and the history of the church and also more likely to reveal God's will.[21] In taking this stance, Wyclif is both stressing that only God can elevate a man to the papacy and arguing that the establishment of the church's supreme seat at Rome was contingent upon human politics, thus leaving open the possibility that the pope need not always be the Bishop of Rome. (Though startling, this argument was familiar in medieval discussions of the office of *apostolicus*.[22] Wyclif does not, however, explore at any length the practical consequences of the possibility of a non-Roman pope.) Where contemporary politics are

---

[17] For the chronology of Wyclif's writings, see Lahey, *John Wyclif*.

[18] *De potestate pape*, 43–62.

[19] Ibid., 47–8.

[20] Ibid., 62: 'non solum accepit primatum pro se ipso sed pro eius vicariis succedentibus in ecclesia militante. Cum enim Christus non potest ecclesiam suam deserere...sic oportet continue esse capitaneum in ecclesia militante.'

[21] Ibid., 63–72.

[22] Michael Wilks, 'The *Apostolicus* and the Bishop of Rome', 2 parts, *Journal of Theological Studies*, n.s. 13 (1962), 290–317, and n.s. 14 (1963), 311–54 at 331; see also Levy, 'John Wyclif and the primitive papacy', 185–6.

concerned, he repeatedly refers to the Roman Pope Urban VI as 'our Urban', but elsewhere in *De potestate pape* he asserts that both claimants to the papal throne are Antichrists.[23] Yet the force of this epithet, for Wyclif as for later writers and heresy suspects, is not to reject the papacy as a diabolical institution: 'But let not the faithful believe, that if one pope is Antichrist, then every pope is Antichrist; even if Caiaphas was a great Antichrist, nevertheless not every bishop; and if Nero was a great Antichrist, nevertheless not every secular lord; and if Sergius was a great Antichrist, nevertheless not every monk.'[24]

De potestate pape is a work whose arguments veer between a moderate, if critical, assessment of papal power and a caustic condemnation of the two rival popes. The latter trend became more pronounced in what has traditionally been seen as the third stage in the development of Wyclif's views on the papacy. In works produced after 1381, in the wake of his exile from Oxford, Wyclif welcomes the schism as proof of the outright corruption of the papacy.[25] Nevertheless, he rarely stated that the papacy should be abolished as an institution; his arguments are instead directed against overly expansive claims about papal authority. It is likely that Wyclif despaired of the possibility that papal elections by the college of cardinals could produce the sort of morally upright candidate who alone would be eligible to take on the office of pope, but that does not imply that he changed his views on whether there should be an office for such a candidate to assume. As Andrew Larsen has recently pointed out, Wyclif's *De citationibus frivolis*, written late in 1383 or early in 1384 to explain why he could not obey Urban VI's summons to appear at the papal curia, seems to reflect a more moderate view of the papacy:

Wyclif explains that he cannot go because he is 'disabled and crippled' and because the Crown has prohibited him from going, and in a letter to Urban, he states that God 'has obliged me to the contrary.' The statement that God has not allowed it seems to refer both to his physical infirmity and the royal prohibition, rather than to an argument that God requires him to reject the authority of the pope on this point.[26]

Though it is possible that the royal command which prevented Wyclif from undertaking the journey to Rome also required him to write respectfully to a man he once denounced as Antichrist, it seems on balance more likely that

---

[23] *De potestate pape*, 247, 255.

[24] Ibid., 328: 'Sed absit fidelem credere, si papa sit Antichristus, tunc omnis papa est Antichristus, ut magnus Antichristus fuit Cayfas, et tamen non omnis episcopus; magnus Antichristus fuit Nero et tamen non omnis secularis dominus; magnus Antichristus fuit Sergius et tamen non omnis monachus.'

[25] *Trialogus*, 424.

[26] Andrew Larsen, 'John Wyclif, c. 1331–1384' in *Companion*, 1–66 at 61–2.

since Wyclif's most extreme statements about the papacy were made in the heat of polemical confrontation, his broader views may have been more moderate than some critics have allowed.

Indeed, several coherent themes run through those passages of Wyclif's writings in which he discusses the papacy at length, a fact which calls further into question the traditional periodization of his thought. First, as we have already seen, no one but Christ is the head of the true church, and no one can know for certain whether she or he is even a member of that church without a special revelation from God.[27] Accordingly, only Christ possesses *plenitudo potestatis* in the church; even though he may have commissioned Peter, he did not pass on the fullness of his authority to Peter, and whatever (potentially geographically circumscribed) power a pope might have in the visible church flows directly from Christ's gift.[28] By extension, the spiritual powers of bishops and other ecclesiastical leaders depend not on Peter and his successors but on Christ.[29] Second, the pope enjoys Peter's primacy, but only insofar as his actions are in conformity with Scripture and with the example of the primitive church.[30] Third, the papacy is not necessary for salvation. Instead, to borrow terminology from Wyclif's theology of grace, the papacy is 'necessary' in only a hypothetical sense: that is, even though Christ chose to institute the papacy as the highest form of governance in the church (and even though, as a result, the papacy exists *iure divino*, not *iure humano*, as some earlier critics have suggested Wyclif believed), Christ could have chosen otherwise.[31]

It is unsurprising that these nuances of Wyclif's arguments about the papacy have received less critical attention, both in his own time and later, than his more controversial statements identifying the pope as Antichrist. We have already seen that the condemnation of Wyclif's writings by the Canterbury convocation of 1396 alluded to his use of the epithet Antichrist for the pope and his subordinates; similarly sensational claims appear in the list of Wycliffite articles produced by the Oxford commission appointed to examine his writings in 1412. For instance, the commissioners found in Wyclif's late polemical tract *De sermone Domini in monte* the propositions that the pope is Antichrist, that along with his cardinals and bishops he comprises a 'monstrous composite person of Antichrist', that the pope is the 'abomination of desolation' foretold by the prophet Daniel, and that the

---

[27] *De ecclesia*, 1, 66, 94; *Dialogus sive speculum ecclesie militantis*, 92; on this point, see also William E. Farr, *John Wyclif as Legal Reformer* (Leiden, 1974), 32.

[28] *De ecclesia*, 314.

[29] *De civili dominio*, i.38, 282–4.

[30] *De ecclesia*, 562; *De potestate pape*, 62.

[31] *De potestate pape*, 245; on Wyclif's use of the concept of hypothetical necessity, see pp. 33–5 above.

papacy and cardinalate were not established by God but by the devil.[32] The Council of Constance included a series of articles about the papacy in its first condemnation of Wyclif: that a pope foreknown as damned has no authority; that no one should be considered as pope after Urban VI; that Pope Silvester and the Emperor Constantine wrongly endowed the clergy; that the pope and his clergy are heretics on account of owning property; that 'the Roman church is Satan's synagogue; and the pope is not the immediate and proximate vicar of Christ and the apostles'; and that the process of papal elections was instituted by the devil.[33] A second set of articles condemned at Constance also included several propositions dealing with the papacy: that the pope has no status in the gospel, his office not having been endorsed by Christ; that the pope is Antichrist made manifest; and that Peter and Clement were not popes. The council also repeated the claim about the twelve ranks of Antichrist's agents first condemned in 1396.[34]

Some of these articles do in fact reflect Wyclif's views. We have already seen that Wyclif repeatedly stressed that a true pope must be among the predestinate, and the propositions which reject the authority of those popes who are foreknown to damnation accord both with Wyclif's ecclesiology and his broader ideas about dominion. Likewise, the Oxford commission of 1412 as well as the Council of Constance seem rightly to have understood Wyclif's objections to the process of election by the college of cardinals. And the documents of Constance acknowledge a particularly important vein of Wyclif's views about exemplarity and papal authority when they identify as his the proposition that 'it is clear that whoever is the humbler, of greater service to the church, and the more fervent in Christ's love towards his church, is the greater in the church militant and to be reckoned the most immediate vicar of Christ'.[35]

In general, however, those who compiled lists of Wycliffite propositions for condemnation seem to have laid greatest stress on the claims Wyclif made in the final phase of his career, in writings which are more polemical than otherwise. The various commissions and councils which rejected Wyclif's views seem at times also to have confused his opinion that particular popes were evil with the broader claim that the papacy as an institution is irretrievably corrupt. Whilst Wyclif indeed wrote that both rival popes are Antichrist and that no pope who is not among the predestined can rightly claim authority in the church, he did not reject the institution of the papacy.

---

[32] Wilkins, iii.340, nos. 4, 5, 8, 12.
[33] Tanner, *Decrees*, i.412–13, nos. 9, 33, 36–7, 40.
[34] Ibid., i.422–6, nos. 17–24, 28, 35, 39.
[35] Ibid., i.424, no. 24.

Hence, many of the claims imputed to him by his adversaries do not do justice to the full range of his thought. The Oxford committee's article that 'it would be useful to the church if there were not a pope', for instance, contradicts Wyclif's claim in *De potestate pape* that the papacy was instituted *iure divino* as the highest form of ecclesiastical authority, so long as the occupants of the office stay within the bounds set by the example of Peter and the primitive church.

HEAD OR 'CAPTEYN'? THE POPE IN WYCLIFFITE WRITINGS

Much more deserves to be said about Wyclif's view of the papal office, but the outline I have been sketching should provide sufficient room for comparisons between Wyclif and those who came after him. Just as in Wyclif's own writings, there is something of a disjunction in the works of his followers between, on the one hand, a virulent condemnation of the abuses of the contemporary papacy and, on the other, an endorsement (tacit or otherwise) of the papacy as the highest structure of ecclesiastical governance. Only a small minority of Wycliffite writers envisioned the outright abolition of the papal office.

As in earlier chapters, the long cycle of English Wycliffite sermons can serve as a helpful point of entry into a discussion of dissenting views on the papacy. Hudson and Gradon have commented that the sermons:

reflect Wyclif's final view, one of outright condemnation of the papacy, of all its associates and activities. The theoretical discussion of the appropriateness of having a single man as head of the church on earth is largely ignored in favour of consideration of separate abuses of the current manifestation of the papacy, though Wyclif's eventual dismissal of the necessity for such a head underlies many of the objections.[36]

It cannot be denied that many of the sermons which comprise the cycle castigate the papacy for its presumption, worldliness, and corruption. Thus, for instance, one sermon condemns the papacy as the head of 'Antichrist's school': 'þese popys ben fadrys, and þer chirches ben modris, þese byschopis ben breþren, and oþre prelates cosines; secler men for muc ben to þese prelates frendys, and alle þese bytrayen cristene men to torment'.[37] The pope arrogantly claims that he knows that he will be among the saved; the process by which he is elected is likely to produce an erroneous, worldly

---

[36] *EWS*, iv.93.   [37] *EWS*, ii.67/47–50.

result; and the endowment of the papacy, whether in the time of 'Seluester or oþur', has rendered it a sinful institution and increased the burden of taxation on the commons.[38]

Beyond these familiar objections to the manner in which the papal office is exercised, however, the sermon-cycle also contains more theoretical treatments of the papacy and its place in the life of the church. The most extensive of these appears in the long sermon *Of Mynystris in þe Chirche*, which runs to more than a thousand lines in the printed edition and can be found in thirteen of the extant manuscripts of the cycle. In the main, it reflects the moderate and nuanced position of Wyclif's *De potestate pape*. The preacher begins by recalling Jesus' prediction of the destruction of the Temple, arguing that among the evils Jesus had foreseen was the assumption of the papal throne by Antichrist, 'heued of alle þes yuel men'.[39] Whereas Peter and his successors should be the poorest and humblest men in the world, contemporary popes are rich, proud, vengeful, and covetous. It is heresy, the preacher continues, to believe that popes cannot sin; in fact, some contemporary popes are the pseudo-prophets against whom Christ had warned.[40] Thus far, the text seems to be articulating what Hudson and Gradon have called 'the most extensive, and most explicitly extreme discussion of the papacy' among the constituent texts of the English sermon-cycle.[41] But half-way through his sermon, the preacher poses a series of awkward questions that, ultimately, generate more judicious responses:

But heere men gruchchen aȝenys þe wyt þat is here ȝouen to þis gospel; and specially herfore þat it sowneþ aȝeyn þe pope and so aȝenys hooly chyrche. . . . For ȝif þer were no pope, and þe chyrche were not dowyd, how schulde þe chyrche stonde oþurwise þon heþone men? Also Crist ordeynede Petre to be aftur hym heed of þe chyrche; how schulde þis body be wiþowten heed, siþ Crist and Petre weron heedis þerof? Also Crist by graunt of his word may not forsake his chirch, and so he mot gouerne hit in byleue and oþre poyntus. But siþ hymself comeþ not down aftur his ascencion, he mot nedis haue a viker to reule þe chirche aftur hym.[42]

These questions, framed from the standpoint of fourteenth-century orthodoxy, lead the preacher into a lengthy excursus on ecclesiology. Like Wyclif,

---

[38] On the pope's salvation, see *EWS*, ii.69/110–14; on the method of election, ii.87/86–116, ii.101/25–40, ii.118/20–1; on endowment, ii.89/83, iii.140/39–45, iii.154/29–33, among others.

[39] *EWS*, ii.MC/39 (MC = 'Of Mynistris in þe Chirche').

[40] On the common antifraternal trope of friars as biblical pseudo-prophets, see Szittya, *The Antifraternal Tradition in Medieval Literature*, 3–4. Wyclif had discussed, and rejected, the ideas of papal infallibility and impeccability in his treatises *De veritate sacre scripture* and *De civili dominio*.

[41] *EWS*, iv.93.   [42] *EWS*, ii.MC/598–609.

his starting point is that Christ, not any human being, is head of the church.[43] It would be monstrous for the church to have two heads, but that does not mean there are no distinctions among its members; Christ, after all, chose Peter and the other apostles to lead his flock. The language, possibly drawn from Wyclif's *De potestate pape*, in which the preacher describes these early church leaders is crucial: 'And so Petre was not *heed* of þe chyrche but *a capteyn* of þe chyrche. And certis werriours wolon scorne þis resoun þat ȝif a man be capteyn he is heed. Petre was capteyn for a tyme and aftur hym was Poule capteyn; and þer was no strif in þis, which of hem schulde be capteyn.'[44]

The sermon seems to argue not only that Peter was only 'captain', not head, of the church, but also that Peter was only *a* captain; there can be multiple captains, and as the preacher also points out, 'yche apostle hadde in his cuntre pleyn power wiþ help of Crist, so þat noon hadde need of Petre to rennon and be confermed of hym'.[45] Whilst this might seem to imply almost a congregationalist understanding of ecclesiastical authority, the preacher does not elaborate further. Instead, he turns to the process of papal election, condemning election by cardinals as a corrupt practice introduced by human law. The cardinal-electors choose neither the most able man, as Christ did, nor the man most likely to remain in a state of evangelical poverty; instead, not knowing whether they are choosing a truly holy and predestinate man, 'þes cardinals lokon by þer lawe who is moste myȝty to þe world'.[46] Like Wyclif, the preacher concludes by recommending election by lot.

The attenuated account of papal authority to be found in *Of Mynystris in þe Chirche*, already of a piece with Wyclif's views on the papacy, appears in other vernacular Wycliffite writings as well. The guiding theme of these texts, that since the pope is not and cannot be head of the church, papal authority must keep within its proper bounds, is familiar to a reader of any of Wyclif's ecclesiological writings. The *Thirty-Seven Conclusions*, for instance, dedicate eight of their number to the powers of the papacy, claiming among other things that the pope is not head nor even necessarily a member of the church; that the laws of the pope are to be obeyed only insofar as they contain 'leful thingis and spedeful to saluacioun and no ferthere'; that the pope's powers are not unlimited but extend only insofar as God has allowed; that the pope has no greater power to forgive sin than any other apostle; and that the pope, like every other priest, has the power of the keys only insofar as he can bind or

---

[43] *EWS*, ii.MC/629–30.

[44] *EWS*, ii.MC/654–8, emphasis mine. For a possible source of the preacher's use of the term 'captain', see the quotation from *De potestate pape* at n. 20 above.

[45] *EWS*, ii.MC/650–2.

[46] *EWS*, ii.MC/668–9.

loose what God has already bound or loosed.[47] That the pope can only command that which Christ has already commanded, a commonplace of Wyclif's views on such diverse subjects as confession, excommunication, and marriage, is a recurring theme in both the English sermon-cycle and other tracts. Thus, for instance, the *Apology for Lollard Doctrines* argues in two places that 'whan he [the pope] filliþ not in dede, but doþ contrarily to his behest in degre, he semiþ not to be þe vicar of Crist in dede'.[48] The vernacular tract *De papa* stresses that men should obey popes only insofar as they follow the example of Christ, and likewise, the Middle English version of the Wycliffite theological dictionary the *Rosarium* warns people to judge their popes carefully: 'þof al he be þe vicarie of Petre, neuþerles þer ow noȝt liȝtly to be had of hym presumpsioun ... noȝt euery pope is seynt or holy, bot somtyme he is punysched of God in þis present life as a reproued man'.[49] Of these three texts, the *Apology* seems most sceptical of the papal office, suggesting in its opening section that the pope is not Christ's vicar, and perhaps not even Peter's. But, as we have seen with other Wycliffite texts, what seems at first a stark condemnation of the papacy may in fact be a qualified assertion of limited papal authority. The author argues that the pope *loses* the powers of Peter's vicar when he fails to do 'þe office of Petir in ȝerþ, ne doiþ not þe þing in þat office þat he is holden to do: but doþ contrarili'.[50] The logical corollary of this position, namely, that the pope is in fact Peter's vicar when he follows Peter's example, goes unstated but also unrefuted.

Wycliffite writers employed a range of tactics to set boundaries to the exercise of papal power. First, some authors focused on the interpretation of Matthew 16:18. We have already seen that Wyclif suggested that Christ himself is the 'rock' upon which he pledged to build the church, and several Wycliffite preachers advanced the same idea. Here is a passage from the English sermon for the feast of the Chair of St Peter: 'And þus *Crist seiþ to hym here þat he is Petre, and vpon þis ston schal he grownde hys chyrche.* Þis corner ston is Crist, of whom Petre haþ þis name, and on þis same stoon is holy chyrche groundud. And þus Petre and eche man signifieþ þis ston.'[51] By making the biblical stone represent Christ in the first instance, and Peter only secondarily, the preacher emphasizes that authority in the church comes not from apostolic succession but, instead, divine gift. The same kind of exegesis appears in the *Tractatus de oblacione iugis sacrificii*:

---

[47] *Remonstrance*, nos. 17–21, 23, 25, 27; quotation at 47.
[48] *An Apology for Lollard Doctrines*, 4; see also 6.
[49] von Nolcken, *The Middle English Translation of the Rosarium Theologie*, 79.
[50] *An Apology for Lollard Doctrines*, 1.
[51] *EWS*, ii.100/54–7, original emphasis.

þis [the misinterpretation of Christ's words] is a grete cause of errour and striff þat is in þe chirche. For of þis worde þe pope and al cristendom, and nameli the clergi, presumen þe pope to be hede of, and grounde of alle holi chirche [but] . . . Suppose we þan here þat onli Crist is þe stone þat þe gospel spekiþ of, whan Crist seiþ 'Upon þis stone I schal bilde my chirche.' For þis is þe stone and þe fundament þat mai not be meued, as seint Poule techiþ.[52]

Second, some Wycliffites emphasized that the power of the keys, from which medieval popes derived many of their claims to authority, was given to all the apostles equally; this claim can be found in both the English sermon-cycle and the *Tractatus*.[53] Third, a number of texts link the proper exercise of papal authority with the poverty the pope should seek to emulate; thus the tract *The Church and Her Members* argues that 'verry cristis viker shulde be porerste man of oþire and mekerst of oþir men', and the vernacular sermon *Omnis plantacio* suggests that contemporary artists wrong Peter by depicting him 'wiþ a diademe upon his heed and an ymage of þe emperour vndir hise feet'.[54] Finally, like Wyclif and the preacher of the sermon *Of Mynystris in þe Chirche*, some texts recommend that election by lot be brought in as a way to avoid the problems created by jockeying for position among the cardinals.[55]

Thus far, the texts we have encountered have either castigated papal abuses without recommending specific remedies or else have articulated a moderate ecclesiology in which a reformed papacy, occupied by godly men, would imitate Peter's style of governing the church. Did any Wycliffite writers go beyond this model of attenuated papal authority by recommending that the papacy be abolished? Several texts which seem to point in this direction are in fact ecclesiological red herrings. For instance, an English epistle-sermon and the *Tractatus de oblacione iugis sacrificii* both contain the suggestion that the papacy is not necessary. On closer inspection, however, these texts seem to be making a less controversial, and in fact a more hopeful, claim: that Christ's power will continue to remain with his church despite the sinfulness of clergymen and the possibility of change in its organizational structure. Since 'Petre ne ony oþre apostle durste not seye þat he was so nedful, þat wiþowten his gouernayle moste þe chyrche nedis perische', the church could continue to function without a pope, but there is a substantial intellectual gap

---

[52] Titus, ll. 2314–17, 2337–40; cf. I Corinthians 3:10 and Ephesians 2:20. For a more detailed discussion of Wycliffite hermeneutics and biblical exegesis, and their relationship to the mainstream of medieval Christianity, see Ghosh, *The Wycliffite Heresy*.

[53] *EWS*, ii.74/81–3; Titus, lines 2408–12.

[54] *The Church and Her Members*, in Conrad Lindberg (ed.), *English Wyclif Tracts 1–3* (Oslo, 1991), 115; *Omnis plantacio*, in *Works*, ll. 1907–8.

[55] See, for instance, the vernacular *De pontificum Romanorum schismate*, in Arnold, iii. 242–66 at 251; *EWS*, ii.101/25–35.

between the negative argument that the papacy is unnecessary (or, to follow Wyclif, necessary in only a hypothetical sense) and the positive suggestion that it should be abolished.[56]

A similar degree of ambiguity can be found in texts which argue that no mention of the papacy can be found in the church's foundational documents, the Bible and the Creed. Wyclif himself makes such a claim in *Dialogus*, where his character Veritas argues that 'since this name "pope" is outside the faith of scripture, it seems that it was contrived by Caesar when he presumed to endow the church'.[57] The same view appears in the anonymous tract entitled *Sixteen Points on which Bishops Accuse Lollards*, whose author affirms that:

we beleuen þat oure lord Iesu Crist was and is cheffe bischoppe of his chirche, as seint Peter seiþ, and schal be vnto þe dai of dome. And we supposen þat þer ben many hooli faderris, popis, siþen seint Petrus tyme, þou3 þis name 'pope' be not seid in Goddis lawe, as seint Clement, seint Clete and oþer many moo. And so we graunten þat þe pope of Rome schulde next folowe Crist and seint Peter in maner of lyuynge, and, if he do so, he is worþily pope, and, if he contrarie hem moost of al oþer, he is most anticrist.[58]

Likewise, the vernacular text *Of Prelates* protests that it should be enough to believe in Christ and to be baptized, without having to add beliefs about papal primacy to the articles of the Creed: 'certis þe apostlis if ihu crist constreyneden neuere ony man to bileue þis of hem self, and 3it þei weren certeyn of here sauynge in heuene; hou schulde þan ony sinful wrecche, þat wot neuere where he schal be dampnyd or sauyd, constreyne men to bileue þat he is heuyd of holy chirche?'[59] The authors of these texts, like Wyclif before them, oscillate between critical comments about the contemporary papacy and affirmations of the possibility that there might one day be a pope worthy of the name.

Indeed, it is difficult to find vernacular Wycliffite texts which explicitly favour the abolition over the reform of the papacy. In some cases, the vigour of the polemic suggests that individual authors may have judged the papacy to be beyond repair. A passage in *Of Prelates* provides perhaps the best example:

of alle prestis he is most contrarie to crist boþe in lif and techynge, and he meynteneþ most synne bi preuylegies, exempcions and longe plees, and he is most proud a3enst cristis mekenesse, most coueitous of worldly goodis and lordschipis a3enst þe pouert of crist and his apostlis, and most idel in gostly werkis and occupied in worldly causes.[60]

---

[56] *EWS*, i.E11/80–2; see also Titus, ll. 2429–40.

[57] *Dialogus*, 49: 'cum hoc nomen papa sit terminus extra fidem scripture, videtur quod in dotacione ecclesie presumpta per cesarem est inventum'.

[58] *Selections*, no. 2, 21.

[59] *Of Prelates*, in Matthew, 52–107 at 84.

[60] *Of Prelates*, 89–90.

The author proceeds to castigate the pope for selling sacraments as well as benefices, for creating unnecessary obstacles to preaching, and for legislating against the will of Christ. Uncompromisingly critical passages such as this suggest that a vocal minority of Wycliffite writers did not entertain the notion that the papacy might ever successfully be reformed. It may be to a certain degree surprising, however, that such views were not in the majority; most of the extended discussions of papal authority in vernacular dissenting texts take the more moderate view we have explored in the pages of Wyclif's *De potestate pape* and the sermon *Of Mynystris in þe Chirche.*

PAPAL ANTICHRIST: THE POPE IN ANTI-WYCLIFFITE TEXTS

Despite the presence and persistence of this moderate strand of Wycliffite thinking about the papacy, anti-Wycliffite authors portrayed their opponents as fundamentally opposed to the headship and primacy of the Bishop of Rome. Roger Dymmok, for instance, mounted a spirited, if predictable, defence of papal prerogatives in the first book of his response to the twelve 'Lollard conclusions' of 1395. He emphasized the role of the papacy in preserving the unity of the church: 'since the church militant is a single kingdom of Christ, surpassing all other kingdoms in precedence, according to the prophecy of Daniel, chapter 2, it follows that there is one principal ruler of this kingdom here with us, who cannot be anyone other than the pope'.[61] Christ specifically designated Peter as supreme pastor and leader (*princeps*) of the church, likewise extending that commission to his successors 'lest the church ever exist without a head'.[62] Accordingly, Dymmok argued, quoting at length from Thomas Aquinas, the papacy is an essential feature of church governance, and it is a 'presumptuous error' not to recognize Peter's successors as heads of the church.[63] Dymmok also identified precedents for papal primacy in the decrees of the Council of Nicaea and in both the Old and New Testaments, where Jewish high priests prefigured Christian popes by serving as a focus of unity among their followers.[64]

---

[61] Dymmok, *Liber contra XII errores et haereses Lollardorum,* 33: 'cum ecclesia militans sit unum regnum Christi, superans omnia precedencia regna, secundum prophetiam Danielis II°, sequitur quod ipsius regni sit unus rex principalis hic nobiscum, qui alius fingi non potest nisi Papa'.

[62] Ibid., 34: 'ne unquam ecclesia sine capite remaneret.'

[63] Ibid., 36.   [64] Ibid.

The dissenting views against which Dymmok wrote can be traced in the records of many of the heresy trials conducted in late medieval England, at least fifty-three of which involved claims about the papacy. But unlike the topics we have considered in earlier chapters, for which the extant records preserve a surprising quantity of detail about defendants' views, the records of many trials in which the papacy figured as a locus of controversy are more terse. The majority of defendants who abjured articles about the pope and his prerogatives were simply said to have called the pope Antichrist (or a similar epithet), though a small group of heresy suspects seem to have articulated the more nuanced view that the pope's authority depends on the extent to which he imitates Christ and Peter.

The view that the pope is Antichrist, or at least *an* Antichrist, was among the most contentious claims attributed to late medieval heresy defendants. It was, however, hardly unique to Wycliffite dissenters. As Bernard McGinn has shown, apocalyptic terms of abuse were applied to the papacy as early as the tenth century, when in 991, a bishop attacked Pope John XV in these words: 'Reverend Fathers, who do you think he is, this man sitting in the highest chair, dressed in purple and glowing with gold? Doubtless, if he is bereft of charity and blown up and lifted on high with knowledge alone, he is Antichrist seated in the Temple of God and showing himself as if he were God!'[65] Similar claims appeared during the tumultuous times of the Gregorian reform, the controversy over the prophecies of Joachim of Fiore, and the struggles between several high medieval popes and emperors.[66] In addition, as we have already seen, Wyclif employed the trope of a papal Antichrist in both his moderate and more polemical works.

In all, at least thirty-two English heresy defendants were accused of having said that the pope is Antichrist. Among them was the itinerant preacher William Swinderby, who in response to charges laid against him by John Trefnant, the bishop of Hereford, wrote in 1391 that if the pope tries to make himself equal with Christ, then he blasphemes as much as Lucifer. 'Gif Crist then came to saufe men and nohte to slee hem, who that doith the reverse hereoffe is ageyn Crist, and then he ys Anticrist.'[67] Later in his written

---

[65] Quoted in Bernard McGinn, 'Angel pope and papal Antichrist', *Church History*, 47 (1978), 155–73 at 156.

[66] It is worth mentioning in this connection the rather unexpected discovery at the Dissolution in 1539 of a stained-glass window depicting the pope as Antichrist in the abbot's lodgings at Bury St Edmunds, Suffolk: Montgomery Carmichael, 'Picture at Hardwick House of a window formerly in the Abbey of Bury St Edmunds', *Proceedings of the Suffolk Institute of Archaeology and Natural History*, 14 (1911), 275–79. I am grateful to Diarmaid MacCulloch for this reference.

[67] Hereford reg. Trefnant, 269.

statement, Swinderby claimed that he had deliberately ignored canon law because the pope is Antichrist.[68] Bishop Trefnant heard similar sentiments from Walter Brut, the enigmatic *laicus litteratus* who in the same year was charged with teaching 'that the pope is Antichrist and the seducer of the people, contrary to all the law and life of Christ'.[69] In his first written reply to his accusers, Brut made clear that his condemnation of the pope was a conditional one: the pope is only to be rejected if he legislates against the Gospel. Brut did not state explicitly what authority a rightly living pope might enjoy; he did, however, make it clear that a pope who abuses his authority is the contemporary equivalent of the beasts of the earth and the sea depicted in the book of the Apocalypse.[70]

Later defendants did not have the same opportunity as Swinderby and Brut to expand upon their views, and in many cases all that is recorded of their beliefs about the pope is the epithet or series of epithets they used. Thus, William Apleward of Henley was accused in 1467 of saying that 'oure holy ffadre the pope of Rome is a grete best and a devyll of hell and a Synagoge: and that he shall lye depper in hell vp sithes then lucyfer'.[71] Thomas Bikenore, tried before Bishop William Aiscough of Salisbury in 1442, rejected the papacy with an extended eschatological metaphor:

the Pope of Rome ys antecriste and like to the hede of a dragon this wiche is specified in the apocolips and that Bisshopes and other astatis of the churche ar discipils of antecrist: like to the body of the seide dragon and that Religious men as monkys chanons freris and suche other be the tayle of that dragon and that the power whiche crist gaff to Petre was yven to hym alone and to none of his successouris popes nor prestos aftir hym.[72]

While no other suspect is recorded as having used such colourful language to describe the papacy and other organs of church government, at least two other defendants argued, as Bikenore did, that the primacy which Christ had given to Peter could not be handed on to his successors. John Skylan of Norwich diocese, tried in 1430, and John Blumston of Coventry and Lichfield diocese, tried more than half a century later in 1486, both argued that, in Skylan's words, 'ther was never pope aftir the decesse of Petir'.[73]

---

[68] Ibid., 275.

[69] Ibid., 279: 'quod papa est Anticristus et seductor populi ac omnino legi Cristi et vite contrarius'.

[70] Ibid., 287–8.

[71] Lincoln reg. Chedworth, fol. 61r.

[72] Salisbury reg. Aiscough, fol. 53r.

[73] *Norwich*, 147; *Coventry*, 64. On a related note, the Salisbury defendant Augustine Sterne argued in 1491 that Peter was not a priest until just before his death; it might seem that Sterne was rejecting the anachronistic view that Jesus' earliest disciples understood themselves as

Some defendants linked their identification of the pope as Antichrist with other ecclesiological claims, many of which resonate with the views we have traced in Wyclif's writings and those of his early followers. Skylan added that the pope does not have the power to create bishops, nor does he have any more power at all than any other man 'but [i.e., except] if he be more holy in lyvyng'.[74] Hawisia Mone of Loddon, whose village neighboured Skylan's, agreed that the pope does not have the power to confer orders and argued that 'he oonly that is moost holy and moost perfit in lyvyng in erthe is verry pope'.[75] Another subset of defendants, including Brut and the Bath and Wells suspect William Emayn, argued that only Christ can claim to be head of the church and that other claims to authority are hence blasphemous.[76] Emayn, like Skylan, drew a correlation between moral rectitude and ecclesiastical authority: 'the hed of the church is Crist, and thoo that be most virtuous in lyuyng be most highest in the church, and thoo that be in dedly synne be out of the church of Goddes ordinance and on the sinagog of Sathanas'.[77] This sort of language may have given at least one set of inquisitors the idea for a question to root out antipapal heretics—an article in bishop Polton of Worcester's 1428 questionnaire asks 'whether the pope is the head of the church?'[78]

It would be redundant to chronicle in detail the many other cases in which defendants were accused of or admitted to having called the pope Antichrist; with few exceptions, the extant court books and bishops' registers preserve little else of their views of the papacy.[79] In two localities, inquisitors seem to have been particularly intent upon recording suspects' opinions about the pope; Bishop Alnwick of Norwich and bishop Blythe of Salisbury both presided over a disproportionately large number of cases which involved the assertion that the pope is Antichrist. In the absence of additional information, however, it is impossible to determine whether these numbers reflect strong antipapal feeling or strong inquisitorial zeal. Equally unclear is a strange

---

priests in the same way as contemporary clergymen did, but we cannot be certain (Salisbury reg. Langton, 71–3).

[74] *Norwich*, 147.

[75] Ibid., 141; see also the case of William Ramsbury, who likewise maintained that the pope cannot confer episcopal orders: Hudson, 'A Lollard Mass?', 111–23, no. 1.

[76] Hereford reg. Trefnant, 287; Bath and Wells reg. Stafford, i.76–8.

[77] Bath and Wells reg. Stafford, i.76–8.

[78] Hudson, 'The examination of Lollards', 133–5: articles *per theologos*, no. 7.

[79] *Norwich*, 53, 61, 67, 108, 116, 122, 127, 135, 141, 147, 170, 197; Lambeth reg. Chichele, iii.197–208; Lincoln reg. Chedworth, fols. 12v–14r; Ely reg. Grey, fol. 130b; Salisbury reg. Blythe, fols. 70–70v, 74r–75r, 77r–77v, 78r–78v; Lambeth reg. Morton, ii.158–60; Hereford reg. Mayew, 66–7; Salisbury reg. Audley, fols. 148v–149r; J. B. Sheppard (ed.), *Literae cantuarienses*, 3 vols. (London, 1887–9), iii.312.

epithet applied to the pope by two Salisbury defendants: Augustine Sterne and Thomas Taillour, tried in 1491, both called the pope a 'panyer maker'.[80] In the fifteenth century, a panyer or pannier was a basket for foodstuffs usually carried by a beast of burden, and hence Sterne and Taillour may have been suggesting that the pope had created unnecessary burdens for the Christian faithful.

Whereas labels such as these seem to betray strong antipapal sentiments on the part of some English heresy defendants, others qualified their views by arguing that popes would be more deserving of their privileges if they behaved better. Hence Thomas Cole, appearing in 1460 before the bishop of Bath and Wells, was charged with teaching 'that god yave power to Petir, being a good man and an holy man, to bynde and to lose, and to his successours being as good as he was, and els not'.[81] Six Norwich defendants detected during Bishop Alnwick's investigations of 1428–31 likewise maintained that the pope can only enjoy Peter's primacy if he follows his example.[82] It is interesting to note that all of these defendants also abjured the belief that the pope is Antichrist, perhaps reflecting a distinction in their minds between the present, corrupt papacy and its ideal counterpart. A related, but ultimately dissimilar, point of view can be found in the trials of three defendants, two from Norwich and one from the diocese of Bath and Wells, who argued that the true pope, the vicar of Christ, is the holiest person in the world.[83] As with Wyclif's earlier suggestion along the same lines, what practical force these defendants imagined their claims to have is unclear. Did they intend to suggest that the papacy should be conferred upon the person who is holiest and hence most likely to use the office for good, or did they mean that Peter's successors should devote themselves to personal holiness rather than church governance? The answers, unfortunately, lie irretrievably behind the brevity of the records.

CONCLUSIONS

But where it is possible to determine the attitudes of English dissenters toward the papacy, we have discovered a surprising degree of moderation. That lollards criticized the abuses of contemporary popes without thereby demanding the abolition of the papacy may represent in large part an

---

[80] Salisbury reg. Langton, 70–3.
[81] Bath and Wells reg. Bekynton, 334–7.
[82] *Norwich*, 108, 116, 122, 127, 135, 170.
[83] *Norwich*, 141, 147; Bath and Wells reg. Bekynton, 120–7.

appropriation of John Wyclif's views on the subject. Whilst we have already discovered in other contexts why theological coherence between Wyclif and later dissenters can never simply be assumed, the extent to which Wyclif's ideas about the papacy recur in Wycliffite writings is striking. The sermon *Of Mynystris in þe Chirche*, for instance, borrows Wyclif's use of the appellation 'captain', rather than head, of the church for the apostle Peter; repeats Wyclif's view that the apostles, and their successors the bishops, receive their authority directly from Christ, not mediately through the pope; and echoes Wyclif's condemnation of papal elections as unscriptural. Similar resonances abound, as we have seen, in other Wycliffite writings; one of the authors of the long sermon-cycle as well as the author of the *Tractatus de oblacione iugis sacrificii* both appropriate Wyclif's interpretation of Jesus' words in Matthew 16:18.

The theological consensus which emerges from these texts is thus one which castigated contemporary popes for a multitude of sins, but this was rarely tantamount to arguing for wholesale change in the church's structures. It is accordingly difficult to endorse unqualifiedly the traditional description of Wyclif's and Wycliffite thought as 'antipapal', and it is even more so to argue that Wyclif's view was 'one of outright condemnation of the papacy, of all its associates and activities'.[84] Instead, it seems that Wyclif, the majority of Wycliffite writers, and even many lay heresy defendants would have preferred to see the papacy, like the clergy as a whole, brought forcibly back to ideal standards of behaviour. Only a few heresy suspects, such as Thomas Bikenore of Salisbury, John Skylan of Norwich, and John Blumston of Coventry and Lichfield, seem to have rejected the power of the papacy outright; Bikenore's claim that Peter's primacy was 'yven to hym alone and to none of his successouris', for instance, seems to require the interpretation that Petrine primacy ceased with the apostle's death.

Had Wyclif and those who followed him been able to implement their programme of reform, what would their ideal papacy have looked like? It would have been almost unrecognizable in late medieval Christendom. The papacy would be required to moderate its claim to *plenitudo potestatis* in the church. The process of papal elections would be changed to the biblical model of selection by lot. The pope, in order to remain the legitimate 'captain' of the church of Rome, would have to model his life and ministry on the example of Peter and the other leaders of the *ecclesia primitiva*. The pope might have to think of himself as one of several captains in the church, none of whom would owe him automatic obedience or be dependent upon him for their authority.

---

[84] See nn. 1, 36 above.

Most controversially, the pope might have to confront the possibility of deposition if in his actions he departed from the model of the apostles. If, as the *Sixteen Points* argues, a man is 'worþily pope' when he follows Peter and 'most anticrist' when he fails to do so, then some provision might have to be made for removing popes whose reigns (a term Wycliffite writers would no doubt deplore) begin in one fashion and then veer off in an unbecoming direction. If Wyclif or later writers envisioned this possibility, they provided little if any indication how to respond to it in practice. Together with Wycliffite views on the clergy more broadly, these reforms point away from an institutional ecclesiology and toward one modelled more closely on the perceived example of the apostolic era and focused primarily on the church's responsibility to proclaim the gospel.[85]

Much of why Wyclif and other dissenting writers have been perceived to have favoured the abolition of the papacy, and indeed the clergy as a whole, and likewise why their suggestions for remedying the corruption of the clerical estate are piecemeal at best, has to do with genre. The claim that the pope is Antichrist, for instance, appears most often in Wyclif's polemical writings, which lack the caveats and qualifications of his more systematic treatises. A similar dynamic operates where vernacular texts are concerned. To the extent that they were written with a polemical purpose in mind, Wycliffite writings seem to deny the possibility that the papacy can be reformed, whereas when they were written from the standpoint of reflective theology, they tend to argue that a papacy stripped of its extravagant claims was the structure Christ intended for his church.

For many Wycliffite writers, to call the pope 'Antichrist' was not simply to condemn the papacy as an institution of the devil; it was rather to point out that contemporary popes, like many of their subjects in the ecclesiastical hierarchy, had strayed from the example of the apostles. Both Wyclif and a substantial majority of those who came after him retained the hope that the papacy might be reformed, whether by force of argument or force of arms. If the pope were to understand his role properly and exercise it faithfully, the man who deserved to be called Antichrist yesterday could well merit the title 'captain' tomorrow.

---

[85] I allude here to two of the five archetypical ecclesiological models described by the late Avery Dulles in his classic survey *Models of the Church*, exp. edn. (New York, 1987).

Conclusion

Our five case studies of lollard views on salvation, the eucharist, marriage and sexuality, the clergy, and the papacy have revealed that, where a number of crucial theological issues were concerned, late medieval dissenters often differed sharply from one another. Their beliefs also often diverged from those of John Wyclif, whose theology has, in many quarters and for many centuries, been the standard by which later heresy suspects have been judged. On the contrary, the findings presented in these pages endorse the trajectory of a more recent scholarly consensus: that the notions of a monolithic lollard movement and a linear dissemination of heterodox views from the academic to the popular context are vastly oversimplified, if not in fact simply inaccurate. Just as some of the individuals whom we have encountered identified themselves as 'known men and women', others called themselves 'sons and daughters of grace', and still others used no such label, so also did these women and men not subscribe to a single way of thinking about the central issues of the late medieval religious world. Nor did they, especially in the wake of the abortive uprising of Sir John Oldcastle and the vigorous anti-heresy initiatives which followed it, always articulate ideas congruent with the theological framework set forth in Wyclif's writings. Whilst in some cases it *is* possible to find traces of the highly nuanced views of Wyclif and early Wycliffites in the writings and abjurations of later heresy suspects, these convergences are not nearly common enough for us to regard the places where Wyclif and later dissenters diverged as exceptional.

Likewise, it does not seem to be the case that dissenting views always became 'popularized and debased' as they moved further away from Wyclif and his circle.[1] Such a judgement reveals a bias—ironically one similar to that held by many late medieval churchmen—against the vernacular and toward Latin, whilst it also ignores the nuanced theological arguments that do appear in writings and trial records removed decades (if not more than a century)

---

[1] Hudson, 'A Lollard compilation', 66, though it must be noted that Hudson's views on the subject are much more complex and nuanced than this simple phrase suggests.

from Wyclif. It is fortunate that recent research has highlighted the complexity of Wycliffite and lollard beliefs; like the similarly porous binary of 'orthodox' and 'lollard', the distinction between 'academic' and 'popular' heresy seems to have little purchase on the polyvalent and intertwined strands of belief we have encountered here.

The 'overlapping and criss-crossing' sets of ideas I have attempted to map in this book reflect a network of allegiances between and within families, villages, and somewhat more loosely defined textual communities. Whilst I have taken as my theoretical guide Wittgenstein's theory of family resemblance, that model is hardly a panacea for all of the complex hermeneutical challenges which surround the study of late medieval heresy. I will return to its advantages and disadvantages in a moment, but it is helpful to note how, by placing the theological leanings of dissenting texts and heresy suspects not on a two-dimensional continuum between 'orthodox' and 'heterodox' but, instead, within a three-dimensional matrix of individuals' beliefs, texts, and social circumstances, Wittgenstein's model can shed new light on the theological complexity of lollardy. It can highlight, for instance, the persistence of works-oriented theologies of salvation within communities whose members nevertheless used epithets reminiscent of predestinarian views; or it can suggest how the distribution of a text such as *Wycklyffes Wycket* among the community of dissenters brought to trial before bishop Richard Fox of Winchester in 1512 might have informed their commemorative theologies of the eucharist. In short, Wittgenstein's model can provide a flexible way of conceiving of communities of dissenters who, as the evidence has shown, communicated and sympathized with one another without necessarily sharing the same beliefs.

But, the objection might fairly be raised, is a Wittgensteinian approach not some form of a theoretical 'cop-out', a delightfully philosophical but ultimately insubstantial way of avoiding the 'real' historical questions? What, after all, are the various characteristics that might help to identify an individual as a member of the lollard 'family', or at least as some sort of distant relative? One of the advantages of the family-resemblance model is that any such list need not be exhaustive, nor fixed in stone; additional characteristics can be added as new similarities among dissenters and their texts become apparent. As a starting-point, however, some attributes have emerged from this study as markers of lollard affiliation:

1. Lollards locate religious and theological authority outside the structures of the visible, institutional church; instead they locate authority in scripture as interpreted by the right-minded individual. A prime example of this attitude can be found in *The Testimony of William Thorpe*, where Thorpe

tells his inquisitor, Archbishop Arundel, that he would be glad to obey him insofar as he acts in accordance with Scripture.

2. Lollards are sceptical of what they perceive to be the excessive entanglement of the 'spiritual' and the 'secular'; in particular, this takes the form of criticizing the involvement of the church in temporal affairs. Churchly endowments, tithes, and the practice of churchmen simultaneously holding secular office are all targets of this criticism.

3. Lollards are concerned about what they take to be an excess of unscriptural ecclesiastical regulations. For example, as we saw in Chapter 4, whilst many dissenters embraced traditional views about marriage and sexuality, they rejected the limitations the institutional church placed on who could marry whom, just as they roundly criticized the requirement that marriages must be solemnized in church. The same can be said of the many dissenters, again including William Thorpe, who rejected the doctrine of transubstantiation as something the institutional church had illegitimately added to the simple faith of Scripture.

4. Lollards use apocalyptic and, in some cases, predestinarian imagery to bifurcate the world into those with them (the 'trewe men') and those against them ('disseyveres').[2] This is often the case even if a particular text or heresy suspect appears not to have subscribed to a doctrine of predestination: as I argued in Chapter 2, predestinarian language does not always betoken predestinarian theology.

5. Lollards reject the doctrine of transubstantiation, condemning it as something either philosophically untenable, scripturally ungrounded, or simply idolatrous, if not all of the above.

6. As many commentators have noted, lollards demonstrate a high regard for the theological and rhetorical possibilities of the English language, using the vernacular as a means not only of communicating their theological convictions but also of disseminating the message of Scripture. Nevertheless, while lollards favoured the vernacular over Latin, it is important not to draw too firm an association between lollardy and English and 'orthodoxy' and Latin. As we have seen, some dissenters wrote in Latin, just as some mainstream writers like Nicholas Love wrote in the vernacular.

7. Lollards know other lollards; with the exception of very few individuals, such as the Pembrokeshire knight Sir Roger Burley, the vast majority of the

---

[2] Hudson, 'A Lollard sect vocabulary?', 167; see also Peikola, *Congregation of the Elect*, who uses the phrase 'Lollard idiom' rather than 'sect vocabulary' for the rhetorical patterns to be discerned among lollard texts.

heresy suspects whom we have encountered in these pages were associated with at least one other dissenter. As Richard Davies argued almost two decades ago, 'If Wycliffism was what you know, Lollardy was whom you knew.'[3] Having social and other contacts with dissenters is among the most likely predictors of being a dissenter oneself, a fact on which many bishops and inquisitors capitalized in asking heresy suspects with whom they associated.

8. Finally, and perhaps most self-evidently, lollards either were excluded (whether by physical markers such as badges to be worn on their clothing, by the public performance of acts of penance, or in the most extreme cases by capital punishment) from full membership in the institutional church or would, if they had been discovered, have been so excluded.

These are, of course, simply the most prominent characteristics that seem likely to mark out an individual as a member of the lollard 'family'. They necessarily discount some aspects of lollard identity for which there is little evidence, such as the forms of affective spirituality that lollard dissenters embraced, and likewise, for the most part they highlight the negative aspects of lollard theology at the expense of the positive. It is essential to note that these characteristics are not the only markers of lollardy; nor is it the case that an individual must demonstrate a certain number of these characteristics to be treated as a lollard. The key insight of the family-resemblance model, after all, is that the question should never be 'is such and such a person a Lollard?' but, instead, 'how can we situate such and such a person in relationship to others?' And there are manifold answers to this latter question: in the case of William Thorpe, for instance, his personal connections with Wyclif and other Wycliffites, the similarities between his views and theirs, and his use of the vernacular, among other factors, all help to locate Thorpe in a prominent place on the lollard family tree. In the case of Sir Roger Burley, on the other hand, his singular claim about his power to celebrate the eucharist, along with the substantial geographical distance between him and almost every other potential lollard, help to situate him on the very margins of the lollard 'family', if he is to be included in it at all.

Even for those within the family, our expectation should be difference, rather than conformity, in beliefs and practices. That does not mean, however, that the theological convictions of English dissenters diverged in entirely arbitrary ways. In keeping with my hypothesis in Chapter 1 that the religious views of communities outside the mainstream may evolve in ways similar to those of more established institutions, several broad patterns of doctrinal

---

[3] Davies, 'Lollardy and locality', 212.

variation appear in the results of our case studies. First, there is *chronological variation.* In Chapter 2, for example, I argued that predestinarian beliefs appear to have been held less frequently over time. It is not that most dissenters made conscious decisions to abandon a predestinarian soteriology in favour of a works-oriented one, but rather that the combination of a decline in the number of Wycliffite preachers who articulated doctrines of predestination and the cumulative background influence of the highly works-oriented culture of mainstream medieval religion may, over time, have made predestinarianism less attractive. As doctrines of predestination may in fact have never been widespread, even among early Wycliffites, works-oriented views may have had to overcome much less doctrinal inertia than much of the historiographical tradition has implied.

A second pattern is that of *geographical variation.* Whilst on a number of occasions we observed differences in belief between dissenters living in different communities or regions of England, geography became an especially important theme in Chapter 3 where, among the records of heresy trials, we discovered that theologies of eucharistic remanence, on the one hand and figuration or commemoration, on the other, seem to have been concentrated in particular areas of the country. Thus, inquisitors in Salisbury, Winchester, and Coventry and Lichfield dioceses encountered far more proponents of commemorative theologies of the eucharist than did their counterparts in Norwich and Lincoln dioceses, where dissenters seem to have placed greater emphasis on the persistence of the substances of bread and wine after the words of consecration. As is also the case with chronological variation, these divergences in belief might reflect differences in inquisitorial expectations rather than dissenting theology, but geographical variation can also be the result of the circulation of individual preachers and texts within particular local contexts, as with the case of the dissemination of the *Wycket* in early sixteenth-century Winchester diocese.

Third, dissenting beliefs are not isolated from the discourse of mainstream religion. I have already mentioned the ways in which the prevailing works-oriented attitude of late medieval Christianity may have informed the reception of predestinarianism, but it is important to note that the *interface between mainstream and dissenting religious culture* operated in both directions. Not only can dissenting groups be affected by developments within the wider community, but the presence of dissenting viewpoints can provide the impetus for mainstream institutions to stress certain ideas over others. We observed this latter phenomenon in Chapter 4: in East Anglia, the interplay of dissenting and 'orthodox' religious culture shaped the theological emphases of both communities. The ideas of preachers such as William White may have contributed both to the proliferation among dissenters of scepticism about the requirement of clerical celibacy and to concern among inquisitors to maintain the church's traditional role in solemnizing marriages. Texts like the N-Town cycle play 'The Marriage of Mary and Joseph' may have reinforced traditional ideas about sexuality across the theological spectrum.

Fourth, dissenting beliefs were often conditioned by the *textual forms in which they were inscribed.* Throughout this book, I have attempted to negotiate the challenges created by what Hudson has called 'the problem of sources': that in many cases, we have access to dissenters' beliefs only through the documents prepared by their antagonists, and even in the case of most lollard texts, crucial questions of authorship, chronology, and geography cannot be resolved.[4] The influence of genre on theological content became a particularly important issue in Chapters 5 and 6, where we saw that the stylistic differences between theological reflection and polemic helped alternately to highlight and to conceal the nuances of dissenting views about the reform of the clergy and the status of the papacy. To the extent that texts were written with a polemical purpose in mind, they seemed to deny the possibility that the papacy could be reformed, whereas when they were written from the standpoint of reflective theology, they tended to argue that a papacy stripped of extravagant claims to power was the structure Christ had in mind for his church.

It should go without saying that none of these four models exists in isolation and, likewise, that they are not the only patterns to be found in the sources. Neither chronology nor geography nor any other factor is ever sufficiently determinative to predict the religious convictions of English dissenters. In fact, all four of the models I have described are highly interdependent; dissenting ideas were always embedded in a broader, itself diverse, culture of mainstream religion, and it is impossible to analyse their chronological and geographical distribution apart from the textual forms in which they are articulated.[5] Nevertheless, these models suggest patterns that might help, if our analysis proves true, to explain how the doctrinal variations we have observed among English dissenters came first to be and then to evolve. It cannot sufficiently be stressed that these models, and any others to which the extant sources might give rise, are inductive rather than deductive, *ad hoc* rather than *a priori.*

The many intertwined and shifting ways in which dissenting ideas varied over time lends credibility to the suggestion that theologians and historians should begin to think systematically about 'the development of heresy' as a

---

[4] *PR*, ch. 1.

[5] For a similar point about the interdependence of the various strata of medieval society—a point not without its applications to Wittgenstein's model—see S. H. Rigby, *English Society in the Later Middle Ages: Class, status, and gender* (New York, 1995), esp. 283.

concept parallel to the development of doctrine. It might be objected that in contrast to the more formal guidelines proposed for the development of official church teachings by such writers as John Henry Newman, the development of religious ideas within dissenting groups seems to follow few rules. Recent scholarship, however, has drawn attention to the many inadequacies of Newman's approach as well as to the highly contingent nature of the development of doctrine within mainstream contexts. John Thiel, for instance, has described several different forms of doctrinal development, including the 'dramatic development' which leads to the reversal of previously accepted norms, whereas Terrence Tilley has pointed out the inability of grand theories to account for every particular set of relationships between history, theology, and faith.[6] 'There are no simple or general solutions to the problem of history. Rather, there are numerous particular problems that historical investigations create for religious believing and theological construction. These need to be solved individually, not *en masse.*'[7]

So if traditional theories of the development of doctrine fail or at least decline to address the changes and variations in belief among dissenting communities, what can this study of dissent in late medieval England contribute to the building up of a theology of the development of heresy? It is beyond the scope of this book to articulate such a theology, and indeed to do so would require a comparative study of the development of dissenting movements across a spectrum of historical and geographical locations, but a few suggestions about the ways in which the development of heresy differs from the development of doctrine within mainstream religion seem appropriate here. First, unlike the development of doctrine, which tends to be regulated by some central authority (whether in the form of a magisterium, a single individual such as a bishop, or the collective voice of the congregation), the development of heresy permits greater scope for theological self-determination and, hence, doctrinal variation. In the absence of the sort of coercive power which affirms one form of theological expression as orthodox and anathematizes others as erroneous, individuals are more likely to possess the self-confidence and socio-political space to express their convictions more idiosyncratically. In the case of late medieval England, there is little if any evidence of individuals being excluded from dissenting communities on account of their views; on the contrary, shared opposition to the doctrines and practices of the institutional church, along with a pledge to keep the

---

[6] Thiel, *Senses of Tradition*, 26, and 'Tradition and authoritative reasoning', *Theological Studies*, 56 (1995), 627–51.

[7] Terrence Tilley, *History, Theology and Faith: Dissolving the modern problematic* (Maryknoll, NY, 2004), 4; see also Nichols, *From Newman to Congar*, 216–7.

secrets of the community, seem alone to have been necessary for membership. Lollards played the role of theological automata much more rarely than earlier scholarship has suggested.

Yet even if dissenting groups lacked structures capable of compelling the acceptance of some centrally authorized set of beliefs, that is not to say they lacked for authorities. Texts such as *Wycklyffes Wycket* and charismatic leaders such as William White and John Stilman provided focal points for resistance to the institutional church and its teachings. Likewise, at least in the late fourteenth and early fifteenth centuries, the recurrence of a stock of common phrases and expressions in Wycliffite writings suggests that individuals learned from and consciously strove to imitate the style of those whom they considered authoritative. Nevertheless, the sources of authority that shaped the development of dissenting communities were much more local and personal than those which exercised influence within mainstream religion. Individual dissenters were likely to adopt the beliefs and the style of the text which they read or heard, or the wandering preacher whose 'incarnate textuality' led to their conversion, rather than to ascribe authority to figures of national importance.[8] The name of John Wyclif, for instance, appears rarely in lollard writings, and even less often in the trials of heresy suspects.

Finally, whilst both mainstream and dissenting communities defined themselves in opposition to one another, they did so differently. On the side of orthodoxy, the Wycliffite controversies and their aftermath highlight a pattern which appears elsewhere in the history of Christianity: a tendency to regard dissent as a threat to the existence of the institutional church and to respond by defining and shoring up the boundaries between right belief and error. Circling the wagons, church leaders from the Council of Nicaea onwards have reacted to the emergence of theological disagreements by developing formal creedal statements and by persecuting, excommunicating, or putting to death those who subsequently failed to endorse them. Dissenters, on the other hand, have responded somewhat differently. In the case of lollardy, dissenters tightened their sense of in-group identity, using a range of devices to distinguish who was and who was not of their number; they attempted to remain integrated into mainstream society, in some cases by continuing to serve in positions of civil and ecclesiastical responsibility; and they borrowed, intentionally and otherwise, from mainstream theology. Accordingly, among some dissenting groups at least, sectarian identity came to be formed chiefly along the lines of broad themes and attitudes, rather than the precise language of creeds and other church formularies.

---

[8] The phrase is Swanson's: 'Literacy, heresy', 286.

These three themes—that dissenting communities tend to erect few if any structures of coercive authority, that such authorities as do exist are local and personal, and that dissenters define themselves by broad attitudes rather than narrow theological propositions—are some of the most prominent differences between the development of doctrine and the development of heresy. Additional claims about the development of heresy must, however, await broader investigations, not least among them studies of the sorts of relationships between beliefs and religious practices which the scarce data on lollard spirituality have almost totally obscured.

Nevertheless, as I suggested in the Preface, to re-examine the ways in which the beliefs of late medieval dissenters differed from one another is to fill an important gap in recent studies of lollardy, not to mention medieval heresy more generally. It is entirely laudable that long-overdue studies of the social structures and textual practices of dissenting communities have proliferated in recent years, but the many gains to be realized from such work must be balanced by equally sophisticated accounts of the theological convictions which, at their core, separated dissenters from their contemporaries. If, by concentrating on the beliefs of dissenting writers and heresy suspects and by sketching an outline of a new model for identifying and explaining the many variations among those beliefs, I have been able to rehabilitate doctrine as a locus of scholarly enquiry, then the result may be a more comprehensive approach to the study of heresy. Only by bringing together our findings about beliefs, texts, and social circumstances can we successfully appreciate the many different contexts which gave rise in late medieval England to so many varieties of dissent.

Trial Records Discussed in Text

	Name	Date(s)/Year(s) of Trial	Diocese	Occupation (if given)	Notes
1	Abell, Thomas	22, 29 Nov. 1511	Coventry and Lichfield	Shoemaker	Referred by name to Wyclif, E
2	Acton, Thomas	5–6 Nov. 1511	Coventry and Lichfield	Purser	Used term 'known man', B
3	Apleward, William	1 Oct. 1467	Lincoln	—	Previously arrested on charge of sorcery, B, E, Bapt, P, Pope, Ch/St, Pilg
4	Archer, Edmund	5 Aug. 1430	Norwich	Cordwainer	E, Bapt, M, P, Orders, T, Saints, I
5	Aston, John	1382	—	Scholar	Associate of Wyclif, E
6	Atcombe, Richard	1 Mar. 1469	Hereford	—	Tried with (19) and (37), Salv, B, E, Bapt, M, P, T, Saints, I, Pilg
7	Badby, John	1409	Canterbury	—	E
8	Baron, John	after 1 Oct. 1467	Lincoln	—	Salv, B, E, Saints
9	Barret, John	1521	Lincoln	—	B
10	Bartlet, Isabel	1521	Lincoln	—	Sister of (11), (12), (112)
11	Bartlet, Richard	1521	Lincoln	—	Brother of (10), (12), (112), called 'known man', B, I, Pilg

	Name	Date(s)/Year(s) of Trial	Diocese	Occupation (if given)	Notes
12	Bartlet, Robert	1521	Lincoln	—	Brother of (10), (11), (112), called 'known man', B, I, Pilg
13	Bate, William	5 Aug. 1430	Norwich	Tailor	E, Bapt, M, P, T, Saints, I, Pilg
14	Baxter, Margery	7 Oct 1428–1 Apr. 1429	Norwich	—	Student of (113), whom she called a saint, Salv, E, Bapt, M, P, Orders, Pope, Saints, I, Pilg
15	Benet, John junior	7 Feb. 1507	Salisbury	—	E
16	Bikenore, Thomas	25 Oct. 1443	Salisbury	—	Salv, E, Bapt, M, T, Pope, Pilg
17	Blumston *alias* Phisicion, John	9 Mar. 1486	Coventry and Lichfield	—	Rejects special powers of Mary, Salv, Pope, I, Pilg
18	Braban, Philip	19 Feb. 1512	Winchester	—	Associate of (39), (56), (58), later servant to (33) B, E, P, Pope, I
19	Breche, John	28 Feb. 1469	Hereford	—	Tried with (6) and (37), Salv, B, E, Bapt, M, P, T, Saints, I, Pilg
20	Brut, Walter	1393	Hereford	—	'*Laicus litteratus*', vouched for orthodoxy of (103), E, Orders, T, Pope
21	Burell, John	18 Apr. 1429–9 Dec. 1430	Norwich	Servant of (67)	Salv, E, M, P, T, I, Pilg
22	Burley, (Sir) Roger	10 Nov, 9 Dec. 1487	St David's	—	E

No.	Name	Date	Diocese	Occupation	Notes
23	Butler, Thomas	9 Mar. 1486	Coventry and Lichfield	—	Tried with (54), Salv, Pilg
24	Canon, Nicholas	1431	Norwich	—	E, P
25	Carpenter *alias* Harford *alias* Daniell, William	10 Feb. 1491	Salisbury	—	Mentioned 'lollards', P, Orders, I, Pilg
26	Cavell, Robert	2–3 Mar. 1430	Norwich	Chaplain	E, Bapt, M, P, T, Saints, I, Pilg
27	Chapell, Robert	12 Jul. 1416	Rochester	Chaplain	Suspected of associations with (71), E, P, I, Pilg
28	Chapleyn, Isabel	2 Mar. 1431	Norwich	—	E, Bapt, M, P, T, I
29	Chase, Thomas	1506?	Lincoln	—	Murdered in prison, B
30	Claydon, John	17 Aug.–19 Sep. 1415	London	Currier	Blind, B (*Lanterne*), E, T, Pope, I, Pilg
31	Clifford, (Sir) Lewis	1402?	—	Knight	Salv, E, Bapt, M
32	Cole *alias* Baker, Thomas	18–23 Jan. 1459	Bath and Wells	—	Salv, E
33	Colins, Richard	1521	Lincoln	—	Son of (34), B
34	Colins, Thomas	1521	Lincoln	—	Father of (33), B
35	Colyn, William	23 Oct. 1429–20 Mar. 1430	Norwich	Skinner	E, M, I
36	Corby, Agnes	22 Jan. 1512	Coventry and Lichfield	—	E, I, Pilg

	Name	Date(s)/Year(s) of Trial	Diocese	Occupation (if given)	Notes
37	Cornewe, John	28 Feb. 1469	Hereford	—	Tried with (6) and (19), Salv, B, E, Bapt, M, P, T, Saints, I, Pilg
38	Cowper, Baldwin	18 Apr. 1430	Norwich	—	E, Bapt, M, P, T, Pope, Saints, I, Pilg
39	Denys, Thomas	19 Feb. 1512	Winchester	—	Associate of (18), (56), (58), B (*Wycket*), E, P, I
40	Dexter, Alice	31 Oct.–17 Nov. 1389	Lincoln	—	Wife of (41), tried with (88), (111), E, P, Orders, I
41	Dexter, Roger	31 Oct.–17 Nov. 1389	Lincoln	—	Husband of (40), tried with (88), (111), E, P, Orders, I
42	Emayn, William	10–14 Mar. 1428	Bath and Wells	—	P, Pope, Saints, Ch/St, I, Pilg
43	Fleccher, Matilda	18 Apr. 1430	Norwich	—	Wife of (44), E, Bapt, M, P, Saints, I, Pilg
44	Fleccher, Richard	27 Aug. 1429	Norwich	—	Husband of (43), E, Bapt, M, P, Orders, Pope, Saints, I, Pilg
45	Fynche, John	20 Sep. 1430–14 Feb. 1431	Norwich	—	Bapt, M, P, T, Saints, I, Pilg
46	Gilmyn, Richard	9 Mar. 1486	Coventry and Lichfield	—	B, T
47	Godesell, John	18–21 Mar. 1429	Norwich	—	Husband of (48), Salv, E, Bapt, M, P, Orders, T, Pope, I, Pilg

48	Godesell, Sybil	22 Mar. 1429	Norwich	—	Wife of (47), E, Bapt, M, P, Orders, T, Pope, I, Pilg
49	Godson, John	22 Jun. 1499	Salisbury	—	E, T, Pope, I, Pilg
50	Grace, Richard	18 Apr. 1430	Norwich	Skinner	E, Bapt, M, P, T, Pope, Saints, I, Pilg
51	Gryggs, Robert	17 Feb. 1431	Norwich	Carpenter	E, Bapt, M, P, T, Pope, I, Pilg
52	Haddam *alias* Brede, Joan	19 Jan. 1508	Winchester	—	E, I
53	Hardy, William	4–7 Aug. 1430	Norwich	Tailor	Salv, E, Bapt, M, P, Orders, T, Saints, I, Pilg
54	Hegham, Richard	9 Mar. 1486	Coventry and Lichfield	—	Salv, Pope, I, Pilg
55	Hereford, Nicholas	1382?	—	Scholar	Associate of Wyclif, E
56	John, Lewis	1512	Winchester/ London	—	Associate of (18), (39), (58), E, Pope, Pilg
57	Jonson, John	28 Oct. 1511, 16 Jan. 1512	Coventry and Lichfield	Cutler	—
58	Jopson, Margery	5 Mar. 1512	Winchester	—	Associate of (39), (56), I
59	Jurdan, John	5 Apr. 1441	Bath and Wells	—	E, Bapt, P, Orders
60	Knobbyng, Richard	18 Apr. 1430	Norwich	—	E, Bapt, M, P, T, Pope, Saints, I, Pilg
61	Kynget, John	20 Aug. 1429	Norwich	—	E, Bapt, M, P, Saints, Pilg

	Name	Date(s)/Year(s) of Trial	Diocese	Occupation (if given)	Notes
62	Landesdale, Roger	29, 31 Oct., 5–6 Nov., late Nov./early Dec. 1511	Coventry and Lichfield	Tailor	Associate of (63), B, E, I, Pilg
63	Lodge, William	29 Nov. 1511	Coventry and Lichfield	Mercer	Associate of (62), used phrase 'son of grace'
64	Man, Thomas	29 Mar. 1518	Lincoln/ London	—	Salv, E, P, Orders, I
65	Masse, William	14 Mar. 1431	Norwich	—	E (struck out), Bapt, P, Orders, I, Pilg
66	Mone, Hawisia	4 Aug. 1430	Norwich	—	Wife of (67), E, Bapt, M, P, Orders, T, Pope, Saints, Ch/St, I, Pilg
67	Mone, Thomas	19–21 Aug. 1430	Norwich	—	Husband of (66), Bapt, M, P, Orders, T, Saints, I, Pilg
68	Morthrop, Christopher	8 Jan. 1499	Rochester	—	Salv
69	Mundy, William	15 Feb. 1412	Salisbury	—	E, Orders, Saints, I, Pilg
70	Nowers, John	12 Feb. 1488	Lincoln	Deacon	M
71	Oldcastle, (Sir) John, Lord Cobham	7 Nov. 1413	Canterbury	Minor noble	E, P, I, Pilg
72	Pert, John	5 Aug. 1430	Norwich	—	E, Bapt, M, P, T, Pope, Saints, I, Pilg
73	Petesyne, Richard	19 Feb. 1490	Winchester	—	Salv, E, M, P, Orders, Pope, I, Pilg

74	Ploman, Thomas	8 Mar. 1430	Norwich	Shipman	T
75	Purvey, John	29 Feb. 1400	—	Wyclif's 'secretarius'	E, M, P, Orders, Pope, Ch/St
76	Qwyrk, John	30 Mar. 1463	Lincoln	Labourer	Salv, E, M, T
77	Ramsbury, William	3 Jun. 1389	Salisbury	—	'Lollard mass' suspect, E, M, P, Orders
78	Repingdon, Philip	1382	—	Scholar	Associate of Wyclif, later bishop of Lincoln, E
79	Reve, John	18 Apr. 1430	Norwich	Glover	E, Bapt, M, P, T, Pope, I, Pilg
80	Rowley, Alice	31 Oct., 5 Nov. 1511, 16, 24 Jan. 1512	Coventry and Lichfield	Widow of William Rowley, merchant	E, I
81	Russell, John, OFM	Oct. 1424	Canterbury	Friar	M
82	Sampson, Elizabeth	1508?	London	—	Salv
83	Sawtre, William	12 Feb. 1401	Canterbury	Priest	E, I, Pilg
84	Seynon, John	before 27 Jul. 1400	Lincoln	—	E, I
85	Shoemaker, Christopher	1518	London	—	E, Saints, Pilg
86	Skylan, John	4–7 Aug. 1430	Norwich	—	Salv, E, Bapt, M, P, Orders, T, Pope, Ch/St, I, Pilg
87	Skylly, John	15–18 Mar. 1429	Norwich	Miller	Student of (113)?, E, Bapt, M, P, Orders, T, Pope, Saints, I, Pilg

	Name	Date(s)/Year(s) of Trial	Diocese	Occupation (if given)	Notes
88	Smith, William	31 Oct.–17 Nov. 1389	Lincoln	—	Tried with (40) (41), (111), E, P, Orders, I
89	Smyth, Joan	4–5 Nov. 1511	Coventry and Lichfield	Wife of Richard Smith, mercer	B, E, I, Pilg
90	Sparke, Richard	27 May 1457	Lincoln	—	Brother of (91), E, Bapt, M, P, Pope, I, Pilg
91	Sparke, William	27 May 1457	Lincoln		Brother of (90), E, Bapt, M, P, Pope, I, Pilg
92	Sterne, Aug.ine	28 Jan. 1491	Salisbury	—	E, Orders, Pope
93	Stevyne, William	after 1 Oct. 1467	Lincoln	—	E, Pilg
94	Stilman, John	25 Oct. 1518 (relapsed from Salisbury, 1507)	London	—	B, E, Pope, I
95	Swaffer, Elizabeth	30 Sep. 1512	Winchester	—	Wife of (96), associate of (109), (110), (114), (115), (116), Salv, E, P, I
96	Swaffer, Laurence	30 Sep. 1512	Winchester	—	Husband of (95), associate of (109), (110), (114), (115), (116), Salv, B, E, P, I, Pilg
97	Swallow, Stephen	3 Jul. 1489	London	—	Salv, E, Bapt, P, Pope
98	Sweeting, William	1511	London	—	B, E, I

99	Swinderby, William	1391	Hereford	—	E, Bapt, P, Orders, T, Ch/St
100	Taillour, Thomas	22 Jan. 1491	Salisbury	—	B, Bapt, P, Orders, Pope, Pilg
101	Tanner, John	15 Jul. 1491	Salisbury	—	E, I
102	Upton, John	20 Jun. 1428	Salisbury	—	T
103	Villers, Thomas	27–29 Nov., 3 Dec. 1511	Coventry and Lichfield	Spicer	I, Pilg
104	Wakeham, William	7 Oct. 1437 (relapse from 24 Sep. 1434)	Salisbury	—	E, I, Pilg
105	Walker, Edward	8 May–3 Oct. 1511	Canterbury	—	E, Bapt, M, P, Orders, Saints, I, Pilg
106	Warde *alias* Wasshingburn, Joan	17 Nov. 1511, 24 Jan. 1512, 11–12 Mar. 1512	Coventry and Lichfield	—	E, I, Pilg
107	Wardon, John	2 Sep. 1428	Norwich	—	E, M, P, T, Saints, I, Pilg
108	Wassyngborn, Thomas	12 Sep. 1482	London	—	E
109	Wattys, Anne	30 Sep. 1512	Winchester	—	Wife of (110), associate of (95), (96), (114), (115), (116), Salv, B, E, P, I, Pilg
110	Wattys, Thomas	30 Sep. 1512	Winchester	—	Husband of (109), associate of (95), (96), (114), (115), (116), Salv, B, E, P, I, Pilg
111	Waystache, Richard	31 Oct.–17 Nov. 1389	Lincoln	Chaplain	E, P, Orders, T, I
112	Wellis, Agnes	1521	Lincoln	—	Sister of (10), (11), (12), B, E, M, I, Pilg

	Name	Date(s)/Year(s) of Trial	Diocese	Occupation (if given)	Notes
113	White, William	5 Jul. 1422, 1428	Canterbury	—	Regarded as saint by (14), teacher of (87)?, E, Bapt, M, P, Orders, Pope, Saints, Ch/St, I
114	Wickham *alias* Bruar, Alice	30 Sep. 1512	Winchester	—	Wife of (115), associate of (95), (96), (109), (110), (116) E, I
115	Wickham *alias* Bruar, William	30 Sep. 1512	Winchester	—	Husband of (114), associate of (95), (96), (109), (110), (116) E, I
116	Winter, Robert	30 Sep. 1512	Winchester	—	Associate of (95), (96), (109), (110), (114), (115), E, I
117	Wroxham, John	22 Sep. 1430	Norwich	Souter	Bapt, M, P, Saints, I, Pilg
118	Wyllis, James	after 20 Mar. 1461	Lincoln	—	Salv, E, P, I

Notes: This table contains entries on the trials of each of the heresy suspects discussed in the main text, but excluding the footnotes, of this book; the notations in the 'Notes' column indicate which theological topics figured in each process. Salv = salvation; B = possession of forbidden vernacular books or texts; E = the eucharist; Bapt = baptism; M = marriage; P = penance; Orders = the sacrament of orders; T = tithes; Pope = the papacy; Saints = prayers to the saints; Ch/St = questions of the relationship between ecclesiastical and civil authority; I = images; and Pilg = pilgrimage. Where possible I have provided the full range of dates for each trial; otherwise, the date listed is the date of the suspect's first appearance in court. The sources for each set of trial records may be found in notes to the main text.

Bibliography

Manuscripts, excluding bishops' registers

Cambridge, Gonville and Caius College 354/581
Dublin, Trinity College 775
London, Westminster Diocesan Archives B.2
Maidstone, Centre for Kentish Studies PRC 3/1

Bishops' registers

Bath and Wells diocese

John Stafford (r. 1425–43): Thomas Scott Holmes (ed.), *The Register of John Stafford, Bishop of Bath and Wells, 1425–1443*, 2 vols. (Somerset Record Society 31–32, 1915)
Thomas Bekynton (r. 1443–65): H. C. Maxwell-Lyte and M. C. B. Dawes (eds.), *The Register of Thomas Bekynton, Bishop of Bath and Wells, 1443–1465*, 2 vols. (Somerset Record Society 49–50, 1934)

Canterbury diocese

Thomas Arundel (r. 1396–7, 1399–1414): London, Lambeth Palace Library, Register of Thomas Arundel
Henry Chichele (r. 1414–43): E. F. Jacob (ed.), *The Register of Henry Chichele*, 4 vols. (Canterbury and York Society 42, 45–47, 1937–47)
John Morton (r. 1486–1500): Christopher Harper-Bill (ed.), *The Register of John Morton, Archbishop of Canterbury 1486–1500*, 3 vols. (Canterbury and York Society, 75, 78, 89)

Ely diocese

William Grey (r. 1454–78): Cambridge, Cambridge University Library, Ely Diocesan Records MS G/1/5

Hereford diocese

John Trefnant (r. 1389–1404): W. W. Capes (ed.) *The Register of John Trefnant, Bishop of Hereford, A.D. 1389–1404* (Hereford, 1914)
John Stanbury (r. 1453–74): Joseph H. Parry and A. T. Bannister (eds.), *The Register of John Stanbury, Bishop of Hereford 1453–1474* (Hereford, 1918)
Richard Mayew (r. 1504–16): A. T. Bannister (ed.), *Registrum Ricardi Mayew, Episcopi Herefordensis, 1504–1516* (Canterbury and York Society 27, 1921)

Lincoln diocese

John Chedworth (r. 1452–71): Lincoln, Lincoln Archive Office, Episcopal Register XX

London diocese

Richard Fitzjames (r. 1506–22): London, Guildhall Library 9531/9

Rochester diocese

Richard Fitzjames (r. 1497–1503): Maidstone, Centre for Kentish Studies Z/3, no. 4

Salisbury diocese

Robert Hallum (r. 1407–17): J. M. Horn (ed.), *The Register of Robert Hallum, Bishop of Salisbury 1407–1417* (Canterbury and York Society 72, 1982)
Robert Nevill (r. 1427–38): Chippenham, Wiltshire and Swindon History Centre D1/2/9
William Aiscough (r. 1438–50): Chippenham, Wiltshire and Swindon History Centre D1/2/10
Thomas Langton (r. 1485–93): Chippenham, Wiltshire and Swindon History Centre D1/2/12
John Blythe (r. 1494–99): Chippenham, Wiltshire and Swindon History Centre D1/2/13
Edmund Audley (r. 1502–1524): Chippenham, Wiltshire and Swindon History Centre D1/2/14

St David's diocese

Collected records: R. A. Roberts and R. F. Isaacson (eds.), *The Episcopal Registers of the Diocese of St David's, 1397 to 1518*, 3 vols. (Cymmrodorion Record Series 6, 1917–20)

Winchester diocese

Peter Courtenay (r. 1487–92): Winchester, Hampshire Record Office A1/15
Richard Foxe (r. 1501–28): Winchester, Hampshire Record Office A1/17–20

Printed primary sources

Arnold, Thomas (ed.), *Select English Works of John Wyclif*, 3 vols. (Oxford, 1869–71)
Astey, Henry (ed.), *Munimenta Academica, or Documents Illustrative of Academical Life and Studies at Oxford* (London, 1868)
Augustine of Hippo, *De bono coniugali, c. 401. The Good of Marriage*, trans. C. T. Wilcox (Washington, DC, 1955)
The Awntyrs off Arthur, in *Sir Gawain: Eleven romances and tales*, ed. Thomas Hahn (Kalamazoo, Mich., 1995)
Barnum, Priscilla Heath (ed.), *Dives and Pauper*, 2 vols., 3 parts (EETS o.s. 275, 280, 323, 1976–2004)
Barr, Helen (ed.), *The Piers Plowman Tradition* (London, 1993)
Biel, Gabriel, 'The circumcision of the Lord' in Heiko A. Oberman, *Forerunners of the Reformation: The shape of late medieval thought illustrated by key documents* (Philadelphia, 1981), 165–74

Bright, William (ed.), *Select Anti-Pelagian Treatises of St Augustine and the Acts of the Second Council of Orange* (Oxford, 1880)

Calendar of Close Rolls: Richard II, 6 vols. (London, 1914–27)

Capgrave, John, *Abbreuiacion of Cronicles*, ed. P. J. Lucas (EETS o.s. 285, 1983)

Chronicon Angliae, ed. E. M. Thompson (London, 1874)

Cigman, Gloria (ed.), *Lollard Sermons* (EETS o.s. 294, 1989)

Dahmus, J. H. (ed.), *The Metropolitan Visitations of William Courtenay, Archbishop of Canterbury, 1381–1396* (Urbana, Ill., 1950)

Devlin, Mary Aquinas (ed.), *The Sermons of Thomas Brinton, Bishop of Rochester (1373–1389)*, 2 vols. (Camden Third Series 85–6, 1954)

Dymmok, Roger, *Liber contra XII errores et haereses Lollardorum*, ed. H. S. Cronin (London, 1922)

Embree, Dan (ed.), *The Chronicles of Rome* (Woodbridge, 1999)

The examinacion of Master William Thorpe... [with] The examinacion of... syr Jhon Oldcastell (Antwerp, 1530)

Fasciculi Zizaniorum, ed. W. W. Shirley (London, 1858)

Forshall, Josiah (ed.), *Remonstrance against Romish Corruptions in the Church* (London, 1851)

——, and Frederic Madden (eds.), *The Holy Bible... Made from the Latin Vulgate by John Wyclif and His Followers*, 4 vols. (Oxford, 1850)

Foxe, John, *The... Ecclesiasticall History Contaynyng the Actes and Monuments* (London, 1570)

Gerson, Jean, 'Considérations sur saint Joseph' in P. Glorieux (ed.), *Oeuvres complètes* (Paris, 1960–73), vol. 7, part 1

Hale, William (ed.), *A Series of Precedents and Proceedings in Criminal Causes from 1475 to 1640, extracted from the Act-Books of Ecclesiastical Courts in the Diocese of London* (London, 1847)

Heyworth, P. L. (ed.), *Jack Upland, Friar Daw's Reply and Upland's Rejoinder* (London, 1968)

Horae Eboracenses: the Prymer or Hours of the Blessed Virgin Mary according to the Use of the Illustrious Church of York, ed. Christopher Wordsworth (Surtees Society 132, 1920)

Hudson, Anne (ed.), *Selections from English Wycliffite Writings*, rev. edn (Toronto, 1997)

—— (ed.), *Tractatus de oblacione iugis sacrificii*, in *The Works of a Lollard Preacher* (EETS o.s. 317, 2001)

—— (ed.), *Two Wycliffite Texts* (EETS o.s. 301, 1993)

——, and Pamela Gradon (eds.), *English Wycliffite Sermons*, 5 vols. (Oxford, 1983–97)

Knighton, Henry, *Knighton's Chronicle*, ed. and trans. G. H. Martin (Oxford, 1995)

Knox, John, *The Historie of the Reformation of the Church of Scotland* (London, 1644)

Langland, William, *The Vision of Piers Plowman: A critical edition of the B-Text*, ed. A. V. C. Schmidt, 2nd edn (London, 2001)

The Lanterne of Liȝt, ed. Lilian M. Swinburne (EETS 151, 1917)

The Lay Folks' Catechism, ed. Thomas Frederick Simmons and Henry Edward Nolloth (EETS o.s. 118, 1901)

Lindberg, Conrad (ed.), *English Wyclif Tracts 1–3* (Oslo, 1991)

Love, Nicholas, *The Mirror of the Blessed Life of Jesus Christ: A reading text*, ed. Michael G. Sargent (Exeter, 2004)

Matthew, F. D. (ed.), *The English Works of Wyclif Hitherto Unprinted*, rev. edn (EETS o.s. 74, 1902)

McSheffrey, Shannon, and Norman Tanner (eds. and trans.), *Lollards of Coventry, 1486–1522* (Camden Fifth Series 23, 2003)

Mirk, John, *Mirk's Festial: A collection of homilies*, ed. Theodor Erbe (EETS e.s. 96, 1905)

——, *Instructions for Parish Priests*, ed. Edward Peacock (EETS o.s. 31, rev. edn., 1902)

More, Thomas, *The Confutation of Tyndale's Answer*, in *The Complete Works of St Thomas More*, ed. Louis A. Schuster, Richard C. Marius, et al., vol. 8 (New Haven, Conn., 1973)

Netter, Thomas, *Doctrinale antiquitatum fidei catholicae ecclesiae*, ed. B. Blanciotti, 3 vols. (Venice, 1757–9)

Ockham, William, *Predestination, God's Foreknowledge, and Future Contingents*, trans. Marilyn McCord Adams and Norman Kretzmann, 2nd edn (Indianapolis, 1983)

Parker, Douglas H. (ed.), *The Praier and Complaynte of the Ploweman vnto Christe* (Toronto, 1997)

Pecock, Reginald, *The Reule of Crysten Religioun*, ed. William Cabell Greet (EETS o.s. 171, 1927)

Radbert, Paschasius, *De corpore et sanguine domini*, ed. Bede Paulus (Corpus Christianorum Continuatio Medievalis 16, Turnhout, 1969)

Reynes, Robert, *The Commonplace Book of Robert Reynes of Acle*, ed. Cameron Louis (New York, 1980)

Riley, H. T. (ed.), *Annales Ricardi Secundi et Henrici Quarti, Regum Angliae*, in *Chronica Monasterii S. Albani* (London, 1866)

Sheppard, J. B. (ed.), *Literae cantuarienses*, 3 vols. (London, 1887–9)

Spector, Stephen (ed.), *The N-Town Play: Cotton MS Vespasian D.8*, 2 vols. (EETS s.s. 11–12, 1991)

Tanner, Norman (ed.), *Decrees of the Ecumenical Councils*, 2 vols. (Washington, 1990)

—— (ed.), *Heresy Trials in the Diocese of Norwich, 1428–1431* (London, 1977)

—— (ed.), *Kent Heresy Proceedings, 1511–12* (Kent Records 26, 1997)

Todd, J. H. (ed.), *An Apology for Lollard Doctrines* (Camden Society 20, 1842)

Vergil, Polydore, *Anglicae historiae*, 2 vols. (Ghent, 1556–8)

von Nolcken, Christina (ed.), *The Middle English Translation of the Rosarium Theologie* (Heidelberg, 1979)

Walsingham, Thomas, *Historia anglicana*, ed. Matthew Parker and Henry Thomas Riley, 2 vols. (London, 1863–4)

Wilkins, David (ed.), *Concilia Magnae Brittaniae et Hiberniae*, 4 vols. (1737, repr. Bruxelles, 1964)

Wycklyffes Wycket (London, 1546)

Wyclif, John, *De blasphemia*, ed. M. H. Dziewicki (London, 1893)

——, *De civili dominio*, ed. R. L. Poole, 4 vols. (London, 1885)

——, *De ecclesia*, ed. J. Loserth (London, 1886)

——, *De eucharistia tractatus maior*, ed. J. Loserth (London, 1892)

——, *De officio regis*, ed. Alfred W. Pollard and Charles Sayle (London, 1887)

——, *De potestate pape*, ed. J. Loserth (London, 1907)

——, *De veritate sacrae scripturae*, ed. R. Buddensieg, 3 vols. (London, 1906)

——, *Dialogus sive speculum ecclesie militantis*, ed. A. W. Pollard (London, 1886)

——, *Opera minora*, ed. J. Loserth (London, 1913)

——, *Opus evangelicum*, ed. J. Loserth, 2 vols. (London, 1895)

——, *Polemical Works*, ed. R. Buddensieg, 2 vols. (London, 1883)

——, *Trialogus cum supplemento trialogi*, ed. G. Lechler (Oxford, 1869)

——, *On Universals*, ed. and trans. Anthony Kenny (Oxford, 1985)

Secondary studies

Adams, Robert, 'Piers's Pardon and Langland's semi-Pelagianism', *Traditio*, 39 (1983), 367–418

Aers, David, *Sanctifying Signs: Making Christian tradition in late medieval England* (Notre Dame, Ind., 2004)

——, and Lynn Staley, *The Powers of the Holy: Religion, politics, and gender in late medieval English culture* (University Park, Pa., 1996)

Arnold, John H., *Inquisition and Power: Catharism and the confessing subject in medieval Languedoc* (Philadelphia, 2001)

——, 'Lollard trials and inquisitorial discourse' in Christopher Given-Wilson (ed.), *Fourteenth Century England II* (Woodbridge, 2002), 81–94

Asad, Talal, 'Medieval heresy: An anthropological view', *Social History*, 11 (1986), 345–62

Aston, Margaret, ' "Caim's Castles": Poverty, politics, and disendowment' in R. B. Dobson (ed.), *The Church, Politics, and Patronage in the Fifteenth Century* (Gloucester, 1984), 94–131

——, *England's Iconoclasts* (Oxford, 1988)

——, 'John Wycliffe's Reformation reputation', repr. in *Lollards and Reformers: Images and literacy in late medieval Religion* (London, 1984), 243–72

——, 'Lollard women priests?', repr. in *Lollards and Reformers: Images and literacy in late medieval religion* (London, 1984), 49–70

——, 'Lollard women' in Diana Wood (ed.), *Women and Religion in Medieval England* (Oxford, 2003), 166–85

——, 'Lollardy and sedition', repr. in *Lollards and Reformers: Images and literacy in late medieval religion* (London, 1984), 1–48

——, 'Were the Lollards a sect?' in *The Medieval Church: Universities, Heresy, and the Religious Life: Essays in honour of Gordon Leff* (Studies in Church History, Subsidia 11, Woodbridge, 1999), 163–91

——, 'William White's Lollard followers', repr. in *Lollards and Reformers: Images and literacy in late medieval religion* (London, 1984), 71–100

——, 'Wyclif and the vernacular' in Anne Hudson and Michael Hudson (eds.), *From Ockham to Wyclif* (Studies in Church History, Subsidia 5, Oxford, 1987), 281–330

Atkins, Anselm, 'Religious assertions and doctrinal development', *Theological Studies*, 27 (1966), 523–52

Baker, Denise, 'From plowing to penitence: *Piers Plowman* and fourteenth-century theology', *Speculum*, 55 (1980), 715–25

Bambrough, Renford, 'Universals and family resemblances', *Proceedings of the Aristotelian Society*, 61 (1960–61), 207–22

Barr, Helen, *Signes and Sothe: Language in the Piers Plowman tradition* (Cambridge, 1994)

——, 'Wycliffite representations of the third estate' in Fiona Somerset, Jill C. Havens, and Derrick Pitard (eds.), *Lollards and Their Influence in Late Medieval England* (Woodbridge, 2003), 197–216

Barstow, Anne Llewellyn, *Married Priests and the Reforming Papacy: The eleventh-century debates* (New York, 1982)

Beckner, Morton, *The Biological Way of Thought* (New York, 1959)

Biller, Peter, '"Deep is the heart of man, and inscrutable": Signs of heresy in medieval Languedoc' in Helen Barr and Ann M. Hutchinson (eds.), *Text and Controversy from Wyclif to Bale: Essays in honour of Anne Hudson* (Turnhout, 2005), 267–80

Blamires, Alcuin, 'The Wife of Bath and Lollardy', *Medium Aevum*, 58 (1989), 224–42

Boehner, Philotheus, 'Ockham's *Tractatus de Praedestinatione et de Praescientia Dei et de Futuris Contingentibus* and its main problems' in *Collected Articles on Ockham* (New York, 1958), 420–41

Bonner, Gerald, 'Augustine and Pelagianism', *Augustinian Studies*, 24 (1993), 27–47

Bose, Mishtooni, 'The opponents of John Wyclif' in Ian Christopher Levy (ed.), *A Companion to John Wyclif: Late medieval theologian* (Leiden, 2006), 407–46

Boyarin, Daniel, *Border Lines: The partition of Judaeo-Christianity* (Philadelphia, 2004)

Boyle, Leonard E., '*Montaillou* revisited: Mentalité and methodology' in J. Raftis (ed.), *Pathways to Medieval Peasants* (Toronto, 1981), 119–40

Brooke, Christopher N. L., *The Medieval Idea of Marriage* (Oxford, 1994)

Brown, L. B., and J. P. Forgan, 'The structure of religion: A multi-dimensional scaling of informal elements', *Journal for the Scientific Study of Religion*, 19 (1980), 423–31

Brundage, James A., *Law, Sex, and Christian Society* (Chicago, 1987)

——, 'Impotence, frigidity, and marital nullity in the decretists and early decretalists', repr. in *Sex, Law, and Marriage in the Middle Ages* (Aldershot, 1993), ch. 10

——, 'Marriage and sexuality in the decretals of Pope Alexander III' in Filippo Liotta (ed.), *Papa Alessandro III* (Siena, 1986), 57–83

Bullough, Vern, 'Postscript: Heresy, witchcraft, and sexuality' in Vern L. Bullough and James Brundage (eds.), *Sexual Practices and the Medieval Church* (Buffalo, NY, 1982), 206–10

Burr, David, 'Ockham, Scotus, and the censure at Avignon', *Church History*, 37 (1968), 144–59 at 144

Campbell, Keith, 'Family resemblance predicates', *American Philosophical Quarterly*, 2 (1965), 238–44

Cannon, H. L., 'The poor priests: A study in the rise of English Lollardry' in *Annual Report of the American Historical Association for the Year 1899*, 2 vols. (Washington, 1900), i.451–82

Carlson, Eric Josef, *Marriage and the English Reformation* (Oxford, 1994)

Carmichael, Montgomery, 'Picture at Hardwick House of a window formerly in the Abbey of Bury St Edmunds', *Proceedings of the Suffolk Institute of Archaeology and Natural History*, 14 (1911), 275–9

Catto, Jeremy, 'Fellows and helpers: The religious identity of the followers of Wyclif' in *The Medieval Church: Universities, heresy, and the religious life: Essays in honour of Gordon Leff* (Studies in Church History, Subsidia 11, Woodbridge, 1999), 141–61

——, 'John Wyclif and the cult of the Eucharist' in K. Walsh and D. Wood (eds.), *The Bible in the Medieval World: Essays in memory of Beryl Smalley* (Studies in Church History, Subsidia 4, Oxford, 1985), 269–86

——, 'Religious change under Henry V' in G. L. Harriss (ed.), *Henry V: The practice of kingship* (Oxford, 1985), 97–115

——, 'Wyclif and Wycliffism at Oxford, 1356–1430' in Catto and Ralph Evans (eds.), *The History of the University of Oxford*, vol. 2 (Oxford, 1984), 175–261

Chadwick, Owen, *From Bossuet to Newman* (Cambridge, 1957)

Chenu, M.-D., 'Orthodoxie et Hérésie: le point de vue du théologien' in J. Le Goff (ed.), *Hérésies et sociétés dans l'Europe pre-industrielle* (Paris, 1968)

Cigman, Gloria, letter, *Review of English Studies*, 43 (1992), 250

Clarke, F. Stuart, 'Lost and foundation: Athanasius' doctrine of predestination', *Scottish Journal of Theology*, 29 (1976), 435–50

Cole, Andrew, *Literature and Heresy in the Age of Chaucer* (Cambridge, 2008)

——, 'William Langland and the invention of Lollardy' in Fiona Somerset, Jill C. Havens, and Derrick Pitard (eds.), *Lollards and Their Influence in Late Medieval England* (Woodbridge, 2003), 37–58

Coleman, Janet, *Piers Plowman and the Moderni* (Rome, 1981)

Coleman, Peter, *Christian Attitudes to Marriage: From ancient times to the third millennium* (London, 2004)

Collinson, Patrick, 'Night schools, conventicles, and churches' in Peter Marshall and Alec Ryrie (eds.), *The Beginnings of English Protestantism* (Cambridge, 2002), 209–35

Compston, H. F. B., 'The thirty-seven conclusions of the Lollards', *English Historical Review*, 26 (1911), 738–49

Conti, Alessandro, 'John Wyclif', *Stanford Encyclopedia of Philosophy*, sect. 3.1, <http://plato.stanford.edu/entries/Wyclif> (accessed 5 March 2006)

Coulton, G. G., *Ten Medieval Studies* (Cambridge, 1930)

Courtenay, William J., 'Inquiry and inquisition: Academic freedom in medieval universities', *Church History*, 58 (1989), 168–81

Crompton, James, 'John Wyclif: A study in mythology', *Transactions of the Leicestershire Archaeological and Historical Society*, 42 (1966–7), 6–34

——, 'Leicestershire Lollards', *Transactions of the Leicestershire Archaeological and Historical Society*, 44 (1968–9), 11–44

Cross, Claire, '"Great reasoners in scripture": The activities of women Lollards 1380–1530' in Derek Baker (ed.), *Medieval Women* (Studies in Church History, Subsidia 1, 1978), 358–80

Daly, L. J., *The Political Theory of John Wyclif* (Chicago, 1962)

Davies, Catherine, '"Poor persecuted little flock" or "Commonwealth of Christians": Edwardian Protestant concepts of the church' in Peter Lake and Maria Dowling (eds.), *Protestantism and the National Church* (London, 1987), 78–94

Davies, Richard, 'Lollardy and locality', *Transactions of the Royal Historical Society*, 6th ser. 1 (1991), 191–212

De Vooght, Paul, 'Du *De consideratione* de saint Bernard au *De potestate papae* de Wyclif', *Irénikon*, 25 (1953), 114–32

Deane, Jennifer, '"Beguines" reconsidered: Historiographical problems and new directions', <http://monasticmatrix.org/MatrixTextLibrary/3461Text.html> (accessed 29 January 2009)

Denery, Dallas G. II, 'From sacred mystery to divine deception: Robert Holkot, John Wyclif, and the transformation of fourteenth-century Eucharistic discourse', *Journal of Religious History*, 29 (2005), 129–44

Dickens, A. G., *The English Reformation*, 2nd edn (London, 1989)

——, 'The shape of anticlericalism and the English Reformation', repr. in *Late Monasticism and the Reformation* (London, 1994), 151–75

Dove, Mary, *The First English Bible* (Cambridge, 2008)

Doyle, Robert, 'The death of Christ and the doctrine of grace in John Wycliffe', *Churchman*, 99 (1985), 317–35

Duffy, Eamon, *Saints and Sinners: A history of the popes* (New Haven, 1997)

——, *The Stripping of the Altars: Traditional religion in England c. 1400–c. 1580*, 2nd edn (New Haven, Conn., 2005)

Dugmore, C. W., *The Mass and the English Reformers* (London, 1958)

Dulles, Avery, *Models of the Church*, exp. edn (New York, 1987)

Duminuco, Vincent, *The Jesuit Ratio Studiorum: 400th anniversary perspectives* (New York, 2000)

Dunnan, D. S., 'A note on the three churches in *The Lanterne of Liȝt*', *Notes and Queries*, 38 (March 1991), 20–2

Edwards, A. S. G., review of *Lollard Sermons*, *Speculum*, 67 (1992), 124–6

Elliott, Dyan, 'Lollardy and the integrity of marriage and the family' in Sherry Roush and Cristelle L. Baskins (eds.), *The Medieval Marriage Scene: Prudence, passion, policy* (Tempe, Ariz., 2005), 37–53

Evans, G. R., *John Wyclif: Myth and reality* (Oxford, 2005)

Fairfield, Leslie P., *John Bale, Mythmaker for the English Reformation* (West Lafayette, Ind., 1976)

Farr, William E., *John Wyclif as Legal Reformer* (Leiden, 1974)

Fendt, Gene, 'Between a Pelagian rock and a hard predestinarianism: The currents of controversy in *City of God* 11 and 12', *Journal of Religion*, 81 (2001), 211–27

Fines, John, 'William Thorpe: An early Lollard', *History Today*, 18 (1968), 495–503

Flanagan, Kieran, 'The return of theology: Sociology's distant relative' in Richard K. Fenn (ed.), *The Blackwell Companion to Sociology of Religion* (Oxford, 2001)

Fleming, Peter, *Family and Household in Medieval England* (Basingstoke, 2001)

Fletcher, Alan J., 'John Mirk and the Lollards', *Medium Aevum*, 56 (1987), 217–24

Ford, Judy Ann, *John Mirk's Festial: Orthodoxy, Lollardy, and the common people in fourteenth-century England* (Cambridge, 2006)

Forde, Simon, 'Nicholas Hereford's Ascension Day sermon, 1382', *Mediaeval Studies*, 51 (1989), 205–41

Forrest, Ian, *The Detection of Heresy in Late Medieval England* (Oxford, 2005)

Frankis, John, review of *Lollard Sermons, Review of English Studies*, 42 (1991), 437–8

Freeman, Thomas, 'Texts, lies, and microfilm: Reading and misreading Foxe's "Book of Martyrs"', *Sixteenth Century Journal*, 30 (1999), 23–46

Ghosh, Kantik, *The Wycliffite Heresy: Authority and the interpretation of texts* (Cambridge, 2002)

Girard, René, *The Scapegoat*, trans. Yvonne Freccero (London, 1986)

Given, James B., *Inquisition and Medieval Society: Power, discipline, and resistance in Languedoc* (Ithaca, NY, 1997)

Gorski, Philip S., 'Historicizing the secularization debate: Church, state, and society in late medieval and early modern Europe, ca. 1300 to 1700', *American Sociological Review*, 65 (2000), 138–67

Guarino, Thomas G., 'Tradition and doctrinal development: Can Vincent of Lérins still teach the church?', *Theological Studies*, 67 (2006), 34–72

Hägglund, Bengt, *The Background of Luther's Doctrine of Justification in Late Medieval Theology* (Philadelphia, 1971)

Haigh, Christopher, 'Anticlericalism and the English Reformation', repr. in *The English Reformation Revised* (Cambridge, 1987), 56–74

Hall, Louis Brewer, *The Perilous Vision of John Wyclif* (Chicago, 1983)

Halverson, James, *Peter Aureol on Predestination* (Leiden, 1998)

Hamilton Thompson, A., *The English Clergy and Their Organization in the Later Middle Ages* (Oxford, 1947)

Hammond, T. C., 'The schoolmen of the middle ages' in A. J. Macdonald (ed.), *The Evangelical Doctrine of Holy Communion* (Cambridge, 1930), 118–50

Hampshire, Annette, and James A. Beckford, 'Religious sects and the concept of deviance: The Mormons and the Moonies', *British Journal of Sociology*, 34 (1983), 208–29

Hanson, R. P. C., *The Continuity of Christian Doctrine* (New York, 1981)

Happé, Peter, *John Bale* (New York, 1996)

Harbert, Bruce, 'A will without a reason: Theological developments in the C-Revision of *Piers Plowman*' in Piero Boitani and Anna Totti (eds.), *Religion in the Poetry and Drama of the Later Middle Ages* (Cambridge, 1990), 149–61

Hargreaves, Henry, 'Sir John Oldcastle and Wycliffite views on clerical marriage', *Medium Aevum*, 42 (1973), 141–6

Harrison, Michael I., and John K. Maniha, 'Dynamics of dissenting movements within established organizations: Two cases and a theoretical interpretation', *Journal for the Scientific Study of Religion*, 17 (1978), 207–24

Harvey, Margaret, *Solutions to the Schism: A study of some English attitudes, 1378–1409* (St Ottilien, 1983)

Havens, Jill C., 'Shading the grey area: Determining heresy in Middle English texts' in Helen Barr and Ann M. Hutchinson (eds.), *Text and Controversy from Wyclif to Bale: Essays in honour of Anne Hudson* (Turnhout, 2005), 337–52

Helmholz, R. H., *Marriage Litigation in Medieval England* (Cambridge, 1974)

Hick, John, *An Interpretation of Religion: Human responses to the transcendent* (Basingstoke, 1989)

Hodgson, Phyllis, '*Ignorantia Sacerdotum*: A fifteenth-century discourse on the Lambeth Constitutions', *Review of English Studies*, 24 (1948), 1–11

Hope, Andrew, 'The lady and the bailiff: Lollardy among the gentry in Yorkist and early Tudor England' in Margaret Aston and Colin Richmond (eds.), *Lollardy and the Gentry in the Later Middle Ages* (Sutton, 1997), 250–77

Hornbeck, J. Patrick II, 'Lollard sermons? Soteriology and late-medieval dissent', *Notes and Queries*, 53 (2006), 26–30

——, 'Of captains and Antichrists: The papacy in Wycliffite thought', *Revue d'histoire ecclésiastique*, 103 (2008), 806–38

——, 'Theologies of sexuality in English "Lollardy"', *Journal of Ecclesiastical History*, 60 (2009), 19–44

——, Stephen E. Lahey, and Fiona Somerset (eds. and trans.), *Wycliffism* (forthcoming)

——, '*Wycklyffes Wycket* and eucharistic heresy: Two series of cases from sixteenth-century Winchester' in Hornbeck and Mishtooni Bose (eds.), *Wycliffite Controversies* (forthcoming)

Hoskins, Edgar, *Horae Beatae Mariae Virginis or Sarum and York Primers* (London, 1901)

Houlbrooke, R. A., 'Persecution of heresy and Protestantism in the diocese of Norwich under Henry VIII', *Norfolk Archaeology*, 35 (1972), 308–26

Hudson, Anne, 'The examination of Lollards', repr. in *Lollards and Their Books* (London, 1985), 124–40

——, 'Hermafrodita or Ambidexter: Wycliffite views on clerks in secular office' in Margaret Aston and Colin Richmond (eds.), *Lollardy and the Gentry in the Later Middle Ages* (Sutton, 1997), 41–51

——, 'A Lollard compilation and the dissemination of Wycliffite thought', repr. in *Lollards and Their Books* (London, 1985), 13–29

——, 'A Lollard Mass?', repr. in *Lollards and Their Books* (London, 1985), 111–23

——, 'A Lollard quaternion', repr. in *Lollards and Their Books* (London, 1985), 192–200

——, 'A Lollard sect vocabulary?', repr. in *Lollards and Their Books* (London, 1985), 165–80

——, 'Lollardy and eschatology' in Alexander Patschovsky and František Šmahel (eds.), *Eschatologie und Hussitismus* (Prague, 1996), 99–113

——, 'The mouse in the pyx: Popular heresy and the Eucharist', *Trivium*, 26 (1991), 40–53

——, 'A neglected Wycliffite text', repr. in *Lollards and Their Books* (London, 1985), 43–65

——, '"No newe thyng": The printing of medieval texts in the early Reformation period', repr. in *Lollards and Their Books* (London, 1985), 227–48

——, 'Notes of an early fifteenth-century research assistant, and the emergence of the 267 articles against Wyclif', *English Historical Review*, 108 (2003), 685–97

——, *The Premature Reformation: Wycliffite texts and Lollard history* (Oxford, 1988)

——, 'The problems of scribes: The trial records of William Swinderby and Walter Brut', *Nottingham Medieval Studies*, 49 (2005), 80–104

——, 'Which Wyche? The framing of the Lollard heretic and/or saint' in Peter Biller and Caterina Bruschi (eds.), *Texts and the Repression of Medieval Heresy* (Woodbridge, 2002), 221–37

——, 'William Thorpe and the question of authority' in G. R. Evans (ed.), *Christian Authority: Essays in Honour of Henry Chadwick* (Oxford, 1988), 127–37

——, and Anthony Kenny, 'Wyclif, John (d. 1384)', *Oxford Dictionary of National Biography*, <http://www.oxforddnb.com/view/article/30122> (accessed 28 Feb 2007)

Jacob, E. F., *Essays in the Conciliar Epoch*, 3rd edn (Manchester, 1963)

Johnson, Benton, 'A critical appraisal of the church-sect typology', *American Sociological Review*, 22 (1957), 88–92

Jurkowski, Maureen, 'Heresy and factionalism at Merton College in the early fifteenth century', *Journal of Ecclesiastical History*, 48 (1997), 658–81

——, 'Lollard book producers in London in 1414' in Helen Barr and Ann M. Hutchinson (eds.), *Text and Controversy from Wyclif to Bale: Essays in honour of Anne Hudson* (Turnhout, 2005), 201–26

——, 'Lollardy and social status in East Anglia', *Speculum*, 82 (2007), 120–52

——, 'Lollardy in Oxfordshire and Northamptonshire: The two Thomas Compworths' in Fiona Somerset, Jill C. Havens, and Derrick Pitard (eds.), *Lollards and Their Influence in Late Medieval England* (Woodbridge, 2003), 73–95

——, 'New light on John Purvey', *English Historical Review*, 110 (1995), 1180–90

Justice, Steven, 'Inquisition, speech, and writing: A case from late-medieval Norwich', *Representations*, 48 (1994), 1–29

——, 'Lollardy' in David Wallace (ed.), *The Cambridge History of Medieval Literature* (Cambridge, 1999), 662–89

Kane, George, 'Some fourteenth-century "political" poems' in Gregory Kratzman and James Simpson (eds.), *Medieval English Religious and Ethical Literature* (Cambridge, 1986), 82–91

Karras, Ruth Mazo, 'Two models, two standards: Moral teaching and sexual mores' in Barbara A. Hanawalt and David Wallace (eds.), *Bodies and Disciplines: Intersections of literature and history in fifteenth-century England* (Minneapolis, Minn., 1996), 123–38

Kaufman, Peter Iver, 'John Colet's *Opus de sacramentis* and clerical anticlericalism: The limitations of "ordinary wayes"', *Journal of British Studies*, 22 (1982), 1–22

Keen, Maurice, 'Wyclif, the Bible, and transubstantiation' in Anthony Kenny (ed.), *Wyclif in His Times* (Oxford, 1986), 1–14

Kelly, H. A., 'Lollard inquisitions: Due and undue process' in A. Ferreiro (ed.), *The Devil, Heresy, and Witchcraft in the Middle Ages* (Leiden, 1998), 279–303

Kenny, Anthony, 'Realism and determinism in the early Wyclif' in Anne Hudson and Michael Wilks (eds.), *From Ockham to Wyclif* (Studies in Church History, Subsidia 5, Oxford, 1987), 165–78

——, *Wyclif* (Oxford, 1985)

Kerby-Fulton, Kathryn, *Books Under Suspicion: Censorship and tolerance of revelatory writing in late medieval England* (South Bend, Ind., 2006)

——, '*Eciam Lollardi*: Some further thoughts on Fiona Somerset's "*Eciam Mulier*: Women in Lollardy and the Problem of Sources"' in Linda Olson and Kathryn Kerby-Fulton (eds.), *Voices in Dialogue: Reading women in the middle ages* (Notre Dame, Ind., 2005), 261–8

Kümin, Beat A., *The Shaping of a Community: The rise and reformation of the English parish c. 1400–1560* (Aldershot, 1996)

Lahey, Stephen E., *John Wyclif* (Oxford, 2009)

——, *Philosophy and Politics in the Thought of John Wyclif* (Cambridge, 2003)

Lambert, Malcolm, *Medieval Heresy: Popular movements from the Gregorian Reform to the Reformation*, 2nd edn (Oxford, 1992)

Larsen, Andrew E., 'Are all Lollards Lollards?' in Fiona Somerset, Jill C. Havens, and Derrick Pitard (eds.), *Lollards and Their Influence in Late Medieval England* (Woodbridge, 2003), 59–72

——, 'John Wyclif, c. 1331–1384' in Ian Christopher Levy (ed.), *A Companion to John Wyclif: Late medieval theologian* (Leiden, 2006), 1–66

Lash, Nicholas, *Change in Focus: A study of doctrinal change and continuity* (London, 1981)

Lawton, D. A., 'Lollardy and the "Piers Plowman" tradition', *Modern Language Review*, 76 (1981), 780–93

Le Bras, Gabriel, *Institutions ecclesiastiques de la chrétienté médiévale*, 2 vols. (Paris, 1959)

Lea, Henry Charles, *A History of the Inquisition in the Middle Ages*, 3 vols. (London, 1888)

Lechler, Gotthard Victor, *John Wycliffe and His English Precursors*, trans. P. Lorimer (London, 1884)

Leclercq, Jean, 'The priesthood in the patristic and medieval church' in Nicholas Lash and Joseph Rhymer (eds.), *The Christian Priesthood* (London, 1970), 53–73

Leff, Gordon, *Bradwardine and the Pelagians* (Cambridge, 1957)

——, *Heresy in the Later Middle Ages: The relation of heterodoxy to dissent, c. 1250–c. 1450*, 2 vols. (Manchester, 1967)

——, 'John Wyclif's religious doctrines', *Churchman*, 98 (1984), 319–28

——, 'Ockham and Wyclif on the Eucharist', *Reading Medieval Studies*, 2 (1976), 1–13

——, 'The place of metaphysics in Wyclif's theology' in Anne Hudson and Michael Wilks (eds.), *From Ockham to Wyclif* (Studies in Church History, Subsidia 5, Oxford, 1987), 217–32

Levine, Joseph M., 'Reginald Pecock and Lorenzo Valla on the Donation of Constantine', *Studies in the Renaissance*, 20 (1973), 118–43

Levy, Ian Christopher, '*Christus Qui Mentiri Non Potest*: John Wyclif's rejection of transubstantiation', *Recherches de Théologie et Philosophie Médiévales*, 66 (1999), 316–34

——, 'Grace and freedom in the soteriology of John Wyclif', *Traditio*, 60 (2005), 279–337

——, 'John Wyclif and Augustinian realism', *Augustiniana*, 48 (1998), 87–106

——, *John Wyclif: Scriptural logic, real presence, and the parameters of orthodoxy* (Milwaukee, Wis., 2003)

——, 'Was John Wyclif's theology of the Eucharist Donatistic?', *Scottish Journal of Theology*, 53 (2000), 137–53

Lipton, Emma, *Affections of the Mind: The politics of sacramental marriage in late medieval English literature* (South Bend, Ind., 2007)

——, 'Performing reform: Lay piety and the marriage of Mary and Joseph in the N-Town cycle', *Studies in the Age of Chaucer*, 23 (2001), 407–35

Little, Katherine, *Confession and Resistance: Defining the self in late medieval England* (South Bend, Ind., 2006)

Littlehales, H., 'On the origin of the prymer' in Edmund Bishop (ed.), *Liturgica Historica* (Oxford, 1918), 211–37

Lossky, Nicholas, *Lancelot Andrewes the Preacher (1555–1626): The origins of the mystical theology of the Church of England*, trans. Andrew Louth (Oxford, 1991)

Lutton, Robert, 'Godparenthood, kinship, and piety in Tenterden, England, 1449–1537' in I. Davis, M. Muller, and S. Rees Jones (eds.), *Love, Marriage, and Family Ties in the Middle Ages* (Turnhout, 2003), 217–34

——, *Lollardy and Orthodox Religion in Pre-Reformation England* (Woodbridge, 2006)

MacCulloch, Diarmaid, *Tudor Church Militant: Edward VI and the Protestant Reformation* (London, 1999)

Macy, Gary, 'The dogma of transubstantiation in the middle ages', *Journal of Ecclesiastical History*, 45 (1994), 11–41

Marshall, Peter, *Beliefs and the Dead in Reformation England* (Oxford, 2002)

——, *The Catholic Priesthood and the English Reformation* (Oxford, 1994)

Martin, Dennis D., 'Popular and monastic pastoral issues in the later middle ages', *Church History*, 56 (1987), 320–32

Matthew, F. D., 'The trial of Richard Wyche', *English Historical Review*, 5 (1890), 530–44

Maxfield, Ezra Kempton, 'Chaucer and religious reform', *PMLA*, 39 (1924), 64–74

Maynell, Hugo A., 'Newman on revelation and doctrinal development', *Journal of Theological Studies*, n.s. 30 (1979), 138–52

McCarthy, Conor, *Marriage in Medieval England: Law, literature, and practice* (Woodbridge, 2004)

McDermott, Robert, 'The religion game: Some family resemblances', *Journal of the American Academy of Religion*, 38 (1970), 390–400

McFarland, K. B., *Lancastrian Kings and Lollard Knights* (Oxford, 1972)

McGinn, Bernard, 'Angel pope and papal Antichrist', *Church History*, 47 (1978), 155–73

McGrath, Alister, 'The anti-Pelagian structure of "nominalist" doctrines of justification', *Ephemerides Theologicae Lovanienses*, 57 (1981), 107–19

——, 'Augustinianism? A critical examination of the so-called "medieval Augustinian tradition"', *Augustiniana*, 31 (1981), 247–67

——, 'Forerunners of the Reformation? A critical examination of the evidence for precursors of the Reformation doctrine of justification', *Harvard Theological Review*, 75 (1982), 219–42

——, *Iustitia Dei: A history of the Christian doctrine of justification*, 3rd edn (Cambridge, 2005)

McHardy, A. K., 'Bishop Buckingham and the Lollards of Lincoln diocese', *Studies in Church History*, 9 (1972), 131–45

——, 'The dissemination of Wyclif's ideas' in Anne Hudson and Michael Wilks (eds.), *From Ockham to Wyclif* (Studies in Church History, Subsidia 5, Oxford, 1987), 361–8

McNeill, John Thomas, 'Some emphases in Wyclif's teaching', *Journal of Religion* 7 (1927), 447–66

McNiven, Peter, *Heresy and Politics in the Reign of Henry IV* (Woodbridge, 1987)

McSheffrey, Shannon, *Gender and Heresy: Women and men in Lollard communities, 1420–1530* (Philadelphia, 1995)

——, 'Heresy, orthodoxy, and English vernacular religion, 1480–1525', *Past and Present*, 186 (2005), 47–80

Meier-Ewart, Charity, 'A Middle English version of the "Fifteen Oes"', *Modern Philology*, 68 (1971), 355–61

Melia, Richard, ' "Non-controversial Lollardy"? The Lollard attribution of the "Diuers Treatises of John Wiclife in English" (John Rylands Library, English MS 85)', *Bulletin of the John Rylands Library*, 83 (2001), 89–102

Minnis, Alastair, ' "Respondet Walterus Bryth . . .": Walter Brut in debate on women priests' in Helen Barr and Ann M. Hutchison (eds.), *Text and Controversy from Wyclif to Bale* (Turnhout, 2005), 229–49

Mohler, James A., *The Origin and Evolution of the Priesthood* (Staten Island, NY, 1970)

Morris, Colin, *The Papal Monarchy: The Western Church from 1050 to 1250* (Oxford, 1991)

Needham, Rodney, *Belief, Language, and Experience* (Oxford, 1972)

——, 'Polythetic classification: Convergence and consequences', *Man*, 10 (1975), 349–69

Nelson, Janet, 'Society, theodicy, and origins of heresy: Towards a reassessment of the medieval evidence', *Studies in Church History*, 9 (1972), 65–77

Newman, John Henry, *An Essay on the Development of Christian Doctrine* (repr. Notre Dame, Ind., 1989)

Nichols, Aidan, *From Newman to Congar: The idea of doctrinal development from the Victorians to the Second Vatican Council* (Edinburgh, 1990)

——, *Holy Order: The apostolic ministry from the New Testament to the Second Vatican Council* (Dublin, 1990)

Nichols, Ann Eljenholm, *Seeable Signs: The iconography of the seven sacraments, 1350–1544* (Woodbridge, 1994), 274–85

Oakley, Francis, *The Conciliarist Tradition: Constitutionalism in the Catholic Church, 1300–1870* (Oxford, 2003)

——, 'Pierre D'Ailly and the absolute power of God: Another note on the theology of nominalism', *Harvard Theological Review*, 56 (1963), 59–63

Oberman, Heiko A., '*Facientibus quod in se est Deus non denegat gratiam*: Robert Holcot, O.P., and the beginnings of Luther's theology', *Harvard Theological Review*, 55 (1962), 317–42

Palliser, D. M., 'Popular reactions to the Reformation during the years of uncertainty, 1530–70' in Christopher Haigh (ed.), *The English Reformation Revised* (Cambridge, 1987), 94–113

Palmer, J. J. N., 'England and the great Western schism, 1388–1399', *EHR*, 83 (1968), 519–22

Pedersen, Frederik, *Marriage Disputes in Medieval England* (London, 2000)

Pegg, Mark Gregory, *The Corruption of Angels: The great inquisition of 1245–1246* (Princeton, NJ, 2001)

Peikola, Matti, *Congregation of the Elect: Patterns of self-fashioning in English Lollard writings* (Turku, 2000)

Pelikan, Jaroslav, *The Christian Tradition: A history of the development of doctrine*, 5 vols. (Chicago, 1971–89)

——, *Development of Christian Doctrine: Some historical prolegomena* (New Haven, Conn., 1969)

Pennington, Kenneth, *Pope and Bishops: The papal monarchy in the twelfth and thirteenth centuries* (Philadelphia, 1984)

Penny, D. Andrew, *Freewill or Predestination: The battle over saving grace in mid-Tudor England* (Woodbridge, 1990)

Peters, Christine, 'Gender, sacrament, and ritual: The making and meaning of marriage in late medieval and early modern England', *Past and Present*, 169 (2000), 63–96

Petry, Ray C., 'Unitive reform principles of the late medieval concilarists', *Church History*, 31 (1962), 164–81

Pineas, Rainer, 'William Tyndale's influence on John Bale's polemical use of history', *Archiv für Reformationsgeschichte*, 53 (1962), 79–96

Plumb, Derek J., 'A gathered church? Lollards and their society' in Margaret Spufford (ed.), *The World of Rural Dissenters* (Cambridge, 1995), 132–63

——, 'The social and economic spread of rural Lollardy: A reappraisal' in W. J. Sheils and Diana Wood (eds.), *Voluntary Religion* (Studies in Church History, 23, Oxford, 1986), 111–29

Pounds, N. J. G., *A History of the English Parish* (Cambridge, 2000)

Powell, Susan, 'Mirk, John', *Oxford Dictionary of National Biography*, <http://www.oxforddnb.com/view/article/18818> (accessed 6 December 2005)

Power, David N., *Ministers of Christ and His Church* (London, 1969)

Resnick, Irvin M., 'Marriage in medieval culture: Consent theory and the case of Joseph and Mary', *Church History*, 69 (2000), 350–71

Rex, Richard, *The Lollards* (London, 2002)

Rhodes, Jim, *Poetry Does Theology* (Notre Dame, Ind., 2001)

Rigby, S. H., *English Society in the Later Middle Ages: Class, status, and gender* (New York, 1995)

Robson, J. A., *Wyclif and the Oxford Schools* (Cambridge, 1961)

Rondet, Henri, *Do Dogmas Change?* trans. Mark Pontifex (London, 1961)

Roper, Lyndal, *Witch Craze: Terror and fantasy in baroque Germany* (New Haven, Conn., 2004)

Rubin, Miri, *Corpus Christi: The Eucharist in late medieval culture* (Cambridge, 1991)

Russell, Jeffrey, 'Interpretations of the origins of medieval heresy', *Mediaeval Studies*, 25 (1963), 26–53

Ryan, E. A., 'Three early treatises on the church', *Theological Studies*, 5 (1944), 113–40

Scase, Wendy, 'The audience and framers of the *Twelve Conclusions of the Lollards*' in Helen Barr and Ann M. Hutchinson (eds.), *Text and Controversy from Wyclif to Bale: Essays in honour of Anne Hudson* (Turnhout, 2005), 283–302

——, ' "Heu! quanta desolatio Angliae praestatur": A Wycliffite libel and the naming of heretics, Oxford 1382' in Fiona Somerset, Jill C. Havens, and Derrick Pitard (eds.), *Lollards and Their Influence in Late Medieval England* (Woodbridge, 2003), 19–36

——, *Piers Plowman and the New Anticlericalism* (Cambridge, 1989)

Scattergood, John, '*Pierce the Ploughman's Crede*: Lollardy and texts' in Margaret Aston and Colin Richmond (eds.), *Lollardy and the Gentry in the Later Middle Ages* (Sutton, 1997), 77–94

——, 'The two ways: An unpublished religious treatise by Sir John Clanvowe', *English Philological Studies*, 10 (1967), 33–56

Schillebeeckx, Edward, *The Church with a Human Face* (London, 1985)

——, *Clerical Celibacy under Fire: A critical appraisal* (London, 1968)

Sheehan, Michael M., 'The formation and stability of marriage in fourteenth-century England: Evidence of an Ely register' in *Marriage, Family, and Law in Medieval Europe: Collected studies* (Cardiff, 1996), 38–76

——, 'Marriage and family in English conciliar and synodal legislation' in *Marriage, Family, and Law*, 77–86

Shogimen, Takashi, 'Wyclif's ecclesiology and political thought' in Ian Christopher Levy (ed.), *A Companion to John Wyclif: Late medieval theologian* (Leiden, 2006), 199–240

Smalley, Beryl, *English Friars and Antiquity* (Oxford, 1960)

Smart, Ninian, *Concept and Empathy* (London, 1986)

Smith, David, *Guide to Bishops' Registers of England and Wales* (London, 1981)

Snow, David A., and Richard Machalek, 'On the presumed frailty of unconventional beliefs', *Journal for the Scientific Study of Religion*, 21 (1982), 15–26

Sokal, Robert R., and Peter H. A. Sneath, *Principles of Numerical Taxonomy* (San Francisco, 1963)

Somerset, Fiona, *Clerical Discourse and Lay Audience in Late Medieval England* (Cambridge, 1998)

——, '*Eciam Mulier*: Women in Lollardy and the problem of sources' in Linda Olson and Kathryn Kerby-Fulton (eds.), *Voices in Dialogue: Reading women in the Middle Ages* (Notre Dame, Ind., 2005), 245–60

——, 'Here, there, and everywhere? Wycliffite conceptions of the Eucharist and Chaucer's "other" Lollard joke' in Fiona Somerset, Jill C. Havens, and Derrick G. Pitard (eds.), *Lollards and Their Influence in Late Medieval England* (Woodbridge, 2003), 127–33

——, 'Introduction' in Fiona Somerset, Jill C. Havens, and Derrick Pitard (eds.), *Lollards and Their Influence in Late Medieval England* (Woodbridge, 2003), 9–16

——, 'Professionalizing translation at the turn of the fifteenth century: Ullerston's *Determinacio*, Arundel's *Constitutions*' in Somerset and Nicholas Watson (eds.), *The Vulgar Tongue: Medieval and postmedieval vernacularity* (University Park, Pa., 2003), 145–57

——, 'Wycliffite spirituality' in Helen Barr and Ann M. Hutchison (eds.), *Text and Controversy from Wyclif to Bale: Essays in honour of Anne Hudson* (Turnhout, 2005), 375–86

Stacey, John, 'John Wyclif as theologian', *Expository Times*, 101 (1990), 134–41

Stark, Rodney, *For the Glory of God: How monotheism led to reformations, science, witch-hunts, and the end of slavery* (Princeton, NJ, 2003)

——, and William Sims Bainbridge, *A Theory of Religion* (New Brunswick, NJ, 1996)

——, and Roger Finke, 'Beyond church and sect: Dynamics and stability in religious economics' in Ted G. Jelen (ed.), *Sacred Markets and Sacred Canopies* (Lanham, Md., 2002), 33–49

——, and Laurence R. Iannaccone, 'A supply-side reinterpretation of the secularization of Europe', *Journal for the Scientific Study of Religion*, 33 (1994), 230–52

Stock, Brian, *The Implications of Literacy: Written language and models of interpretation in the eleventh and twelfth centuries* (Princeton, NJ, 1983)

——, *Listening for the Text: On the uses of the past* (Philadelphia, 1996)

Storey, R. L., 'Recruitment of English clergy during the period of the conciliar movement', *Annuarium Historiae Concilorum*, 7 (1975), 290–313

Strohm, Paul, 'Counterfeiters, Lollards, and Lancastrian unease' in Wendy Scase, Rita Copeland, and David Lawton (eds.), *New Medieval Literatures*, vol. 1 (Oxford, 1997), 31–58

——, *England's Empty Throne: Usurpation and the language of legitimation, 1399–1422* (New Haven, Conn., 1998)

Summers, W. H., *The Lollards of the Chiltern Hills* (London, 1906)

Swanson, R. N., 'Before the Protestant clergy: The construction and deconstruction of medieval priesthood' in C. Scott Dixon and Luise Schorn-Schütte (eds.), *The Protestant Clergy of Early Modern Europe* (Basingstoke, 2003), 39–59, 200–9

——, *Church and Society in Late Medieval England* (Oxford, 1989)

——, '. . . "Et examinatus dicit . . .": Oral and personal history in the records of English ecclesiastical courts' in Michael Goodich (ed.), *Voices from the Bench: The narratives of lesser folk in medieval trials* (New York, 2005), 203–25

Swanson, R. N., 'Literacy, heresy, history, and orthodoxy: Perspectives and permutations for the later Middle Ages' in Peter Biller and Anne Hudson (eds.), *Heresy and Literacy, 1000–1530* (Cambridge, 1996), 279–93

——, 'Pastoralia in practice: Clergy and ministry in pre-Reformation England' in T. Clemens and W. Janse (ed.), *The Pastor Bonus: Papers read at the British-Dutch colloquium at Utrecht, 18–21 September 2002* (Leiden, 2004), 104–28

——, 'Problems of the priesthood in pre-Reformation England', *English Historical Review*, 105 (1990), 846–69

——, 'Titles to orders in medieval English episcopal registers' in Henry Mayr-Harting and R. I. Moore (eds.), *Studies in Medieval History Presented to R. H. C. Davis* (London, 1985), 233–45

Szittya, Penn R., *The Antifraternal Tradition in Medieval Literature* (Princeton, NJ, 1986)

——, review of Scase, *Piers Plowman and the New Anticlericalism, Speculum*, 67 (1992), 1040–2

Tanner, Norman, 'Penances imposed on Kentish Lollards by Archbishop Warham, 1511–12' in Margaret Aston and Colin Richmond (eds.), *Lollardy and the Gentry in the Later Middle Ages* (Sutton, 1997), 229–49

Thiel, John, *Senses of Tradition: Continuity and development in Catholic faith* (Oxford, 2000)

——, 'Tradition and authoritative reasoning', *Theological Studies*, 56 (1995), 627–51

Thompson, Samuel Harrison, 'The philosophical basis of Wyclif's theology', *Journal of Religion*, 11 (1931), 86–116

Thomson, J. A. F., 'John Foxe and some sources for Lollard history: Notes for a critical appraisal' in G.J. Cuming (ed.), *Studies in Church History* 2 (London, 1965), 251–7

——, *The Later Lollards: 1414–1520* (Oxford, 1965)

Thomson, S. Harrison, 'John Wyclif's "lost" *De Fide Sacramentorum*', *Journal of Theological Studies*, 33 (1932), 359–65

Tierney, Brian, *Foundations of the Conciliar Theory: The contribution of the medieval canonists from Gratian to the Great Schism* (Cambridge, 1968)

Tilley, Terrence W., *History, Theology and Faith: Dissolving the modern problematic* (Maryknoll, NY, 2004)

——, *Inventing Catholic Tradition* (Maryknoll, NY, 2000)

Van Engen, John H., 'Anticlericalism among the Lollards' in Peter A. Dykema and Heiko A. Oberman (eds.), *Anticlericalism in Late Medieval and Early Modern Europe* (Leiden, 1993), 53–63

von Nolcken, Christina, 'Richard Wyche, a certain knight, and the beginning of the end' in Margaret Aston and Colin Richmond (eds.), *Lollardy and the Gentry in the Later Middle Ages* (Sutton, 1997), 127–54

Wakefield, Walter L., and Austin P. Evans (eds. and trans.), *Heresies of the High Middle Ages* (New York, 1991)

Walgrave, Jan Hendrik, *Unfolding Revelation: The nature of doctrinal development* (London, 1972)

Wallace, D. D., 'The doctrine of predestination in the early English Reformation', *Church History*, 43 (1974), 201–15

Walsh, Katherine, *Richard FitzRalph in Oxford, Avignon, and Armagh: A fourteenth-century scholar and primate* (Oxford, 1981)

Watson, Nicholas, 'Censorship and cultural change in late-medieval England: Vernacular theology, the Oxford translation debate, and Arundel's *Constitutions* of 1409', *Speculum*, 70 (1995), 822–64

——, 'Vernacular apocalyptic: On *The Lanterne of Liȝt*', *Revista canaria de estudios ingleses*, 47 (2003), 115–26

——, 'Visions of inclusion: Universal salvation and vernacular theology in pre-Reformation England', *Journal of Medieval and Early Modern Studies*, 27 (1997), 146–70

Weaver, Rebecca Harden, *Divine Grace and Human Agency: A study of the semi-Pelagian controversy* (Macon, Ga., 1996)

Welsby, Paul A., *Lancelot Andrewes, 1555–1626* (London, 1958)

Wenzel, Siegfried, *Latin Sermon Collections from Later Medieval England* (Cambridge, 2005)

Wetzel, James, 'Predestination, Pelagianism, and foreknowledge' in Eleonore Stump and Norman Kretzmann (eds.), *The Cambridge Companion to Augustine* (Cambridge, 2001), 49–58

White, Peter O. G., *Predestination, Policy, and Polemic: Conflict and consensus in the English church from the Reformation to the Civil War* (Cambridge, 1992)

Wiles, Maurice, *Archetypal Heresy: Arianism through the centuries* (Oxford, 1996)

——, *The Making of Christian Doctrine: A study in the principles of early doctrinal development* (Cambridge, 1967)

Wilks, Michael, 'The *Apostolicus* and the Bishop of Rome', *Journal of Theological Studies*, n.s. 13 (1962), 290–317, and n.s. 14 (1963), 311–54

——, 'Predestination, property, and power: Wyclif's theory of dominion and grace', repr. in Anne Hudson (ed.), *Wyclif: Political ideas and practice* (Oxford, 2000), 16–32

——, 'Royal patronage and anti-papalism: From Ockham to Wyclif', repr. in Anne Hudson (ed.), *Wyclif: Political ideas and practice* (Oxford, 2000), 117–46

Williams, Rowan, *Arius: Heresy and tradition*, 2nd edn (London, 2001)

Wilson, Bryan, *The Social Dimensions of Sectarianism* (Oxford, 1990)

——, 'A typology of sects in dynamic and comparative perspective', *Archives de Sociologie des Religions*, 16 (1963), 49–63

Wittgenstein, Ludwig, *Philosophical Investigations*, trans. G. E. M. Anscombe, 2nd edn (repr. Oxford, 1997)

Wood, Rega, 'Ockham's repudiation of Pelagianism' in Paul Vincent Spade (ed.), *The Cambridge Companion to Ockham* (Cambridge, 1999), 350–74

Workman, H. B., *John Wyclif: A study of the English medieval church*, 2 vols. (Oxford, 1926)

Wunderli, Richard M., *London Church Courts and Society on the Eve of the Reformation* (Cambridge, Mass., 1981)

Yearley, Lee H., 'St Thomas Aquinas on providence and predestination', *Anglican Theological Review*, 49 (1967), 409–23

Unpublished papers and theses

Catto, Jeremy, 'William Woodford, O.F.M. (*c.* 1330–*c.*1397)' (D.Phil. thesis, Oxford University, 1969)

D'Alton, Craig, 'The suppression of heresy in early Henrician England' (Ph.D. thesis, University of Melbourne, 1999)

Fines, John, 'Studies in the Lollard heresy' (Ph.D. thesis, Sheffield University, 1964)

Forrest, Ian James, 'Ecclesiastical justice and the detection of heresy in England, 1380–1430' (D.Phil. thesis, Oxford University, 2003)

Fraser, Craig James, 'The religious instruction of the laity in late medieval England with particular reference to the sacrament of the Eucharist' (D.Phil. thesis, Oxford University, 1995)

Hargrave, O. T., 'The doctrine of predestination in the English Reformation' (Ph.D. thesis, Vanderbilt University, 1966)

Hudson, Anne, '*Robustissimus Antichristi Achilles*: Thomas Netter, Wyclif, and the Lollards', Open Lecture, Society for the Study of Medieval Languages and Literature, Oxford, 28 February 2004

Kightly, Charles, 'The early Lollards: A survey of popular Lollard activity in England, 1382–1428' (Ph.D. thesis, York University, 1975)

Phillips, Heather, 'John Wyclif's *De Eucharistia* in its medieval setting' (Ph.D. thesis, University of Toronto, 1980)

Plumb, Derek J., 'John Foxe and the later Lollards of the Thames Valley' (Ph.D. thesis, University of Cambridge, 1987)

von Nolcken, Christina, 'An edition of selected parts of the Middle English translation of the *Rosarium Theologie*', 2 vols. (D.Phil. thesis, Oxford University, 1977)

Yarnell, Malcolm, 'Royal priesthood in the English Reformation' (D.Phil. thesis, Oxford University, 2000)

Index